Manual o
Objective Tests

to accompany

Basic Marketing
A Global-Managerial Approach

Fourteenth Edition

William D. Perreault, Jr.
University of North Carolina

E. Jerome McCarthy
Michigan State University

Boston   Burr Ridge, IL   Dubuque, IA   Madison, WI   New York   San Francisco   St. Louis
Bangkok   Bogotá   Caracas   Kuala Lumpur   Lisbon   London   Madrid   Mexico City
Milan   Montreal   New Delhi   Santiago   Seoul   Singapore   Sydney   Taipei   Toronto

McGraw-Hill Higher Education

A Division of The McGraw-Hill Companies

Manual of Objective Tests to accompany
BASIC MARKETING: A GLOBAL-MANAGERIAL APPROACH
William D. Perreault, Jr. and E. Jerome McCarthy

2 3 4 5 6 7 8 9 0 QSR/QSR 0 9 8 7 6 5 4 3 2

ISBN 0-07-243014-1

www.mhhe.com

Contents

Introduction

Introduction

How to Use the Manual of Tests

This *Manual of Objective Tests* contains about 3,500 true-false and multiple-choice questions which have been specially prepared by the authors for use with *Basic Marketing, 14th edition*. They provide flexible, comprehensive, and thorough coverage of the text material.

All of the questions in this manual are also available in microcomputer form. Easy-to-use software allows you to select (and, if you desire, edit) any of the questions and/or add your own-- and then print out the questions you want for your test (or, if you desire, various forms of the same test with questions in different orders). The software also allows you to administer the test you create over a computer network. Alternatively, you can call a toll-free telephone number and a test with the questions you want will be printed for you. All of this makes it even more convenient to develop a finished test. Use of computerized test generation is described in greater detail later in this chapter, but first it's useful to review several other special features that have been built into this manual (and the computerized question database that accompanies it).

For your convenience, several special features have been built into this manual.
1. The questions are arranged in the order in which the related material is presented in the text--and a page reference is given for each question to indicate where the correct answer (or the related discussion) can be found in the text.

2. Each multiple-choice question has been classified according to:
   (a) the *type of question* (e.g., definitional, comprehension, application, integrating, or mathematical), and
   (b) the *level of difficulty* (e.g., easy, medium, or hard).
These classifications are explained in the next section.

3. For most key topics, there are a variety of different types of questions and questions at different levels of difficulty. In addition, the answer key, classification information, and page reference are given in the margin right beside the question. This format makes it fast and easy to select the questions you want. With the test generating software, you can quickly select questions based on the question numbers that appear in this manual and then print out a finished test (or alternative versions of the test with the order of questions and/or response alternatives rotated).

Using the multiple-choice question classification system

Beside each multiple-choice question in this manual we have provided information that can be helpful to you in selecting questions that fit your testing needs. A sample question is given on the next page, and it illustrates the format used and the information provided.

As you can see in the example above, set off from each multiple-choice question in the left margin are five important pieces of information in the following order:

1. The question number (for example, 1-**1** means chapter 1 - question **1**)
2. The correct answer (*D*)
3. The type of question (Definitional)
4. The level of difficulty of the question (Easy)
5. The page (or range of pages) in the text where the correct answer can be found (page 3)

Similarly, the margin beside true-false questions gives the question number, the correct answer (*True* or *False*), and a page reference for the answer--in that order.

The multiple-choice question classification information is discussed in more detail below, along with some suggestions you may wish to consider when you are preparing a test.

Type of question

Each multiple-choice question has been classified as follows:

Definitional (Def.)--questions which focus on definitions of important terms or concepts introduced in the text--or which stress knowledge of facts presented in the text (e.g., "Price-fixing is prohibited by the _____ Act.").

Comprehension (Comp.)--questions which a require a more in-depth understanding of important terms or concepts--including their assumptions and implications--and which go beyond a simple recognition of definitions and facts (e.g., "What circumstances favor the use of penetration pricing?"). This classification also includes questions which test the students' understanding of text material that is not definitional in nature and which may extend over several paragraphs or pages (e.g., "When trying to segment a market, a marketing manager should _____.")

Application (App.)--questions which ask students to apply important terms or concepts introduced in the text. This might involve identifying terms or concepts described in short "caselets" or applying the terms or concepts to real-life situations (e.g., "Which of the following business products is most likely to involve new task buying?").

Integrating (Int.)--questions which cover several important terms or concepts in a single question--or which cover material discussed in several sections in the text. This type of question sometimes requires that a student demonstrate an understanding of how different concepts relate to each other.

Mathematical (Math.)--questions which require students to do some kind of arithmetic calculations--such as calculating a markup or break-even point.

Level of difficulty

Each multiple-choice question has been classified as either easy, medium, or hard--according to its approximate level of difficulty. "Easy" questions generally test a basic familiarity and understanding of terms and concepts discussed in the text (assuming, of course, that the students have actually read the text--those who haven't may not find any of the questions "easy!"). True-false questions are not classified according to difficulty in this manual--as almost all of them are "easy." "Medium" questions generally require more thought and understanding than "easy" questions. "Hard" questions involve unusually difficult text material--or questions where a well informed "judgment" is required. Alternatively, this type of question sometimes focuses on fine points in the text (including percentages and data presented in tables or figures) which might be overlooked by all but your more thorough students. *If you plan to use questions which draw information from tables and figures, you might want to warn students in advance so that they are not surprised at test time.*

WARNING!

The terms "easy," "medium," and "hard" are general indicators of the level of difficulty of each multiple-choice question. If used with discretion, this classification should aid your test preparation. However, it cannot be overstressed that how well *your* students perform on these test questions will depend on a multitude of variables, including:

 • The course level (e.g., freshmen and sophomores, juniors and seniors, or graduate students).
 • The reading level and analytical ability of your students.
 • The degree to which lectures and other materials used in the course are in agreement with the text.
 • How much the textbook is stressed in the course.
 • Whether or not your students use some or all parts of the accompanying *Learning Aid*.
 • The number of chapters that are covered on a particular exam.
 • The number of questions that are included in a particular exam.
 • How much time students are allowed to complete the exam.

Note: Questions which require students to perform mathematical calculations are generally classified as either "medium" or "hard." However, many students have considerable difficulty working with numbers and may find all such questions "hard." In general, the authors recommend that you avoid questions which involve calculations or interpretation of graphs *unless* you have devoted considerable time in class to discussing such calculations or graphs.

Page numbers for correct answer

There are several important potential uses of the page number that appears beside each question.

First, in preparing an exam, the instructor can quickly judge the extent to which questions sample evenly from across the reading assignments. Or--if students have been instructed to devote extra study to some assigned pages, these reference pages help the instructor to quickly identify material from those pages (i.e., if additional questions are desired).

Often, an important concept from the text will be represented in the test bank with a variety of questions--questions of different types and difficulty levels. This increases flexibility--since you can choose those questions that are well suited to the way you teach and what you expect your students to know. In addition, the ample selection of questions allows you to "rotate" test items from one term to the next. Since the questions appear in the manual in sequential order *by page number*, the instructor can easily see the complete set of available questions and select accordingly.

The page number references can also be very handy when returning graded tests to students. Students like feedback on what they missed and what they got correct--and the teaching/learning value of a test can be enhanced when students get more information about questions they have missed. Discussing every item on the test and answering individual questions can be very time consuming--especially if you have a large class. However, being able to easily give students the page numbers where a topic is discussed and a question is answered can be a good way to keep class discussion focused on topics that seem to warrant the time of the whole class--while still providing feedback. Some instructors provide students a copy of the answer key for the test that includes these page numbers (perhaps along with dates related material was covered in class) so a student can easily pinpoint areas that need additional study.

General tips on exam preparation

1. When selecting questions for exams, we *strongly recommend* that you test yourself on each question before looking at the suggested correct answer--because your own lecture material, supplementary reading materials, or other assignments may lead the students to think that another alternative is a better choice. This is especially true for "application" questions which are sometimes rather subjective in nature. Where an individual instructor's lecture material conflicts with material in the text, some alternatives may need to be modified or changed altogether. (This is easy with the Diploma computer test-generator software.)

2. Most exams should probably consist of a variety of question types and a balanced number of "easy" and "medium" questions (although some instructors may wish to rely almost exclusively on easy or medium questions--depending on their students' abilities). It may be desirable to also include some "hard" questions to help distinguish between the very good and average students. However, the use of hard questions probably should be minimized when more than a few chapters are covered on a particular exam.

3. Depending on the length and difficulty of the questions--and your students' reading abilities--40 multiple-choice questions is usually a reasonable number for a 50-minute exam. If all the questions are "easy," as many as 60 questions might be asked; but if all the

questions are "medium" and "hard"--requiring considerable weighing of alternatives--even 40 questions may be too many. In general, using too many questions will force guessing and may reduce the validity of the exam results. Keep in mind that some questions that are "easy" in terms of rated difficulty may still involve more reading--and take more time on the exam.

4. One way to reduce the difficulty and/or the length of an exam is to eliminate one or more incorrect alternatives for various questions. However, reducing the number of alternatives obviously increases a student's probability of guessing the correct answer.

5. The authors have seen that many students do better on multiple-choice questions when it is explained that multiple-choice questions often can be thought of as complex true-false questions--for which they are expected to choose the best or wholly correct alternative. Selecting the best answer may be facilitated by the student actually marking a small plus or minus or T or F by each alternative as she or he reads through a question. Then, if the student is looking for the best alternative and finds that three of the five alternatives have a plus or T in front of them, she or he must go back to these three alternatives and determine whether they are wholly correct. Those which are wholly correct are marked with another plus or T. If two alternatives still remain after this second step, then the remaining two alternatives must be weighed to determine which is best. This approach emphasizes the importance of not "jumping" at the first *seemingly* correct answer. Once the student accepts the idea that it is important to carefully read and consider all of the alternatives, then the idea of marking a small plus or T will not appear as extra effort--but rather as a way to economize on time as some alternatives need not be reread.

6. Some instructors try to motivate their students to make heavier use of the self-test quizzes on the Student CD-ROM and in the *Learning Aid* by including some true-false and/or multiple-choice questions from the *Learning Aid* in their exams. Many instructors report to us that their students appreciate the instructor having the *Learning Aid* available at the book store, even if it is not a required part of the course or used as a source of test questions, as this can help the students be certain that they really understand course material.

7. Where time permits and your classes are not too large, it would be desirable to include some essay questions in your exams--along with the multiple-choice questions. Many of the "Questions and Problems" at the end of each chapter in the text are very suitable for use as essay questions on exams. Some instructors also use selected application exercises from the *Learning Aid* as examination problems. Suggested answers to these questions and exercises can be found in the *Instructor's Manual to Accompany Basic Marketing*. Similarly, if you are using the *Computer-Aided Problems* in your class, you can test knowledge in this area. The *Instructor's Manual* provides printed copies of spreadsheets for all of the questions. Thus, you can reproduce one or more of these spreadsheets in a test for students to use in answering a question from one of the problems.

8. If you are using *The Marketing Game!* in your course, the separate *Instructor's Manual* that accompanies the game includes additional true-false and multiple-choice questions on that material. Those questions are also available in computerized form and can be intermixed with the questions from this text.

**Information about computerized test generation:
Diploma and Teletest**

Questions from this *Manual of Objective Tests for Basic Marketing* are available in two computerized forms--to make it easier to produce tests in "ready-to-be-duplicated" form.

One alternative is the new *Diploma Exam software (developed by Brownstone Research).* It is a test generating and editing system you can use locally on your own Windows-based PC. The second alternative is *Teletest*, a service designed to allow you to simply call a toll-free number (or fax, mail, or email) an order form and have the publisher, McGraw-Hill/Irwin, prepare the test and send it back to you (attached to an email or by regular mail) ready to be printed.

A number of different options make each of these testing systems flexible and easy to use. Each alternative is fully explained in separate instructions, so our review here will just briefly describe the major features. You can get the detailed and "user-friendly" instructions for each system by contacting your local Irwin sales representative or call Irwin's toll-free line at 1-800-634-3963 and ask for faculty service. If you don't know how to contact your McGraw-Hill/Irwin sales rep, there is also a sales rep "locator" available at the Irwin/McGraw-Hill web site (www.mhhe.com) on the Internet.

Diploma exam generating software system (for Windows™ computers)

Diploma is a microcomputer testing system provided free of charge to adopters of *Basic Marketing*. (It is a new and enhanced replacement for the *Computest* program that was available with earlier editions of *Basic Marketing*). It gives instructors a fast, easy and flexible way to create and print exams (and answer keys) in their offices or computer labs. It uses a combination of menu selections and toolbar buttons--which will be familiar for anyone who has previously used a Windows-based word processor (or other Windows software). It has a good online Help system so even a computer novice can have it running in just a few minutes. The *Diploma* system includes several separate programs. *Exam* is used to quickly create and print tests--or output them into a "portable" word processing format; it can also be used to add new questions in the test bank or delete or edit the ones already there. Another program, *Proctor* is designed to make it easy to administer exams online with a computer network. *Gradebook* provides a variety of helpful features to make it easy to manage grades and the grading process. The system makes it easy to "publish" a test to a website and/or capture and analyze student responses.

Diploma was designed for Windows and it can run on nearly any desktop system that can run the Windows operating system. The absolute minimum configuration is a 486 machine running Windows 95, 4 megabytes of RAM, at least 10 MB disk space free, and a VGA video driver. However, the recommended minimum is a Pentium processor, Windows 98, 16 megabytes of RAM, at least 50 MB disk space free, and a Super VGA driver.

Select, edit, delete, or add questions as you wish

Diploma allows you to select and print questions from the *Manual of Objective Tests*. Further, you can easily edit (or delete) any of the existing questions or use the built-in question editor to write your own and add them to the question bank. The software basically creates a "fill in the form" type template so that it is very clear what you need to do to create your own test questions and add them to the test bank database. You can also select questions from the test bank according to criteria you set (for example, number of questions per chapter or difficulty level). When choosing questions by criteria, *Diploma Exam* gives you the option of previewing and accepting or rejecting the questions. It is very easy to produce several versions of a test.

It's now easier than ever to select the questions you want and to print them with *Diploma*. In the margin beside each question in *this* manual is a number that indicates the chapter number and the question number within that chapter. All you need to do is check off the questions you want to use--and then "click" on the corresponding question number in the software to add it to the test you create. More specifically, to create a new exam with the *Diploma Exam* software:

1. Click the New Exam button in the Question Bank window.
2. Select the Basic Marketing question file (its questions match the ones in this manual).
3. Point your mouse at a question that you want to incorporate into the new exam and double click. Repeat to add other questions. (Note: You may also select questions randomly, based upon their properties, when viewing them, or in groups.)
4. Repeat steps 2-3 as needed.
5. Write the instructions at the top of the question list in the new exam.
5. Save the new exam and/or print it.

Although the software makes it easy to randomly select questions or to quickly select a set of questions that match certain criteria, these features should be used with care. Because there are usually a number of different questions on any given topic, random selection may result in a test with more questions than intended on a given topic. Of course, you can randomly select a set of questions and then review them to see if there are any that you would prefer not to use (for whatever reason). Then, those can be deleted before the others are added to the final test.

Diploma Exam also allows you to save the test you have created on disk as a standard "rich text" formatted file. Most Windows word processing software--including Microsoft Word and Corel WordPerfect--can directly import this type of file and preserve all the formatting information. This makes it easy, if you wish, to make additional changes with favorite word processing software. This is not required--but rather is a convenience for those who want the added flexibility. For example, this approach might be used by an instructor who wants to do additional formatting before printing the test with a laser printer.

Summaries keep track of the process

Diploma Exam displays summary information concerning the tests (including the source number of each question) as it is being created. The summary lists the number of questions of a particular type (multiple-choice, true-false, or essay) and of a particular level of difficulty (easy, medium, or hard), and the chapter range. When you choose questions by number, the numbers of those questions are displayed in the summary. If you change your mind at any time, you can delete questions from a test before printing it--or save questions for further refinement or reuse at a later time.

"Cut and paste" a finished-form test without using a computer

If for any reason you do not wish to take advantage of "computerized test generation," exam preparation can be simplified by following the steps outlined below:

a. Select the questions which you wish to use on an exam.
b. Make photocopies of the pages in the test manual on which the selected questions appear.
c. Using the photocopies, cut out the selected questions--omitting the information in the left margin--and tape them in the desired sequence on a blank sheet of paper. (Save the information for the answer key).
d. Number the questions.
e. Student copies of the exam can then be photocopied directly from this "master."

Note that the above procedure eliminates almost all typing and, consequently, the need for extensive proofreading of exams.

Ideas on grading objective tests

There are many advantages to using objective questions on tests. They make it possible to sample broadly from the material covered in the course. They provide a uniform basis for grading. With the extensive set of questions in the test bank and the test generator software it is quick and easy to create a test that is consistent with what you want students to know and be evaluated on. Such tests can be graded more quickly than some other types of test questions--and this means that students can be provided feedback more quickly than might be possible otherwise.

Most instructors assign grades on objective tests by adding up the number of *correct* answers, perhaps looking at the number correct as a percentage relative to the total number of questions on the test. There are, however, other approaches which may be used.

For example, there are different approaches to how missed answers affect the final grade. Some instructors try to discourage "guessing" by giving students the option of not selecting an answer if they simply do not know the material well enough to make an "educated" guess. Then, in computing a test score a question with a "wrong" answer is weighted more heavily than a question that is not answered. For example, the total score might be computed as:

   Score = (number of questions) - (number not answered) - 1.2*(number wrong).

Note in the scoring formula above that an additional weight (.2) is applied to wrong answers. Sometimes this weight is viewed as a "correction" for guessing because it adjusts the total score based on the probability of a guess (i.e., with five answers there is a 1 in 5 chance that a correct answer is based on a guess). Of course, others argue that using such an adjustment discourages students from making judgments when they have some information on which to arrive at an answer--and it does complicate scoring.

Another idea that has been used by one of the authors with some success involves a different approach--allowing students to "justify" answers when they think that something is ambiguous. For example, students are instructed to select the "best" answer on their answer sheet. But, if they think that what is "best" depends on unstated assumptions or how a particular wording is interpreted, they are allowed to write out a very brief explanation on the back of their answer sheet. The idea is for them to concisely show that they really *understand* the concept tested in the question. Then, the instructor can consider the comments and count an answer as correct if the student reveals an understanding of the material--even if the answer sheet alone would have suggested a "wrong" answer.

This approach preserves most of the advantages of traditional objective testing approaches, and it may have other advantages as well. One advantage is that students seem to have a good reaction to this approach. They perceive it as adding another element of "fairness" to objective tests. It can also eliminate some of the potential problems of student questions during the exam. A student who asks for a "clarification" during the exam may be given some type of advantage by a response from the instructor--if the rest of the class does not hear the same explanation. On the other hand, there may be a dilemma if a student's question suggests that he really does understand the material, and when repeating the question to the whole class would provide more of a "hint" than the instructor prefers to give to those who may not know the material as well. An obvious disadvantage of this approach is that it does add to the grading effort--perhaps significantly in large classes. The authors' experience here may help the instructor in considering the advantages and limitations of using this approach, or some modification of it. First, how many "comments" are written is a key issue. If a substantial amount of "extra" time is allowed for such comments relative to the number of questions, more should be expected. On the other hand, actual experience suggests that students will on average write comments on only two or three questions on a test which includes 40 or 50 questions--if students are told that they are not "expected" to write a lot of comments--but rather should reserve use of comments for questions where they really think that added clarification is needed. This can cut down on "boiler-plate" explanations--and instructor time in reading unnecessary comments. It typically takes a few minutes per exam to consider comments.

Another consideration is whether or not allowing such comments makes any real difference in grades. Experience here suggests that this approach has a slightly different effect for different types of students. The very best students may write quite a few comments, but often they end up "justifying" a correct answer with the type of logic that the instructor had in mind in selecting a question in the first place. Thus, their grades may not change very much. Conversely, students who in general do poorly on the test will tend to write few comments (or none), and quite frequently the comment does not support a good choice. This is perhaps expected--as it simply confirms that those who don't know enough to select good answers usually don't know enough to write a comment! It seems that allowing comments has the most effect on the grades of students who are in the "middle ranges" on a test. As such, using this approach may tend to provide additional discrimination in the middle of the class "grade distribution"--but not result in significant shifts in the overall scores. The point, however, is that some students appreciate the opportunity to show that they understand the concepts behind a question--and some students may fare a bit better by having that opportunity.

Most instructors who use objective questions on tests provide students with a standardized "answer sheet" so that all answers are consolidated in one place. This eliminates the time of "flipping pages" on many--perhaps hundreds of--test booklets to check answers. It makes it easier and more accurate to compare student responses to an answer key. Another advantage is that the instructor can return the answer sheet (with incorrect responses marked or with a key). That way, each student will have personal feedback for going over the test results in class--even if the instructor does not want students to be able to retain copies of the test booklets. Many instructors "control" distribution of the actual test questions in this fashion--so that some future students are not given an unfair advantage by having access to an unauthorized "quiz file." This, of course, is a matter of individual instructor preferences--and perhaps joint decisions when different instructors teach different sections of the course.

When a separate answer sheet is used, one simple approach is to provide students with a sheet that has question numbers and a place for a correct answer to be written in. A variation on this approach is to use an answer form that makes it convenient for students to select an answer by simply marking the correct answer in a standard format. This approach has an additional advantage in scoring exams--especially when a large number of students take the test. Specifically, the instructor can mark the answers on the standard form, and then use a hole-punch or a razor-knife to cut out the area around the correct answers. This leaves a template that can be placed over a student's answers. It is easy to spot incorrect answers--by simply looking at cut-outs in the template to see if the student has marked a correct answer. The template can also make it easy and fast to show correct answers on the answer sheet--by drawing a line (with the proverbial red pen!) across the area where an answer should have been marked. Of course, when using this approach it is wise to scan the answer sheet to make certain that the student has not marked more than one answer per question!

Many schools provide standard forms of this sort--and sometimes even provide scanner services for computer grading. For the convenience of faculty who do not have such help, an answer form is provided on the next page. This can be removed at the perforated line, duplicated and distributed to students with test booklets--and also used for making a template of the answer key. Space has been left at the top of the form for the instructor to insert the date, test identification information, and to label other information that might be requested from students.

CONCLUDING REMARKS

In summary, the *Manual of Objective Tests* and associated computerized test generating systems provide you with high quality, flexible alternatives to meet your *Basic Marketing* testing needs. They are part of our comprehensive set of teaching and learning materials for the first marketing course. We have carefully developed these materials ourselves so they will be the very best available anywhere and really WORK for you and your students. We hope you find them helpful. If you have comments, criticisms or suggestions concerning the test bank please let us know. The most efficient approach is to send an email message to the address Bill_Perreault@unc.edu.

William D. Perreault, Jr. and E. Jerome McCarthy

ANSWER SHEET

Date: _____   Test: _____

Please Print the Information Requested Below:

_____   _____
(last name, first name)   (identification number)

_____   _____

Instructions: For each question, please indicate the *best* answer by marking out the letter for the answer you select in the space provided. Please erase any errors completely.

EXAMPLE: =A= —B— =C= =D= =E= [if you want answer "B"]

SELECT ANSWERS BELOW

1 =A= =B= =C= =D= =E=	2 =A= =B= =C= =D= =E=	3 =A= =B= =C= =D= =E=
4 =A= =B= =C= =D= =E=	5 =A= =B= =C= =D= =E=	6 =A= =B= =C= =D= =E=
7 =A= =B= =C= =D= =E=	8 =A= =B= =C= =D= =E=	9 =A= =B= =C= =D= =E=
10 =A= =B= =C= =D= =E=	11 =A= =B= =C= =D= =E=	12 =A= =B= =C= =D= =E=
13 =A= =B= =C= =D= =E=	14 =A= =B= =C= =D= =E=	15 =A= =B= =C= =D= =E=
16 =A= =B= =C= =D= =E=	17 =A= =B= =C= =D= =E=	18 =A= =B= =C= =D= =E=
19 =A= =B= =C= =D= =E=	20 =A= =B= =C= =D= =E=	21 =A= =B= =C= =D= =E=
22 =A= =B= =C= =D= =E=	23 =A= =B= =C= =D= =E=	24 =A= =B= =C= =D= =E=
25 =A= =B= =C= =D= =E=	26 =A= =B= =C= =D= =E=	27 =A= =B= =C= =D= =E=
28 =A= =B= =C= =D= =E=	29 =A= =B= =C= =D= =E=	30 =A= =B= =C= =D= =E=
31 =A= =B= =C= =D= =E=	32 =A= =B= =C= =D= =E=	33 =A= =B= =C= =D= =E=
34 =A= =B= =C= =D= =E=	35 =A= =B= =C= =D= =E=	36 =A= =B= =C= =D= =E=
37 =A= =B= =C= =D= =E=	38 =A= =B= =C= =D= =E=	39 =A= =B= =C= =D= =E=
40 =A= =B= =C= =D= =E=	41 =A= =B= =C= =D= =E=	42 =A= =B= =C= =D= =E=
43 =A= =B= =C= =D= =E=	44 =A= =B= =C= =D= =E=	45 =A= =B= =C= =D= =E=
46 =A= =B= =C= =D= =E=	47 =A= =B= =C= =D= =E=	48 =A= =B= =C= =D= =E=
49 =A= =B= =C= =D= =E=	50 =A= =B= =C= =D= =E=	51 =A= =B= =C= =D= =E=
52 =A= =B= =C= =D= =E=	53 =A= =B= =C= =D= =E=	54 =A= =B= =C= =D= =E=
55 =A= =B= =C= =D= =E=	56 =A= =B= =C= =D= =E=	57 =A= =B= =C= =D= =E=
58 =A= =B= =C= =D= =E=	59 =A= =B= =C= =D= =E=	60 =A= =B= =C= =D= =E=
61 =A= =B= =C= =D= =E=	62 =A= =B= =C= =D= =E=	63 =A= =B= =C= =D= =E=
64 =A= =B= =C= =D= =E=	65 =A= =B= =C= =D= =E=	66 =A= =B= =C= =D= =E=
67 =A= =B= =C= =D= =E=	68 =A= =B= =C= =D= =E=	69 =A= =B= =C= =D= =E=
70 =A= =B= =C= =D= =E=	71 =A= =B= =C= =D= =E=	72 =A= =B= =C= =D= =E=
73 =A= =B= =C= =D= =E=	74 =A= =B= =C= =D= =E=	75 =A= =B= =C= =D= =E=
76 =A= =B= =C= =D= =E=	77 =A= =B= =C= =D= =E=	78 =A= =B= =C= =D= =E=
79 =A= =B= =C= =D= =E=	80 =A= =B= =C= =D= =E=	81 =A= =B= =C= =D= =E=
82 =A= =B= =C= =D= =E=	83 =A= =B= =C= =D= =E=	84 =A= =B= =C= =D= =E=
85 =A= =B= =C= =D= =E=	86 =A= =B= =C= =D= =E=	87 =A= =B= =C= =D= =E=
88 =A= =B= =C= =D= =E=	89 =A= =B= =C= =D= =E=	90 =A= =B= =C= =D= =E=
91 =A= =B= =C= =D= =E=	92 =A= =B= =C= =D= =E=	93 =A= =B= =C= =D= =E=
94 =A= =B= =C= =D= =E=	95 =A= =B= =C= =D= =E=	96 =A= =B= =C= =D= =E=
97 =A= =B= =C= =D= =E=	98 =A= =B= =C= =D= =E=	99 =A= =B= =C= =D= =E=
100 =A= =B= =C= =D= =E=	101 =A= =B= =C= =D= =E=	102 =A= =B= =C= =D= =E=
103 =A= =B= =C= =D= =E=	104 =A= =B= =C= =D= =E=	105 =A= =B= =C= =D= =E=
106 =A= =B= =C= =D= =E=	107 =A= =B= =C= =D= =E=	108 =A= =B= =C= =D= =E=
109 =A= =B= =C= =D= =E=	110 =A= =B= =C= =D= =E=	111 =A= =B= =C= =D= =E=
112 =A= =B= =C= =D= =E=	113 =A= =B= =C= =D= =E=	114 =A= =B= =C= =D= =E=
115 =A= =B= =C= =D= =E=	116 =A= =B= =C= =D= =E=	117 =A= =B= =C= =D= =E=
118 =A= =B= =C= =D= =E=	119 =A= =B= =C= =D= =E=	120 =A= =B= =C= =D= =E=

Chapter 1

Marketing's Role in the Global Economy

True-False Questions:

1-1.
False
p. 4

Marketing is basically selling and advertising.

1-2.
True
p. 5

Customer satisfaction is the extent to which a firm fulfills a consumer's needs, desires and expectations.

1-3.
False
p. 5

If a firm produces the right goods or services, marketing has little role to play in creating customer satisfaction.

1-4.
False
p. 5

Marketing is a necessary economic activity, while production is not.

1-5.
True
p. 6

Marketing can provide needed direction for production and help make sure that the right goods and services find their way to interested consumers.

1-6.
False
p. 6

Marketing creates task utility, but not time or place utility.

1-7.
True
p. 6

The job of marketing is to guide the development of form and task utility, and to provide time, place and possession utilities.

1-8.
False
p. 7

In advanced economies, marketing costs only about 10 percent of each consumer's dollar.

1-9.
False
p. 8

Marketing is a set of activities performed by organizations--i.e., it is not a social process.

1-10.
False
p. 8

Marketing is a social process--i.e., it is not a set of activities performed by organizations.

1-11. *True* p. 8 — Micro-marketing is the performance of activities that seek to accomplish an organization's objectives by anticipating customer or client needs and directing a flow of need-satisfying goods and services from producer to customer or client.

1-12. *True* p. 9 — Micro-marketing is mainly concerned with the activities performed by organizations.

1-13. *False* p. 9 — Micro-marketing activities are performed only by profit-oriented organizations.

1-14. *True* p. 9 — Marketing activities should begin with potential customer needs, not with the production process.

1-15. *False* p. 9 — Production, not marketing, should determine what products are to be made.

1-16. *False* p. 9 — Marketing should begin with the production process.

1-17. *False* p. 9-10 — Marketing is concerned with individual transactions rather than with building ongoing relationships with customers because that is the job of people in the public relations department.

1-18. *True* p. 10 — Macro-marketing emphasizes how the whole marketing system works.

1-19. *False* p. 10 — Macro-marketing emphasizes the activities of individual organizations.

1-20. *True* p. 11 — Whether a particular macro-marketing system is judged fair and effective depends on the objectives of the society.

1-21. *True* p. 11 — An economic system is the way an economy organizes to use scarce resources to produce goods and services and distribute them for consumption among various people and groups in the society.

1-22. *False* p. 11 — Only industrial nations need an economic system to decide what and how much is to be produced and distributed by whom, when, to whom, and why.

1-23. *False* p. 11 — In a planned economy, the individual decisions of many producers and consumers make the macro-level decisions for the whole economy.

1-24.
False
p. 12

A market-directed economy is one in which government planners decide what and how much is to be produced and distributed by whom, when, to whom, and why.

1-25.
True
p. 12

Market-directed systems tend to provide consumers with greater freedom of choice than planned economic systems.

1-26.
False
p. 12

In a market-directed economy, consumers enjoy complete freedom of choice.

1-27.
False
p. 12

In a market-directed economy, profit is guaranteed.

1-28.
True
p. 12

Gun control is an example of a micro-macro dilemma.

1-29.
True
p. 14

No economic system--whether centrally planned or market directed--can achieve its objectives without an effective macro-marketing system.

1-30.
True
p. 14

Marketing does not occur unless there are two or more parties who want to exchange something for something else.

1-31.
True
p. 14

A market is a group of potential customers with similar needs who are willing to exchange something of value with sellers offering various goods and/or services.

1-32.
False
p. 16

The development of marketing middlemen in central markets increases the total number of transactions necessary to carry out exchange between producers and consumers.

1-33.
True
p. 16-17

The advantages of working with intermediaries (middlemen) increase as the number of producers and customers, their distance apart, and the number and variety of competing products increase.

1-34.
False
p. 18

A more effective macro-marketing system is caused by more economic development.

1-35.
True
p. 18

Before a nation can achieve a high level of economic development, it must have an effective macro-marketing system.

1-36.
True
p. 19

Tariffs and quotas are often used to discourage foreign firms from entering a country's markets.

1-37.
True
p. 19

A tariff is simply a tax on imported products.

1-38.
True
p. 19

Countertrade is a special type of bartering in which products from one country are traded for products from another.

1-39.
True
p. 19-20

Soft-drink bottlers in Mexico who trade locally grown broccoli for Pepsi concentrate from the U.S. are using countertrade.

1-40.
False
p. 20

Less than 1 percent of all U.S. exports rely on countertrade.

1-41.
True
p. 20

The World Trade Organization (WTO) is an international body dealing with the rules of trade between nations.

1-42.
False
p. 20

The main purpose of the World Trade Organization (WTO) is to help firms find countertrade partners in other countries.

1-43.
False
p. 20

The WTO agreements try to discourage competition and protectionism.

1-44.
False
p. 20

"Economies of scale" means that as a company produces more of a product the total cost of production goes up.

1-45.
True
p. 20

"Economies of scale" means that as a company produces more of a product the cost of each unit produced goes down.

1-46.
False
p. 21

In advanced societies, all goods and services can be produced with mass production and its economies of scale.

1-47.
True
p. 21

Both mass production and effective marketing are needed to satisfy the economic needs of an advanced economy.

1-48.
True
p. 21

Buying, selling, transporting and storing are all universal marketing functions.

1-49.
False
p. 21

The universal functions of marketing are performed in the same way in all macro-marketing systems.

1-50.
True
p. 24

A market-directed macro-marketing system encourages the development and spread of new ideas and products.

1-51.
True
p. 24-25

E-commerce refers to exchanges between individuals and organizations--and the activities that facilitate those exchanges--based on applications of information technology.

1-52.
False
p. 24-25

E-commerce refers to exchanges between organizations, but not exchanges between individuals.

1-53.
False
p. 24

Compared to other innovations, firms have been relatively slow to adopt e-commerce.

1-54.
False
p. 25

Marketing costs go down and customer satisfaction goes up in all exchanges handled by e-commerce.

1-55.
True
p. 26

Marketing ethics are the moral standards that guide marketing decisions and actions.

1-56.
True
p. 26-27

Moral standards often vary from one society to another and among groups within a society, so there is likely to be disagreement about what opinion is correct when it comes to marketing ethics.

1-57.
False
p. 27

A manager shouldn't be criticized for making an unethical marketing decision unless the ethical breach was intentional.

Multiple Choice Questions

1-58.
A
Def.
Easy
p. 4

According to the text, marketing means:
  A. much more than selling and advertising.
  B. selling.
  C. producing and selling.
  D. advertising.
  E. selling and advertising.

1-59.
A
Def.
Easy
p. 4

According to the text, marketing means:
  A. much more than just selling and advertising.
  B. advertising.
  C. producing a product that provides task and form utility.
  D. selling.
  E. making a good product that sells itself.

1-60.
B
Def.
Med.
p. 4

According to the text, marketing means:
A. making a good product that sells itself.
B. much more than selling and advertising.
C. selling and advertising.
D. producing goods and/or services.
E. doing whatever it takes to be able to offer consumers a "better mousetrap."

1-61.
B
Comp.
Easy
p. 5

The production of a new mountain bike model includes which of the following activities?
A. determining how to get the new model to likely bike purchasers.
B. actually making the new mountain bikes.
C. predicting what types of bikes different types of bike riders will want.
D. all of the above.
E. none of the above.

1-62.
E
Def.
Easy
p. 5

Customer satisfaction is the extent to which a firm fulfills a consumer's:
A. needs.
B. desires.
C. expectations.
D. only A and B above.
E. all of the above.

1-63.
C
App.
Easy
p. 6

A bicycle manufacturer designs and produces a new model that is fun and safe. This is an example of providing:
A. place utility.
B. time utility.
C. form utility.
D. possession utility.
E. all of the above.

1-64.
B
App.
Easy
p. 6

A credit union handles financial transactions for its customers. This is an example of providing _____ utility.
A. time
B. task
C. place
D. form
E. all of the above

1-65.
E
Def.
Easy
p. 6

Production provides _____ utility.
A. form and possession
B. possession
C. form
D. task
E. form and task

1-66.
C
Def.
Easy
p. 6

Production supplies _____ utility.
A. form and possession.
B. time and place.
C. form and task.
D. all of the above.
E. none of the above.

1-**67.**
D
Comp.
Med.
p. 6

The old saying--"build a better mousetrap and the world will beat a path to your door":
    A. looks at exchange from the customer's point of view.
    B. recognizes the importance of economies of scale.
    C. overemphasizes the importance of place utility.
    D. considers only form utility, not other types of utility.
    E. is true only in market-directed economies.

1-**68.**
B
Comp.
Easy
p. 6

"Build a better mousetrap and the world will beat a path to your door" implies that there is little need for marketing when a company can provide:
    A. consumers with all of the different types of economic utility.
    B. form utility.
    C. task utility.
    D. place utility.
    E. possession utility.

1-**69.**
E
Comp.
Easy
p. 6

The old saying -- "build a better mousetrap and the world will beat a path to your door" -- focuses on:
    A. form, place, and time utility.
    B. only task utility.
    C. only place utility.
    D. both form and place utility.
    E. only form utility.

1-**70.**
D
Comp.
Easy
p. 6

Marketing and production combine to provide economic utility. But production by itself is concerned primarily with:
    A. task utility.
    B. time utility.
    C. form utility.
    D. only A and C above.
    E. all of the above.

1-**71.**
B
Comp.
Easy
p. 6

Both production and marketing contribute to providing:
    A. time and place utility.
    B. form and task utility.
    C. possession utility.
    D. place utility.
    E. None of the above.

1-**72.**
B
Comp.
Med.
p. 6

According to the text:
    A. marketing is a more important economic activity than production.
    B. production and marketing combine to provide the five basic economic utilities.
    C. only marketing provides form utility.
    D. only marketing provides economic utility.
    E. a good product is all you need for success in business.

1-**73.**
B
Comp.
Easy
p. 6

Marketing and production combine to provide five economic utilities. Which of the following is NOT one of these five?
 A. possession.
 B. product.
 C. place.
 D. time.
 E. form.

1-**74.**
C
Def.
Easy
p. 6

Having the right to use or consume a product is:
 A. task utility.
 B. place utility.
 C. possession utility.
 D. form utility.
 E. time utility.

1-**75.**
B
Comp.
Med.
p. 6

Which of the following statements about economic utility is NOT true?
 A. Possession utility gives a customer the right to use a product.
 B. Place utility means making the product wherever it can be done most efficiently.
 C. Time utility means having the product available when the customer wants it.
 D. Form utility is provided by making something out of something else.
 E. Task utility is provided when someone performs a task for someone else.

1-**76.**
D
Comp.
Med.
p. 6

Which of the following statements about economic utility is NOT true?
 A. Task utility is provided when someone performs a task for someone else.
 B. Place utility means having a product available where consumers want it.
 C. Possession utility means having the right to use or consume the product.
 D. Time utility means getting a new product onto the market in as short a time as possible.
 E. Form utility means making something tangible.

1-**77.**
E
App.
Hard
p. 6

Bullseye Stores recently bought several truckloads of chairs from a furniture manufacturer in North Carolina. The chairs were shipped to Bullseye stores in Atlanta, where they were put on the retail floor and--eventually--sold to customers. In this situation, Bullseye Stores created:
 A. task, time, place, and possession utility.
 B. only place utility.
 C. only time and place utility.
 D. only place and possession utility.
 E. only time, place, and possession utility.

1-**78.**
A
Def.
Easy
p. 6

Marketing guides production in providing _____ utility.
 A. form and task
 B. time and place
 C. place and form
 D. only possession
 E. none of the above is correct.

1-**79.**
C
Comp.
Easy
p. 6

Marketing provides:
A. task, place, and possession utility.
B. place and time utility.
C. place, possession, and time utility.
D. form, place, and possession utility.
E. form, possession, and time utility.

1-**80.**
C
Int.
Easy
p. 7

Which of the following statements about marketing is FALSE?
A. Marketing concepts and techniques apply for nonprofit organizations--as well as for profit-seeking organizations.
B. Marketing offers many rewarding career opportunities.
C. The cost of marketing is about 10 percent of the consumer's dollar.
D. Marketing affects almost every part of your daily life.
E. Marketing is vital for economic growth and development.

1-**81.**
D
Def.
Easy
p. 8-9

Marketing is:
A. a set of activities performed by individual organizations.
B. relevant to both business and nonprofit organizations.
C. a social process.
D. all of the above are correct.
E. only A and B above.

1-**82.**
A
Comp.
Med.
p. 8

The statement that marketing is "the creation and delivery of a standard of living" focuses on:
A. macro-marketing.
B. possession utility.
C. marketing in planned economic systems.
D. micro-marketing.
E. marketing by nonprofit organizations.

1-**83.**
E
Comp.
Med.
p. 8

The statement that marketing is "the creation and delivery of a standard of living" focuses on:
A. form utility.
B. both form and place utility.
C. place utility.
D. the micro-macro dilemma.
E. macro-marketing.

1-**84.**
C
Def.
Easy
p. 8

Looking at marketing as a set of activities focuses on
A. macro-marketing.
B. business marketing.
C. micro-marketing.
D. time utility.
E. personalized marketing.

1-**85.**
A
Def.
Easy
p. 8-9

Micro-marketing:
A. tries to accomplish a company's objectives by anticipating customers' needs and trying to satisfy them.
B. begins with the production process.
C. involves persuading customers to buy your product.
D. is a social process involving all producers, middlemen, and consumers.
E. tries to make the whole economic system fair and effective.

1-**86.**
E
Def.
Easy
p. 8-9

MICRO-marketing:
A. is concerned with whether the whole system is fair and effective.
B. applies only to profit organizations.
C. consists only of personal selling and advertising.
D. is a social process.
E. tries to anticipate and satisfy customer needs and accomplish an organization's objectives.

1-**87.**
A
Def.
Med.
p. 9

MICRO-marketing:
A. applies to both profit and nonprofit organizations.
B. says that marketing should take over all production, accounting, and financial activities.
C. should begin as soon as goods are produced.
D. does away with the need for advertising.
E. All of the above are true.

1-**88.**
C
Def.
Easy
p. 9

Micro-marketing:
A. emphasizes mass selling over personal selling.
B. allows production, rather than marketing, to determine what products to make.
C. applies to both profit and nonprofit organizations.
D. concentrates on production, rather than advertising.
E. none of the above.

1-**89.**
E
App.
Med.
p. 9-10

Which of the following organizations would be least likely to need marketing skills?
A. an accountant
B. an electronics retailer
C. a toy manufacturer
D. a financial advisor
E. All of the above would need marketing skills.

1-**90.**
C
App.
Easy
p. 9-10

Which of the following is the best example of micro-marketing?
A. Korea unveils a new five year production plan
B. China and the U.S. agree on a new trade agreement
C. The American Red Cross seeks more blood donors
D. The Internet makes it possible for firms to reach customers in other countries.
E. none of the above is a good example.

1-91.
E
Comp.
Hard
p. 9-10

Which of the following statements by a U.S. president best reflects a MICRO-marketing point of view?
A. "A tax cut will give consumers more spending money."
B. "Many young people can no longer afford to buy a new home."
C. "In the United States we have a better choice of products than in any other country."
D. "My administration will spend 25 percent more on purchases related to domestic security during the next year."
E. "Tourism firms should advertise more to attract more international visitors."

1-92.
C
Comp.
Med.
p. 9

Which of the following statements best describes the modern view of marketing?
A. Marketing is only necessary for profit-oriented firms.
B. Marketing consists mainly of advertising and personal selling.
C. Marketing anticipates customer needs.
D. Marketing begins as soon as products are produced.
E. Firms that don't rely on e-commerce should put more emphasis on marketing.

1-93.
B
Comp.
Med.
p. 9

Effective MICRO-marketing should begin with
A. an effort to persuade unwilling customers to buy the firm's products.
B. potential customer needs.
C. a decision about what the firm can produce efficiently.
D. evaluation of the effect of the firm's decisions on the MACRO-marketing system.
E. the marketing manager making important production, accounting, and financial decisions for the firm.

1-94.
E
Int.
Easy
p. 9-10

Which of the following statements about marketing is FALSE?
A. Marketing affects the products you buy.
B. Marketing applies to nonprofit organizations too.
C. Marketing affects the advertising you see and hear.
D. Marketing offers many good job opportunities.
E. Marketing can help with individual transactions but not in building relationships with customers.

1-95.
C
Def.
Easy
p. 10

Viewing marketing as a social process focuses on
A. marketing by non-profit organizations.
B. planned economic systems.
C. macro-marketing.
D. micro-marketing.
E. none of the above.

1-96.
E
Def.
Easy
p. 10-11

MACRO-marketing:
A. is a social process.
B. is concerned with the objectives of society.
C. tries to effectively match supply and demand.
D. directs an economy's flow of goods and services from producers to consumers.
E. All of the above are true statements.

1-**97.**
C
Def.
Easy
p. 10-11

Macro-marketing:
A. assumes that all countries have the same social objectives.
B. focuses on the activities of individual organizations.
C. tries to effectively match supply and demand.
D. all of the above.
E. none of the above.

1-**98.**
C
Comp.
Easy
p. 10-11

A "good" MACRO-marketing system should:
A. increase output of consumer goods.
B. support and encourage mass production.
C. match heterogeneous supply and heterogeneous demand.
D. fill all consumer needs.
E. eliminate differences between rich and poor consumers.

1-**99.**
B
Def.
Med.
p. 10-11

MACRO-marketing:
A. is concerned with the activities performed by individual business organizations.
B. tries to match heterogeneous supply capabilities with heterogeneous demands for goods and services.
C. is concerned with how effectively and fairly an individual business organization performs.
D. assumes that the effectiveness and fairness of all macro-marketing systems must be evaluated in terms of the same social objectives.
E. All of the above are true.

1-**100.**
C
Comp.
Med.
p. 11

A MACRO-marketing system should:
A. provide everyone with the same goods and services.
B. be market-directed, not centrally planned.
C. accomplish a particular society's objectives, whatever they are.
D. all of the above are true.
E. none of the above is true.

1-**101.**
E
App.
Med.
p. 11

Which of the following BEST describes what is necessary for a country's MACRO-marketing system to be "fair and effective"?
A. No low quality or dangerous products are sold.
B. Product shortages never exist.
C. There is a big choice of goods and services.
D. All consumers get the same opportunity to enjoy a high standard of living.
E. There is not enough information to select an answer.

1-**102.**
B
Comp.
Hard
p. 11

The following headlines are from Business Week magazine. Which article is most likely to be reporting on a MACRO-marketing topic?
A. "Two-Person Engineering Firm Offers Unique Service."
B. "Russia Increases Output of Consumer Goods."
C. "Pepsi Sells in India."
D. "BankAmerica Offers New Internet Banking Services."
E. "Donations to Terrorist Victims Fund Increase after TV Broadcast."

1-**103.**
E
Comp.
Med.
p. 11

The following headlines are for articles from the WALL STREET JOURNAL. Which article is most likely to be reporting a MACRO-marketing topic?
A. "Cadillac Goes after Luxury Sport Utility Buyers."
B. "Adidas Jumps as Footwear Competition Heats Up."
C. "Drugstore Chain Aims at Seniors."
D. "Hardee's Fried Chicken Takes on KFC."
E. "DVD Popularity Leads to More DVD Retailers."

1-**104.**
B
Comp.
Hard
p. 11

Of the following headlines from the WALL STREET JOURNAL, which is most likely to be about a MACRO-marketing topic?
A. "Rubbermaid Has a New Strategy."
B. "Thailand Has Unusually Large Number of Wholesalers."
C. "Military Supplier Shifts to Selling Gas Masks to Private Citizens."
D. "Coke Plans Beverage Line to Compete with Lipton's."
E. "Dow Chemical Adds Shipping Safeguards."

1-**105.**
A
Comp.
Hard
p. 11

Of the following headlines from a business magazine, which is most likely to be about a MACRO-marketing topic?
A. "Chinese Students Demand More Consumer Goods."
B. "Girl Scouts Organize Nationwide Cookie Sale."
C. "L'eggs Sells Direct in Hungary."
D. "Kraft Offers New Low-Fat Products."
E. "Coke Again Available in Belgium."

1-**106.**
E
Def.
Med.
p. 11

An economic system in which government planners determine production levels is known as
A. a subsistence economic system.
B. a central market economic system.
C. a macro-marketing economic system.
D. a market-directed economic system.
E. a planned economic system.

1-**107.**
D
Def.
Med.
p. 11

In planned economic systems:
A. producers generally have a lot of choice about what and how much to produce.
B. prices usually fluctuate according to supply and demand.
C. marketing activities such as advertising, branding, and market research are not allowed.
D. consumers usually have some freedom of choice--but it is quite limited.
E. All of the above are true.

1-**108.**
E
Def.
Easy
p. 11

In a planned economic system, government planners decide:
A. who is to produce and distribute what to whom.
B. how much is to be produced.
C. how much is to be distributed to whom.
D. what is to be produced.
E. all of the above.

1-109.
E
Def.
Easy
p. 12

In a market-directed economic system:
   A. marketing managers make all the important economic decisions.
   B. government planners make all the important economic decisions.
   C. all the important economic decisions are made by voters in political elections.
   D. consumers make all the important economic decisions.
   E. the individual decisions of the many producers and consumers make the macro-level decisions for the whole economy.

1-110.
C
Comp.
Med.
p. 12

In a market-directed economic system:
   A. profit, survival, and growth are all guaranteed for producers.
   B. consumers have little freedom of choice.
   C. consumers decide what is to be produced and by whom through their dollar votes.
   D. prices usually do not change according to supply and demand.
   E. only the needs of the majority are served.

1-111.
E
Def.
Easy
p. 12

The role of price in a market-directed economy is to:
   A. allocate resources and distribute income according to consumer preferences.
   B. serve as a rough measure of the social importance of consumer goods and services.
   C. coordinate the economic activity of many people and institutions.
   D. serve as a rough measure of the value of resources used to produce goods and services.
   E. All of the above are true.

1-112.
A
Comp.
Med.
p. 12

Which of the following statements about economic systems is true?
   A. Consumers usually have more freedom of choice in a market-directed economy.
   B. Planned economies are most effective for countries with large and complicated varieties of goods and services.
   C. Branding is less common in a market-directed economy than in a planned economy.
   D. The United States is a good example of a planned economy.
   E. None of the above is true.

1-113.
D
Comp.
Easy
p. 12

Which of the following is NOT true about a market-directed economic system?
   A. Consumers enjoy maximum freedom of choice.
   B. Producers enjoy maximum freedom of choice.
   C. The interaction between consumers and producers is great.
   D. Government is responsible for setting up central markets.
   E. The price of a consumer product serves as a measure of its value.

1-114.
C
Comp.
Med.
p. 12

Which of the following statements about economic systems is NOT true?
   A. Government has less of a role in market-directed economies than in planned economies.
   B. A market-directed economy self-adjusts through producer and consumer choices.
   C. Producers always make a profit in a market-directed system.
   D. A planned economy is more likely to work if the variety of goods and services is small.
   E. Both market-directed and planned economies need a macro-marketing system.

1-115.
A
Comp.
Hard
p. 12

Which of the following is TRUE about the micro-macro dilemma?

A. What is good for some producers and consumers may not be good for society as a whole.
B. Marketing people cannot agree on whether marketing should be viewed as individual activities or a social process.
C. In a multiproduct company, one product should not be emphasized over another.
D. Most people don't want much freedom of choice.
E. Middlemen facilitate exchange but they add to the cost of goods.

1-116.
E
Def.
Hard
p. 12

The term "micro-macro dilemma" means that:

A. most people are both producers and consumers.
B. marketing people cannot agree on whether marketing should be viewed as activities or as a social process.
C. every economy needs a micro-marketing system--but not necessarily a MACRO-marketing system.
D. MICRO-marketing is concerned with the flow of goods and services from producers to consumers--while MACRO-marketing is not.
E. what is "good" for some producers and consumers may not be good for society as a whole.

1-117.
D
App.
Med.
p. 12-13

Trying to balance the interests of people who want to drink beer and the dangers of drunk driving is an example of:

A. the role of a central market.
B. subsistence marketing.
C. political action.
D. the macro-micro dilemma.
E. the exchange process in marketing.

1-118.
D
App.
Med.
p. 12-13

Which of the following is an example of the micro-macro dilemma?

A. Disposable packages are convenient, but contribute to environmental problems.
B. Children like to ride bicycles, but accidents are common.
C. Sulfites help to keep restaurant salads looking fresh, but some people have a dangerous allergic reaction to sulfites.
D. All of the above.
E. A and C, but not B.

1-119.
B
App.
Med.
p. 12-13

Which of the following is NOT an example of the micro-macro dilemma?

A. Many people like beer and wine, but drunk driving is a big social problem.
B. Some people like to eat a lot, but later feel guilty about eating too much.
C. A "good" lawnmower can be produced cheaply, but its price must be higher if its design must be safe for "ignorant" users.
D. A smoker may enjoy a cigar, but the smell can make other people sick.
E. Downhill snow skiing is fun, but really quite dangerous.

1-120. Which of the following is the BEST example of the micro-macro dilemma?
B
App.   A. Many consumers buy imported cars, even though they say they like American
Med.   cars better.
p. 12-13   B. High performance cars are fun to drive but may be dangerous to others.
         C. Buying an imported car may cost buyers more to buy now but may have better
             resale value later.
         D. A fuel efficient car may cost more to buy but less to operate.
         E. The economy may be growing, but many people still are not able to buy a new
             car.

1-121. Which of the following is the BEST example of the micro-macro dilemma?
D
App.   A. 7-Up sales went up, but total sales of all soft drinks went down.
Med.   B. A small group of loyal consumers really like RC Cola best, but most consumers
p. 12-13   don't like it at all.
         C. The deposit on returnable soft drink bottles is about equal to the cost of the
             bottle.
         D. Paper cups for soft-drinks are convenient, but they often end up as litter along
             the highway.
         E. Gatorade is more popular in Texas than in the rest of the U.S.

1-122. Which of the following is LEAST LIKELY to be a government role in a
E   market-directed economic system?
Comp.   A. To set rules to protect individual rights and freedom.
Hard   B. To supervise the economic system.
p. 13-14   C. To provide things such as mass transportation and highways, national defense,
             police and fire protection, and public health services.
         D. To control interest rates and the supply of money.
         E. To determine prices--and thereby allocate resources and distribute income.

1-123. In a pure subsistence economy,
D
Def.   A. each family unit is self-sufficient.
Easy   B. exchanges are not important.
p. 14   C. there is no need for middlemen.
         D. All of the above are true.
         E. None of the above is true.

1-124. If the family units on a South Pacific-island nation made all the products they consume,
A   it would be a good example of:
App.   A. a pure subsistence economy.
Easy   B. a pure market-oriented economy.
p. 14   C. a micro-marketing system.
         D. a planned economy.
         E. none of the above.

1-125. Marketing could NOT take place without:
C
App.   A. central markets.
Easy   B. middlemen.
p. 14   C. two or more parties who each have something they want to exchange for
             something else.
         D. a money system.
         E. all of the above.

1-**126.**
D
Comp.
Med.
p. 14

Marketing will not happen unless:
A. producers and consumers can meet at some central location for face-to-face bargaining.
B. an economy has a money system.
C. middlemen are present to facilitate exchange.
D. two or more parties each have something they want to exchange for something else.
E. an economy is market-directed rather than planned.

1-**127.**
E
Def.
Easy
p. 14

According to the text, a "market" is:
A. a convenient place to shop.
B. a meeting place for producers and consumers.
C. a convenient place for social gatherings.
D. a display area for producers' goods.
E. a group of buyers who are willing to exchange something of value with sellers offering various goods and services.

1-**128.**
A
Def.
Easy
p. 14

A "market" is:
A. a group of buyers who are willing to exchange something of value with sellers offering various goods and services.
B. a group of producers and consumers located close to each other.
C. a set of middlemen in one location.
D. a convenient physical location.
E. a small place consisting of a few families.

1-**129.**
E
Def.
Med.
p. 14-16

Central markets:
A. allow more time for production, consumption, and recreation.
B. help provide time, place, and possession utility.
C. provide a convenient place for social gatherings.
D. facilitate exchange.
E. All of the above.

1-**130.**
D
Def.
Med.
p. 14-16

Central markets:
A. facilitate exchange.
B. help provide time, place, and possession utility.
C. allow more time for production, consumption, and recreation.
D. All of the above.
E. None of the above.

1-**131.**
D
Comp.
Med.
p. 16

Exchanges between buyers and sellers are simplified by:
A. use of money as a medium of exchange.
B. use of middlemen.
C. use of a central market as a trading location.
D. all of the above.
E. none of the above.

1-**132.** What happens after the development of a central market in a primitive society?
C
Comp.   A. one central middleman controls the market and ensures that all producers are
Med.   represented.
p. 16   B. specialization in production is discouraged.
        C. the number of exchange transactions needed will decrease--if a middleman
           develops.
        D. total form utility will decrease.
        E. all of the above are true.

1-**133.** A middleman:
E
        A. is a wholesaler--not a retailer.
Def.   B. usually increases the number of transactions required.
Easy   C. tends to make the exchange process more difficult and costly.
p. 16   D. reduces economic utility in more complex economies.
        E. is someone who specializes in trade rather than production.

1-**134.** Which of the following is NOT true about middlemen?
B
        A. They save time for other participants in a transaction.
Comp.   B. They provide additional form utility.
Med.   C. They specialize in trade rather than production.
p. 16   D. All of the above.
        E. None of the above.

1-**135.** A middleman is LEAST likely to provide:
D
        A. place utility.
Comp.   B. possession utility.
Easy   C. economic utility.
p. 16   D. form utility.
        E. time utility.

1-**136.** When a central market develops in a primitive society,
C
        A. specialization in production decreases because trade is more important.
Comp.   B. the next stage of development is likely to be a pure subsistence economy.
Med.   C. the number of exchange transactions needed will remain high unless a
p. 16   middleman appears.
        D. each family has less overall utility--at least until a middleman emerges.
        E. None of the above is true.

1-**137.** The advantages of working with an intermediary usually increase when there is
E
        A. difficulty communicating with customers
Comp.   B. a greater number of customers.
Med.   C. greater distance between customers
p. 16-17   D. a larger number of competing products
        E. all of the above

1-**138.** A MACRO-marketing system is NOT needed in a _____ economy.
C
        A. consumer-oriented
Comp.   B. planned
Hard   C. pure subsistence
p. 18   D. pure market-directed
        E. ALL of the above types of economies would need a macro-marketing system.

1-**139.**   A MACRO-marketing system is NOT needed in a _____ economy.
C
Comp.   A. pure market-directed
Hard   B. planned
p. 18   C. pure subsistence
           D. central market
           E. All of the above

1-**140.**   An effective MACRO-marketing system is:
B
Comp.   A. not really related to economic development.
Easy   B. necessary for economic development.
p. 18   C. the only cause of economic development.
           D. the result of greater economic development.
           E. None of the above is true.

1-**141.**   Which of the following is necessary for economic development?
E
Comp.   A. tariffs that reduce competition from imported products.
Med.   B. eliminating at least some of the universal marketing functions.
p. 18   C. government planners who decide what and how much is to be produced.
           D. low wages.
           E. an effective macro-marketing system.

1-**142.**   Tariffs:
E
Def.   A. are customs quotas.
Easy   B. set the quantities of products which can move in or out of a country.
p. 19   C. are "bribes" paid to foreign officials.
           D. are the same as quotas.
           E. are taxes on imported products.

1-**143.**   Tariffs (in international trade):
E
           A. may have the same effect as import quotas.
Comp.   B. sometimes are set very high to limit trade.
Easy   C. are basically taxes on imported products.
p. 19   D. are the same as quotas.
           E. A, B, and C are true, but not D.

1-**144.**   Countertrade is
D
           A. impossible if there is no middleman.
Def.   B. a substitute for exchange.
Med.   C. found only in planned economies.
p. 19   D. a special type of bartering.
           E. found only in subsistence economies.

1-**145.**   Countertrade is
D
           A. defined as the exchange of money for something of value.
Def.   B. illegal in the United States.
Med.   C. found only in planned economies.
p. 19   D. a type of transaction that may involve no exchange of money.
           E. found only in subsistence economies.

1-**146.**
E
Comp.
Med.
p. 19-20

Countertrade is
   A. more likely to be used in economies where distribution systems and middlemen have not yet developed.
   B. a special type of bartering.
   C. used by many U.S. firms that export their products.
   D. a type of transaction that may involve no exchange of money.
   E. all of the above are true.

1-**147.**
E
Def.
Med.
p. 20

The World Trade Organization (WTO)
   A. was created in 1995.
   B. tries to encourage competition and discourage protectionism.
   C. is an international body dealing with rules of trade between nations.
   D. has no means to settle actual disputes.
   E. A, B, and C are true, but not D.

1-**148.**
E
Def.
Med.
p. 20

The World Trade Organization WTO)
   A. encourages competition.
   B. helps to settle disputes.
   C. discourages protectionism.
   D. is an international body that deals with trade rules.
   E. All of the above.

1-**149.**
A
Def.
Med.
p. 20

"Economies of scale" means that:
   A. as a company produces larger numbers of a particular product, the cost of each of these products goes down.
   B. the more producers there are in an economy the greater the need for middlemen.
   C. larger countries enjoy more economic growth than smaller countries.
   D. as a company produces larger numbers of a particular product, the total cost of producing these products goes down.
   E. All of the above are true.

1-**150.**
C
Def.
Med.
p. 20

When a firm produces a large quantity of a product, the cost of producing each individual unit usually goes down. This is known as:
   A. the central market phenomenon.
   B. exchange efficiency.
   C. economies of scale.
   D. macro-marketing.
   E. form utility.

1-**151.**
B
Def.
Easy
p. 20

The term "economies of scale" means that:
   A. The largest producers are always the most efficient.
   B. The cost of a product goes down as a company produces larger numbers of it.
   C. The more one produces, the greater the profit.
   D. it is more efficient for an economy to have a large number of transactions.
   E. None of the above.

1-**152.**
A
Int.
Hard
p. 20-21

In advanced economies:
A. mass production is a necessary--but not the only condition--for satisfying consumer needs.
B. creating time, place, and possession utilities is less complex.
C. exchange is facilitated by discrepancies of quantity and assortment.
D. both supply and demand tend to be homogeneous.
E. All of the above are true.

1-**153.**
D
Int.
Hard
p. 21

In advanced economies:
A. both supply and demand tend to be heterogeneous.
B. creating time, place, and possession utilities is more complex.
C. exchange is hampered by discrepancies of quantity and assortment.
D. All of the above are true.
E. None of the above is true.

1-**154.**
E
Def.
Easy
p. 21-22

Exchange between producers and consumers is more difficult in an advanced economy because of:
A. separation in time.
B. separation in values.
C. spatial separation.
D. separation of information.
E. All of the above.

1-**155.**
C
Comp.
Med.
p. 21-22

The primary purpose of the transporting and storing functions of marketing is to overcome:
A. the need for marketing specialists.
B. separation of information.
C. spatial separation.
D. discrepancies of assortment.
E. separation of values.

1-**156.**
A
Def.
Med.
p. 21-22

The fact that producers usually prefer to produce products in large quantities, while most consumers prefer to buy in small quantities, results in:
A. discrepancies of quantity.
B. separation of ownership.
C. discrepancies of assortment.
D. spatial separation.
E. temporal separation.

1-**157.**
A
App.
Hard
p. 21-22

In a simple economy, one family may produce only cooking pots families-but many of them. Others may specialize in farming, making clothing, and building shelters. This
A. shows why "discrepancies of assortment" occur.
B. is so simple that the universal functions of marketing don't have to be done.
C. cannot work without a middleman.
D. is an example of "separation in values" since the different families choose to produce different things.
E. All of the above are true.

1-**158.**   The "universal functions of marketing" do NOT include:
C
Def.   A. financing and risk taking.
Easy   B. standardization and grading.
p. 21   C. producing.
             D. transporting and storing.
             E. buying and selling.

1-**159.**   The "universal functions of marketing":
E
Comp.   A. must be performed in all MACRO-marketing systems.
Easy   B. are performed differently and by different parties in different economic systems.
p. 21-22   C. create economic utility.
             D. are needed to help overcome various separations and discrepancies.
             E. All of the above are true.

1-**160.**   The "universal functions of marketing":
B
Comp.   A. can be eliminated in advanced MACRO-marketing systems.
Easy   B. are performed differently and by different parties in different economic systems.
p. 21-22   C. create form utility.
             D. create various separations and discrepancies between producers and consumers.
             E. All of the above are true.

1-**161.**   After seeing a "sale" ad in a local newspaper, Silvia Peta went to a local pet supply
D   store and bought a year's supply of high protein dog food. Which marketing
App.   functions--if any--did she perform?
Med.   A. Financing and risk taking
p. 21-22   B. Buying, transporting, and storing
             C. Market information
             D. All of the above
             E. None of the above--only producers and middlemen perform marketing functions.

1-**162.**   A large advertising agency is planning a national promotion to introduce a new type of
D   of MP3 player. Which of the universal functions of marketing is it performing?
App.   A. risk-taking.
Easy   B. financing.
p. 21   C. buying.
             D. selling.
             E. none of the above.

1-**163.**   _____ involve(s) sorting products according to size and quality.
C
Def.   A. Transporting and storing
Med.   B. Financing
p. 22   C. Standardization and grading
             D. Marketing
             E. Buying

1-**164.**   The standardization and grading function of marketing involves:
C
Def.   A. promoting goods and services.
Med.   B. collection, analysis, and distribution of marketing information.
p. 22   C. sorting products according to size and quality.
             D. looking for and evaluating goods and services.
             E. movement of goods from one place to another.

1-**165.**
C
Comp.
Med.
p. 21

The "universal functions of marketing":
A. are usually performed in the same way and by the same types of institutions in all MACRO-marketing systems.
B. can sometimes be eliminated--in very efficient macro-marketing systems.
C. must be performed in both market-directed and planned economic systems.
D. must all be performed by every firm at the MICRO-marketing level.
E. All of the above are true.

1-**166.**
C
Comp.
Med.
p. 22

The universal functions of marketing
A. can be eliminated if a central market develops.
B. are not all needed in planned economies.
C. can be performed by producers, consumers, and a variety of marketing specialists.
D. All of the above are true.
E. None of the above is true.

1-**167.**
D
Def.
Easy
p. 22

The "universal functions of marketing" can be performed by:
A. producers.
B. middlemen and marketing specialists.
C. consumers.
D. All of the above.
E. Only A and C above.

1-**168.**
A
Int.
Med.
p. 22

Concerning the "universal functions of marketing," it is true that:
A. these functions must be performed in all MACRO-marketing systems.
B. these functions can be performed by producers or middlemen--but not by consumers.
C. from a MICRO viewpoint, every firm must perform all of the functions.
D. responsibility for performing these functions can be shifted and shared--and some functions can be completely eliminated to reduce costs.
E. All of the above are true.

1-**169.**
E
Def.
Easy
p. 24

Firms that specialize in providing marketing functions other than buying or selling are known as:
A. suppliers.
B. middlemen.
C. consultants.
D. agents.
E. facilitators.

1-**170.**
E
Def.
Easy
p. 24

Which of the following types of firms are facilitators?
A. Marketing research firms
B. Trucking companies
C. Advertising agencies
D. Product-testing labs
E. All of the above

1-**171.**
E
Comp.
Med.
p. 24

Which of the following is LEAST likely to be classified as a marketing facilitator?
A. Mayflower Transport Company.
B. Internet Advertising, Inc.
C. Southern States Bank.
D. Market Survey Research, Inc.
E. Quality Coatings Company.

1-**172.**
D
Comp.
Med.
p. 24

Which of the following is LEAST likely to be classified as a marketing facilitator?
A. United Parcel Service (UPS).
B. Public Warehouse Corporation.
C. Broadband Communications Company.
D. Valley Aluminum Company.
E. Product Safety Testing Laboratories, Inc.

1-**173.**
D
Comp.
Med.
p. 24

Marketing middlemen and facilitators can often perform marketing functions:
A. better than producers or consumers can perform them.
B. which leaves producers and consumers more time for production and consumption.
C. at a low cost--because of specialization or economies of scale.
D. all of the above are true.
E. none of the above are true.

1-**174.**
E
Comp.
Easy
p. 22-24

Concerning the "universal functions of marketing," which of the following statements is FALSE?
A. These functions can be performed by producers, middlemen, facilitators, or consumers.
B. Responsibility for performing these functions can be shared and shifted.
C. From a micro viewpoint, not every company must perform every function.
D. From a macro viewpoint, all these functions must be performed by someone.
E. None of the above.

1-**175.**
E
Comp.
Med.
p. 24

A market-directed MACRO-marketing system encourages:
A. links between an economy's production and consumption sectors.
B. widespread distribution of new products.
C. the shift of goods from producing areas to consuming areas.
D. the development and spread of new products.
E. All of the above.

1-**176.**
C
Comp.
Hard
p. 26

Which of the following criticisms focuses most directly on our MACRO-marketing system rather than on micro-marketing:
A. often products wear out right after the warranty expires.
B. much TV advertising is annoying.
C. marketing exploits the poor and the uneducated.
D. prices for very similar products vary a lot from store to store.
E. door-to-door salespeople are trained to be pushy.

1-**177.** Concerning marketing ethics:
D
Comp. A. Individuals develop moral standards based on their own values.
Med. B. Opinions about what is right or wrong vary from one society to another.
p. 26-27 C. The prevailing practice of most businesspeople is to be fair and honest.
  D. All of the above are true.
  E. None of the above is true.

Chapter 2

Marketing's Role within the Firm or Nonprofit Organization

True-False Questions:

2-1.
True
p. 34

During the "production era" a company focuses on production--because few products are available in the market.

2-2.
False
p. 34

During the "sales era," the firm tries to improve short-run marketing policy planning to tie together its activities.

2-3.
True
p. 34

The "marketing department era" is a time when all marketing activities are brought under the control of one department.

2-4.
False
p. 34

During the "marketing company era," the total company effort is guided by the idea that customers exist to buy the firm's output.

2-5.
False
p. 34

The "marketing concept" means that a firm emphasizes attracting new customers above all other objectives.

2-6.
True
p. 34

A firm that adopts the "marketing concept" will aim all its efforts at satisfying customers, while trying to make a profit.

2-7.
True
p. 35

A firm that makes products which are easy to produce and then tries to sell them has a production orientation.

2-8.
True
p. 35

A marketing-oriented firm would try to produce what customers want, while a production-oriented firm would try to get customers to buy what the firm has produced.

2-9.
False
p. 35

The three basic ideas in the marketing concept are 1) putting the marketing manager in charge of the whole firm, 2) a competitive orientation, and 3) an emphasis on profit.

2-10.
True
p. 35

When a firm makes a total company effort to satisfy its customers, and profit--not just sales--is an objective of the firm, the company is practicing the "marketing concept."

2-11.
False
p. 35

Adopting the marketing concept rarely requires any change in a firm's attitudes, organization structure, or management methods and procedures.

2-12.
False
p. 35-36

Adopting the marketing concept requires that a business firm eliminate all functional departments.

2-13.
False
p. 36

In a firm which practices the marketing concept, the efforts of each functional department are guided by what it does best.

2-14.
True
p. 36-37

Service industries were initially slow to adopt the marketing concept, but this has changed dramatically since the 1980s.

2-15.
True
p. 38

Customer value is the difference that a customer sees between the benefits of a firm's offering and the costs of obtaining those benefits.

2-16.
False
p. 38

Customer value is just another term for customer satisfaction.

2-17.
False
p. 38

Setting a low price for a firm's offering is a sure way of creating high customer value.

2-18.
True
p. 39

When it comes to customer value, it is the customer's view that matters, not the view of the marketing manager.

2-19.
True
p. 39

Offering superior customer value is especially important when competition is intense.

2-20.
True
p. 39

Often the best way for a firm to beat the competition is to be first to find and satisfy a need that others have not even considered.

2-21.
True
p. 39

To develp lasting relationships with customers, marketing-oriented firms need to focus on customer satisfaction both before and after each sale.

2-22.
False
p. 39-40

When trying to build relationships with customers, salespeople must be particularly well-trained because they are usually the only employees whose actions influence customers directly.

2-23.
False
p. 40-41

The text credits L.L. Bean's marketing success to its great location.

2-24.
True
p. 40-41

L.L. Bean has achieved success because its customers typically view the benefits of buying its products as greater than the costs.

2-25.
True
p. 41

The marketing concept applies to nonprofit organizations as well as to businesses.

2-26.
False
p. 41

The marketing concept cannot be applied to nonprofit organizations because they are not profit-oriented.

2-27.
True
p. 41

In nonprofit organizations, support may not come directly from satisfied customers.

2-28.
False
p. 43

The marketing concept says that it is a firm's obligation to improve its positive effects on society and reduce its negative effects.

2-29.
True
p. 43

Organizations that adopt the marketing concept should be concerned about marketing ethics as well as broader issues of social responsibility.

2-30.
True
p. 44-45

The American Marketing Association has adopted a code of ethics that sets specific ethical standards for many aspects of the management job in marketing.

2-31.
True
p. 45

The three basic jobs in the marketing management process are planning, implementation, and control.

2-32.
True
p. 45

Strategic planning is the managerial process of developing and maintaining a match between an organization's resources and its market opportunities.

2-33.
True
p. 46

Finding attractive opportunities and developing profitable marketing strategies are the tasks included in the marketing manager's marketing strategy planning job.

2-34.
True
p. 46

A marketing strategy is composed of two interrelated parts--a target market and a marketing mix.

2-35.
False
p. 46

A marketing strategy is composed of two interrelated parts--planning and implementation.

2-**36.**
False
p. 46

The two parts of a marketing strategy are an attractive opportunity and a target market.

2-**37.**
False
p. 47

Mass marketing means focusing on some specific customers, as opposed to assuming that everyone is the same and will want whatever the firm offers.

2-**38.**
True
p. 47

"Mass marketers" like Kmart usually try to aim at clearly defined target markets.

2-**39.**
False
p. 48

The "four Ps" of the marketing mix are People, Products, Price, and Promotion.

2-**40.**
True
p. 48

Product, Place, Promotion and Price are the four major variables (decision areas) in a firm's marketing mix.

2-**41.**
True
p. 48

Although the customer should be the target of all marketing efforts, customers are not part of a marketing mix.

2-**42.**
False
p. 48

According to the text, a firm that sells a service rather than a physical good does not have a product.

2-**43.**
True
p. 48

The Product area of the marketing mix may involve a service and/or a physical good which satisfies some customers' needs.

2-**44.**
True
p. 48

The Place decisions are concerned with getting the right product to the target market at the right time.

2-**45.**
True
p. 48

Any series of firms (or individuals) from producer to final user or consumer is a channel of distribution.

2-**46.**
False
p. 49

A channel of distribution must include a middleman.

2-**47.**
True
p. 50

Personal selling, mass selling, and sales promotion are all included in the Promotion area of the marketing mix.

2-**48.**
False
p. 50

Personal selling is relatively inexpensive, but using it means a firm can't adapt its marketing mix to different potential customers.

2-49.
True
p. 50

Advertising is any paid form of nonpersonal presentation of ideas, goods, or services by an identified sponsor.

2-50.
True
p. 50

Sales promotion can involve point-of-purchase materials, store signs, catalogs, and circulars.

2-51.
False
p. 50

According to the text, Promotion is the most important of the "four Ps."

2-52.
True
p. 51-52

As in the Toddler University case, the needs of a target market virtually determine the nature of an appropriate marketing mix.

2-53.
True
p. 53

A marketing strategy and all the time-related details for carrying out the strategy is a "marketing plan."

2-54.
False
p. 53-54

Marketing strategy planning should specify all of the operational decisions to implement the plan.

2-55.
True
p. 54

A "marketing program" blends all of a firm's marketing plans into one "big" plan.

2-56.
True
p. 55-56

Many of the conventional watchmakers failed because they were not marketing oriented.

2-57.
False
p. 57

"Death-wish" marketing refers to the idea that some firms do such a good job satisfying customers that customers say they'd "almost rather die than switch to some other firm's product."

2-58.
True
p. 57

"Death-wish" marketing refers to the idea that too many managers do a poor job planning and implementing marketing strategies and programs.

Multiple Choice Questions

2-59.
E
Def.
Med.
p. 33

The text considers five "eras" of marketing evolution. Which of the following shows the logical order in which these eras occur?
  A. Marketing department, production, sales, simple trade, marketing company
  B. Sales, production, marketing department, marketing company, simple trade
  C. Sales, simple trade, marketing company, production, marketing department
  D. Simple trade, production, sales, marketing company, marketing department
  E. Simple trade, production, sales, marketing department, marketing company

2-60.
C
Def.
Easy
p. 33

The text discusses the evolution of business through five "eras." Which of the following is NOT one of these eras?
- A. Simple trade era
- B. Sales era
- C. Facilitator era
- D. Marketing department era
- E. Production era

2-61.
A
Def.
Easy
p. 33

The text discusses the evolution of business through five "eras." Which of the following is NOT one of these eras?
- A. Diversification era
- B. Sales era
- C. Production era
- D. Marketing company era
- E. Simple trade era

2-62.
E
Comp.
Med.
p. 33-34

Regarding the five stages in marketing evolution,
- A. in the marketing department era, firms do both short-run and long-run planning.
- B. the first era to evolve was the sales era.
- C. in the marketing company era, firms do short-run planning only.
- D. most firms operate in the production era.
- E. None of the above are true.

2-63.
E
App.
Med.
p. 34

Which of the following is the BEST example of management thinking during the "production era"?
- A. "Production provides form utility and marketing provides time, place, and possession utility."
- B. "We need to find out what the customer wants."
- C. "The more salespeople we have, the more we can sell."
- D. "We need to work hard to sell the product to our customers."
- E. "If we produce a good product, customers will find us and buy it."

2-64.
C
App.
Med.
p. 34

Which of the following is the BEST example of management thinking during the "production era"?
- A. "The more we advertise a product, the more we can sell."
- B. "We need to increase our sales effort--to sell what we can produce."
- C. "If we can produce it, customers will buy it."
- D. "We need to be selective and produce what customers want."
- E. "Production provides time, place, and possession utility."

2-65.
E
App.
Med.
p. 34

Until recently, good microcomputer software for producing digital videos was not available, but was much in demand by businesses. The first companies to produce a specific type of program had good sales even though they did little promotion and their programs were not "user-friendly." It seems that many of these "innovators" operated as if they were in the:
- A. simple trade era.
- B. marketing department era.
- C. sales era.
- D. marketing company era.
- E. production era.

2-**66.**   Regarding the five stages in marketing evolution:
E   A.   Many firms have graduated to the marketing company era.
Comp.   B.   For most firms, the sales era continued until at least 1950.
Med.   C.   In the marketing department era, firms began to do short-run planning.
p. 33-34   D.   The simple trade era was the first era to evolve.
               E.   All of the above are true.

2-**67.**   Because of increased competition during the _____ era, firms put new effort
B   into winning customers.
Comp.   A.   simple trade
Easy   B.   sales
p. 34   C.   production
               D.   marketing company
               E.   marketing department

2-**68.**   During the _____ era, concern about increased competition lead firms to
A   focus on selling to attract customers.
Def.   A.   sales
Easy   B.   simple trade
p. 34   C.   marketing department
               D.   production
               E.   marketing company

2-**69.**   The owner of a company that produces electronic circuit boards sees many competitors
B   with extra capacity and says the "only hope is that our sales manager, who makes all of
App.   our marketing decisions, will find a way to sell more boards." It seems that this
Med.   company is run as if it were in the:
p. 34   A.   production era.
               B.   sales era.
               C.   simple trade era.
               D.   marketing company era.
               E.   marketing department era.

2-**70.**   The president of a company that produces cardboard boxes is concerned about the large
D   number of competitors with extra capacity. As he put it, "our best shot is in the hands
App.   of our sales manager--she makes all of our marketing decisions and is creative enough
Med.   to figure out how to sell more boxes." It seems that this company is run as if it were in
p. 34   the:
               A.   production era.
               B.   marketing company era.
               C.   simple trade era.
               D.   sales era.
               E.   marketing department era.

2-**71.**   Which of the following statements regarding the "sales era" is true?
D   A.   The emphasis was on selling.
Comp.   B.   A business problem was to beat the competition.
Easy   C.   More production capability was available than ever before.
p. 34   D.   All of the above.
               E.   None of the above.

2-**72.**
C
App.
Med.
p. 34

Shaq Hewell was just named Poldston, Inc.'s sales manager, with responsibilities for all marketing planning. Poldston's president told hhim that his job is to "outsell the competition." Apparently, Poldston is operating in the _____ era.
    A. market-oriented
    B. production
    C. sales
    D. marketing company
    E. marketing department

2-**73.**
B
Def.
Med.
p. 34

The _____ era is a time when all marketing activities are brought under the control of one department to improve short-run planning.
    A. production
    B. marketing department
    C. sales
    D. simple trade
    E. marketing company

2-**74.**
B
Comp.
Med.
p. 34

As a firm moves from the sales era to the marketing department era it is likely to:
    A. have marketing people who develop long range plans--sometimes 5 or more years ahead.
    B. begin to integrate all the firm's marketing activities.
    C. place less emphasis on earning a profit and more emphasis on what customers will buy.
    D. adopt a more narrow view of marketing.
    E. be more concerned with its ability to produce enough to meet demand.

2-**75.**
C
App.
Med.
p. 34

Susan Brett-Newell was just named Holiday, Inc.'s "marketing manager"--with responsibilities for short-run policy planning of the firm's advertising, sales, marketing research, purchasing, and distribution efforts. Apparently, Holiday is operating in the _____ era.
    A. market-oriented
    B. production
    C. marketing department
    D. marketing company
    E. sales

2-**76.**
D
Int.
Hard
p. 34

The main difference between the "marketing department era" and the "marketing company era" is:
    A. more emphasis on selling and advertising in the marketing department era.
    B. whether the president of the firm has a background in marketing.
    C. more emphasis on short-run planning in the marketing company era.
    D. whether the whole company is customer-oriented.
    E. There is no difference.

2-**77.**
C
Def.
Med.
p. 34

When marketing people do long-range planning and the whole company is guided by the "marketing concept," the company has entered the _____ era.
    A. production
    B. customer satisfaction
    C. marketing company
    D. consumerism
    E. marketing department

2-**78.**
A
Def.
Easy
p. 34

A company where the marketing people do both short-run and long-range planning is operating in the
   A. marketing company era.
   B. sales era.
   C. simple trade era.
   D. marketing department era.
   E. production era.

2-**79.**
A
App.
Hard
p. 34

The president of a financial services company says that her new marketing manager has changed things a lot--making long-range plans about where the firm should focus its effort, and coordinating the decisions about what services to offer and how they should be promoted and priced. It seems that this company is just moving into the:
   A. marketing company era.
   B. sales era.
   C. production era.
   D. marketing department era.
   E. simple trade era.

2-**80.**
E
Comp.
Easy
p. 34

Which of the following would be relevant in the marketing company era?
   A. Concentrating on satisfying customers.
   B. Planning for five or more years ahead.
   C. Involving the whole company in the marketing effort.
   D. Making a profit.
   E. All of the above.

2-**81.**
B
App.
Med.
p. 34

Smith Corporation just named Lavonne Birch to a marketing management position. One of the reasons she accepted a position with this company was its reputation for market-oriented long-range planning. Smith Corp. is probably operating in the
_____ era.
   A. planning.
   B. marketing company.
   C. marketing research.
   D. marketing department.
   E. none of the above.

2-**82.**
C
Comp.
Med.
p. 35

A "production-oriented" firm typically:
   A. views customer credit as a customer service.
   B. sets inventory requirements with customer needs in mind.
   C. tries to sell the products it can make easily.
   D. focuses advertising on need-satisfying product benefits.
   E. operates as an integrated unit.

2-**83.**
A
Comp.
Med.
p. 35

A manager with a "production orientation" is likely to think that:
   A. customers exist to buy the firm's output.
   B. customers' needs should guide decisions about what the firm produces.
   C. the company should find out what product customers want to buy, and then produce that product.
   D. production managers should handle all marketing activities.
   E. people in the production department should work closely with people from all the firm's other departments.

2-**84.**
B
App.
Med.
p. 35

AmazoTech Corporation has been experiencing declining profits. AmazoTech's salespeople blame the production people for making inferior products, and the production people complain that the salesmen are just not getting enough orders. AmazoTech seems to have
    A. implemented the marketing concept.
    B. a production orientation.
    C. a customer orientation.
    D. a sales orientation.
    E. a marketing orientation.

2-**85.**
E
App.
Med.
p. 35

AmazoTech Corporation has been experiencing declining profits. The accounting department blames the AmazoTech marketing staff for "out of control" sales costs. The salespeople blame the warehouse for being slow to fill orders. And the warehouse manager says that the production department can't meet its schedule. AmazoTech Stars seems to have
    A. implemented the marketing concept.
    B. a customer orientation.
    C. a marketing orientation.
    D. a sales orientation.
    E. a production orientation.

2-**86.**
C
Comp.
Easy
p. 35

Which of the following is LEAST LIKELY to be found in a production-oriented firm?
    A. Disagreements among departments about how to improve the company's product.
    B. Making products that are easy to produce.
    C. Producing goods that exactly meet the customer's needs.
    D. a mass marketing approach.
    E. None of the above.

2-**87.**
B
Comp.
Easy
p. 35

Which of the following is MOST LIKELY to be found in a production-oriented firm?
    A. Agreements among departments about how to improve customer satisfaction.
    B. Making products that are easy to produce.
    C. Producing goods that exactly meet the customer's needs.
    D. a focus on profit rather than sales.
    E. None of the above.

2-**88.**
C
Def.
Easy
p. 35

Accepting the "marketing concept" means that a firm should have a _____ orientation.
    A. production
    B. sales
    C. marketing
    D. All of the above.
    E. None of the above.

2-**89.**
A
Def.
Easy
p. 35

Accepting the "marketing concept" means that a firm should have a _____ orientation.
    A. marketing.
    B. research.
    C. production.
    D. sales.
    E. planning.

2-**90.**   A firm with a marketing orientation:
C   A. has little need for salespeople.
Comp.   B. sells what it can make easily.
Med.   C. tries to determine customers' needs before developing its product.
p. 35   D. focuses advertising on product features.
               E. all of the above.

2-**91.**   A firm with a marketing orientation is MOST likely to:
C   A. view advertising as an unnecessary expense.
Comp.   B. recognize that effective advertising is the key to sales.
Hard   C. advertise how a product meets customers' needs.
p. 35   D. focus advertising on product features and quality.
               E. not use any advertising.

2-**92.**   The three basic ideas in the "marketing concept" are:
E   A. customer satisfaction, resource efficiency, sales maximization.
Def.   B. customer satisfaction, total company effort, sales growth.
Med.   C. resource efficiency, sales growth, profit maximization.
p. 35   D. customer satisfaction, marketing manager as chief executive, profit.
               E. customer satisfaction, total company effort, profit.

2-**93.**   Which of the following is one of the three basic ideas in the "marketing concept?"
B   A. resource efficiency.
Def.   B. total company effort.
Easy   C. obtain economies of scale.
p. 35   D. maximize sales.
               E. the president has a marketing background.

2-**94.**   Which of the following is one of the three basic ideas in the "marketing concept?"
C   A. resource efficiency.
Def.   B. obtain economies of scale.
Easy   C. profit as an objective.
p. 35   D. maximize sales.
               E. the president has a marketing background.

2-**95.**   Which of the following is one of the three basic ideas in the "marketing concept?"
B   A. resource efficiency.
Def.   B. customer satisfaction.
Easy   C. obtain economies of scale.
p. 35   D. maximize sales.
               E. the president has a marketing background.

2-**96.**   An important step in applying the marketing concept is:
E   A. changing the firm's organizational structure.
Comp.   B. changing the firm's management methods and procedures.
Easy   C. appointing someone with a marketing management background to be the firm's
p. 35   president.
               D. hiring a marketing consultant.
               E. committing to customer satisfaction.

2-**97.**
B
Def.
Med.
p. 35

The "marketing concept" says that a business firm should:
- A. Aim all its efforts at meeting society's needs--regardless of profitability.
- B. Aim all its efforts at satisfying its customers--at a profit.
- C. Sell those products which it can make at lowest cost.
- D. Place heavy emphasis on developing new products.
- E. Treat advertising and selling as its priority.

2-**98.**
D
Def.
Med.
p. 35

The "marketing concept" says that a business firm should aim all of its efforts at:
- A. doing more advertising and selling than competitors.
- B. selling what the company produces.
- C. satisfying customers--regardless of profitability.
- D. satisfying its customers--at a profit.
- E. producing those products which it can make at lowest cost.

2-**99.**
A
Comp.
Med.
p. 35-38

Which of the following is NOT likely to be found in a company with a marketing orientation?
- A. The company sells whatever it can make.
- B. The company sees customer credit as a service.
- C. The company designs its packaging as a selling tool.
- D. The company uses marketing research to see if it is satisfying its customers.
- E. The company focuses on locating new opportunities.

2-**100.**
A
Int.
Med.
p. 35-36

Complete acceptance of the "marketing concept" would require:
- A. making sure that all departments focus their efforts on satisfying customer needs.
- B. having all production, finance, accounting, and personnel managers report directly to the marketing manager.
- C. placing less emphasis on profit as the objective of the firm.
- D. trying to satisfy the needs of each and every customer.
- E. All of the above.

2-**101.**
E
Def.
Easy
p. 35

"Production orientation" refers to the attitudes of:
- A. sales managers.
- B. accountants.
- C. financial managers.
- D. production managers.
- E. anyone who doesn't practice the marketing concept.

2-**102.**
A
Comp.
Med.
p. 36

In a firm operating as a total "system" to implement the marketing concept:
- A. the whole company is customer-oriented.
- B. there are no departments.
- C. product planning is under the control of the production or engineering departments.
- D. the marketing manager directs and controls all company activities.
- E. None of the above are true.

2-**103.**
D
Comp.
Med.
p. 36

The total system view of the marketing concept builds on the idea that
- A. sales should be the firm's high-level objective.
- B. a company should not have specialized departments.
- C. each department in an organization should do what it does best.
- D. all departments--not just marketing--should be guided by customer needs.
- E. Both B and D are correct.

2-**104.**
B
App.
Med.
p. 36

Which of the following organizations would most likely be the first to adopt the marketing concept?
   A. A producer of industrial plastics.
   B. A producer of soap.
   C. A hardware store.
   D. A community zoo.
   E. A doctor's office.

2-**105.**
E
App.
Med.
p. 36

Which of the following organizations would most likely be the first to adopt the marketing concept?
   A. A producer of industrial solvents.
   B. A department store.
   C. A hospital.
   D. A local post office.
   E. A producer of health and beauty aids.

2-**106.**
D
App.
Med.
p. 36

Which of the following organizations would most likely be the first to adopt the marketing concept?
   A. a German producer of textile equipment.
   B. a steel producer.
   C. a group of dentists in San Francisco.
   D. a manufacturer of snack foods.
   E. a bank in San Antonio.

2-**107.**
A
Comp.
Easy
p. 36

The marketing concept was first accepted by:
   A. consumer products manufacturers.
   B. Internet retailers.
   C. service industries.
   D. producers of industrial commodities.
   E. all firms equally.

2-**108.**
E
App.
Easy
p. 37

The marketing concept can be applied by:
   A. a nurses association.
   B. cosmetic manufacturers.
   C. nonprofit hospitals.
   D. national parks.
   E. all of the above.

2-**109.**
E
App.
Easy
p. 37

The marketing concept can be applied by:
   A. nonprofit hospitals.
   B. symphony orchestras.
   C. private universities.
   D. manufacturers of consumer products.
   E. All of the above.

2-110.
C
App.
Med.
p. 37

Which of the following is the best example of the marketing concept in action?
A. A product manager tells her sales force "the inventory in the warehouse must be sold if we are to make a profit, so redouble your sales efforts."
B. A manufacturer of industrial chemicals adapts its formulas and goes after the big consumer cleaning market.
C. A cleaning supplies firm learns that many consumers are having trouble hiring maids--so it develops a plan to offer customers complete house cleaning services.
D. An Internet retailer finds that shoppers are abandoning their shopping carts before checking out, so it promotes its $10 discount on each customer's first purchase.
E. A student group wants to hold an awards banquet, so it buys Krispy Kreme donuts and sells them to friends who want to help the club achieve its objectives.

2-111.
A
App.
Hard
p. 37

A public utility that has adopted the marketing concept would be most likely to
A. set up a special service to help consumers reduce expensive peak-hours energy consumption.
B. lower prices until almost all consumers felt that prices were fair.
C. advertise its "public service role" to improve its image with the public.
D. use email to send customers a personal apology if a blackout were to occur.
E. None of the above.

2-112.
C
App.
Hard
p. 37

A local symphony group that has adopted the marketing concept would be most likely to
A. lower ticket prices until all its concerts sell out.
B. advertise so consumers know about the quality of the musicians who play in its concerts.
C. find out what kind of music local residents want to hear.
D. use only its best musicians to handle solo performances.
E. All of the above.

2-113.
E
App.
Med.
p. 37

Which of the following illustrates the marketing concept in action?
A. Three doctors set up a group practice--so that at least one is always available for emergencies.
B. Bank ATMs that dispense cash are placed in fast-food restaurants.
C. The Florida auto registration office mails license tags to people, to reduce inconvenient waiting in line.
D. A veterinarian has office hours in the evening to see pets whose owners must work during the day.
E. All of the above.

2-114.
B
App.
Med.
p. 37

Which of the following illustrates the marketing concept in action?
A. A young lawyer gives free legal advice to poor people.
B. A local police department organizes a "community crime watch" program in a neighborhood that has had many burglaries.
C. Several lawyers set up a group practice--so that the costs of the office and equipment can be shared.
D. All of the above.
E. None of the above has anything to do with the marketing concept.

2-115.
A
Comp.
Med.
p. 38

Which of the following statements about customer value is true?
A. Customer value is the difference between the benefits a customer sees from a market offering and the costs of obtaining those benefits.
B. The greater the competition, the less important customer value is.
C. The sure was to achieve high customer value is to offer a lower price.
D. It is the manager's view of customer value that matters, not the customer's.
E. None of the above is true.

2-116.
E
Comp.
Med.
p. 38

A major limitation of the customer value idea is that:
A. It can't be applied in competitive situations.
B. It considers price but not other elements of the marketing mix.
C. It applies to goods but not services.
D. It's emphasis on what the customer sees as the positive things about a marketing mix means that the negatives are likely to be ignored.
E. None of the above is a limitation.

2-117.
E
Comp.
Med.
p. 38

Customer value typically would NOT be impacted by a marketing manager's decisions concerning:
A. product.
B. place.
C. promotion.
D. price.
E. Any of the above might impact customer value.

2-118.
D
Comp.
Easy
p. 41-42

Given the nature of their work, which of the following should have a marketing orientation?
A. Girl Scouts of America.
B. Boston Symphony.
C. American Cancer Society.
D. All of the above.
E. None of the above.

2-119.
B
Comp.
Med.
p. 41

Nonprofit organizations
A. do not have a profit objective, so the marketing concept does not apply.
B. can benefit by adopting the marketing concept.
C. are fundamentally different than business firms--so they should embrace a production orientation rather than a marketing orientation.
D. do not need to be concerned with marketing activities.
E. none of the above.

2-120.
E
App.
Hard
p. 43

A marketing manager made a speech in which he described his company as having "really embraced the marketing concept over ten years ago." A critic in the audience argued that the manager didn't understand the "socially conscious" view of the marketing concept. Given the critic's argument, the marketing manager may work for:
A. a fruit processor.
B. an Internet service provider.
C. a firm that recycles aluminum cans.
D. a soap producer.
E. a motorcycle producer.

2-**121.**
E
Def.
Easy
p. 45

The three basic tasks of ALL managers, according to the text, are:
A. planning, staffing, and evaluating.
B. marketing, production, and finance.
C. execution, feedback, and control.
D. hiring, training, and compensating.
E. planning, implementation, and control.

2-**122.**
D
Def.
Easy
p. 45

The managerial process of developing and maintaining a match between the resources of an organization and its market opportunities is called:
A. management by objective.
B. marketing programming.
C. marketing strategy planning.
D. strategic (management) planning.
E. market planning.

2-**123.**
A
Def.
Med.
p. 46

"Marketing strategy planning" means:
A. finding attractive opportunities and developing profitable marketing strategies.
B. finding attractive opportunities and selecting a target market.
C. selecting an attractive target market.
D. selecting an attractive marketing mix.
E. selecting a target market and developing a marketing strategy.

2-**124.**
A
Def.
Easy
p. 46

A marketing strategy specifies:
A. a target market and a related marketing mix.
B. all the company's resources.
C. a target market.
D. a target market and the company's objectives.
E. a marketing mix.

2-**125.**
B
Def.
Easy
p. 46

A marketing strategy specifies:
A. a marketing mix.
B. a target market and a related marketing mix.
C. a target market.
D. the resources needed to implement a marketing mix.
E. both A and D.

2-**126.**
C
Comp.
Med.
p. 47

The difference between target marketing and mass marketing is that target marketing
A. means focusing on a small market.
B. focuses on short-run objectives, while mass marketing focuses on long-run objectives.
C. focuses on specific customers, while mass marketing aims at an entire market.
D. does not rely on e-commerce but mass marketing does.
E. aims at increased sales, while mass marketing focuses on increased profits.

2-**127.**
B
Comp.
Med.
p. 47

Good marketing strategy planners know that:
A. firms like Colgate Foods and Wal-Mart are too large to aim at clearly defined target markets.
B. target marketing does not limit one to small market segments.
C. mass marketing is often very desirable and effective.
D. the terms "mass marketing" and "mass marketer" mean basically the same thing.
E. target markets cannot be large and spread out.

2-**128.**   "Target marketing," in contrast to "mass marketing,"
D
Def.   A. is limited to small market segments.
Med.   B. assumes that all customers are basically the same.
p. 47   C. ignores markets that are large and spread out.
              D. focuses on fairly homogeneous market segments.
              E. All of the above.

2-**129.**   "Target marketing," in contrast to "mass marketing,"
E
Def.   A. ignores the need for the firm to obtain a competitive advantage.
Med.   B. ignores markets that are large and spread out.
p. 47   C. is limited to small market segments.
              D. assumes that all customers are basically the same.
              E. None of the above is correct.

2-**130.**   The "four Ps" of a marketing mix are:
E
Def.   A. Production, Personnel, Price, and Physical Distribution
Med.   B. Promotion, Production, Price, and People
p. 48   C. Potential customers, Product, Price, and Personal Selling
              D. Product, Price, Promotion, and Profit
              E. Product, Place, Promotion, and Price

2-**131.**   A firm's "marketing mix" decision areas would NOT include:
B
Def.   A. Promotion.
Easy   B. People.
p. 48   C. Price.
              D. Product.
              E. Place.

2-**132.**   A firm's "marketing mix" decision areas would NOT include:
E
Def.   A. Price.
Easy   B. Promotion.
p. 48   C. Product.
              D. Place.
              E. Profit.

2-**133.**   Which of the following is NOT one of the four variables in a marketing mix?
D
Def.   A. Price
Easy   B. Product
p. 48   C. Promotion
              D. Payment
              E. Place

2-**134.**   When one considers the strategy decisions organized by the four Ps, branding is related
D   to packaging as:
Comp.   A. branding is to pricing.
Hard   B. production is to marketing.
p. 49   C. store location is to sales force selection.
              D. personal selling is to mass selling.
              E. pricing is to promotion.

2-**135.**   "Product" is concerned with:
E
Def.   A. branding.
Easy   B. packaging and warranty.
p. 49   C. physical goods.
               D. services.
               E. all of the above might be involved.

2-**136.**   "Product" is NOT concerned with:
C
Def.   A. quality level.
Easy   B. branding.
p. 49   C. wholesale price.
               D. packaging.
               E. warranty.

2-**137.**   "Product" is concerned with:
E
Def.   A. branding and warranties.
Med.   B. physical goods and/or services.
p. 49   C. packaging.
               D. developing the right new product for a market.
               E. all of the above might be involved.

2-**138.**   "Product" is concerned with:
E
Def.   A. services.
Med.   B. developing products which will satisfy some customers' needs.
p. 49   C. designing, packaging, and branding new products.
               D. physical goods.
               E. All of the above might be involved.

2-**139.**   Which of the following is NOT considered a product?
E
App.   A. tax advice from a financial consultant.
Easy   B. a computer.
p. 49   C. a haircut.
               D. a chair.
               E. All of the above are considered products.

2-**140.**   Nissan's 3 year/36,000 mile new car warranty is part of which marketing mix decision
D   area?
App.   A. price
Easy   B. target market
p. 49   C. place
               D. product
               E. promotion

2-**141.**   "Place" is concerned with:
E
Def.   A. middlemen.
Easy   B. transporting.
p. 49   C. channel members.
               D. storing.
               E. all of the above might be involved.

2-**142.**   "Place" is concerned with:
E   A. getting the product to its intended market.
Def.   B. middlemen located between producers and consumers.
Med.   C. where, when, and by whom goods are offered for sale.
p. 49   D. when and where products are wanted.
               E. all of the above might be involved.

2-**143.**   "Place" is NOT concerned with:
E   A. storing.
Def.   B. middlemen.
Med.   C. transporting.
p. 49   D. channels of distribution.
               E. sales reps.

2-**144.**   "Place" is NOT concerned with:
D   A. who handles storing and transporting.
Def.   B. when and where products are wanted.
Easy   C. kinds of middlemen needed to reach customers.
p. 49   D. telling the target market what products are available--and where.
               E. channels of distribution.

2-**145.**   Scott Paper uses many middlemen to reach its target markets; Citibank uses none.
D   Which of the marketing mix variables is being considered here?
App.   A. penetration
Med.   B. product
p. 49   C. promotion
               D. place
               E. price

2-**146.**   A "channel of distribution":
B   A. usually has three members--a manufacturer, a distributor, and a retailer.
Def.   B. is any series of firms (or individuals) from producer to final user or consumer.
Med.   C. should be as short as possible.
p. 48-49   D. is not involved if a firm sells directly from its own website to final customers.
               E. All of the above are true.

2-**147.**   "Promotion" may include:
E   A. personal selling to middlemen.
Def.   B. point-of-purchase materials.
Easy   C. mail-order selling.
p. 49-50   D. advertising on the Internet.
               E. all of the above.

2-**148.**   "Promotion" is NOT concerned with:
B   A. creating billboard ads.
Def.   B. designing new products.
Easy   C. publicity.
p. 49-50   D. television commercials.
               E. personal selling.

2-**149.**
E
Def.
Easy
p. 50

"Promotion" includes:
A. advertising.
B. personal selling.
C. sales promotion.
D. publicity.
E. All of the above.

2-**150.**
A
Def.
Easy
p. 50

_____ is direct spoken communication between sellers and potential customers.
A. Personal selling
B. Sales promotion
C. Advertising
D. Publicity
E. Mass selling

2-**151.**
C
Def.
Easy
p. 50

Personal selling lets the salesperson adapt the firm's marketing mix to a specific customer. This is an aspect of which marketing mix variable?
A. price
B. place
C. promotion
D. product
E. all of the above

2-**152.**
C
Def.
Med.
p. 50

Advertising is:
A. the designing and distribution of novelties, point-of-purchase materials, store signs, catalogs, and circulars.
B. direct communication between sellers and potential customers.
C. any paid form of nonpersonal presentation of ideas, goods, or services by an identified sponsor.
D. the main form of publicity.
E. All of the above.

2-**153.**
C
Def.
Med.
p. 50

Catalogs, point-of-purchase materials, and free samples are all examples of:
A. publicity.
B. personal selling.
C. sales promotion.
D. advertising.
E. none of the above.

2-**154.**
C
Comp.
Med.
p. 50

Sales promotion:
A. lets the salesperson adapt the firm's marketing mix to each potential customer.
B. is the main form of advertising.
C. tries to help the personal selling and mass selling people.
D. is free.
E. consists of both advertising and personal selling.

2-**155.**   When developing a marketing mix, a marketing manager should remember that:
C   A. "Promotion" includes only personal selling and publicity.
Int.   B. A channel of distribution includes at least one middleman.
Med.   C. "Price" includes markups, discounts, allowances, and geographic terms.
p. 50   D. "Product" includes physical goods but not services.
                      E. All of the above are true.

2-**156.**   "Price":
A   A. is affected by the kind of competition in the target market.
Def.   B. includes markups and discounts, but not allowances and freight charges.
Med.   C. is not affected by customer reactions.
p. 50   D. is the most important part of a marketing mix.
                      E. None of the above is true.

2-**157.**   The most important variable in a firm's marketing mix is:
E   A. Product.
Def.   B. Price.
Easy   C. Promotion.
p. 50   D. Place.
                      E. None of the above--all contribute to one whole.

2-**158.**   An office supplies producer sells a variety of office supplies to final consumers and
E   businesses using its own mail order catalog. Here,
App.   A. there is no channel of distribution.
Med.   B. there is no opportunity to apply target marketing.
p. 50   C. no promotion is involved.
                      D. a production orientation is just as effective as a marketing orientation.
                      E. None of the above is true.

2-**159.**   From the perspective of the four Ps, personal selling is to advertising as
E   A. mass selling is to branding.
Comp.   B. Place is to Product.
Hard   C. sales promotion is to pricing.
p. 49   D. warranties are to channel type.
                      E. geographic terms are to price allowances.

2-**160.**   An appropriate marketing mix should be determined PRIMARILY by
B   A. what has worked for the company in the past.
Comp.   B. the needs of a target market.
Med.   C. the budget available to spend.
p. 51   D. the past experiences of the marketing manager.
                      E. what product the firm can produce with economies of scale.

2-**161.**   The text's "Toddler University" example shows that:
B   A. parents are not price sensitive when it comes to assuring that their kids will get a
Comp.   good college education.
Hard   B. the needs of a target market determine the nature of the appropriate marketing
p. 51-52   mix.
                      C. a small producer can't compete effectively against large competitors.
                      D. in the long run, a firm cannot make a profit without its own production facilities.
                      E. All of the above are true.

2-**162**.
B
Comp.
Hard
p. 51-52

The text's "Toddler University" example shows that:
A. no mass market exists for general-purpose baby shoes.
B. the needs of a target market determine the nature of the appropriate marketing mix.
C. a small producer can't compete effectively against large competitors.
D. no target market exists for high-quality baby shoes.
E. All of the above are true.

2-**163**.
A
Comp.
Med.
p. 53

The main difference between a "marketing strategy" and a "marketing plan" is that:
A. time-related details are included in a marketing plan.
B. a marketing plan includes several marketing strategies.
C. a marketing strategy provides more detail.
D. a marketing strategy omits pricing plans.
E. a marketing plan does not include a target market.

2-**164**.
B
Comp.
Med.
p. 53

Which of the following is part of a complete marketing plan?
A. Competitors' marketing strategies.
B. What company resources (costs) are required and at what rate.
C. How different marketing mixes (for different target markets) relate to each other.
D. All of the above.
E. None of the above.

2-**165**.
C
Def.
Med.
p. 53

A "marketing plan" is:
A. a marketing program.
B. a marketing strategy.
C. a marketing strategy--plus the time-related details for carrying it out.
D. a target market and a related marketing mix.
E. a plan that contains the necessary operational decisions.

2-**166**.
B
Comp.
Med.
p. 53

Which of the following would probably NOT be in a proposed marketing plan?
A. A list of what company resources (costs) would be required.
B. A statement of how frequently the design of the web site will be changed.
C. Expected sales and profit results.
D. A description of the target market and marketing mix.
E. All of the above would normally be part of a marketing plan.

2-**167**.
E
Comp.
Easy
p. 53

A "marketing plan" should include:
A. some control procedures.
B. what company resources will be needed--at what rate.
C. what marketing mix is to be offered to whom--and for how long.
D. what sales and profit results are expected.
E. all of the above.

2-**168**.
E
Def.
Med.
p. 53

Which of the following is NOT included in a marketing plan?
A. the control procedures to be used
B. the costs involved
C. the results expected
D. what marketing mix is to be offered
E. All of the above should be included.

2-**169.**   Which of the following statements about operational decisions is FALSE?
C   A. They help to carry out a marketing strategy.
Def.   B. They are made regularly, sometimes on a daily basis.
Med.   C. They usually require ongoing changes in the basic strategy to be effective.
p. 53   D. They sometimes take up a good part of an advertising manager's time.
               E. They sometimes take up a good part of a sales manager's time.

2-**170.**   Which of the following statements by a marketing manager refer to operational
B   decisions, rather than strategy decisions?
App.   A. "Our target customers view most existing luxury sedans as dull, and they want
Med.   performance as well as luxury."
p. 53-54   B. "Newspaper ads will be more cost effective than 30 second radio ads--given the
                   price increase for radio this month.
               C. "We hope to earn a 15 percent return on investment with our plan."
               D. All of the above.
               E. None of the above.

2-**171.**   Which of the following is an operational decision--rather than a strategy decision?
D   A. a decision to seek distribution only through the best retailers.
App.   B. selection of a specific target market.
Med.   C. a decision to maintain a "one price" policy.
p. 53-54   D. selection of a specific cable TV channel on which to advertise.
               E. All of the above are good examples of operational decisions.

2-**172.**   Which of the following is an example of an operational decision?
C   A. focus promotion on the economy of the product.
App.   B. make the product available in every possible retail outlet.
Med.   C. have a salesperson visit the manager of a new hardware store that will open next
p. 53-54   week.
               D. set a price that is no higher than competitors' prices.
               E. None of the above is an operational decision.

2-**173.**   A "marketing program":
A   A. blends all of a firm's marketing plans into one big plan.
Def.   B. is a description of a firm's marketing mix.
Easy   C. is a detailed plan of how to implement a strategy.
p. 54   D. is a marketing strategy plus the time-related details.
               E. None of the above.

2-**174.**   The text's discussion of Timex's marketing strategy highlights the fact that:
A   A. it's not wise for managers to just define a business in terms of the products they
Comp.   currently produce or sell.
Hard   B. there is little alternative but to stick with the traditional distribution channels for
p. 55-56   a product.
               C. most consumers see basic products--like watches--as close substitutes for each
                   other.
               D. once a firm establishes a position as the market leader, competitors are not likely
                   to be a big problem.
               E. all of the above.

2-175.
A
Comp.
Hard
p. 55-56

The text's discussion of Timex's marketing strategy highlights the fact that:
A. creative strategy planning is needed for survival.
B. there is little alternative but to stick with the traditional distribution channels for a product.
C. most consumers want only high-quality products.
D. once a firm establishes a position as the market leader, competitors are not likely to be a big problem.
E. all of the above.

2-176.
D
Comp.
Hard
p. 57

Based on the discussion (and exhibit) in Chapter 2 that considers the effectiveness of different firms' marketing programs, you would conclude that in the majority of firms:
A. market share is growing rapidly.
B. most new product introductions are a success.
C. most marketing decisions are effective and only a very small percentage of customers are dissatisfied.
D. marketing programs are not producing great results.
E. customer retention and loyalty rates are very high.

Chapter 3

Focusing Marketing Strategy with Segmentation and Positioning

True-False Questions:

3-**1.**
False
p. 62

The single most important factor in screening possible marketing opportunities is the long-run trends facing the company.

3-**2.**
True
p. 62

Attractive opportunities for a particular firm are those that the firm has some chance of doing something about--given its resources and objectives.

3-**3.**
True
p. 62

A "breakthrough opportunity" is an opportunity that helps innovators develop long-term, hard-to-copy marketing strategies that will be very profitable.

3-**4.**
True
p. 62

Finding "competitive advantages" is important because they are needed for survival in increasingly competitive markets.

3-**5.**
True
p. 65

Differentiation means that the marketing mix is distinct from and better than what is available from a competitor.

3-**6.**
True
p. 65

Differentiation often requires a firm to fine-tune its marketing mix to meet the specific needs of its target market(s).

3-**7.**
True
p. 65

Differentiation emphasizes uniqueness rather than similarity.

3-**8.**
False
p. 65

Differentiation emphasizes similarity rather than uniqueness.

3-**9.**
False
p. 66

A S.W.O.T. analysis identifies the "special weapons or tactics" used by the competitor in a product market that has the most profitable marketing mix.

3-10.
False
p. 66

S.W.O.T. analysis is based on the idea that one of the best ways to develop a strategy is to identify and copy the marketing "strategies, weapons, outlook and tactics" of the firm's most effective competitor.

3-11.
True
p. 66

A good S.W.O.T. analysis helps a manager focus on a strategy that takes advantages of the firm's opportunities and strengths while avoiding its weaknesses and threats to its success.

3-12.
True
p. 66

The letters in "S.W.O.T. analysis" are an abbreviation for the first letters of the words "strengths, weaknesses, opportunities and threats"

3-13.
False
p. 66

The letters in "S.W.O.T. analysis" are an abbreviation for the first letters of the words "special weapons or tactics."

3-14.
True
p. 67

Marketing opportunities involving present products and present markets are called "market penetration" opportunities.

3-15.
False
p. 67

The Martinez Company has just modified and enlarged its product line to meet the changing needs of its current customers. This is an example of "market development."

3-16.
False
p. 67

When Cadillac added a new sport utility vehicle to the "luxury-oriented" selection at its existing dealers, it was seeking "market development" opportunities.

3-17.
False
p. 67

If Burger King added tacos to the "burger-oriented" menu in its existing restaurants, it would be seeking "market development" opportunities.

3-18.
False
p. 67

A firm which tries to increase sales by selling new products in new markets is purusing "market development" opportunities.

3-19.
True
p. 67

When a firm tries to increase sales by offering new or improved products to its present markets, this is called "product development."

3-20.
True
p. 68

Marketing opportunities that involve moving into totally different lines of business are "diversification" opportunities.

3-21.
False
p. 68

The least risky--but most challenging--marketing opportunities are diversification opportunities.

3-22.
False
p. 68

Marketing managers almost always find that opportunities in international markets are less profitable than in domestic markets.

3-23.
True
p. 69

Unfavorable trends in the domestic marketing environment may make the international marketing environment very attractive.

3-24.
False
p. 70

A market is a group of two or more sellers who offer substitute ways of satisfying customer needs.

3-25.
False
p. 71

The main difference between a "product-market" and a "generic market" is whether customer needs are similar or different.

3-26.
False
p. 71

A "generic market" is a market in which sellers offer substitute products which are so similar that customers see them as "all the same."

3-27.
True
p. 71

A firm's "relevant market for finding opportunities" should be bigger than the present product-market but not so large that it couldn't expand and still be an important competitor.

3-28.
True
p. 73

The definition of a product-market includes a product type while the definition of a generic market does not include a product type.

3-29.
True
p. 73

Effective market segmentation is a two-step process that starts with naming broad product-markets and then goes on to segmenting these broad product-markets into more homogeneous submarkets.

3-30.
True
p. 74

Using one or two demographic dimensions to describe market segments usually does not provide enough detail for planning a marketing strategy.

3-31.
False
p. 74

Market segmentation says that target marketers should develop one good marketing mix aimed at a fairly large market.

3-32.
True
p. 74

Marketing-oriented managers see segmenting as a process of aggregating people with similar needs into a group.

3-33.
True
p. 75

Ideally, segmenters should start with the idea that each person is "one of a kind" and can be described by a special set of dimensions that may be used to aggregate similar customers together.

3-34.
True
p. 75

One of the difficult things about segmenting is that not every customer will neatly fit into some market segment.

3-35.
True
p. 76

A "good" market segment should be composed of people who are as homogeneous as possible with respect to their likely responses to marketing mix variables.

3-36.
True
p. 76

"Good" market segments should be homogeneous (similar) within, heterogeneous (different) between, substantial, and operational.

3-37.
False
p. 76

"Good" market segments should be heterogeneous within and homogeneous between.

3-38.
False
p. 76

If a product-market segment is "homogeneous within," it is called a "substantial" target market.

3-39.
True
p. 76

A "substantial" market segment is one which is big enough to be profitable.

3-40.
True
p. 76

Planning place and promotion elements of a marketing mix is especially difficult if the dimensions of a product-market are not operational.

3-41.
False
p. 76

A product-market segment is "operational" if it is big enough to be profitable to the firm.

3-42.
False
p. 76

A personality trait like moodiness is a good example of an "operational" segmenting dimension.

3-43.
False
p. 76

The correct number of submarkets in a broad product-market is usually obvious, so the likelihood of managerial error is small.

3-44.
False
p. 76

With the "multiple target market approach" the marketer combines two or more homogeneous submarkets into one larger target market as a basis for one strategy.

3-45.
True
p. 77

A manager who aggregates all potential customers into a single product-market segment is likely to find that the segment is not homogeneous.

3-46.
True
p. 77

The more heterogeneous a firm's target market becomes, the more likely the firm will see competition from an innovative segmenter.

3-47.
False
p. 77

A profit-oriented firm will usually want to continue aggregating potential customers into larger submarkets until every consumer fits neatly into some segment.

3-48.
True
p. 79

Cost considerations usually favor more aggregating and larger market segments, but smaller segments may be required to satisfy needs more exactly.

3-49.
True
p. 80

Dimensions that should be looked at when segmenting consumer markets are: geographic location and other demographic characteristics, behavioral needs, urgency to get needs satisfied, and willingness to compare and shop.

3-50.
False
p. 80

When segmenting markets, one should look at geographic location and demographic characteristics as well as customers' desire and willingness to compare and shop, but behavioral needs aren't important for this purpose.

3-51.
True
p. 80

A determining dimension for segmenting markets actually affects the purchase of a specific brand in a product-market.

3-52.
False
p. 80

A marketing manager who is able to use qualifying dimensions in forming market segments will not need to worry about determining dimensions.

3-53.
False
p. 79-82

Market segmentation applies only to consumer goods and services; it cannot be applied to business products.

3-54.
True
p. 83

A firm involved in international marketing should pay even more attention to segmenting than a firm that sells only in the United States.

3-55.
False
p. 83

The first step in segmenting international markets is to group countries that are close to each other into "common markets."

3-56.
False
p. 83-84

Computer-aided segmenting approaches eliminate the need for managerial judgment and intuition in selecting segmenting dimensions.

3-57.
True
p. 83-84

Clustering techniques can be used in segmenting to help find similar patterns within sets of data--to identify homogeneous groups of people.

3-58.
False
p. 84

A firm is most likely to rely on customer relationship management (CRM) approaches when it does not have a database of information on individual customers.

3-59.
False
p. 84

CRM is a variation of the positioning approach.

3-60.
True
p. 84

CRM approaches are based on information from detailed customer databases.

3-61.
False
p. 84

Firms that operate on the Internet are at a disadvantage when it comes to using approaches like CRM.

3-62.
True
p. 85

"Positioning" shows how proposed and/or present brands are located in a market--as seen by customers.

3-63.
False
p. 86

"Positioning" means using a map to show where a firm's products are distributed geographically.

Multiple Choice Questions

3-64.
E
Def.
Easy
p. 62

"Breakthrough opportunities" are opportunities that:
A. help innovators develop hard-to-copy marketing strategies.
B. may be turned into marketing strategies that will be profitable for a long time.
C. help the firm develop a "competitive advantage."
D. help a firm satisfy customers better than some competitor.
E. All of the above.

3-65.
C
Def.
Easy
p. 62

It's best to think of "breakthrough opportunities" as opportunities which:
A. appeal to the mass market.
B. will quickly create a whole new industry of firms competing with similar marketing mixes
C. help innovators develop hard-to-copy marketing mixes.
D. increase sales.
E. All of the above.

3-66.
B
App.
Med.
p. 62

Which of the following best illustrates a "breakthrough opportunity?"
A. A recording company's new CD gets unexpected national publicity on MTV and almost every teenager wants a copy for Christmas.
B. A drug company develops a patented pill that people can take once a year and safely avoid catching a cold.
C. A bank puts its credit card machines in convenient drive-up locations--so they will be more convenient for customers.
D. A nurse realizes that the growing number of older people will increase the demand for nursing home services, so she quits her job and opens a quality nursing center for the elderly.
E. A wireless phone company introduces a new service that offers more free weekend minutes than any other service in its market area.

3-67.
E
App.
Med.
p. 62

Which of the following would be likely to help you develop a "breakthrough opportunity?"
A. A two-month advantage over competitors in introducing a new product.
B. An idea for a new website animation that will attract consumer attention.
C. Accurate marketing research information about how much of a planned product the target market is likely to buy.
D. All of the above.
E. None of the above.

3-**68.**
D
App.
Med.
p. 62

Which of the following could be a "breakthrough opportunity?"
- A. A unique technical invention that competitors could not legally copy.
- B. A contract with the best middlemen to reach your market--ensuring that they will handle your product and no competitors' offerings.
- C. A head start in a market so you can win target customers who will be really loyal to your firm and its offering.
- D. All of the above.
- E. None of the above.

3-**69.**
B
Def.
Med.
p. 65

Differentiation refers to the _____ of the firm's marketing mix to meet the needs of the target market.
- A. similarity
- B. uniqueness
- C. unsuitability
- D. willingness
- E. none of the above

3-**70.**
D
Def.
Med.
p. 66

A S.W.O.T. analysis
- A. focuses on what a firm plans to do to "Satisfy Wishes Of a Target" customer.
- B. summarizes a firm's "strategy, wishes (of its customers), outlook and tactics."
- C. helps defend against potential competitors by developing a set of competitive "safeguards, weapons, offensives, and tactics."
- D. identifies a firm's "strengths, weaknesses, opportunities and threats."
- E. seeks to reduce the risk of competitive surprises by scanning the market for "signals, warnings, omens, and tips."

3-**71.**
D
Comp.
Med.
p. 66

A S.W.O.T. analysis
- A. seeks to improve strategy planning by "Scanning for Warnings, Omens, and Tips" about competitors' plans.
- B. is not necessary if competitors have already entered the market.
- C. defends against potential competitive threats by planning specific "safeguards, weapons, or tactics."
- D. should help a manager develop a strategy that leads to a competitive advantage.
- E. None of the above is a good answer.

3-**72.**
E
Comp.
Med.
p. 66

A S.W.O.T. analysis can help a marketing manager:
- A. define what business and markets the firm wants to compete in.
- B. narrow down to a specific target market and marketing mix from the many alternatives available.
- C. see the pros and cons of different possible strategies.
- D. develop a competitive advantage.
- E. all of the above.

3-**73.**
D
Comp.
Med.
p. 66

Ideally, the ingredients of a good marketing mix should:
- A. match the ingredients typically used by key competitors.
- B. be determined by which ingredients cost the least.
- C. not include much advertising because it's expensive.
- D. flow logically from all the relevant dimensions of a target market.
- E. All of the above are true.

3-**74.**
B
Def.
Easy
p. 67

_____ means trying to increase sales of a firm's present products in its present markets.
  A. Product development
  B. Market penetration
  C. Market development
  D. Mass marketing
  E. Diversification

3-**75.**
B
App.
Easy
p. 67

Lipton has increased sales by developing ads that encourage it current customers to drink Lipton tea instead of coffee at morning "coffee breaks." This effort focuses on
  A. diversification.
  B. market penetration.
  C. product development.
  D. mass marketing.
  E. market development.

3-**76.**
A
App.
Easy
p. 67

Tropicana is trying to get its customers to drink orange juice more often with ads that say "It's not just for breakfast anymore." What type of opportunity is the company pursuing?
  A. market penetration
  B. diversification
  C. market development
  D. product development
  E. mass marketing

3-**77.**
A
App.
Med.
p. 67

Kraft Foods recently increased its advertising and couponing to its present cheese customers. It appears that Kraft is pursuing what kind of opportunity?
  A. Market penetration
  B. Product development
  C. Market development
  D. Mass marketing
  E. Diversification

3-**78.**
B
App.
Med.
p. 67

If Frito-Lay (which has products in almost all the submarkets for snack foods) were to try to increase its share of one of these markets, it would be pursuing a _____ opportunity.
  A. diversification
  B. market penetration
  C. product development
  D. mass marketing
  E. market development

3-**79.**
C
App.
Med.
p. 67

When IBM realized that other companies were attracting its customers by advertising that their personal computers were "IBM compatible," IBM tried to promote the differences between its products and the "compatibles." It was pursuing a _____ opportunity.
  A. market development.
  B. diversification.
  C. market penetration.
  D. product development.
  E. None of the above.

3-80.
E
Def.
Easy
p. 67

When a firm tries to increase sales by selling its present products in new markets, this is called:
    A. product development.
    B. diversification.
    C. market penetration.
    D. mass marketing.
    E. market development.

3-81.
E
App.
Easy
p. 67

The Wall Street Journal has been trying to attract new customers by promoting its newspaper for student use in business courses. This is an example of
    A. target marketing.
    B. product development.
    C. diversification.
    D. market penetration.
    E. market development.

3-82.
C
App.
Easy
p. 67

An Embassy Suites hotel offers an inexpensive "Family Luncheon Buffet" on Sundays to get customers for its restaurant that is filled by business travelers during week days. This effort to get new customers for the available facility is an example of
    A. a production orientation.
    B. product development.
    C. market development.
    D. diversification.
    E. market penetration.

3-83.
A
App.
Easy
p. 67

Coca-Cola is taking advantage of the new willingness of Chinese leaders to engage in international trade by marketing its soft drinks in China. What type of opportunity is Coke pursuing?
    A. market development
    B. diversification
    C. product development
    D. market penetration
    E. none of the above

3-84.
A
App.
Med.
p. 67

Avon, which in the past relied on door-to-door personal selling, is trying to reach new customers by distributing mail-order catalogs, adding toll-free telephone ordering, and ordering from websites. Avon is pursuing a _____ opportunity.
    A. market development
    B. market penetration
    C. target marketing
    D. product development
    E. mass marketing

3-85.
A
App.
Med.
p. 67

A mail-order marketer of flower bulbs to gardening hobbyists decides to sell the bulbs in grocery stores--to reach nonhobbyists who might be interested in pretty flowers. This is an example of:
    A. market development.
    B. diversification.
    C. market penetration.
    D. product development.
    E. None of the above.

3-86.
A
App.
Med.
p. 67

GreatGadgets, an Internet-based marketer of innovative gift items, decides to sell products in its own retail stores--to reach consumers who don't like to buy without first seeing the item in person. This is an example of:
   A. market development.
   B. diversification.
   C. market penetration.
   D. product development.
   E. None of the above.

3-87.
A
App.
Med.
p. 67

An Australian wine producer, facing declining sales at home, set up a new channel of distribution to sell wine in the United States. This seems to be an effort at
   A. market development.
   B. diversification.
   C. market penetration.
   D. product development.
   E. None of the above.

3-88.
E
App.
Med.
p. 67

In an effort to increase its total sales, Champion has started exporting its spark plugs for use by several German auto producers. Champion is pursuing a _____ opportunity.
   A. diversification
   B. market penetration
   C. product development
   D. mass marketing
   E. market development

3-89.
B
Def.
Easy
p. 67

When a firm tries to increase sales by offering new or improved products to its present markets, this is called:
   A. mass marketing.
   B. product development.
   C. market penetration.
   D. diversification.
   E. market development.

3-90.
D
App.
Med.
p. 67

To compete more successfully with its many competitors offering packaged cookies, Famous Amos added its own line of "extra chunky" premium cookies. This seems to be an effort at:
   A. combination.
   B. market penetration.
   C. market development.
   D. product development.
   E. diversification.

3-**91.**
D
App.
Hard
p. 67

A producer of frozen pasta dinners finds that its current target customers select among its frozen pasta dinners, going to a pizza restaurant, or staying home and eating an Italian sub sandwich. So the company set up a chain of pizza restaurants that also serve Italian sub sandwiches. This seems to be an effort at:
   A. market development.
   B. diversification.
   C. market penetration.
   D. product development.
   E. None of the above.

3-**92.**
C
App.
Med.
p. 67

Wendy's continues to test possible new toppings for hamburgers, including grilled mushrooms and provolone cheese. This suggests that Wendy's is pursuing
_____.
   A. marketing myopia.
   B. mass marketing.
   C. product development.
   D. market development.
   E. diversification.

3-**93.**
C
App.
Med.
p. 67

Wendy's continues to come out with new offerings like stuffed pitas. This suggests that Wendy's is pursuing _____.
   A. marketing myopia.
   B. mass marketing.
   C. product development.
   D. market development.
   E. diversification.

3-**94.**
D
App.
Med.
p. 67

Hewlett-Packard decided that too many other companies were attracting its customers by advertising their computer printers as "having all of the features of Hewlett-Packard's Laserjet." So Hewlett-Packard designed a new color printer with a completely new set of features which no competitors' equipment offered. Hewlett-Packard then introduced it to the same market with the hope that it could develop a larger and more profitable share. This was an effort at:
   A. market development.
   B. diversification.
   C. market penetration.
   D. product development.
   E. None of the above.

3-**95.**
C
App.
Med.
p. 67

To improve its profits, Delta Tool Corp. has redesigned its entire line of rechargeable power drills--adding several new or improved features and three new models. Apparently, Delta Tool is pursuing a _____ opportunity.
   A. combiner
   B. market development
   C. product development
   D. diversification
   E. market penetration

3-**96.**
A
Def.
Med.
p. 68

When a firm tries to increase its total sales by offering new products to new markets, it's pursuing:
  A. diversification.
  B. product development.
  C. market development.
  D. market penetration.
  E. All of the above.

3-**97.**
B
App.
Med.
p. 68

A beer distributor, concerned about increasing regulation of alcoholic beverages, decides to start a new business distributing children's toys. This company seems to be pursuing
  A. market development.
  B. diversification.
  C. product development.
  D. market penetration.
  E. None of the above.

3-**98.**
E
App.
Med.
p. 68

Industrial Plastics Corporation has decided to manufacture and sell electric motors for fishing boats. The firm appears to be pursuing a _____ opportunity.
  A. combiner
  B. product development
  C. market development
  D. market penetration
  E. diversification

3-**99.**
B
App.
Med.
p. 68

A producer of home burglar alarm devices decides to start manufacturing portable video cameras for use in industrial security situations. This is an example of
  A. market development.
  B. diversification.
  C. product development.
  D. market penetration.
  E. None of the above.

3-**100.**
B
App.
Med.
p. 68

If a cola producer bought out a Mango juice producer in an attempt to appeal to health-conscious consumers who do not drink soft drinks, it would be pursuing a _____ opportunity.
  A. market development.
  B. diversification.
  C. market penetration.
  D. product development.
  E. None of the above.

3-**101.**
A
Comp.
Med.
p. 68

Because companies are likely to be most familiar with their own operations, _____ opportunities are usually the easiest to pursue.
  A. market penetration
  B. product development
  C. market development
  D. diversification
  E. All of the above are equally easy.

3-**102.**
D
App.
Hard
p. 68

Professional Dental Supply has been successfully selling dental instruments to dentists for the past twenty years, and has developed strong customer relations. When looking for new marketing opportunities, Professional Dental Supply will most likely look first at _____ .
   A. market penetration
   B. diversification
   C. market development
   D. product development
   E. They will look at all opportunities equally.

3-**103.**
C
Comp.
Med.
p. 68

The most risky and challenging opportunities usually involve:
   A. market development.
   B. product development.
   C. diversification.
   D. market penetration.
   E. all of the above are similar in terms of risk.

3-**104.**
C
Comp.
Easy
p. 68

The most risky types of marketing opportunity to pursue usually involve
   A. market development.
   B. market penetration.
   C. diversification.
   D. product development.
   E. All of the above are equally risky.

3-**105.**
D
Def.
Easy
p. 70

A "market" consists of:
   A. customers who are willing to exchange something of value.
   B. a group of potential customers with similar needs.
   C. sellers offering various ways of satisfying customer needs.
   D. all of the above.
   E. none of the above.

3-**106.**
D
Int.
Hard
p. 71

A marketing manager has just learned about generic markets. This may lead the manager
   A. to see a larger set of potential competitors.
   B. to put less emphasis on market penetration or market development opportunities and more emphasis on product development opportunities.
   C. to think about new ways of satisfying the needs of her current customers.
   D. All of the above.
   E. None of the above.

3-**107.**
B
Int.
Hard
p. 71

A basic difference between a "generic market" and a "product-market" is:
   A. whether or not sellers in the market rely on e-commerce.
   B. how similar the competing sellers' products are.
   C. whether customer needs are similar or different.
   D. whether the market includes only buyers--or both buyers and sellers.
   E. There is NO DIFFERENCE--the terms mean the same thing.

3-**108.**
A
Comp.
Med.
p. 71

The main difference between a generic market and a product-market is that:
   A. a generic-market involves a less similar set of needs than does a product-market.
   B. a product-market is usually larger than a generic market.
   C. product-markets usually don't involve competition, but generic markets do.
   D. sellers in a generic market are more concerned with prices than sellers in a product-market.
   E. There is no difference between the two.

3-**109.**
D
Def.
Med.
p. 71

A _____ market is a market with broadly similar needs and sellers offering various--and often diverse--ways of satisfying those needs.
   A. planned
   B. target
   C. central
   D. generic
   E. relevant

3-**110.**
D
Def.
Med
p. 71

A _____ market is a market with broadly similar needs and sellers offering various--and often diverse--ways of satisfying those needs.
   A. homogeneous
   B. product
   C. relevant
   D. generic
   E. target

3-**111.**
D
Def.
Med.
p. 71

A "product-market" is a market in which:
   A. all sellers offer exactly the same product.
   B. one firm has achieved a competitive advantage.
   C. all sellers offer products that are unique and innovative.
   D. sellers offer very close substitute ways of satisfying potential customers' needs.
   E. sellers offer substitute products which are quite different physically or conceptually.

3-**112.**
C
Comp.
Med.
p. 71

Which of the following is NOT true of a product-market?
   A. Competing suppliers offer close substitutes to satisfy needs.
   B. Customers in a product-market have very similar needs.
   C. Very different types of products may compete for consumer dollars.
   D. Naming product-markets includes consideration of where the customers are.
   E. None of the above statements is true.

3-**113.**
B
Comp.
Med.
p. 71

A generic market
   A. related to a consumer's functional need is smaller than a related product-market.
   B. might involve competition among skis, roller blades, bicycles, and ice skates.
   C. might logically include rubber cement, a lamp, and a CD player.
   D. is usually narrower than the firm's target market.
   E. All of the above are correct.

3-114.
D
Def.
Hard
p. 71

A generic market
A. may include sellers who compete in different product-markets.
B. would probably be broader than the firm's target market.
C. might be composed of several different product-markets.
D. All of the above are true.
E. None of the above is true.

3-115.
D
Comp.
Med.
p. 71

In a generic market,
A. diverse types of products may compete for customers.
B. customers have broadly similar needs.
C. there may be many ways to satisfy customers' needs.
D. All of the above are true.
E. None of the above is true.

3-116.
D
App.
Easy
p. 71

A product-market is one
A. in which exchanges are based on barter rather than money.
B. where one seller has a patent for a superior product and other firms try to imitate the leader the best they can.
C. where all of the customers want the same product but will consider a substitute if their preferred brand is not available.
D. in which competing sellers offer physically or conceptually similar products.
E. in which no middlemen operate.

3-117.
E
Comp.
Med.
p. 71

A product-market is one in which
A. products from different industries compete for customers by trying to satisfy the same basic need.
B. price is the determining factor in deciding which brand to buy.
C. all of the customers want the exact same product but will consider a substitute if their preferred brand is not available.
D. one seller has a monopoly and there is no competition.
E. None of the above is true.

3-118.
A
Comp.
Med.
p. 71

A generic market is one in which
A. products from different industries compete for customers by trying to satisfy the same basic need.
B. no firm can establish a competitive advantage.
C. a number of firms are all offering new or improved products in an effort to increase sales.
D. one seller has a patent for a superior product and other competitors imitate the leader with inferior products.
E. None of the above is true.

3-119.
B
Comp.
Med.
p. 71

A product-market is one in which
A. demand is inelastic.
B. products that are close substitutes for each other compete for customers by trying to satisfy very similar needs.
C. breakthrough opportunities are no longer possible.
D. one seller has a patent for a superior product and other competitors try to imitate the leader.
E. All of the above are true.

3-**120.**   Which of the following is the best example of a "product-market?"
B
App.   A. The MP3 player market
Med.   B. The young adult exercise market
p. 71   C. The software market
              D. The convenience market
              E. The status symbol market

3-**121.**   Which of the following is LEAST likely to compete in the same generic market with
C   the others?
App.   A. pop corn.
Med.   B. soft drink.
p. 71   C. napkin.
              D. cookie.
              E. ice cream.

3-**122.**   Which of the following is LEAST likely to compete in the same generic market with
E   the others?
App.   A. garlic powder.
Hard   B. pepper.
p. 71   C. tabasco sauce.
              D. salt.
              E. potato chips.

3-**123.**   Which of the following is LEAST LIKELY to compete in the same generic market with
B   the others?
App.   A. Long-stem roses
Med.   B. A tomato
p. 71   C. Champagne
              D. A greeting card
              E. A telegram

3-**124.**   Which of the following is the BEST example of a "generic market?"
A
App.   A. The senior citizen recreation market
Med.   B. The designer shoes market
p. 71   C. The frozen yogurt market
              D. The transportation market
              E. The Hispanic-American market

3-**125.**   Which of the following is the BEST example of a "generic market?"
E   A. the meat market.
App.   B. the minivan market.
Easy   C. the e-commerce market.
p. 71   D. the beer market.
              E. the "singles" entertaining market.

3-**126.**   Which of the following is the BEST example of a "generic market?"
A   A. The adult "personal expression" market
App.   B. The roller blade market
Easy   C. The female exercise shoes market
p. 71   D. The sports drink market
              E. The sporting goods market

3-127.
B
App.
Med.
p. 71

A digital camera, a computer video-cam, and a computer scanner might compete in the same

    A. single target market.
    B. generic market.
    C. multiple target market.
    D. combined target market.
    E. product-market.

3-128.
E
App.
Med.
p. 71

A transistor radio, an MP3 player, and a portable CD player might compete in the same

    A. single target market.
    B. multiple target market.
    C. product-market.
    D. combined target market.
    E. generic market.

3-129.
B
App.
Med.
p. 71

A pencil, a dictating machine, and a word processor might compete in the same
    A. target market.
    B. generic market.
    C. product-market.
    D. Any of the above.
    E. None of the above.

3-130.
B
Comp.
Med.
p. 71

A firm's "relevant market for finding opportunities" should:
    A. have no geographic boundaries.
    B. be bigger than the firm's present product-market--but not so big that the firm couldn't be an important competitor.
    C. be no larger than the firm's present product-market.
    D. usually be named in product-related terms.
    E. have no strong competitors.

3-131.
B
Comp.
Med.
p. 71

A firm's "relevant market for finding opportunities" should:
    A. be limited to products the firm already produces.
    B. be bigger than the firm's present product-market--but not so big that the firm could not be an important competitor.
    C. have no geographic boundaries.
    D. be as large a possible.
    E. be no larger than the firm's present product-market.

3-132.
E
Def.
Easy
p. 72

A product-market definition should include:
    A. product type.
    B. customer types.
    C. customer needs.
    D. geographic area.
    E. All of the above.

3-**133**.   Which of the following is NOT part of a product-market definition?
C
           A.   information about consumer needs
Def.
           B.   information about the final customer (or user) of the product
Med.
           C.   information about which specific retailers will sell the product
p. 72
           D.   a description of the type of product
           E.   All of these should be included.

3-**134**.   A generic market description should NOT include any:
C
           A.   customer needs.
Def.
           B.   geographic area.
Med.
           C.   product type.
p. 73
           D.   customer types.
           E.   none of the above.

3-**135**.   A generic market description should NOT include any:
C
           A.   customer needs.
Def.
           B.   geographic area.
Med.
           C.   competitors' names.
p. 73
           D.   customer types.
           E.   It should include all of the above.

3-**136**.   _____ is the process of naming broad product-markets and then segmenting
A   these broad product-markets in order to select target markets and develop suitable
Def.   marketing mixes.
Easy
           A.   Market segmentation
p. 73
           B.   Strategic planning
           C.   Mass marketing
           D.   Market positioning
           E.   Implementation

3-**137**.   _____ is the process of naming broad product-markets and then segmenting
B   these broad product-markets in order to select target markets and develop suitable
Def.   marketing mixes.
Easy
           A.   Market positioning
p. 73
           B.   Market segmentation
           C.   Mass marketing
           D.   Diversification
           E.   Strategic planning

3-**138**.   The first step in market segmentation should be:
E
           A.   deciding what new product you could develop.
Comp.
           B.   evaluating what segment(s) you currently serve.
Med.
           C.   finding a demographic group likely to use your products.
p. 74
           D.   listing features of your current products.
           E.   defining some generic markets where you may be able to operate profitably.

3-**139.**
C
Comp.
Hard
p. 74

The main difference between naming broad product-markets and market segmentation is:

A. naming is a computerized process, while segmentation requires more thought.
B. naming is concerned with customers, while segmentation is concerned with product features.
C. naming involves breaking down markets, while segmentation involves aggregating customers with similar needs.
D. naming involves looking for similarities, while segmentation involves looking for differences.
E. None of the above is true.

3-**140.**
D
Comp.
Easy
p. 74

According to the text, segmenting:

A. is a disaggregating or "breaking down" process.
B. assumes that each person should be treated as a separate target market.
C. assumes that all customers can be clustered into profitable market segments.
D. is an aggregating process.
E. uses scientific rules to decide how many submarkets exist.

3-**141.**
C
Def.
Easy
p. 74

According to the text, segmenting should be viewed as a(n) _____ process.

A. assorting
B. mechanical, nonjudgmental
C. "clustering" or aggregating
D. "breaking apart" or disaggregating
E. combining

3-**142.**
D
Comp.
Med.
p. 75

Market segmentation:

A. means the same thing as marketing strategy planning.
B. assumes that most submarkets can be satisfied by the same marketing mix.
C. is the same thing as positioning.
D. tries to identify homogeneous submarkets within a product-market.
E. All of the above are true.

3-**143.**
C
App.
Med.
p. 75

Given its interest in the broad product-market for "ready-to-eat, health-conscious snack foods," which of the following should the GoodHealth Foods Co. do FIRST?

A. Develop a plan for getting support from middlemen.
B. Develop each of the four Ps at the same time.
C. Segment the product-market to try to identify homogeneous submarkets and select an attractive target market.
D. Determine whether to compete on a price basis.
E. Decide what low-fat product or products it will offer.

3-**144.**   Which of the following criteria should a marketing manager use when segmenting a
D   broad product-market?
Comp.   A.   The segments should be substantial--big enough to be profitable--and
Med.   operational--useful for identifying customers and deciding on marketing mix
p. 76   variables.
                 B.   The people within a market segment should be as homogeneous as possible with
                 respect to the segmenting dimensions and their likely response to marketing mix
                 variables.
                 C.   The people in different market segments should be as heterogeneous as possible
                 with respect to the segmenting dimensions and their likely response to marketing
                 mix variables.
                 D.   All of the above.
                 E.   Only A and B above.

3-**145.**   "Good" market segments are those which are:
E   A.   heterogeneous between.
Def.   B.   operational.
Easy   C.   substantial.
p. 76   D.   homogeneous within.
                 E.   All of the above.

3-**146.**   Saying that a "good" product-market segment should be substantial means
C   A.   that the company does not have to worry about substantial competition for a long
Comp.   time.
Med.   B.   that people should have substantially different reactions to marketing mix
p. 76   variables.
                 C.   it should be large enough to be profitable.
                 D.   that people in different market segments should be as different as possible.
                 E.   None of the above is true.

3-**147.**   "Good" market segments are those that are:
C   A.   homogeneous between.
Def.   B.   heterogeneous within.
Easy   C.   operational and substantial.
p. 76   D.   international in nature.
                 E.   All of the above.

3-**148.**   Which of the following criteria should a marketing manager use when segmenting a
B   broad product-market?
Comp.   A.   The segments should be operational--i.e., only quantitative dimensions are
Hard   useful.
p. 76   B.   The people in different segments should be as heterogeneous as possible with
                 respect to their likely response to marketing mix variables.
                 C.   The people within a market segment should be as heterogeneous as possible with
                 respect to their likely response to marketing mix variables.
                 D.   The market segments should be substantial--i.e., big enough to minimize the
                 firm's costs.
                 E.   All of the above.

3-149.
B
Comp.
Easy
p. 76

Which of the following segmenting dimensions probably would be LEAST LIKELY to result in segments that would meet the criteria that product-market segments should be "operational?"
A. geographic region.
B. personality.
C. family size.
D. age.
E. income level.

3-150.
C
Comp.
Easy
p. 76

Which of the following is NOT one of the target marketing approaches for developing market-oriented strategies in a broad product-market?
A. multiple.
B. single.
C. exclusive.
D. combined.
E. All of the above are target marketing approaches.

3-151.
C
App.
Med.
p. 76

A food processor considering snack-food opportunities identified three possible market segments and gave them "nicknames": the dieters, health faddists, and nutrition-conscious parents. It developed a marketing mix around a line of good tasting, nutritious children's snacks. The firm is apparently
A. relying on cluster analysis techniques.
B. using a multiple target market approach.
C. using a single target market approach.
D. using a combined target market approach.
E. ignoring the criteria that good market segments should be operational.

3-152.
B
App.
Med.
p. 76

Electro Co. segmented its broad product-market and decided to aim at two different segments, offering each segment a different marketing mix. Electro Co. is following the _____ approach.
A. mass marketing
B. multiple target market
C. combined target market
D. single target market
E. All of the above.

3-153.
A
App.
Med.
p. 76

Quality Ceramic, Inc. (QCI) defined five submarkets within its broad product-market. To obtain some economies of scale, QCI decided NOT to offer each of the submarkets a different marketing mix. Instead, it selected two submarkets whose needs are fairly similar, and is counting on promotion and minor product differences to make its one basic marketing mix appeal to both submarkets. QCI is using the:
A. combined target market approach.
B. single target market approach.
C. multiple target market approach.
D. mass marketing approach.
E. All of the above.

3-**154.**
A
App.
Hard
p. 76

Quality Ceramic, Inc. (QCI) wants to gain some economies of scale and limit its risk. Its broad product-market consists of three reasonably similar submarkets. To identify a target market, QCI should consider using the _____ approach.
- A. combined target market
- B. mass marketing
- C. multiple target market
- D. single target market
- E. All of the above.

3-**155.**
C
App.
Med.
p. 76

Having segmented its broad product-market, Gayle, Inc. feels that three segments are similar enough that--together--they can be treated as one large target market and offered the same marketing mix. Gayle, Inc. is following the _____ approach.
- A. mass marketing
- B. multiple target market
- C. combined target market
- D. single target market
- E. All of the above.

3-**156.**
E
Comp.
Med.
p. 77

Combiners (as opposed to segmenters):
- A. try to satisfy target customers "very well" rather than "pretty well."
- B. try to develop a different marketing mix for each submarket.
- C. want to avoid "inviting" competition.
- D. are not target marketers--they aim at everybody.
- E. try to increase the size of their target markets by combining two or more market segments.

3-**157.**
A
App.
Med.
p. 77

A large firm with ample resources wants to minimize the risk of "inviting" competitors to "chip away" at its target market(s). It has segmented its broad product-market and identified several homogeneous submarkets--each of which is large enough to offer attractive sales and profit potential. Which of the following approaches should the firm use?
- A. Multiple target market approach
- B. Mass marketing approach
- C. Combined target market approach
- D. Single target market approach
- E. All of the above

3-**158.**
B
Comp.
Hard
p. 77

Segmenting, in contrast to combining:
- A. tends to focus more on customer similarities than on differences.
- B. tries to identify homogeneous submarkets and develop different marketing mixes for each submarket.
- C. usually means settling for a smaller sales potential.
- D. relies more on promotion appeals and minor product differences to create general customer appeal among several submarkets.
- E. All of the above are true statements except C.

3-**159.**
A
Def.
Med.
p. 77

Segmenters, in contrast to combiners:
A. try to aim at homogeneous submarkets of larger product-markets.
B. see one aggregate demand curve for a generic market.
C. are accepting the likelihood of lower sales.
D. assume that everyone in a broad product-market has the same needs.
E. develop general-purpose marketing mixes that appeal to several submarkets.

3-**160.**
C
Comp.
Med.
p. 77

The combined target market approach:
A. tends to focus on small, homogeneous market segments.
B. aims at several target markets and offers each target market a unique marketing mix.
C. tries to improve the general appeal of a firm's basic marketing mix rather than tailor it to meet the strongly felt needs of some people.
D. works well only when each submarket of a product-market has a different demand curve.
E. All of the above.

3-**161.**
A
App.
Med.
p. 77

A producer of electrical components combined electrical supply wholesalers and manufacturers of electrical equipment into the same market segment--one of several segments it was targeting. Soon it lost the manufacturers' business to a competitor. It seems that the firm failed to consider the risk of
A. too much aggregating.
B. insulting the manufacturers by putting them in the same market segment with the wholesalers.
C. picking market segments based on qualifying dimensions.
D. selecting market segments that were not substantial.
E. using too many segmenting dimensions.

3-**162.**
A
Comp.
Med.
p. 77

Which of the following is a possible danger when using a combining approach to target marketing?
A. Competitors may do a better job appealing to submarkets.
B. Coordinating the different marketing mixes for the different segments is difficult.
C. The target market may become larger over time.
D. Economies of scale may develop.
E. All are dangers.

3-**163.**
B
Comp.
Easy
p. 77

"Too much" aggregating in market segmenting
A. ignores the criterion that product-market segments should be substantial.
B. leaves the firm vulnerable to competitors.
C. is usually not a very serious error because it results in economies of scale.
D. A and C are both true.
E. All of the above are true.

3-**164.**
B
Int.
Hard
p. 77

Which of the following statements about "segmenting" and "combining" is TRUE?
A. Combiners usually have more sales potential than segmenters.
B. A combiner tries to meet the demand in several segments.
C. Segmenters try to develop a marketing mix that will have general appeal for several market segments--to obtain economies of scale.
D. A segmenter assumes that a broad product-market consists of a fairly homogeneous group of customers.
E. Both segmenters and combiners try to satisfy some people very well rather than a lot of people fairly well.

3-**165.**
E
App.
Easy
p. 78

Which of the following offers a firm the greatest potential for profit?
A. Mass marketing
B. The multiple target market approach
C. The combined target market approach
D. The single target market approach
E. Any of the above--depending on the situation

3-**166.**
D
Def.
Easy
p. 78

A market-oriented strategy planner applies the _____ target market approach.
A. combined
B. multiple
C. single
D. Any of the above.
E. None of the above.

3-**167.**
B
Comp.
Med.
p. 78

Which of the following statements about market-oriented strategy planning is TRUE?
A. Segmenters aim at more heterogeneous markets than combiners.
B. Both "segmenters" and "combiners" can be target marketers.
C. All segmenters follow the single target market approach.
D. Combiners follow a mass marketing strategy.
E. All of the above are true.

3-**168.**
B
Comp.
Med.
p. 79

When segmenting broad product-markets, cost considerations tend
A. to encourage managers to disregard the criterion that a product-market segment should be substantial.
B. to lead to more aggregating.
C. to be unimportant as long as the segmenting dimensions are operational.
D. to lead to a large number of small, but very homogeneous, product-market segments.
E. All of the above are true.

3-**169.**
A
Comp.
Hard
p. 79

When deciding how far to carry the segmenting process,
A. profit should be the balancing point--determining how unique a marketing mix the firm can offer to some target market.
B. it is easier to develop effective marketing mixes for larger, more heterogeneous segments.
C. cost considerations encourage less aggregating.
D. the threat of potential competitors suggests more aggregating.
E. All of the above are true.

3-170.
D
Comp.
Hard
p. 80

Ideally, product-markets should be described in terms of:

A. behavioral needs, attitudes, and how present and potential goods or services fit into customers' consumption patterns.
B. urgency to get needs satisfied and desire and willingness to compare and shop.
C. geographic location and other demographic characteristics of potential customers.
D. All of the above.
E. Only A and B above.

3-171.
E
Def.
Med.
p. 81

BEHAVIORAL (rather than DEMOGRAPHIC) segmenting dimensions include:

A. family life cycle.
B. geographic location.
C. education.
D. social class.
E. purchase frequency.

3-172.
E
Def.
Med.
p. 81

BEHAVIORAL (rather than DEMOGRAPHIC) segmenting dimensions include:

A. type of problem-solving.
B. kind of shopping.
C. brand familiarity.
D. benefits sought.
E. All of the above are behavioral dimensions.

3-173.
B
Def.
Med.
p. 81

Which of the following possible segmenting dimensions is a "demographic" dimension?

A. Benefits sought
B. Social class
C. Purchase frequency
D. Brand familiarity
E. Rate of use

3-174.
E
Int.
Easy
p. 80

The MOST USEFUL dimensions for segmenting markets are:

A. geographic and demographic dimensions.
B. brand familiarity and consumption patterns.
C. social class.
D. benefits sought.
E. It depends on what product-market one is segmenting.

3-175.
B
Comp.
Med.
p. 80

"Qualifying dimensions," in contrast to "determining dimensions,"

A. are the only kind of dimensions useful for marketing strategy planning.
B. indicate whether a person might be a potential customer but do not show which product or brand that person might buy.
C. are the customer-related dimensions in a product-market.
D. affect the product or brand a person is likely to purchase.
E. None of the above is true.

3-**176.**
D
Def.
Easy
p. 80

_____ segmenting dimensions are those which actually affect a person's purchase of a specific product type or brand in a product-market.
A. Operational
B. Qualifying
C. Customer-related
D. Determining
E. Situation-related

3-**177.**
A
Comp.
Med.
p. 80-81

Which of the following is MOST LIKELY to be a DETERMINING dimension with respect to purchase of a particular brand of coffee?
A. taste.
B. income.
C. age.
D. sex.
E. None of the above.

3-**178.**
D
Comp.
Med.
p. 80-81

Compared to qualifying dimensions, determining dimensions
A. are more likely to be related to whether a customer will make a purchase in the product-market at all.
B. are more likely to be related to the specific brand selected.
C. are usually much more specific.
D. Both B and C are true.
E. None of the above is true.

3-**179.**
B
Def.
Easy
p. 80-81

_____ segmenting dimensions help decide whether a person might be a potential customer--but not which specific products or brands that person might buy.
A. Determining
B. Qualifying
C. Operational
D. Customer-related
E. Situation-related

3-**180.**
E
Comp.
Med.
p. 83

Planning marketing strategies for international markets:
A. is usually most effective when the marketing manager uses the same marketing strategy for all markets.
B. is often easier than planning domestic strategies because economic, political, and other uncontrollable variables are less important.
C. is "easy" because each country should be treated as one target market.
D. All of the above are true.
E. None of the above is true.

3-**181.**
B
Comp.
Med.
p. 83

Segmenting international markets (as contrasted with domestic markets):
A. is more complicated because qualifying dimensions are not helpful.
B. may be more difficult because critical data may not be available or dependable.
C. usually involves less risk because more potential target markets are available.
D. usually involves fewer segmenting dimensions.
E. All of the above are true.

3-**182.**
B
Comp.
Easy
p. 83

Segmenting international markets can be more difficult because:
A. the concepts and approaches for segmenting domestic markets simply do not apply.
B. there are more dimensions and many unfamiliar variables.
C. there are fewer useful dimensions.
D. a manager must rely entirely on his or her own judgments about people in other countries.
E. the quantity and quality of available market data are usually greater.

3-**183.**
D
Comp.
Med.
p. 83

When evaluating international markets, the marketing manager should:
A. focus primarily on consumer markets because foreign business markets are in general too risky.
B. not worry very much about segmenting because marketing concepts are not very well developed in most other economies.
C. consider the whole "foreign market" as a segment.
D. use broad criteria, such as geographic region or stage of economic development, to define submarkets before further segmenting.
E. treat each foreign market as a separate segment.

3-**184.**
C
Def.
Easy
p. 83

The first step in segmenting international markets is to:
A. develop a marketing mix.
B. treat all the countries in the "foreign market" as one segment.
C. segment by country or region--looking at demographic, cultural, and other characteristics.
D. list the suppliers who serve the market.
E. consider the number, size, kind, and location of business and organizational customers.

3-**185.**
A
Comp.
Med.
p. 83

Clustering techniques applied to segmenting markets
A. usually require computers to group people based on data from market research.
B. remove the need for managerial judgment.
C. eliminate the need for marketing managers to specify in advance what dimensions might be relevant for grouping consumers.
D. Both B and C are true.
E. All of the above are true.

3-**186.**
C
Comp.
Med.
p. 83

The clustering techniques that can be used in segmenting:
A. eliminate the need for management intuition and judgment.
B. group people together into heterogeneous product-market segments.
C. try to find similar patterns within sets of data.
D. All of the above are true
E. None of the above are true.

3-**187.**
D
Comp.
Med.
p. 84

A cluster analysis of the "toothpaste market" would probably show that:
A. the broad product-market can be served effectively with one marketing mix.
B. most consumers are mainly concerned about brightness of teeth.
C. factors such as taste, price, and "sex appeal" are not important.
D. different market segments seek different product benefits.
E. All of the above.

3-188.
B
Def.
Easy
p. 85

_____ is a marketing management aid which refers to how customers think about proposed and/or present brands in a market.
  A. Brand familiarity
  B. Positioning
  C. Market scanning
  D. Market segmentation
  E. Customer relationship management (CRM)

3-189.
B
Def.
Easy
p. 85

"Positioning" is a marketing management aid which refers to:
  A. a product's ability to provide both immediate satisfaction and social responsibility.
  B. how customers think about proposed and/or present brands in a market.
  C. a firm's ability to distribute products through middlemen who are in the right position to reach target customers.
  D. how a firm approaches customer relationship management.
  E. all of the above.

3-190.
D
Def.
Med.
p. 85-86

"Positioning" is a marketing management aid which refers to:
  A. how closely existing products match customers' ideal preferences.
  B. how customers think about proposed and/or present brands in a market.
  C. if some products are viewed as very similar.
  D. All of the above.
  E. None of the above.

3-191.
E
App.
Med.
p. 86-88

"Positioning" might cause a marketing manager to:
  A. introduce a new product for a segment with unsatisfied needs.
  B. change a product's promotion to make its image fit more closely with the needs and attitudes of the target market.
  C. shift attention to another market segment where competition is weaker.
  D. physically change his or her product to compete more effectively with a competitor aiming at the same target market.
  E. Any of the above.

3-192.
C
App.
Hard
p. 86-88

When doing "positioning," a marketing manager should:
  A. avoid targeting strategies.
  B. focus on specific product features of all generic competitors.
  C. rely on how customers think about proposed and/or existing brands in a market.
  D. plan physical product changes rather than image changes.
  E. All of the above.

3-193.
A
Comp.
Hard
p. 86-88

Which of the following statements about positioning is NOT true? Positioning techniques
  A. position products on a graph based on price level and quantity demanded.
  B. require a firm to collect data about consumer perceptions of products.
  C. are sometimes called "perceptual mapping" techniques.
  D. typically rely on a "product space" diagram to show the relationship among various products.
  E. may use information about consumers' "ideal" products, so that the preferences of different segments of consumers can be considered.

3-**194.**   "Positioning":

B   A. applies to new products--but not existing products.

Comp.   B. helps strategy planners see how customers view competitors' offerings.

Med.   C. is concerned with obtaining the best shelf space in retail outlets.

p. 86   D. is useful for combining but not for segmenting.

               E. eliminates the need for judgment in strategy planning.

Chapter 4

Evaluating Opportunities in the Changing Marketing Environment

True-False Questions:

4-1.
True
p. 95

Earning a profit probably should be one of the objectives of a firm, but it should not be the only one.

4-2.
True
p. 96

A mission statement sets out the organization's basic purpose for being.

4-3.
True
p. 96

A mission statement can help a manager decide which opportunities to pursue and which to screen out.

4-4.
False
p. 96

A mission statement sets out the strengths and weaknesses of a firm as well as the opportunities and threats that it faces.

4-5.
False
p. 97

The objectives of a firm should direct the operation of the marketing department, but aren't important to the rest of the business.

4-6.
True
p. 98

If the cost of production per unit goes down as the quantity produced increases, small producers can be at a great cost disadvantage.

4-7.
False
p. 98

Smaller producers always have a great advantage in competing with larger producers because of their flexibility.

4-8.
True
p. 98

Good relations with middlemen, good location, and good salespeople are some of the many resources of a firm that should be evaluated when searching for new opportunities.

4-9.
True
p. 98

Ownership of patents, a familiar brand name, and financial strength are some of the many resources of a firm that a manager should evaluate when searching for new opportunities.

4-10.
False
p. 99

Over the long run, most product-markets tend toward monopolistic competition.

4-11.
True
p. 100

In market-directed economies, unregulated monopolies are rare.

4-12.
True
p. 100

In monopolistic competition, managers sometimes try to differentiate very similar products by relying on promotion or other elements of the marketing mix.

4-13.
False
p. 101

The major shortcoming of competitor analysis is that it focuses on the weaknesses of competitors--but ignores their strengths.

4-14.
True
p. 101

The first step in a competitor analysis is to identify current and potential competitors.

4-15.
True
p. 102

Competitive barriers are conditions that make it difficult for a firm to compete in a market.

4-16.
True
p. 103

The Internet is a powerful way to get information about competitors.

4-17.
False
p. 103

The Internet is an important aspect of the technological environment, but it isn't very useful for getting information about competitors.

4-18.
False
p. 103

Many people think that it is unethical to spy on competitors to obtain their trade secrets, but it is perfectly legal.

4-19.
True
p. 103

A firm may find that the competitive environment is better in a foreign market than in its domestic market.

4-20.
False
p. 104

Pure competition can always be avoided--if a firm tries hard enough.

4-21.
True
p. 105

Compared to some countries in Latin America, the rate of inflation in the U.S. is low.

4-22.
True
p. 106

Technical skills and equipment affect how an economy's resources are converted to output.

4-23.
True
p. 106

Technology is the application of science to convert an economy's resources to output.

4-24.
True
p. 106

Technology affects marketing through new products and new processes.

4-25.
True
p. 106

Technological advances like the World Wide Web and the Internet are leading to big advances in business.

4-26.
True
p. 106

The Internet can be thought of as a collection of consistent hardware and software standards.

4-27.
False
p. 106

The Internet can be thought of as a collection of inconsistent hardware and software standards.

4-28.
True
p. 107

Changes in technology can have major impacts on marketing strategy planning.

4-29.
False
p. 108

Placing the interests of individual consumers before the interests of business is nationalism.

4-30.
True
p. 108

Nationalism--or the emphasis on a country's interests before anything else--may affect the work of some marketing managers.

4-31.
False
p. 108

Regional groupings of nations outside the United States have little effect on the decisions of marketing managers whose firms are headquartered in the U.S.

4-32.
True
p. 108

The elimination of separate barriers to inter-European trade has made Europe the largest unified market in the world.

4-33.
False
p. 109

Consumerism is a social movement which seeks to punish uncooperative businesses.

4-34.
False
p. 110

President Kennedy's "Consumer Bill of Rights" included the right to safety, the right to be informed, and the right to a clean and safe environment.

4-35.
True
p. 110

The right to safety, the right to be informed, the right to choose, and the right to be heard are all included in President Kennedy's "Consumer Bill of Rights."

4-36.
False
p. 110

A manager could be fined for violating the antimonopoly laws, but he or she could not be sent to jail.

4-37.
False
p. 111

The Sherman Act deals with tying contracts, exclusive dealing contracts, and price discrimination by manufacturers.

4-38.
True
p. 111

The Magnuson-Moss Act regulates product warranties.

4-39.
True
p. 111

The Clayton Act focuses on practices which may substantially lessen competition--such as tying contracts, exclusive dealing contracts and price discrimination by manufacturers.

4-40.
True
p. 111

Before the Pure Food and Drug Act was passed, it was assumed that the common law and the warning "let the buyer beware" would take care of consumers.

4-41.
False
p. 112

The Consumer Product Safety Act provides for the creation of safety standards but has no power to set penalties for failure to meet these standards.

4-42.
False
p. 112

Because the Consumer Product Safety Commission has no power to force a product off the market, safety is not a very important consideration in product design.

4-43.
True
p. 112

Marketers should be aware of federal legislation, as well as state and local laws, when planning marketing strategy.

4-44.
True
p. 113

The old rule about buyer-seller relations of "let the buyer beware" seems to be changing to "let the seller beware."

4-45.
True
p. 113

The cultural and social environment affects how and why people live and behave as they do.

4-46.
True
p. 114

Most changes in the cultural and social environment come slowly.

4-47.
True
p. 115

When evaluating opportunities, quantitative screening criteria help a manager decide what kind of opportunities to pursue.

4-48.
False
p. 115

Screening criteria should be in quantitative form--based on factors such as profit and expected sales--so that they are objective and not subject to qualitative judgments and interpretations by different managers.

4-49.
True
p. 117

The General Electric "strategic planning grid" relies on subjective judgments about business strengths and industry attractiveness.

4-50.
False
p. 117

Opportunities which fall into the red boxes in the General Electric "strategic planning grid" are growth opportunities.

4-51.
True
p. 118

A strategic business unit (SBU) within a larger firm is usually treated as a separate profit center.

4-52.
False
p. 119

In multiproduct firms, the emphasis in portfolio management is usually on the long run rather than the short run.

4-53.
False
p. 120

The "continuum of environmental sensitivity" suggests that industrial products are more sensitive to the cultural environments in which they are placed than high-style consumer products.

Multiple Choice Questions

4-54.
D
Def.
Easy
p. 95

The basic objective of a firm should be to:
  A. engage in some specific business activity that will perform a socially and economically useful function.
  B. develop an organization to carry on the business and implement its strategies.
  C. earn enough profit to survive.
  D. All of the above.
  E. Only B and C above.

4-55.
E
Comp.
Easy
p. 96-97

Overall company objectives should:
  A. be specific.
  B. focus on returning some profit to the business.
  C. be realistic and achievable.
  D. be compatible with one another.
  E. all of the above.

4-56.
A
Comp.
Med.
p. 97

When setting objectives for the whole firm, TOP MANAGEMENT should:
  A. involve the marketing manager in the objective setting process.
  B. set objectives that focus on the highest possible immediate profit potential.
  C. stick to general objectives--in order to maintain flexibility.
  D. set objectives beyond what can actually be achieved--so everyone will work harder.
  E. all of the above.

4-57.
B
Comp.
Med.
p. 97

Of the following objectives, the LAST objective(s) that a firm should specify is its
_____ objective(s).

A. marketing
B. sales promotion
C. price
D. company
E. promotion

4-58.
A
Int.
Med.
p. 97

Along with studying trends in the environment, a first step in looking for attractive
opportunities is to:

A. understand the resources and objectives of the firm.
B. decide which product-markets the firm will enter.
C. find new markets for present products.
D. estimate product-market potentials.
E. hire a marketing strategy planner.

4-59.
B
Comp.
Hard
p. 98

With regard to a firm's resources (when searching for attractive opportunities):

A. a manufacturer needs skilled production people more than skilled salespeople.
B. lack of financial strength is often a barrier to entry.
C. large companies always have an advantage over smaller companies.
D. a good marketing strategy will probably use new facilities rather than present
   facilities.
E. a patent owner has a 5-year monopoly to develop its product.

4-60.
E
Def.
Easy
p. 98

When looking for attractive opportunities, a marketing manager should consider:

A. the firm's producing capability and flexibility.
B. the firm's financial strength.
C. whether the firm has good relations with established middlemen.
D. the firm's marketing strengths.
E. All of the above.

4-61.
B
Def.
Easy
p. 99

The number and types of competitors a marketing manager must face--and how they
might behave--is called the _____ environment.

A. cultural
B. competitive
C. economic
D. political
E. social

4-62.
A
Comp.
Hard
p. 99

Regarding the competitive environment, a marketing manager usually can:

A. choose strategies to avoid head-on competition.
B. control it with the help of the legal environment.
C. control it in the short run.
D. control it with the help of the political environment.
E. control it in the long run.

4-63.
A
Comp.
Hard
p. 104

A firm may find itself in--or moving toward--pure competition because:
   A. production-oriented firms often enter markets without understanding the competitive situation.
   B. a firm with a unique product has no choice.
   C. customers don't have much information about competing suppliers.
   D. when the number of competitors is small, they usually make similar decisions.
   E. None of the above.

4-64.
B
Def.
Easy
p. 104

Rising costs and inflation are part of the uncontrollable _____ environment.
   A. technological
   B. economic
   C. competitive
   D. legal
   E. cultural and social

4-65.
A
App.
Easy
p. 104

The marketing manager for a financial services firm knows that customer preferences for mutual funds and bond accounts will differ depending on the current interest rate. She must plan her offerings with the _____ environment in mind.
   A. economic
   B. social
   C. technological
   D. cultural
   E. legal

4-66.
D
Def.
Easy
p. 106

The way in which an economy's resources are converted to output is part of the _____ environment.
   A. competitive.
   B. economic.
   C. political.
   D. technological.
   E. social.

4-67.
A
Def.
Easy
p. 106

Underlying any economic environment is technology which affects:
   A. how the economy's resources are converted to output.
   B. how quickly technological developments lead to new consumer protection laws.
   C. how competitors react to each other.
   D. how aggressive competitors are in planning new marketing strategies.
   E. how fast consumer attitudes change.

4-68.
D
App.
Easy
p. 106

Which of the following is NOT an example of how the technological environment might affect marketing management?
   A. A manufacturer uses a computer to send orders directly to a supplier's computer.
   B. A retailer installs a computerized checkout scanner to replace a manual cash register system.
   C. A firm develops a substitute for saturated fat in manufactured foods.
   D. All of the above are examples.
   E. None of the above is an example.

4-69.
E
App.
Hard
p. 106

Which of the following is NOT an example of a change in TECHNOLOGY:
- A. a camera producer finds a way to enable a camera to store pictures electronically--without film.
- B. machines are developed to assemble defect-free electronic components.
- C. robots on a production line make it possible to lower cost.
- D. a manufacturer of frozen food is finding that consumers prefer containers that can go from the freezer direct to a microwave oven.
- E. the government passes a law that requires car manufacturers to use antilock brakes.

4-70.
D
App.
Med.
p. 106

AT&T reacted to the popularity of the cellular phone by adding several cellular models to its line of regular phones. Availability and popularity of cellular phones is most likely due to changes in the _____ environments.
- A. political and cultural
- B. technological and legal
- C. legal and economic
- D. social and technological
- E. all of the above

4-71.
B
Def.
Easy
p. 108

A "Buy American" campaign is an example of:
- A. transnationalism.
- B. nationalism.
- C. environmentalism.
- D. consumerism.
- E. federalism.

4-72.
C
Def.
Easy
p. 109

"Consumerism" is a social movement seeking to increase the rights and powers of:
- A. consumer activists.
- B. government planners.
- C. consumers.
- D. public interest groups.
- E. None of the above.

4-73.
E
Def.
Med.
p. 110

President Kennedy's "Consumer Bill of Rights" did NOT include:
- A. the right to be heard.
- B. the right to safety.
- C. the right to be informed.
- D. the right to choose.
- E. the right to low prices.

4-74.
B
Def.
Easy
p. 107-10

"Consumerism" and "nationalism" are issues in the _____ environment.
- A. competitive
- B. political
- C. economic
- D. cultural
- E. technological

4-75.
B
App.
Med.
p. 107-10

Which of the following newspaper headlines would be LEAST likely to involve the political environment?
A. U.S.-Vietnamese Joint Ventures in the Future.
B. Egg Sales Fall as Consumers Switch to Low Cholesterol Diets.
C. U.S. Signs Trade Agreement with Canada.
D. FDA Adopts New Regulations for Generic Drugs.
E. Consumers Urged to "Buy American."

4-76.
D
App.
Easy
p. 107-10

The largest producer of "fuzz-busters" (radar detectors) sees that many states are increasing the penalty for using them. Clearly, this firm's marketing strategy may have to change in response to these changes in the
A. economic and technological environment.
B. resources and objectives of the firm.
C. competitive environment.
D. political and legal environment.
E. cultural and social environment.

4-77.
A
Comp.
Med.
p. 110

American legislative and economic thinking assumes that:
A. competition among many small firms helps the economy.
B. firms must have their prices approved by the Federal Trade Commission.
C. the free enterprise system is dying.
D. anticompetition laws are needed to stop large firms from dominating small firms.
E. government planners are needed to run the economy.

4-78.
D
Comp.
Med.
p. 110-11

The early antimonopoly (or "procompetition") laws passed in the United States:
A. include the Federal Trade Commission Act and the Clayton Act.
B. evolved out of the efforts of some Midwestern farmers.
C. were a reaction against the "robber barons."
D. All of the above are true.
E. None of the above is true.

4-79.
D
Comp.
Hard
p. 111

The Sherman Act and the Clayton Act:
A. were intended to protect small producers.
B. were aimed at efforts to restrain trade or lessen competition.
C. were passed before the Depression of the 1930s.
D. All of the above are true.
E. None of the above is true.

4-80.
E
Comp.
Hard
p. 111

The Sherman Act and the Clayton Act:
A. were intended to protect large producers.
B. were designed to limit competition.
C. were passed during the rash of corporate takeovers in the 1980s.
D. All of the above are true.
E. None of the above is true.

4-81.
C
Def.
Hard
p. 111

The Wheeler-Lea Amendment specifically aims at:
A. product warranties.
B. product safety.
C. unfair or deceptive practices.
D. tying and exclusive dealing contracts.
E. mergers and acquisitions.

4-**82.**
B
Def.
Hard
p. 111

The Robinson-Patman Act specifically aims at:
A. unfair methods of competition.
B. price discrimination.
C. deceptive advertising.
D. firms that rely on salespeople who sell "door to door."
E. attempts to monopolize.

4-**83.**
D
Def.
Hard
p. 111

The Clayton Act specifically aims at:
A. tying contracts.
B. price discrimination by manufacturers.
C. exclusive dealing contracts limiting a buyer's sources of supply.
D. all of the above.
E. none of the above.

4-**84.**
C
Def.
Hard
p. 111

The Federal Trade Commission Act of 1914 focuses on:
A. mergers between competitors.
B. unreasonable practices related to product warranties.
C. unfair methods of competition.
D. tying contracts.
E. attempts to monopolize.

4-**85.**
A
Def.
Hard
p. 111

The Sherman Act sought to:
A. prevent monopolies or conspiracies in restraint of trade.
B. establish the Federal Consumer Protection Agency.
C. eliminate price differences among different competing suppliers.
D. prevent fraud on the Internet.
E. restrict importing into the United States.

4-**86.**
D
Comp.
Hard
p. 111

A company would be charged with product warranty violations under:
A. the Total Quality Management Act
B. the Robinson-Patman Act
C. the Federal Trade Commission Act
D. the Magnuson-Moss Act
E. There are no laws regulating product warranties.

4-**87.**
B
Comp.
Hard
p. 111

Which of the following laws focuses on price discrimination on goods of "like grade and quality" without a cost justification?
A. the Fair Prices Act
B. the Robinson-Patman Act
C. the Federal Trade Commission Act
D. the Magnuson-Moss Act
E. There are no laws regulating price discrimination.

4-**88.**
D
Comp.
Hard
p. 111

Which of the following laws is primarily concerned with product warranties?
A. the Sherman Act
B. the Robinson-Patman Act
C. the Federal Trade Commission Act
D. the Magnuson-Moss Act
E. There are no laws regulating product warranties.

4-89.
C
Comp.
Hard
p. 111

The Sherman Act and the Federal Trade Commission Act:
A. were passed to make it difficult for small companies to win customers away from large companies.
B. are not taken seriously, since there are no penalties for violations.
C. are quite different, with the FTC Act focusing on stopping deceptive business practices and the Sherman Act focusing on controlling monopolies.
D. are just different names for the same thing--a law proposed by Sherman to establish the Federal Trade Commission.
E. were passed to protect consumers from abuses by business, rather than to protect some businesses from others who had an "unfair" advantage.

4-90.
B
Def.
Hard
p. 111

Product warranties are the focus of the _____ Act.
A. Lemon
B. Magnuson-Moss
C. Sherman
D. Federal Trade Commission
E. Robinson-Patman

4-91.
E
Comp.
Med.
p. 111

The Pure Food and Drug Act:
A. regulates branding and labeling of food and drugs.
B. bans the shipment of unsanitary products.
C. gives the FDA the power to seize products.
D. requires testing of drugs.
E. All of the above.

4-92.
A
Def.
Med.
p. 112

Safety standards for products such as bicycles are set by the:
A. Consumer Product Safety Commission.
B. U.S. Department of Transportation.
C. Federal Trade Commission.
D. Office of Consumer Affairs.
E. Food and Drug Administration.

4-93.
D
Comp.
Med.
p. 112

Regarding the current legal environment facing U.S. marketing managers,
A. state and local laws rarely are important because they are always less restrictive than federal laws.
B. the focus has shifted from "let the seller beware" to "let the buyer beware."
C. the emphasis is now on restricting monopolies.
D. most Federal laws convey an intent rather than specific detail--so interpretation and enforcement is left to the courts and government agencies.
E. All of the above are true.

4-94.
A
App.
Easy
p. 112

In recent years the Federal Trade Commission has been lenient in allowing mergers between firms that had been competitors. When considering a merger, companies should take this aspect of the _____ environments into consideration.
A. legal and political
B. cultural and economic
C. technological and legal
D. social and cultural
E. political and economic

4-95.
B
Comp.
Easy
p. 113

Which of the following is NOT an important federal (U.S.) regulatory agency?
A. Office of Consumer Affairs
B. Chamber of Commerce
C. Environmental Protection Agency
D. Federal Communications Commission
E. Consumer Product Safety Commission

4-96.
B
Def.
Easy
p. 113

The attitudes and behavior patterns of people are part of the
A. political environment.
B. social and cultural environment.
C. competitive environment.
D. firm's resources and objectives.
E. economic and technological environment.

4-97.
B
App.
Med.
p. 113

A marketing analyst for a chicken processor reports that a rising percentage of people are eating chicken because it has less fat than beef. Clearly, this firm's opportunities may improve with this change in the
A. technological environment.
B. cultural and social environment.
C. economic environment.
D. political and legal environment.
E. competitive environment.

4-98.
D
App.
Easy.
p. 113

Consumer emphasis on fitness has created opportunities for firms like Nike, Nautilus and Schwinn, and illustrates the impact of the changing:
A. technological environment.
B. economic environment.
C. competitive environment.
D. cultural and social environment.
E. political and legal environment.

4-99.
B
App.
Easy
p. 113

More women working outside the home and greater interest in leisure are examples of changes in the _____ environment.
A. technological.
B. cultural and social.
C. economic.
D. legal.
E. competitive.

4-100.
D
App.
Med.
p. 113

Which of the following is an example of the cultural and social environment?
A. Growing acceptance of women in business.
B. Growing popularity of exercise.
C. Increased desire for satisfaction with life.
D. All of the above.
E. None of the above.

4-101.
B
App.
Hard
p. 113

Which of the following is least likely a result of shifts in the cultural and social environment?
   A. Domino's Pizza finds that demand for pizza delivered at home has expanded as more consumers are willing to pay for more convenience.
   B. A toy manufacturer recalls a playpen with a defective latch and Toys 'R' Us stores remove them from the shelf.
   C. Haagen-Dazs introduces a nonfat yogurt that is also "low cal."
   D. Sony recruits more women graduates for sales management positions.
   E. BMW builds its new plant in South Carolina because of the willingness of "Sun Belt" workers to put in a "full day's work."

4-102.
A
App.
Med.
p. 113

Maria Lopez runs an errand service from her home. For a fee, she will pick up dry cleaning, buy groceries, plan small parties, and do errands for her customers. The demand for this type of service has increased because of changes in the
   A. cultural/social environment.
   B. legal environment.
   C. technological environment.
   D. political environment.
   E. none of the above.

4-103.
E
Def.
Easy
p. 114

In the short run, a marketing manager usually cannot control:
   A. the competitive environment.
   B. the cultural environment.
   C. the legal environment.
   D. the economic environment.
   E. Any of the above.

4-104.
A
Comp.
Med.
p. 114

In which of the external environments do changes usually occur most slowly?
   A. Cultural and social environment
   B. Political and legal environment
   C. Resources and objectives of the firm
   D. Competitive environment
   E. Economic and technological environment

4-105.
A
Comp.
Med.
p. 114-15

The first and most important question to ask when evaluating product-market opportunities is:
   A. "How does it fit with our objectives and resources?"
   B. "What is the sales forecast for this product?"
   C. "How much profit will we make this year?"
   D. "How much do we need to invest in this product?"
   E. "How far along is our research and development effort in this area?"

4-106.
D
Def.
Med.
p. 115

A firm's product-market screening criteria for evaluating existing plans and possible new opportunities should consider:
   A. the objectives of top management.
   B. trends in the marketing environment.
   C. the firm's resources.
   D. All of the above.
   E. Only A and B above.

4-**107.**
E
Comp.
Easy
p. 115

Product-market screening criteria should:
- A. be qualitative.
- B. summarize in one place what the firm wants to accomplish.
- C. be achievable.
- D. be stated in quantitative terms.
- E. All of the above.

4-**108.**
A
Comp.
Med.
p. 115

When evaluating the potential of possible opportunities (product-market strategies), a marketing manager should:
- A. evaluate each opportunity over the life of the project, since short-term losses may hide long-term profitability.
- B. avoid using quantitative criteria because they tend to oversimplify the problem.
- C. look at each opportunity on its own, since there is no good way to compare different plans.
- D. look only at internal resources, since they are controllable.
- E. All of the above are true.

4-**109.**
C
Comp.
Med.
p. 116

A total profit approach to evaluating product-market strategic plans
- A. will not work if the plans are for the same number of years.
- B. will be most useful when the plans require very different levels of investment.
- C. may support a particular plan even if it generates poor profits in some years.
- D. Both A and B are true.
- E. None of the above is true.

4-**110.**
C
Comp.
Med.
p. 116

The "total profit" approach to evaluating possible product-market strategic plans:
- A. is the best approach to use.
- B. cannot be used to compare possible plans unless they are very similar.
- C. may support a plan that is not the most profitable in the short run.
- D. requires only sales forecasts for the life of possible plans.
- E. All of the above are true.

4-**111.**
B
Comp.
Med.
p. 116

When selecting among possible product-market strategic plans,
- A. the total profit approach tends to support plans that will be profitable in the short term even if longer term profits would be higher with another plan.
- B. the total profit approach requires estimates of sales, costs, and profits.
- C. you can only use the ROI approach to compare plans that require the same investment.
- D. All of the above are true.
- E. None of the above is true.

4-**112.**
C
Comp.
Med.
p. 116

The return-on-investment approach to evaluating possible product-market strategic plans is useful when:
- A. the plans are for longer than two years.
- B. there is uncertainty about the profitability of each plan.
- C. the plans differ a lot in terms of investment required.
- D. the total profit approach would be misleading because it ignores costs.
- E. the plans involve very different strategies.

4-113.
C
Def.
Easy
p. 117

General Electric's "strategic planning grid" is an approach for:
    A. evaluating possible marketing objectives.
    B. selecting target markets.
    C. evaluating existing and possible plans.
    D. developing new products.
    E. developing marketing mixes.

4-114.
E
Comp.
Med.
p. 117

General Electric's "strategic planning grid":
    A. focuses on market share and market growth rate.
    B. ignores some important issues--such as competitive structure and the environmental impact of a plan.
    C. requires that all opportunities be judged either "High" or "Low."
    D. substitutes quantitative estimates for management judgment.
    E. None of the above is true.

4-115.
A
App.
Med.
p. 117

Using General Electric's "strategic planning grid," an opportunity rated "medium" in terms of industry attractiveness and "medium" in terms of business strengths would be evaluated as:
    A. yellow--borderline.
    B. red--for no growth.
    C. green--for growth.
    D. could be yellow, red, or green--because the grid really doesn't deal with "medium" ratings.

4-116.
C
App.
Med.
p. 117

Using General Electric's "strategic planning grid," an opportunity rated "medium" in terms of industry attractiveness and "high" in terms of business strengths would be evaluated as:
    A. yellow--borderline.
    B. red--for no growth.
    C. green--for growth.
    D. could be yellow, red, or green--because the grid suggests that opportunities with medium ratings need more analysis.

4-117.
B
Comp.
Hard
p. 117

According to the General Electric strategic planning grid, a business that is the strongest in its industry:
    A. should still be considered as a "no-growth" prospect unless the industry attractiveness is high.
    B. is a good prospect, provided the industry has at least medium attractiveness.
    C. should automatically receive a large investment.
    D. All of the above are true.
    E. None of the above is true.

4-118.
B
Comp.
Med.
p. 117

According to the General Electric strategic planning grid, an opportunity which is low on the "business strengths" dimension but high on the "industry attractiveness" should be:

    A. called a strategic business unit.
    B. supported if it is an existing business, but probably not supported if it is a new opportunity.
    C. immediately supported with large investment.
    D. sold off or discontinued.
    E. viewed as a "green" (high growth) opportunity.

4-119.
B
Comp.
Med.
p. 117

General Electric's "strategic planning grid":

    A. focuses on market share and market growth rate.
    B. requires subjective judgments about business strengths and industry attractiveness.
    C. requires that all opportunities be judged either "High" or "Low."
    D. substitutes quantitative estimates for management judgment.
    E. All of the above are true.

4-120.
E
Comp.
Med.
p. 118

GE's planning grid approach

    A. doesn't work because different managers usually come to different conclusions given the subjective evaluations involved.
    B. is really the same thing as the total profit approach.
    C. overemphasizes short term profitability.
    D. is superficial because it considers only ROI and expected market share, and ignores other possibly important factors.
    E. could be adapted easily by another firm with different objectives.

4-121.
D
Def.
Easy
p. 118

Organizational units (within a larger company) which focus their efforts on selected product-markets and are treated as separate profit centers are called:

    A. marketing departments.
    B. SPMs.
    C. functional departments.
    D. strategic business units.
    E. BTUs.

4-122.
D
Def.
Easy
p. 118

A marketing manager in a large corporation wrote the company's president a memo in which she said: "The performance of our SBU has improved." An "SBU" is a:

    A. struggling business unit.
    B. small business unit.
    C. selective branding unit.
    D. strategic business unit.
    E. secondary bidding unit.

4-123.
C
Comp.
Med.
p. 119

Portfolio management:

    A. heavily emphasizes long-run profitability.
    B. is preferred over the General Electric strategic planning grid.
    C. allows a manager to compare different divisions within the company.
    D. is another name for the combined target market approach.
    E. None of the above is true.

4-124.
E
Comp.
Med.
p. 119

Portfolio management:
A. may place too much emphasis on easy-to-compare quantitative criteria.
B. identifies which opportunities should be supported, "milked," or sold off.
C. tends to overemphasize short-run profitability and return on investment.
D. treats products or SBUs as though they were stock investments.
E. All of the above are true.

4-125.
E
Comp.
Med.
p. 119

Portfolio management:
A. does not consider quantitative screening criteria such as ROI.
B. makes sense only if a manager is interested in comparing very similar alternatives.
C. primarily focuses on the likely long-term potential of a product-market opportunity.
D. is too complex to be helpful except in small companies that have only one product.
E. None of the above is true.

4-126.
A
Comp.
Med.
p. 120

The "continuum of environmental sensitivity" suggests that:
A. some products are more adaptable to international markets than others.
B. it is extremely risky to sell basic commodities in international markets.
C. industrial products need to be adapted more than consumer products for international markets.
D. All of the above are true.
E. None of the above is true.

Chapter 5

Demographic Dimensions of Global Consumer Markets

True-False Questions:

5-1.
False
p. 132-33

The U.S. does not have the largest population of any country in the world, but it does have the largest population growth rate.

5-2.
True
p. 132-33

India has more people than the United States, and China has more people than India.

5-3.
False
p. 128

Less-developed countries usually experience the slowest population growth.

5-4.
False
p. 129

When considering international markets, income is usually not an important demographic dimension.

5-5.
False
p. 129

Gross national product is the total dollar value of a country's exports during a one year period.

5-6.
True
p. 132

Gross domestic product includes foreign income earned in a country.

5-7.
True
p. 129

Both GDP and GNP are widely used measures of national income.

5-8.
True
p. 132-33

GDP income measures can give the impression that people in less-developed nations have more income than they really do.

5-9.
False
p. 132-33

GNP income measures can give the impression that people in less-developed nations have less income than they really do.

5-10.
True
p. 132-33

Generally the nations with the fastest growth in GNP are not the nations with the largest GNPs.

5-11.
False
p. 132-33

The fastest rate of growth in GNP is occurring in the nations with the largest current GNP.

5-12.
True
p. 132-33

Even though the more developed industrial nations don't have the largest populations, they do have the biggest share of the world's GNP.

5-13.
True
p. 132-34

Income and wealth tend to be distributed very unevenly in many countries.

5-14.
True
p. 134

Much of the world's population lives in extreme poverty.

5-15.
False
p. 136

Because almost all of the world's population can read and write, international marketers can rely on printed communications to reach foreign customers who do not have radio or TV.

5-16.
True
p. 136

California is the state with the largest population, and Texas is a distant second.

5-17.
False
p. 136

New York is the state with the largest population, and California is a distant second.

5-18.
True
p. 137

Areas with small populations may still be attractive target markets for some firms--because there may be less competition.

5-19.
True
p. 137

There are about 281 million people living in the United States.

5-20.
True
p. 137

In the United States, the West and the South are growing faster than the Northeast and the North Central areas.

5-21.
True
p. 138

The rate of growth of the world's population is much higher than the rate of growth of the U.S.'s population.

5-22.
True
p. 138

Most of the U.S.'s future population growth is expected to come from immigration.

5-23.
False
p. 139

The birthrate has been steadily increasing for nearly fifty years--and that trend is called the "baby boom."

5-24.
True
p. 139

The average age of the U. S. population will continue to rise for many years because of the post-World War II "baby boom."

5-25.
True
p. 140

The post-World War II "baby boom" produced about 25 percent of the present U.S. population.

5-26.
True
p. 140

The decline in the number of teenagers in the U. S. has now reversed itself.

5-27.
True
p. 140

Between 1995 and 2005, the teenage group will grow about twice as fast as the overall population.

5-28.
False
p. 140

There has been a steady decline in the number of teens for 15 years and that trend will probably continue.

5-29.
False
p. 140

Between 1995 and 2005, the teen group will grow slower than any other segment of the population.

5-30.
False
p. 141

The typical American household consists of a couple with two children living at home.

5-31.
True
p. 141

The United States has the highest divorce rate in the world.

5-32.
True
p. 141

In the U.S., about 80 percent of all divorced people remarry.

5-33.
True
p. 141

In the U.S., about 60 percent of all adults are married.

5-34.
False
p. 141

In the U.S., traditional households are growing at a much higher rate than nontraditional households.

5-35.
False
p. 142

In the U.S., single-adult households account for nearly two thirds of all households.

5-36.
True
p. 142

In the U.S., less than two percent of the population lives in rural areas on farms.

5-37.
True
p. 142

A Metropolitan Statistical Area is an integrated economic and social unit with a large population at the center.

5-38.
True
p. 142

A Metropolitan Statistical Area usually has a population of at least 50,000 people.

5-39.
True
p. 143

Competition for consumer dollars is usually greater inside a MSA than outside a MSA.

5-40.
False
p. 143

Americans are not very mobile--less than 2 percent of all Americans move each year.

5-41.
True
p. 143

About 40 percent of those who move each year are relocating to a new county.

5-42.
False
p. 143

Compared to 50 years ago, fewer American families are now in the middle and upper income levels.

5-43.
False
p. 145

Because the "income pyramid" in the U.S. has turned over, higher-income groups no longer receive a very large share of the total income.

5-44.
True
p. 145

Only about 5 percent of families in the U.S. have incomes over $155,000, but these families get more than 20 percent of the total income.

5-45.
True
p. 145

The lowest 20 percent income group in the U.S. receives less than 5 percent of the country's total income.

5-46.
True
p. 146

It's not unusual for a college graduate to start out earning as much as the median family income.

5-47.
False
p. 146

Discretionary income is what is left after paying taxes.

5-48.
False
p. 147

Stage of family life cycle is usually determined by two demographic dimensions--income and number of children.

5-49.
True
p. 147

Marital status, age, and the age of any children in a household are the three demographic dimensions that determine stage of family life cycle.

5-50.
False
p. 147

Older people seem to be more open to new products and brands than younger people.

5-51.
False
p. 147

Singles and young couples seem less willing to try new products because they earn less.

5-52.
True
p. 147

Younger families with no children are a good market for durable goods such as automobiles and furniture.

5-53.
False
p. 148

Families with teenagers tend to spend more on durables than younger families.

5-54.
False
p. 148

Teens play an increasingly minor role in shaping family purchases.

5-55.
False
p. 148

"Empty nesters" is a term that refers to young couples with no children.

5-56.
True
p. 149

Senior citizens make up almost 13 percent of the population and may be an attractive target market--even though their incomes are lower than in their peak earning years.

5-57.
True
p. 150

Both the birthrate and the buying power of ethnic groups in the U.S. are increasing.

5-58.
True
p. 150

In the U.S., ethnic submarkets are growing at a faster rate than the overall population.

5-59.
False
p. 150

In ethnic markets within the U.S., the median age is higher and the birthrate is lower than the overall population.

5-60.
True
p. 150

The Hispanic population in the U.S. is already larger than the Black population.

5-61.
True
p. 151

Already, more than 36 percent of American children are Black, Hispanic, or Asian.

Multiple Choice Questions

5-62.
D
Def.
Easy
p. 126

When considering a potential product-market, a marketer should decide:
A. where it is.
B. what its relevant segmenting dimensions are.
C. how big it is.
D. All of the above.

5-63.
B
Comp.
Med.
p. 126

In analyzing a potential market, the LEAST RELEVANT question for a marketing manager to answer is:
A. how big is the market?
B. what is the average age in the market?
C. where is the market?
D. what are the market's relevant segmenting dimensions?

5-64.
D
Comp.
Easy
p. 126

Analysis of demographic dimensions:
A. is the most important step to successful segmentation.
B. considers income and sex, but not age.
C. is the most effective way to identify unmet consumer needs.
D. can be used along with analysis of other dimensions to identify attractive target markets.
E. none of the above.

5-65.
D
Comp.
Hard
p. 128

Regarding population growth in the world,
A. Population growth in Japan and Europe is even slower than in the U.S.
B. less-developed countries generally experience the fastest growth.
C. it will take over five times as long for the populations of the U.S. and Canada to double compared to Nicaragua and Saudi Arabia.
D. All of the above are true.
E. None of the above are true.

5-66.
E
Def.
Hard
p. 132-33

Which of the following countries has the fastest annual population growth?
A. United Kingdom
B. Canada
C. Germany
D. United States
E. Tanzania

5-67.
B
Comp.
Hard
p. 129

Regarding population density in the world,
A. high-population density occurs only in highly developed economies.
B. some Western European and Asian urban areas are more crowded than U.S. urban areas.
C. the United States is the only country with crowded urban areas.
D. there is a worldwide movement back to the farm.
E. None of the above is true.

5-**68.**   Which of the following countries has the highest population density?
D   A. Switzerland
Def.   B. United States
Hard   C. Australia
p. 132-33   D. Singapore
              E. Bangladesh

5-**69.**   A widely used measure of income in most countries is:
A   A. gross national product.
Comp.   B. total consumption expenditures.
Easy   C. disposable personal product.
p. 129   D. population times GNP.
              E. socio-economic product.

5-**70.**   Gross national product (GNP):
A   A. is affected by economic conditions and the productivity of workers in the
Comp.   country.
Med.   B. usually rises when there are bad economic conditions in an economy.
p. 129   C. is the amount of new capital invested in business in a year.
              D. is the total cost of producing all goods and services in a year.
              E. is the total market value of goods and services consumed in an economy in a
                  year.

5-**71.**   Gross national product (GNP) is the:
B   A. total cost of producing all goods and services sold in a year.
Def.   B. total market value of goods and services produced in an economy in a year.
Easy   C. total market value of goods (but not services) consumed in an economy in a year.
p. 129   D. total market value of goods and services consumed in a year.
              E. total market value of goods (but not services) produced in an economy in a year.

5-**72.**   Gross national product (GNP) is the:
A   A. total market value of goods and services produced in an economy in a year.
Def.   B. manufacturers' selling price of goods (but not services) produced in a year.
Easy   C. total market value of goods (but not services) produced in an economy in a year.
p. 129   D. total market value of goods and services consumed in a year.
              E. None of the above.

5-**73.**   Gross national product:
C   A. is the total market value of goods, but not services, produced in a year.
Comp.   B. is an excellent basis for comparing consumer well-being across different cultures
Hard   and economies.
p. 129   C. is a widely used measure of income for different countries.
              D. All of the above are true.
              E. A and B are true.

5-**74.**
C
Comp.
Med.
p. 129

Comparing GNP for foreign countries can help a marketing manager evaluate potential markets if the manager remembers that:
A. GNP measures show people's tendency to buy particular products.
B. income tends to be evenly distributed among consumers in most countries.
C. GNP estimates may not be very accurate for very different cultures and economies.
D. GNP measures show the degree of competition in a market.
E. All of the above are true.

5-**75.**
D
Comp.
Med.
p. 129-33

Regarding GDP and GNP:
A. GDP income measures can give the impression that people in less-developed nations have more income than they really do.
B. GDP includes foreign income earned in a country, but GNP does not.
C. Both GDP and GNP are widely used measures of national income.
D. All of the above are true.
E. A and B are true, but not C.

5-**76.**
C
Def.
Hard
p. 132-33

Which of the following countries have the HIGHEST GNP PER CAPITA?
A. Saudi Arabia and Kuwait
B. Mexico and Spain
C. Japan and Switzerland
D. India and China
E. Germany and the United States

5-**77.**
C
Def.
Hard
p. 132-33

Which of the following countries have the LOWEST GNP PER CAPITA?
A. Japan and Switzerland
B. Mexico and Spain
C. Ethiopia and Nepal
D. India and Pakistan
E. Germany and the United States

5-**78.**
B
Def.
Hard
p. 136

Literacy studies show that only about _____ of the world's population can read and write.
A. two-thirds
B. three-fourths
C. one-half
D. one-tenth
E. one-fourth

5-**79.**
A
Def.
Hard
p. 132-33

Which of the following countries has the LOWEST illiteracy rate?
A. Finland
B. Venezuela
C. Greece
D. Algeria
E. Morocco

5-**80.**
C
Def.
Hard
p. 132-33

Which of the following countries has the HIGHEST illiteracy rate?
A. United Kingdom
B. Italy
C. Bangladesh
D. France
E. Egypt

5-**81.**
E
Comp.
Easy
p. 136

The state with the largest population is
A. Texas.
B. Nevada.
C. New York.
D. Florida.
E. California.

5-**82.**
E
Comp.
Easy
p. 136-37

The best marketing opportunity for a consumer products producer is in:
A. California.
B. Florida.
C. New York.
D. Texas.
E. It depends on the marketing strategy.

5-**83.**
C
Comp.
Hard
p. 136-37

Regarding changing population patterns
A. the population of the U.S. will double in about 25 years.
B. nearly one half of the people move in a typical year.
C. areas with rapid population growth may offer the most attractive marketing opportunities.
D. All of the above are true.
E. None of the above is true.

5-**84.**
D
Def.
Hard
p. 137-38

In the period from 1990 to 2000, the population grew most rapidly in:
A. the north central states (around the Great Lakes).
B. every state in the U.S.
C. Sun Belt states.
D. the western states.
E. None of the above is true.

5-**85.**
B
Def.
Med.
p. 137-38

During the next decade, the U.S. population is expected to continue to shift:
A. away from the Southeast to the Northeast.
B. to the South and West.
C. to the north central states.
D. away from the Northeast to all other parts of the country.
E. away from the West to the East.

5-**86.**
B
Def.
Hard
p. 137-38

According to the text, which of the following states had the LARGEST percentage increase in population between 1990 and 2000?
A. North Dakota
B. Nevada
C. West Virginia
D. Florida
E. Iowa

5-87. Smart marketers might respond to the changes in the U.S. population by:
D
Comp.
    A. targeting customers in international markets to take advantage of faster population growth overseas.
Hard
    B. targeting areas where there is less population but also fewer competitors.
p. 136-38
    C. focusing on areas, like the Northeast, where there are large numbers of potential customers.
    D. all of the above.
    E. none of the above.

5-88. In the next 20 years,
B
    A. there should be a continuous increase in the U.S. birthrate.
Comp.
    B. the population of the U.S. will probably decline unless immigration offsets low birthrates.
Hard
p. 138
    C. the growth rate of the U.S. population will rise.
    D. the U.S. population is expected to double.
    E. population will increase at a faster rate in the U.S. than in the rest of the world population.

5-89. The number of babies born per year per 1,000 people is called the:
B
    A. economic index.
Def.
    B. birthrate.
Easy
    C. future market index.
p. 139
    D. baby boom index.
    E. consumer surplus.

5-90. An estimate of the U.S. birthrate for the year 2005 is 14.1. This means that
A
    A. 14.1 babies were born per 1,000 people in the population.
Def.
    B. babies less than 1 year old were 14.1 percent of the population.
Med.
    C. 14.1 percent of population growth was from new births.
p. 139
    D. the birthrate was at an all time high.
    E. the average age of the U.S. population will not increase in the next 10 years.

5-91. The birthrate in the United States
B
    A. has been almost constant for the last thirty years.
Comp.
    B. is falling again because many couples born during the "baby boom" are now past their child-bearing years.
Med.
p. 139
    C. rose when Vietnam vets got married, had children, and created the "baby boom" generation.
    D. will contribute more to U.S. population growth than immigration in the next 25 years.
    E. All of the above are true.

5-92. With respect to marketing opportunities that depend on the age distribution of the U.S.
E population,
Comp.
    A. the 18-24 year old group will see dramatic growth between 2000 and 2010.
Hard
    B. sales of products targeted at senior citizens are likely to rise between 2000 and 2010.
p. 139-41
    C. the size of the 45-64 age group will increase more rapidly between 2000 and 2010 than any other group.
    D. the average age of the U.S. consumer is rising.
    E. All of the above are true.

5-**93.**
A
Comp.
Hard
p. 139-41

During the 1990s, the largest increase in the U.S. population occurred in the:
A. 45-64 age group.
B. 65 or over age group.
C. 18-24 age group.
D. 25-44 age group.
E. 5-17 age group.

5-**94.**
E
Comp.
Med.
p. 139-40

The move of the "Baby Boomers" into middle age has:
A. increased the average age of the population.
B. left many colleges and universities with excess capacity.
C. contributed to increased interest in health and fitness products.
D. lowered the birthrate.
E. All of the above are true.

5-**95.**
A
Comp.
Hard
p. 141

Which of the following U.S. marketing managers is about to make a serious mistake?
A. "We are targeting the pre-school age group, since that group is growing faster than ever before."
B. "We are refocusing on senior citizens, since they will be a growing market for many years."
C. "We are developing special swimsuit designs for older women as that market is very large and growing."
D. "Our company is shifting to international markets, where the population will continue to grow at a more rapid rate."
E. None of the above seems headed for a mistake.

5-**96.**
D
Comp.
Hard
p. 141-42

Which of the following statements about U.S. consumer households is true?
A. More than 80 percent of all households in the U.S. are made up of married couples with no children under 18 years of age.
B. The divorce rate is about 50 percent, and the majority of divorced people stay single.
C. Americans are marrying younger, but delaying child bearing.
D. Single-adult households account for over one-fourth of all households.
E. All of the above are true.

5-**97.**
A
Comp.
Hard
p. 141-42

Which of the following statements about U.S. consumer households is true?
A. The U.S. has the highest divorce rate in the world.
B. The typical American household is a married couple with two children living in the suburbs.
C. One-half of all households in the U.S. are made up of married couples with no children under 18 years of age.
D. Only one-fourth of all adults are married.
E. Single-adult households make up 50 percent of all U.S. households.

5-**98.**
E
Comp.
Hard
p. 141-42

Which of the following statements about U.S. consumer households is true?
  A. About 2 out of every 3 marriages ends in divorce--and at any given time only about 40 percent of all adults are married.
  B. More than half of all U.S. households consist of married couples with no children 18 or younger living at home.
  C. Single-adults account for nearly 40 percent of all households.
  D. Americans are marrying younger, but delaying child bearing compared to the older generation.
  E. None of the above is true.

5-**99.**
E
Comp.
Hard
p. 141-42

Which of the following statements about U.S. consumer households is true?
  A. Married couples with no children 18 or younger account for half of all U.S. households.
  B. The typical American household is a married couple living in the suburbs with two children.
  C. The number of families living "on the farm" has dropped to an all time low of 15 percent.
  D. About two thirds of all adults are now single.
  E. None of the above is true.

5-**100.**
C
Comp.
Hard
p. 141-42

The composition of U.S. households is such that:
  A. the number of unmarried couples living together has sharply declined.
  B. married couples with no children under 18 now account for one-half of all households.
  C. single-adult households account for over 25 percent of all households.
  D. only about one-third of all adults are married.
  E. 75 percent of all marriages end in divorce.

5-**101.**
E
Def.
Hard
p. 142

Single-adult households account for over _____ percent of all households in the United States.
  A. 45
  B. 55
  C. 35
  D. 15
  E. 25

5-**102.**
D
Def.
Hard
p. 142

The number of people living on farms in the United States is _____ percent of the total population.
  A. 20
  B. more than 20
  C. 12
  D. less than 2
  E. 10

5-**103.**
E
Comp.
Med.
p. 142-43

Regarding the population distribution in urban and suburban areas,
  A. more people live in suburbs than in central cities.
  B. the share of the U.S. population living on farms has dropped to less than 2 percent.
  C. professionals with high incomes tend to concentrate in metro areas.
  D. purchase patterns in suburbs are often different from those in central cities.
  E. All of the above are true.

5-**104.**   The largest group of Americans live in:
A   A. suburban areas.
Comp.   B. farm areas.
Med.   C. central cities.
p. 142   D. rural areas.

5-**105.**   A Metropolitan Statistical Area (MSA):
C   A. must contain one city of 10,000 or more people.
Def.   B. is an urbanized area with a population of at least 2,000,000 people.
Med.   C. is an integrated economic and social unit with a large population nucleus.
p. 142   D. usually includes several cities.
               E. Both B and D are true.

5-**106.**   A Metropolitan Statistical Area (MSA):
B   A. contains one city of 500,000 or more.
Def.   B. is an integrated economic and social unit having a large population nucleus.
Med.   C. is a consolidated set of cities and suburbs.
p. 142   D. consists of one or more counties which must contain a total population of at least
                  2,000,000.
               E. Both C and D are required for an area to be designated an MSA.

5-**107.**   A Metropolitan Statistical Area (MSA) is:
C   A. an area where there has been at least a 15 percent change in the population
Def.   during the previous 10 years.
Easy   B. a city with 250,000 or more people.
p. 142   C. generally centered on one city or urbanized area of 50,000 or more inhabitants
                  and includes bordering urban areas.
               D. a Census Bureau term that corresponds to county-by-county political boundaries.
               E. All of the above.

5-**108.**   Consolidated Metropolitan Statistical Areas (CMSA):
B   A. are the "central city" areas of the largest urban areas--such as New York City
Def.   and Los Angeles.
Med.   B. are the largest MSAs--those with a population of more than 1,000,000.
p. 142   C. are of little interest to marketers because they are defined by political boundaries
                  rather than on some other, more useful, segmenting dimensions.
               D. have large populations, but usually are only of interest to marketers who are
                  targeting low income consumers.
               E. Both C and D are true.

5-**109.**   A Consolidated Metropolitan Statistical Area
C   A. is a group of small towns or cities that, taken together, have a total population of
Comp.   100,000.
Med.   B. is smaller than an MSA.
p. 142   C. is a large metropolitan statistical area--with over 1 million population.
               D. is the central city area of a large city.
               E. None of the above is true.

5-**110.**
A
Comp.
Med.
p. 142

Metropolitan Statistical Areas
    A. are attractive to many marketers, but usually are very competitive.
    B. are declining in importance.
    C. offer lower sales potential than might be suggested by the population base involved.
    D. All of the above are true.
    E. None of the above is true.

5-**111.**
C
Def.
Hard
p. 143

The percentage of Americans who move each year?
    A. is less than 3 percent
    B. is more than 50 percent
    C. is about 16 percent
    D. is about 36 percent
    E. difficult to estimate because some people move within the same town.

5-**112.**
E
Comp.
Med.
p. 143

Regarding U.S. population changes,
    A. about 16 percent of all Americans move each year.
    B. some of the areas with the largest populations are losing population.
    C. the overall U.S. population continues to grow rapidly.
    D. All of the above are true.
    E. Only A and B are true.

5-**113.**
B
Comp.
Med.
p. 143

People who move to a new home (that is, "mobile" consumers):
    A. are not good targets for most products since buying a new house usually consumes most of their discretionary income.
    B. are split about 60 percent for "local" (same county) and 40 percent for long-distance moves.
    C. represent only about 5 percent of all Americans in any given year.
    D. create opportunities for marketers only when a long distance move is involved.
    E. All of the above are true.

5-**114.**
B
Comp.
Med.
p. 143

U.S. "mobiles" (consumers who move):
    A. are not a very attractive market--since less than 2 percent of all Americans move each year.
    B. must make many market-oriented decisions fairly quickly after they move.
    C. tend to ignore "national" retailers.
    D. tend to restrict their purchases until they become very familiar with their new area.
    E. generally have less money to spend than other groups.

5-**115.**
D
Def.
Easy
p. 143

Over the last 50 years, the distribution of buying power in the United States has shifted:
    A. very little.
    B. only slightly, but the ongoing trend has been toward a larger percentage of people in the lower income levels.
    C. dramatically--with a much smaller "middle income" group and a much larger group living in poverty.
    D. dramatically--with many more consumers in the middle and upper income levels.

5-**116.**
D
Comp.
Med.
p. 143-45

Regarding the distribution of U.S. family income,
    A. the U.S. income distribution is similar to that of Canada and Japan.
    B. the higher income groups still receive a big share of the total income.
    C. buying power has generally become more evenly distributed in the last 50 years.
    D. All of the above are true.
    E. B and C are true.

5-**117.**
C
Comp.
Med.
p. 144

The median family income in the U.S.:
    A. has increased for the last twenty years, primarily because growth in service industries has created more high paying jobs.
    B. does not vary much from one state to another.
    C. reflects the upward shift in the income distribution.
    D. was about $67,000 in 1996.
    E. has risen continuously since 1960.

5-**118.**
D
Comp.
Hard
p. 145

The 20 percent of U.S. families with the highest incomes receive:
    A. about the same total income as the next highest 20 percent.
    B. about twice as much income, on average, as the lowest 20 percent group.
    C. almost 80 percent of the total income
    D. almost 50 percent of the total U.S. income.
    E. only about 20 percent of the total U.S. income.

5-**119.**
E
Def.
Hard
p. 145

About what percentage of TOTAL U.S. income goes to the 20 percent of families with the top incomes?
    A. About 75 percent
    B. About 95 percent
    C. About 15 percent
    D. About 25 percent
    E. About 50 percent

5-**120.**
A
Def.
Hard
p. 145

The percentage of U.S. families with incomes of $59,400 and over in 1999 was:
    A. About 40 percent
    B. About 60 percent
    C. 10-15 percent
    D. about 20 percent
    E. Less than 5 percent

5-**121.**
E
Def.
Easy
p. 146

"Disposable income" means:
    A. discretionary income.
    B. income before taxes.
    C. income less "necessity" expenditures.
    D. family income
    E. income after taxes.

5-122.
A
App.
Med.
p. 146

Charlene Newsome is a sales rep for a computer producer. Her salary last year was $30,000, and she earned another $5,000 in sales commissions. She paid $6,000 in taxes, and spent $8,000 on food, housing, a car, and other "necessities." What is Charlene's disposable income?
  A. $29,000
  B. $34,000
  C. $15,000
  D. $24,000
  E. $ 8,000

5-123.
A
App.
Med.
p. 146

A young working couple earned $55,000 last year. They paid $16,000 in taxes and $20,000 in rent, food, insurance and other necessities. What was their disposable income for the year?
  A. $39,000.
  B. $55,000.
  C. $30,000.
  D. $35,000.
  E. $19,000.

5-124.
D
App.
Med.
p. 146

A young working couple earned $35,000 last year, and paid $10,000 in taxes. They spent $13,000 on rent, food, insurance, and other "necessities." What is their disposable income?
  A. $12,000
  B. $35,000
  C. $22,000
  D. $25,000
  E. there is not enough information to tell.

5-125.
A
Def.
Easy
p. 146

"Disposable income" means:
  A. a family's income AFTER taxes.
  B. the amount a family spends on consumption.
  C. the amount a family has left to spend AFTER paying for necessities.
  D. a family's income BEFORE taxes.
  E. the amount a family has left to spend AFTER taxes and savings.

5-126.
E
App.
Med.
p. 146

Sonny Cooper earned $20,000 last year as a carpenter. He paid $6,000 for food, rent, medical expenses and other "necessities." There was little construction work in February, so he took a trip to Hawaii and spent $4,000. What was Sonny's disposable income last year?
  A. $ 4,000
  B. $20,000
  C. $10,000
  D. $12,000
  E. There is not enough information to tell.

5-**127.**
A
App.
Med.
p. 146

As the owner of a women's clothing store, Tiffany Chin has an income of $75,000. She pays $30,000 per year in taxes and another $17,000 per year in grocery bills, house mortgage, and car payment. Last year she went to Europe and spent an additional $4,000. What was Tiffany's disposable income last year?
  A. $45,000.
  B. $75,000.
  C. $26,000.
  D. $28,000.
  E. $24,000.

5-**128.**
D
Def.
Med.
p. 146

"Discretionary income":
  A. is a family's income AFTER taxes.
  B. is a measure of a family's total purchasing power.
  C. is the amount of income spent on durable goods.
  D. is the amount of disposable income left AFTER paying for "necessities."
  E. both B and C are true.

5-**129.**
A
Def.
Easy
p. 146

The amount of disposable income a family has left after paying for its "necessities" is called its _____ income.
  A. discretionary
  B. family
  C. marginal
  D. personal
  E. taxable

5-**130.**
B
Def.
Easy
p. 146

The amount of disposable income a family has left after paying for its "necessities" is called its _____ income.
  A. personal.
  B. discretionary.
  C. marginal.
  D. disposable.
  E. modified.

5-**131.**
C
App.
Med.
p. 146

A young working couple earned $50,000 last year. Of that, they paid $16,000 in taxes and $15,000 in rent, food, insurance and other necessities. Their discretionary income for the year was:
  A. $35,000.
  B. $50,000.
  C. $19,000.
  D. $34,000.
  E. $15,000.

5-**132.**
C
App.
Med.
p. 146

Sandy Fontina was just promoted to marketing manager for her company. She also gets a big raise with the promotion. Because her discretionary income will increase, which of the following products is MOST likely to benefit?
  A. furnace repairs.
  B. automobile insurance.
  C. a CD stereo system.
  D. medical services.
  E. grocery staples.

5-**133.**
A
App.
Med.
p. 146

As the owner of a videotape rental store, Sandy Fontina has an income of $72,000. She pays $30,000 per year in taxes and another $22,000 per year in grocery bills, house mortgage, and car payment. Last year she spent an additional $4,000 on a two-week vacation at a Club Med in Cancun, Mexico. What was Sandy's discretionary income last year?
   A. $20,000.
   B. $4,000.
   C. $42,000.
   D. $26,000.
   E. $50,000.

5-**134.**
C
App.
Med.
p. 146

Manuel Hostas has an annual income of $75,000 a year. He pays $25,000 in taxes, and spends another $15,000 on his home, car, food, and other "necessities." Last year, he decided to really enjoy his annual vacation, so he spent $5,000 to go skiing in Austria. What was Manuel's discretionary income last year?
   A. $20,000
   B. $ 5,000
   C. $35,000
   D. $30,000
   E. $50,000

5-**135.**
B
App.
Med.
p. 146

Jon Crosby is a marketing analyst and made $28,000 last year. He paid $5,000 in taxes, and spent another $10,000 for food, housing, a car, and other "necessities." Jon's discretionary income was:
   A. $28,000
   B. $13,000
   C. $23,000
   D. $18,000
   E. There is not enough information to tell.

5-**136.**
A
App.
Med.
p. 146

Dana Longstreet's salary as a sales rep was $32,000 last year. She earned an additional $10,000 in sales commissions. Her tax bill was $14,000 and bills covering other necessities such as food, housing, and transportation amounted to $11,000. Dana's discretionary income last year was:
   A. $17,000.
   B. $11,000.
   C. $32,000.
   D. $28,000.
   E. $42,000.

5-**137.**
E
Comp.
Easy
p. 147

Which of the following dimensions affect family spending?
   A. income
   B. age of children
   C. age
   D. marital status
   E. all of the above

5-**138.**
A
Comp.
Hard
p. 147

Regarding the family life cycle, singles and younger couples without children
A. usually spend a greater proportion of their income on discretionary items.
B. tend to be carefree shoppers who are not very price-conscious.
C. often wait to buy basic durable goods until they have children.
D. feel more financially squeezed than couples with young children.
E. All of the above are true.

5-**139.**
E
Def.
Easy
p. 147

Of the following, which are the most receptive to new products and new brands?
A. families with small children.
B. older people with no children.
C. families with teenagers.
D. families whose children are grown.
E. younger people with no children.

5-**140.**
A
Def.
Easy
p. 147

Of the following, which are the most receptive to new products and new brands?
A. Young people
B. Senior citizens
C. Empty-nesters
D. Middle-aged people
E. All are equally receptive.

5-**141.**
B
Comp.
Med.
p. 147

Peter and Jeannie Talbott were married last year, at age 24. They have no children and both are currently working. Couples like Peter and Jeannie:
A. are likely to be a poor target for firms that are trying to market a new brand or new product concept.
B. usually focus on buying durables--such as furniture and appliances.
C. usually don't spend money on discretionary purchases.
D. All of the above are true.
E. None of the above is true.

5-**142.**
E
App.
Hard
p. 147-49

Baroke Construction Company built large, single-family homes for 25 years. Then there was a shift toward more demand for small luxury condominiums--and Baroke changed its focus. The change in demand could be explained by:
A. the increasing number of senior citizens who are "empty-nesters."
B. the fact that consumers in urban areas have higher incomes.
C. the trend toward smaller family size.
D. the increase in the number of single-adult households.
E. All of the above are likely causes.

5-**143.**
C
Comp.
Med.
p. 148

"Empty nesters":
A. are senior citizens.
B. are people over 65 who live alone.
C. often have high incomes and fewer required expenses.
D. are singles and couples without children--who have much discretionary income.
E. None of the above is true.

5-**144.**   Senior citizens now represent about _____ percent of the population.
D
Def.   A. 23
Hard   B. 43
p. 149   C. 6
              D. 13
              E. 3

5-**145.**   Jesse Jacobs has started "Seasoned Support," a business that provides a number of
D   services--from house and lawn care to grocery shopping--for the elderly. Jesse Jacobs
App.   is apparently
Hard   A. unaware of the lack of success experienced by most other companies that have
p. 149   tried to target this market.
              B. doomed to failure, since older consumers do not need such services.
              C. unaware that very few people who are over 65 have enough money to pay for
                 such services.
              D. targeting the increasing number of older consumers who now have higher
                 incomes than in the past.
              E. None of the above is a good answer.

5-**146.**   Compared to U.S. averages, the median age of Spanish-speaking people in the U.S. is:
C   A. slightly higher.
Def.   B. much higher.
Easy   C. lower.
p. 150   D. about the same.

5-**147.**   Informed marketing managers know that in the U.S.:
A   A. the birthrate for African-Americans is higher than for whites.
Int.   B. "empty nesters" have less income to spend than senior citizens.
Hard   C. young married couples without children spend relatively little on durable goods.
p. 150   D. All of the above are true.
              E. None of the above is true.

5-**148.**   Which of the following statements by marketing managers is NOT logical and true?
E   A. "We are planning to appeal more to Hispanic consumers, since this group has
Comp.   surged more than 60 percent since 1990."
Hard   B. "We're building supermarkets that will appeal to Hispanic consumers; it's a big
p. 150-51   investment, but the Hispanic population in the U.S. spends more than $380
                 billion a year."
              C. "We are adapting our diaper promotion to target Black and Hispanic parents,
                 since the birthrate in those groups is higher than for whites."
              D. "We will target Asian-Americans in San Francisco since they comprise over 20
                 percent of its population."
              E. "Black consumers spend more than $540 billion a year, so we are going to
                 appeal to this large, homogeneous target market."

5-**149.**
D
Comp.
Med.
p. 150-52

The ethnic composition of a market can be important to marketing managers because
A. treating all members of an ethnic group as one target market is often misleading.
B. more than 1 out of 10 families speak a language other than English at home.
C. the geographic distribution of ethnic groups varies across the country.
D. All of the above are true.
E. None of the above is true.

5-**150.**
C
Comp.
Med.
p. 150-52

When looking at demographic dimensions, marketers should:
A. know that it is illegal to segment markets based on membership in some racial or ethnic group.
B. know that demographics are especially helpful in explaining why specific people buy specific brands.
C. recognize that demographics can be very useful for estimating the market potential of possible target markets.
D. understand that ethnic groups are generally homogeneous within.
E. All of the above are correct.

5-**151.**
E
Def.
Easy
p. 152

Which of the following is a consumer market demographic dimension?
A. income distribution.
B. stage in life cycle.
C. geographic distribution.
D. household composition.
E. All of the above are examples.

5-**152.**
E
Def.
Easy
p. 152

Which of the following is a consumer market demographic dimension?
A. income.
B. age.
C. family life cycle.
D. geographic location.
E. All of the above are examples.

Chapter 6

Behavioral Dimensions of the Consumer Market

True-False Questions:

6-1.
True
p. 157

Most economists assume that consumers are "economic buyers" who logically evaluate choices in terms of cost and value received to get the greatest satisfaction from spending their time and money.

6-2.
True
p. 157

The economic-buyer theory assumes that consumers know all the facts and logically compare choices in terms of cost and value.

6-3.
False
p. 157

The "economic buyer" view of consumers says that individuals will only buy the cheapest goods and services available--regardless of quality.

6-4.
False
p. 157

Economic needs are concerned only with getting the best quality at the lowest price.

6-5.
False
p. 157

Economic needs include such things as self-respect, accomplishment, fun, freedom and relaxation.

6-6.
False
p. 157

Most marketing managers think that the economic-buyer theory explains buyer behavior very well.

6-7.
True
p. 157

According to the text, consumer buying decisions are influenced by psychological variables, social influences, and the purchase situation.

6-8.
True
p. 158

Motivation, perception, learning, attitudes and lifestyle are psychological variables which affect consumer buying.

6-9.
False
p. 158

Family, social class, reference groups, and culture are the intrapersonal variables that affect a consumer's buying decisions.

6-10.
True
p. 158

Wants are needs which are learned during a person's life.

6-11.
True
p. 159-60

The "hierarchy of needs" model suggests that we never reach a complete state of satisfaction, and that as lower level needs are satisfied higher level needs become more dominant.

6-12.
False
p. 160

Motivation theory suggests that a consumer would not try to satisfy physiological and safety needs until social and personal needs have been completely satisfied.

6-13.
True
p. 160

Consumers do not usually see or hear all the stimuli that come their way.

6-14.
False
p. 160

"Selective exposure" refers to a person's ability to screen out or modify ideas, messages, and information that conflict with previously learned attitudes and beliefs.

6-15.
True
p. 161-62

According to learning theory, a cue is likely to result in a consumer response only if there is a drive to satisfy.

6-16.
False
p. 161

Reinforcement of a response decreases the likelihood of the same response the next time the drive occurs.

6-17.
True
p. 162

Adding lemon scent to Pledge furniture polish is an example of using a positive cue.

6-18.
True
p. 162

A perfume ad that suggests that people who use the product have more appeal to the opposite sex is an example of a positive cue.

6-19.
True
p. 162

Many needs are culturally (or socially) learned.

6-20.
True
p. 162

Americans' preoccupation with deodorants is an example of a culturally learned need.

6-21.
False
p. 162

The main difference between attitudes and beliefs is that beliefs always involve liking or disliking, but attitudes don't necessarily involve liking or disliking.

6-22.
True
p. 162

Beliefs are not as action-oriented as attitudes.

6-23.
False
p. 162

Beliefs are more action-oriented than attitudes.

6-**24.**
True
p. 162

A consumer's belief about a product may have a positive or negative effect on his or her attitudes about the product.

6-**25.**
False
p. 163

Attitudes are very good predictors of intention to buy.

6-**26.**
True
p. 163

The Purina Dog Chow example in the text is a good example of how consumers' beliefs have an impact on whether or not a strategy is successful.

6-**27.**
True
p. 163

It is easier for a marketer to work with existing attitudes than to try to change them.

6-**28.**
True
p. 163

It is possible for marketing managers to change or create new attitudes about goods and services--but overcoming negative attitudes is a really tough job.

6-**29.**
True
p. 164

Consumers may evaluate a product not just on how well it performs but on how it performs relative to their expectations.

6-**30.**
False
p. 164

In light of the relationships between consumer expectations and satisfaction, it's usually best for promotion to slightly "over promise" what the firm can actually deliver.

6-**31.**
True
p. 165

Activities, Interests and Opinions are the "AIO" variables used in lifestyle analysis.

6-**32.**
False
p. 165

Attitudes, Income and Opinions are the "AIO" variables used in lifestyle analysis.

6-**33.**
True
p. 166

The VALS approach to understanding consumer behavior considers values, attitudes, and lifestyles.

6-**34.**
True
p. 166

A disadvantage of the VALS approach to understanding consumers is that VALS data may not be very specific to the marketing manager's target market.

6-**35.**
False
p. 167

Consumer buying decisions are affected by social influences such as motivation, perception, learning, attitudes, and personality.

6-**36.**
True
p. 167

Buying responsibility and purchase influence between husband and wife vary greatly--depending on the product and the specific family.

6-37.
True
p. 168

According to the text, the U.S. social class system is usually measured in terms of occupation, education, and housing arrangements.

6-38.
False
p. 168

According to the text, the U.S. social class system is much more rigid than those in most countries.

6-39.
False
p. 168

The upper-middle class typically includes small businesspeople, office workers, teachers, technicians, and most "white-collar" workers.

6-40.
False
p. 169

People who have the same amount of income--but who are in different social classes--tend to spend their income in the same way.

6-41.
True
p. 169

Given the same income as middle-class consumers, lower-class consumers will handle themselves and their money very differently.

6-42.
True
p. 169

The group of people to whom an individual looks when forming attitudes about a particular topic is his reference group for that topic.

6-43.
True
p. 169

A person normally has several reference groups.

6-44.
False
p. 169

Reference group influence is likely to be greater for products which will not be seen by other individuals.

6-45.
True
p. 169

Reference groups are more important when others will be able to "see" which product or brand we're using.

6-46.
False
p. 169

An opinion leader is usually wealthier and better educated than the people he or she influences.

6-47.
False
p. 169

Opinion leaders for one subject or product are also usually opinion leaders for many other subjects or products.

6-48.
True
p. 170

Word-of-mouth publicity from opinion leaders can be favorable or unfavorable.

6-49.
False
p. 170

Marketers who want to aim at people within several different cultures usually will be able to use the same marketing mix for all of them.

6-50.
False
p. 170

Planning for cultural differences in international markets is easier than in domestic markets.

6-51.
True
p. 170-71

The reaction of British consumers to iced tea is an example of cultural influence.

6-52.
True
p. 171

Needs, benefits sought, attitudes, motivation, and even how a consumer selects certain products all vary depending on the purchasing situation.

6-53.
True
p. 171

Different purchase situations may require different marketing mixes, even though the same target market is involved.

6-54.
False
p. 174-75

A consumer interested in making a low involvement purchase is most likely to use "limited problem solving"--rather than one of the other levels of problem solving.

6-55.
False
p. 174-75

Finding her favorite brand of shampoo temporarily out of stock, a supermarket shopper is more likely to take part in routinized response behavior than limited problem solving.

6-56.
True
p. 175

The steps in the adoption process are awareness, interest, evaluation, trial, decision and confirmation.

6-57.
False
p. 175

In the adoption process, the confirmation step usually precedes the decision step.

6-58.
True
p. 176

Dissonance takes place when an individual is NOT confident about the rightness of a decision.

6-59.
False
p. 177

In international marketing, it's important to rely on intuition and to generalize the cultural influences on consumer behavior from one country to another.

6-60.
True
p. 177

It's hazardous to rely on intuition in generalizing about cultural influences on consumer behavior from one country to another.

Multiple Choice Questions

6-61.
C
App.
Easy
p. 157

Which of the following would be most helpful for predicting why a final consumer selects one of several similar brands?
A. Population data
B. Consumer expenditure patterns
C. Behavioral science theories
D. Income data
E. All would be equally helpful

6-62.
E
App.
Med.
p. 157

The statement, "Of course people will buy our product--each of its features is better than the competition," most closely reflects which consumer behavior concept?
A. psychographics
B. reference groups
C. needs
D. competitive advantage
E. the economic-buyer theory

6-63.
B
Comp.
Med.
p. 157

Economists' economic-buyer theory assumes that:
A. demographic data are very useful for predicting consumer behavior.
B. buyers logically compare choices in terms of cost and value in order to maximize their satisfaction.
C. consumers should purchase only low-priced products.
D. All of the above.
E. None of the above.

6-64.
A
Comp.
Med.
p. 157

The "economic-buyer" theory of buyer behavior:
A. is seen as too simplistic by most marketing managers.
B. assumes that consumers are affected by psychological variables and social influences.
C. suggests that men and women behave differently as buyers.
D. assumes that buyers don't have enough information to make logical choices--and as a result buy products that are not a good value.
E. None of the above is correct.

6-65.
E
Comp.
Med.
p. 157

The economists' view of buyers
A. puts a great deal of emphasis on differences in buying behavior related to individual differences among consumers.
B. is based on the idea that consumers value time and select the first alternative they learn about.
C. assumes that they always buy the lowest-price alternative.
D. emphasizes psychological variables rather than social influences.
E. None of the above is true.

6-66.
B
App.
Easy
p. 157

Which of the following is NOT an economic need?
A. Dependability in use
B. Hunger
C. Economy of use
D. Convenience
E. Efficiency in use

6-**67.**
A
Def.
Easy
p. 158

Which of the following is NOT a psychological variable?
A. culture.
B. personality.
C. learning.
D. perception.
E. attitudes.

6-**68.**
B
Def.
Easy
p. 158

Which of the following is NOT a psychological variable?
A. Attitudes
B. Social class
C. Motivation
D. Learning
E. Perception

6-**69.**
B
Comp.
Med.
p. 158

Amber Mantel is status-oriented. When she buys clothing she only considers items with well-known "labels" that her friends will notice. This behavior illustrates
A. satisfying a need.
B. satisfying a want.
C. satisfying a belief.
D. the "economic buyer" model of buyer behavior.
E. All of the above are equally good answers.

6-**70.**
B
Comp.
Med.
p. 158

Good marketing managers know that
A. marketing strategies can't influence consumer "wants."
B. marketers can't create internal drives in consumers.
C. it is not that difficult to develop a marketing strategy that gets consumers to do what they don't want to do.
D. All of the above are true.
E. None of the above is true.

6-**71.**
E
Def.
Med.
p. 158

Regarding consumer motivation, the text states that:
A. needs are the basic forces which motivate people to do something.
B. all needs and wants are caused by drives.
C. wants are learned needs.
D. the terms "need" and "wants" mean the same thing.
E. both A and C.

6-**72.**
C
Def.
Hard
p. 158

When a consumer actually purchases a particular product it is the direct result of a
A. need.
B. want.
C. drive.
D. desire for physical well-being.
E. None of the above is more true than the others.

6-**73.**
C
App.
Easy
p. 159-60

According to the "hierarchy of needs" model, the first needs most people try to satisfy are their _____ needs.
A. safety
B. personal
C. physiological
D. social
E. any of the above

6-74.
B
Def.
Easy
p. 159

The text discusses a four-level hierarchy of needs. Which of the following is NOT included in that model?
A. social needs.
B. psychological needs.
C. safety needs.
D. physiological needs.
E. personal needs.

6-75.
B
Def.
Med.
p. 159-60

Ranked from lowest level to highest level, the "hierarchy of needs" model includes:
A. personal, social, safety, and physiological needs.
B. physiological, safety, social, and personal needs.
C. safety, personal, social, and physiological needs.
D. social, personal, safety, and physiological needs.
E. physiological, safety, personal, and social needs.

6-76.
D
Comp.
Med.
p. 160

When studying consumer needs, a marketer should:
A. know that total consumer satisfaction is not likely.
B. try to understand how the marketing mix can satisfy a set of needs, rather than only one.
C. realize that he or she cannot create needs, merely identify them.
D. all of the above.
E. none of the above.

6-77.
E
Comp.
Hard
p. 160

Which of the following statements about "needs" is true?
A. A higher level need may develop before lower level needs are all satisfied.
B. If lower level needs are reasonably satisfied, those at higher levels become more dominant.
C. A particular product may satisfy more than one need at the same time.
D. The order in which needs are satisfied can vary.
E. All of the above are true.

6-78.
B
Comp.
Med.
p. 160

A marketing manager who wants to apply the "hierarchy of needs" model should keep in mind that:
A. most consumers are already satisfied and promotion will be needed to "create a need."
B. the same marketing mix might satisfy two or more levels of need.
C. not enough attention is focused on physiological needs.
D. "social needs" focus on the psychological variables in consumer behavior.
E. None of the above is true.

6-79.
C
Comp.
Hard
p. 160

Which of the following statements about "hierarchy of needs" is FALSE?
A. As soon as lower level needs are reasonably satisfied, those at higher levels become more dominant.
B. A higher level need may develop before lower level needs are satisfied.
C. The order in which needs are satisfied always follows a definite pattern--with lower level needs being satisfied first.
D. A particular product may satisfy more than one need at a time.
E. All of the above are true.

6-**80.**
B
Def.
Easy
p. 160-61

Which of the following is NOT one of the selective processes?
A. selective perception.
B. selective distribution.
C. selective exposure.
D. selective retention.
E. All of the above are selective processes.

6-**81.**
B
Def.
Easy
p. 160

The fact that our eyes and minds seek out and notice only information that interests us is called:
A. conscious cognition.
B. selective exposure.
C. selective retention.
D. preconscious perception.
E. selective perception.

6-**82.**
A
App.
Med.
p. 160

Lucy Hansen has itchy eyes and a stuffy nose, and suddenly becomes aware of many TV ads for allergy products that she never noticed before. This illustrates:
A. selective exposure.
B. selective perception.
C. selective retention.
D. reinforced cognition.
E. None of the above.

6-**83.**
D
App.
Med.
p. 160

Carmen Corley is planning to buy a pair of running shoes. Recently, she has been noticing more Adidas advertising in magazines. This is an example of:
A. a physiological need.
B. dissonance.
C. need satisfaction.
D. selective exposure.
E. a consumer expectation.

6-**84.**
B
Def.
Easy
p. 160

When consumers screen out or modify ideas, messages, and information that conflict with previously learned attitudes and beliefs, this is called:
A. cognitive perception.
B. selective perception.
C. selective retention.
D. conscious perception.
E. selective exposure.

6-**85.**
A
App.
Med.
p. 160

On his way to a GM dealership to pick up a new truck he has purchased, Ben Colavito hears a Ford ad that says that Ford trucks have more power than Chevy trucks. Ben thought that the ad said that the Chevys had more power. This illustrates
A. selective perception.
B. learning.
C. selective retention.
D. reinforcement.
E. selective exposure.

6-**86.**
B
Def.
Easy
p. 161

Consumers remembering only what they want to remember is called:
A. conscious response.
B. selective retention.
C. selective exposure.
D. cognitive learning
E. selective perception.

6-**87.**
E
App.
Easy
p. 161-62

Which of the following is an example of using a cue to attract consumers?
A. using a label with red, white, and blue colors to stir patriotic feelings.
B. adding lemon scent to a soap.
C. using a package that looks like the one for a popular brand.
D. adding pine scent to a cleansing fluid.
E. All of the above are examples.

6-**88.**
E
App.
Hard
p. 161-62

When Taco Bell shows a large close-up of a chicken taco in a television ad, they are:
A. encouraging selective retention.
B. hoping to encourage extensive problem solving by the audience.
C. appealing to the social needs of the audience.
D. appealing to the economic needs of the audience.
E. using a cue to encourage a particular response to the hunger drive.

6-**89.**
D
App.
Med.
p. 161-62

A grocery store sprays an aerosol scent that smells like fresh baked bread near its packaged bakery items. This is
A. a case of a manager developing a need.
B. likely to have no effect because selective retention will eliminate any effect of the smell.
C. a case of linking a response with a drive.
D. an example of trying to link a cue with a marketing mix.
E. a violation of the selective processes.

6-**90.**
D
Comp.
Easy
p. 161

Which of the following statements about learning is NOT correct?
A. Satisfaction with a product purchase is reinforcement.
B. Repeated reinforcement is likely to lead to routine buying.
C. A marketing manager can use a package as a "cue."
D. Reinforcement in the learning process weakens the relationship between a cue and a response.
E. Almost all consumer behavior is learned.

6-**91.**
D
Comp.
Hard
p. 161

Which of the following statements about the learning process is TRUE?
A. A cue is a strong stimulus which drives an individual.
B. Learning occurs only when a drive is satisfied.
C. Cues are the causes of drives.
D. Reinforcement strengthens the relationship between a cue and a response.
E. All of the above are true.

6-**92.**
A
Def.
Med.
p. 161

The order of the steps in the learning process is:
A. drive, cue, response, reinforcement.
B. cue, response, drive, reinforcement.
C. cue, response, reinforcement, drive.
D. drive, response, reinforcement, cue.
E. reinforcement, drive, cue, response.

6-**93.**   Which of the following is NOT a major step in the learning process?
A
Def.   A. Dissonance
Easy   B. Drive
p. 161   C. Response
               D. Cues
               E. Reinforcement

6-**94.**   Attitudes are:
E
Def.   A. things we believe strongly enough to be willing to take some action.
Med.   B. more action-oriented that beliefs.
p. 162   C. reasonably enduring points of view about something.
               D. usually thought of as involving liking or disliking.
               E. All of the above.

6-**95.**   An attitude is:
B
Def.   A. the same as an "intention to buy."
Easy   B. a person's point of view about something.
p. 162   C. easy to change.
               D. the same as a belief.
               E. All of the above.

6-**96.**   The statement, "I like Southwest Air," is an example of a(n):
C
App.   A. belief
Med.   B. intention
p. 162   C. attitude
               D. none of the above

6-**97.**   The statement, "Hershey Kisses are made with real chocolate" is an example of:
A
App.   A. a belief
Med.   B. an intention
p. 162   C. an attitude
               D. none of the above

6-**98.**   The statement, "I plan to see the new Brad Pitt movie," is an example of:
E
App.   A. a drive
Med.   B. reinforcement
p. 162   C. an attitude
               D. a belief
               E. an intention

6-**99.**   Some marketers stretch the meaning of "attitude" to include:
A
Def.   A. intention to buy.
Easy   B. needs.
p. 162   C. beliefs.
               D. psychographics.
               E. actual purchasing behavior.

6-**100.**
D
Comp.
Easy
p. 162-63

Regarding consumer buying behavior,
A. attitudes affect the selective processes and learning.
B. many consumers with a favorable attitude toward a product may have no
   intention to buy it.
C. beliefs are less action-oriented than attitudes.
D. All of the above are true.
E. None of the above is true.

6-**101.**
D
Comp.
Easy
p. 162-63

Consumers' attitudes can be learned from:
A. exposure to the attitudes of others.
B. promotion which is directed toward them.
C. previous experiences.
D. All of the above could be true.
E. None of the above.

6-**102.**
B
Comp.
Hard
p. 163

When dealing with consumer attitudes, marketers should know that:
A. it is usually easier to change a negative attitude about a product than to reinforce
   a positive attitude.
B. consumer attitudes tend to be enduring.
C. attitudes are very good predictors of how people will behave.
D. all of the above.
E. none of the above.

6-**103.**
B
Comp.
Med.
p. 163

Which of the following would be the most difficult task facing a marketing manager?
A. discover the attitudes of the firm's target market.
B. change existing negative attitudes.
C. create new attitudes toward his or her brand.
D. promote existing attitudes.
E. strengthen existing positive attitudes.

6-**104.**
D
Def.
Easy
p. 164

An expectation is
A. an event that a person likes to remember.
B. a positive cue.
C. an unfulfilled need.
D. an outcome that a person looks forward to.
E. None of the above.

6-**105.**
C
Comp.
Med.
p. 165

Personality affects people's behavior, but
A. it is the least useful of all the social influences.
B. it is impossible to observe in an actual situation.
C. personality traits haven't been much help in predicting which specific products or
   brands people actually buy.
D. takes too much research effort to measure economically.
E. none of the above is true.

6-**106.**
D
Def.
Med.
p. 165

The AIO items used in life-style analysis include:
A. activities, intentions, and opinions.
B. attitudes, intentions, and opinions.
C. attitudes, income, and opinions.
D. activities, interests, and opinions.
E. attitudes, interests, and opinions.

6-**107.**   Psychographics or life-style analysis analyzes an individual's:
E   A. opinions.
Def.   B. demographics.
Easy   C. activities.
p. 165   D. interests.
                    E. All of the above.

6-**108.**   Timothy Cole noticed during a weekly grocery shopping that Sprite was on sale. Even
D   though he could have saved money with the Sprite, Timothy bought 7-Up because
App.   that's the brand his children prefer. Timothy was responding to:
Easy   A. selective exposure.
p. 167   B. dissonance.
                    C. marketing influence.
                    D. social influence.
                    E. a drive.

6-**109.**   Which of the following is NOT a social influence in consumer buying?
B   A. Social class
Def.   B. Beliefs
Med.   C. Family
p. 167   D. Reference groups
                    E. Culture

6-**110.**   Current consumer research suggests that the family's purchasing agent is now:
D   A. the husband.
Comp.   B. the children.
Easy   C. the wife.
p. 167   D. it varies, depending on the product and the family.

6-**111.**   "Social class" in the U.S. is usually measured in terms of:
B   A. race, religion, and occupation.
Def.   B. occupation, education, and type and location of housing.
Med.   C. income.
p. 168   D. income, occupation, and education.
                    E. income, occupation, and religion.

6-**112.**   The social class system in the U.S.
B   A. makes it obvious that the upper class is the best target market.
Comp.   B. often groups people with very different incomes in the same social class.
Easy   C. is based on a person's educational level.
p. 168   D. is much more rigid than in Europe and Asia.
                    E. results in social groupings which are about equal in size.

6-**113.**   According to the text, your social class level does not depend directly on your:
B   A. type and location of housing.
Def.   B. income level.
Easy   C. occupation.
p. 168   D. education.
                    E. Any of the above.

6-**114.**   Nadine Debeau has an annual income of $120,000. What social class is she in?
E
Comp.   A. The upper-middle class
Easy   B. The upper class
p. 168   C. The upper-lower class
            D. The lower-middle class
            E. There is not enough information to tell

6-**115.**   The upper-middle class includes:
B
Def.   A. socially prominent new rich.
Med.   B. successful professionals, owners of small businesses, and managers of large
p. 168   corporations.
            C. service people and skilled workers.
            D. unskilled laborers and people in low-status occupations.
            E. small businesspeople, office workers, teachers and technicians.

6-**116.**   What social class is a firm aiming at if its target market consists of small
B   businesspeople, office workers, teachers, and technicians?
App.   A. upper-middle
Med.   B. lower-middle
p. 168   C. upper-lower
            D. lower-lower
            E. upper

6-**117.**   The two social classes which account for about three-fourths of the U.S. population
D   are:
Def.   A. the upper-middle class and the upper-lower class.
Easy   B. the lower-middle class and the lower-lower class.
p. 168   C. the upper-middle class and the lower-lower class.
            D. the lower-middle class and the upper-lower class.
            E. none of the above.

6-**118.**   The upper-lower class includes:
D
Def.   A. unskilled laborers and people in low-status occupations.
Med.   B. small businesspeople, office workers, teachers and technicians.
p. 168   C. successful professionals, owners of small businesses, and managers of large
                corporations.
            D. service people and skilled workers.
            E. socially prominent new rich.

6-**119.**   The largest social class in the United States is the _____ class.
D   A. upper-middle
Def.   B. upper
Hard   C. lower-lower
p. 168   D. upper-lower
            E. lower-middle

6-**120.**   The largest social class in the United States is the:
A   A. upper-lower class.
Def.   B. lower-lower class.
Hard   C. lower-middle class.
p. 168   D. upper class.
              E. None of the above - they are all about equal in size.

6-**121.**   When people talk about America's "blue-collar market" they are probably referring to
B   A. the lower-middle class.
Comp.   B. the upper-lower class.
Hard   C. the middle class.
p. 168   D. the upper-lower and lower-middle classes.
              E. the upper-middle class.

6-**122.**   Which of the following is LEAST likely to be associated with the upper-lower class?
E   A. asking for help in decision-making.
App.   B. relying more on salespeople and advertising.
Hard   C. seeking security.
p. 168   D. feeling "controlled" by the world.
              E. willing to take risks.

6-**123.**   Which of the following is LEAST likely to be associated with the upper-middle class?
B   A. wanting social acceptability.
App.   B. "playing it safe."
Hard   C. saving for the future.
p. 168   D. being community-minded.
              E. wanting quality products.

6-**124.**   Compared to lower class consumers, middle class consumers generally:
D   A. want help with decision-making.
Comp.   B. feel controlled by the world.
Hard   C. live for the present.
p. 168   D. are more self-confident and willing to take risks.
              E. have larger incomes.

6-**125.**   A good marketing manager knows that
A   A. a consumer's reference group may consist of people with whom the consumer
Comp.   has no face-to-face contact.
Med.   B. most consumers have only one reference group.
p. 169   C. a consumer's family is not a reference group.
              D. reference groups usually have the most influence on purchases of products which
                 are not easily seen by others.
              E. None of the above is true.

6-**126.**   Reference-group influence would be WEAKEST for determining which particular
D   _____ a person buys.
App.   A. watch
Hard   B. cosmetics
p. 169   C. clothing
              D. laundry soap
              E. car

6-**127.**
D
App.
Hard
p. 169

Reference group influence is likely to have the strongest effect on the particular
BRAND of _____ purchased.
  A. dishwasher detergent
  B. frozen peas
  C. batteries
  D. watch
  E. Reference group influence would be about the same for each of these products.

6-**128.**
D
Comp.
Hard
p. 169

Reference group
  A. influence is so strong that a person normally has only one reference group.
  B. influence is greatest for older people.
  C. influence is equally strong for all products and brands.
  D. members may not even know the person whose attitudes they influence.
  E. Both B and C are true.

6-**129.**
E
Comp.
Med.
p. 169

Tricia Holland was interested in a new set of golf clubs. She discussed the various
types with some knowledgeable friends and relied on their advice. Tricia's friends
were acting as:
  A. an economic influence.
  B. routinized decision-makers.
  C. a social class.
  D. a lifestyle group.
  E. a reference group.

6-**130.**
E
App.
Easy
p. 159-69

Consumer buying behavior is affected by:
  A. opinion leaders.
  B. social class.
  C. physiological, safety, social, and personal needs.
  D. reference groups.
  E. all of the above.

6-**131.**
C
Comp.
Easy
p. 169

Opinion leaders
  A. for one subject are also usually opinion leaders for other subjects too.
  B. are usually wealthier and better educated than their followers.
  C. for one social class usually are not opinion leaders for another social class.
  D. All of the above are true.
  E. None of the above is true.

6-**132.**
C
Def.
Med.
p. 169

Opinion leaders:
  A. are usually from the upper social classes.
  B. are usually wealthy and highly educated.
  C. are people who influence others.
  D. are rarely actually involved in product-related discussions with the people who
      "follow" them.
  E. All of the above.

6-133.
B
Def.
Easy
p. 170

The whole set of beliefs, attitudes, and ways of doing things of a reasonably homogeneous set of people is called their:
  A. personal environment.
  B. culture.
  C. motivation.
  D. learned set.
  E. opinion set.

6-134.
C
App.
Easy
p. 171-72

A college student on her way to take an exam remembers that she doesn't have a pencil with an eraser--which the instructor asked everyone to bring. The store where she stops doesn't have regular pencils--but it does sell Scripto mechanical pencils priced at $2.95. That is what she buys. This case illustrates the affect of:
  A. personal environment.
  B. culture.
  C. purchase situation.
  D. learned set.
  E. dissonance.

6-135.
D
Comp.
Easy
p. 172-74

The evaluative grid approach to analyzing consumers' attitudes
  A. may show features of a product which are underrated by consumers.
  B. views a product as a bundle of features or attributes.
  C. may reveal that many consumers are rejecting a product because of one below standard feature.
  D. All of the above are true.
  E. None of the above is true.

6-136.
D
App.
Hard
p. 172-74

Marketing managers sometimes find it useful to use evaluative grids like the one below

COMMON FEATURES

BRANDS	PRICE	STYLING	DEPENDABILITY	COMFORT
Brand A	+	+	-	-
Brand B	-	+	+	+
Brand C	+	-	+	+
Brand D	+	+	+	-
Brand E	+	-	-	-

Based on this grid, we can logically conclude that for this consumer
  A. price is more important than styling if the consumer selects Brand C.
  B. dependability is not at all important if the consumer selects Brand A.
  C. Brand C seems better than Brand E.
  D. All of the above are logical conclusions.
  E. None of the above is logical based on the grid.

6-137.
D
App.
Hard
p. 172-74

Marketing managers sometimes find it useful to use evaluative grids like the one below.

COMMON FEATURES

BRANDS	PRICE	STYLING	DEPENDABILITY	COMFORT
Brand A	+	+	-	-
Brand B	-	+	+	+
Brand C	+	-	-	-
Brand D	+	-	+	+
Brand E	+	+	+	-

Based on this grid, we can logically conclude that for this consumer
A. styling is more important than price if the consumer selected Brand B instead of Brand D.
B. Brand D is better than Brand C.
C. styling is more important than comfort if the consumer selects Brand E instead of Brand D.
D. All of the above are logical conclusions.
E. None of the above is logical based on the grid.

6-138.
D
App.
Hard
p. 172-74

Marketing managers sometimes find it useful to use evaluative grids like the one below.

COMMON FEATURES

BRANDS	PRICE	STYLING	DEPENDABILITY	COMFORT
Brand A	+	+	+	-
Brand B	+	-	+	+
Brand C	-	+	+	+
Brand D	+	-	-	-
Brand E	+	+	-	-

Based on this grid, we can logically conclude that for this consumer
A. styling is more important than price if the consumer selected Brand C instead of Brand B.
B. Brand B is better than Brand D.
C. styling is more important than comfort if the consumer selects Brand A instead of Brand B.
D. All of the above are logical conclusions.
E. None of the above is logical based on the grid.

6-139.
A
App.
Hard
p. 172-74

Marketing managers sometimes find it useful to use evaluative grids like the one below.

COMMON FEATURES
```
                -----------------------------------------------
BRANDS          Price    Styling    Dependability    Comfort
                -----------------------------------------------
Brand A          +         +              -              -
Brand B          -         +              +              +
Brand C          +         -              +              +
Brand D          +         -              -              -
Brand E          +         +              +              -
```

Based on this grid, we can logically conclude that for this consumer
  A. styling is more important than price if the consumer selected Brand B instead of Brand C.
  B. Brand D is better than Brand C.
  C. styling is more important than comfort if the consumer selects Brand C instead of Brand E.
  D. All of the above are logical conclusions.
  E. None of the above is logical based on the grid.

6-140.
A
Def.
Easy
p. 174

Which of the following in NOT one of the levels of consumer problem solving discussed in the text?
  A. Dissonance problem solving
  B. Routinized response behavior
  C. Extensive problem solving
  D. Limited problem solving
  E. None of the above, i.e. all four are discussed.

6-141.
E
App.
Easy
p. 174

Extensive problem solving probably would be required by a recent college graduate in the purchase of:
  A. living room furniture.
  B. a color TV set.
  C. a new home.
  D. a sports car.
  E. all of the above.

6-142.
B
App.
Easy
p. 174

Extensive problem solving probably would NOT be required by young newly-marrieds in the purchase of:
  A. a stereo system.
  B. soft drinks.
  C. a home.
  D. a VCR.
  E. a car.

6-143.
C
Comp.
Med.
p. 174

Routinized response behavior by consumers
  A. is most likely when past purchases of similar products have not satisfied the needs.
  B. is more likely when previous behavior has not yet been reinforced.
  C. is most common for purchases where the consumer has much experience in how to meet a need.
  D. increases the time required to make a purchase decision.
  E. is likely in a new purchase situation.

6-**144.**
C
App.
Med.
p. 174

Matthew Garriss went to a grocery store to buy his favorite brand of ice cream. However, the store was temporarily out of that brand, so he looked over the other familiar brands and decided to try a well advertised brand. This case illustrates:
  A. Routinized response behavior
  B. Intensive problem solving
  C. Limited problem solving
  D. Extensive problem solving

6-**145.**
E
App.
Med.
p. 174

Limited problem solving probably would be required by "empty-nesters" in the purchase of:
  A. sports clothes.
  B. restaurant's services.
  C. plumbing repair service.
  D. a replacement garbage disposer.
  E. all of the above.

6-**146.**
E
App.
Easy
p. 174

Routinized response behavior probably would be used by many consumers in the purchase of:
  A. soap.
  B. canned fruit.
  C. salt.
  D. milk.
  E. all of the above.

6-**147.**
E
App.
Easy
p. 174

Limited problem-solving probably would NOT be required in the purchase of:
  A. running shoes.
  B. an encyclopedia.
  C. new suit.
  D. coffee maker.
  E. fast-food restaurant meal.

6-**148.**
B
App.
Easy
p. 174

Which of the following is LEAST likely to be an example of routinized response behavior?
  A. buying a Pepsi.
  B. purchasing a new pair of shoes.
  C. buying soap at a convenient supercenter.
  D. buying a "Whopper" at Burger King.
  E. filling the car with gasoline.

6-**149.**
A
App.
Easy
p. 175

Which of the following products probably would result in the lowest involvement purchase for most consumers?
  A. Paper towels
  B. Summer vacation
  C. CD player
  D. Sweater
  E. Cough syrup

6-**150.**
B
Comp.
Hard
p. 175

The "adoption process" suggests that:
   A. confirmation must come before the decision to adopt or reject.
   B. evaluation usually comes before trial and decision.
   C. the decision to reject may follow confirmation.
   D. confirmation comes from a satisfactory evaluation.
   E. decision usually follows trial and confirmation.

6-**151.**
A
Def.
Easy
p. 175

Which of the following is NOT one of the steps of the "adoption process?"
   A. Involvement
   B. Awareness
   C. Interest
   D. Evaluation
   E. Trial

6-**152.**
B
Def.
Hard
p. 175

Which of the following gives the correct ORDERING of the steps in the "adoption process?"
   A. Interest, awareness, trial, decision, evaluation, dissonance
   B. Awareness, interest, evaluation, trial, decision, confirmation
   C. Awareness, interest, trial, evaluation, decision, dissonance
   D. Awareness, interest, trial, decision, evaluation, confirmation
   E. Awareness, interest, evaluation, decision, trial, confirmation

6-**153.**
A
App.
Med.
p. 175

Jerry Justice has noticed several television commercials for LookYourBest--a new brand of shampoo. While washing his hair, he thinks about what would happen if he replaced his current shampoo with LookYourBest. What stage in the adoption process has Jerry reached?
   A. evaluation
   B. feedback
   C. decision
   D. interest
   E. awareness

6-**154.**
C
App.
Med.
p. 175

A marketing manager for a new brand of bar soap decides to mail free samples to consumers. The logic for using this approach is best explained by
   A. the "economic buyer" model.
   B. the stimulus-response model.
   C. the typical consumer's adoption process.
   D. the need to reduce dissonance.
   E. the high level of problem solving required with such a product.

6-**155.**
B
App.
Med.
p. 176

Pam Walters just bought a cellular telephone for her car after spending several weeks considering all the possibilities. She likes the new phone, but is still wondering if another brand at a slightly higher price would have been better. This is an example of:
   A. the relationship between drives, cues, and reinforcement.
   B. dissonance.
   C. reference group influence.
   D. stimulus-response reaction.
   E. routinized response behavior.

6-156.
D
Comp.
Med.
p. 176

Dissonance
A. discourages a consumer from considering further information once a purchase has been made.
B. is likely to result in a consumer buying the same product next time.
C. is more likely to occur with low involvement products.
D. is less likely to occur when a consumer has repeatedly purchased the same product.
E. occurs in the adoption process after a consumer becomes interested in a product.

6-157.
A
Def.
Easy
p. 176

Dissonance is a:
A. tension caused by uncertainty about the rightness of a decision.
B. conflict between opinion leaders.
C. confirmation in the learning process.
D. kind of belief.
E. form of social influence.

6-158.
C
Comp.
Easy
p. 177-78

When planning strategies for international markets, keep in mind that:
A. a marketing manager must rely primarily on intuition because there is usually little available information about the social and cultural influences on buying behavior.
B. the effects of cultural influences on consumers are usually obvious, if you just take the time to think about the buying situation.
C. cultural changes may make outdated stereotypes even more misleading.
D. All of the above are true.1
E. Only B and C are true.

6-159.
B
Comp.
Med.
p. 179

The present state of our knowledge about consumer behavior is such that:
A. relevant market dimensions can be easily identified and measured using AIO.
B. we still must rely heavily on intuition and judgment to explain and predict consumer behavior.
C. the behavioral sciences provide a marketing manager with a complete explanation of the "whys" of consumer behavior.
D. a marketing manager can rely almost completely on the text's integrating framework--to explain and predict buying behavior.
E. All of the above are true.

Chapter 7

Business and Organizational Customers and Their Buying Behavior

True-False Questions:

7-1.
False
p. 184

There are more final consumers than business and organizational customers, so more is purchased by final consumers.

7-2.
True
p. 184

Organizational buyers are also referred to as industrial or intermediate buyers.

7-3.
True
p. 184

Like final consumers, organizations make purchases to satisfy specific needs, but their basic need is for goods and services that will help them satisfy their own customers or clients.

7-4.
False
p. 185

Dependability of supply is usually much less important than price for most business customers.

7-5.
False
p. 186

The approaches used to serve business customers in international markets are even more varied than those required to reach individual consumers.

7-6.
True
p. 187

Organizational buyers often buy on the basis of a set of purchasing specifications.

7-7.
True
p. 187

A description of what a firm wants to buy is called its purchasing specifications, whether that description is written or electronic.

7-8.
False
p. 187

Purchasing specifications should be used only with products where quality is highly standardized.

7-9.
False
p. 187

Purchase specifications for services are usually very simple because services tend to be very standardized.

7-10.
False
p. 187

Purchasing managers seldom use purchasing specifications to buy on the Internet.

7-11.
True
p. 187

Purchasing specifications may be very simple (with only a brand name or part number) or very detailed (as with services).

7-12.
True
p. 187

ISO 9000 is a way for a supplier to document that its quality procedures meet internationally recognized standards.

7-13.
False
p. 187

ISO 9000 is only relevant to domestic suppliers.

7-14.
False
p. 187

ISO 9000 is only relevant to international suppliers.

7-15.
True
p. 187

ISO 9000 is relevant to both domestic and international suppliers.

7-16.
True
p. 187

With ISO 9000 someone is responsible for quality at every step.

7-17.
True
p. 187

ISO 9000 reduces the need for a customer to conduct its own audit of a supplier's quality procedures.

7-18.
True
p. 187

Purchasing managers are buying specialists for organizations and may have a lot of power.

7-19.
True
p. 188

Multiple buying influence means that the buyer shares the purchasing decision with several people.

7-20.
False
p. 190

The process of organizational buying is entirely different from consumer buying.

7-21.
True
p. 191

A requisition is a request to buy something.

7-22.
False
p. 192

Straight-rebuy buying takes longer than modified-rebuy or new-task buying and offers more chance for promotion impact by the seller.

7-23.
False
p. 192

Few purchasing managers have been able to turn over any of their order placing to computers because so few organizational purchases are routine.

7-24.
False
p. 193

In business markets, suppliers usually want close relationships with customers; however, there's little benefit to the customer of having closer relationships with suppliers.

7-25.
True
p. 194

A close buyer-seller relationship in a business market may reduce a firm's flexibility.

7-26.
False
p. 194

In business markets, a seller would always prefer to have a closer relationship with a customer.

7-27.
False
p. 194

In business markets, buyer-seller relationships tend to be an "all-or-nothing" arrangement--either very close or not at all close.

7-28.
False
p. 194-95

Although we talk about close "relationships" between firms in business markets, in practice it is just the relationship between the salesperson and purchasing manager that becomes close.

7-29.
True
p. 195

In cooperative relationships in a business market, the buyer and seller work together to jointly achieve both mutual and individual objectives.

7-30.
True
p. 196

Just-in-time relationships between buyers and sellers usually require operational linkages and information sharing.

7-31.
False
p. 197

Negotiated contract buying would be used when the buyer knows precisely what he wants and the requirements of the job aren't likely to change as the job is done.

7-32.
True
p. 197

Relationship-specific adaptations involve changes in a firm's product or procedures that are unique to the needs or capabilities of a relationship partner.

7-33.
True
p. 198

To protect themselves from unpredictable events, most purchasing managers seek several dependable sources of supply.

7-34.
True
p. 198

Reciprocity means trading sales for sales.

7-35.
False
p. 199

Reciprocity is usually resisted by sales departments, but purchasing managers usually like it.

7-36.
False
p. 199

So far, B2B e-commerce has had little effect on the way organizations make purchase decisions and deal with suppliers.

7-37.
True
p. 199

Community sites were among the first e-commerce websites because many firms just put in digital form information that was already being distributed in other ways.

7-38.
True
p. 199

Catalog sites make it convenient to search for products by offering digital product catalogs for different producers at one website.

7-39.
True
p. 199

Exchanges bring buyers and sellers together to agree on prices for business products.

7-40.
True
p. 200

Procurement hubs operate for the benefit of buyers by directing suppliers to them at one convenient site.

7-41.
True
p. 200

The Internet is making it faster and easier for organizational buyers to use competitive bidding procedures.

7-42.
True
p. 200

By offering unique items, auction sites operate for the benefit of sellers.

7-43.
True
p. 200

Reverse auctions, unlike regular auctions, operate for the benefit of buyers.

7-44.
False
p. 200

Reverse auctions, unlike regular auctions, operate for the benefit of sellers.

7-45.
True
p. 200

Collaboration hubs go beyond matching buyers and sellers for one-time transactions and instead focus on helping firms work together on a continuing basis.

7-46.
False
p. 200

Unfortunately, collaboration hubs match buyers and sellers for one-time transactions only.

7-47.
True
p. 201

Internet (ro)bots can help a buyer search for products by description.

7-48.
True
p. 201

Internet (ro)bots can help a buyer search for products using purchase specifications.

7-49.
False
p. 201

Internet (ro)bots seach for products by inspection.

7-50.
True
p. 202

A purchasing manager who uses an Internet (ro)bot may reduce the need to arrange for custom-produced items.

7-51.
True
p. 204

The Internet is making even straight rebuys more competitive.

7-52.
True
p. 205

Most manufacturers are quite small, with 250 or fewer employees.

7-53.
False
p. 205

Compared to final consumers, manufacturers tend to be more spread out geographically.

7-54.
True
p. 205

It is very common for manufacturers to concentrate in certain geographic areas and by type of industry.

7-55.
False
p. 206

The term "NAICS" stands for New Auto Industry Classification Survey.

7-56.
True
p. 206

The United States adopted NAICS as its new industrial classification system in 1997.

7-57.
True
p. 206

The U.S. government reports data on the number of firms, sales volume, and number of employees by NAICS code.

7-58.
True
p. 206-207

Firms that are described by NAICS code 3152 are more similar than firms described by NAICS code 31.

7-59.
True
p. 208

Most retail and wholesale buyers see themselves as purchasing agents for their target customers.

7-60.
True
p. 209

Sales reps calling on large food retailers often must make their sales presentations to a buyer who doesn't have the final decision responsibility.

7-61.
False
p. 209

Most wholesalers and retailers pay very close attention to each item they handle, treating most products as new-task purchases.

7-62.
True
p. 210

A retail buyer who is "open to buy" has funds budgeted to spend during the current time period.

7-63.
False
p. 210

If a buyer is "open to buy," this means that he generated more sales than he expected.

7-64.
True
p. 210

Independent buying agents who work in central markets, representing several wholesaler or retailer customers, are called resident buyers.

7-65.
False
p. 210

Resident buyers are employees of chain stores who buy in central markets for their employers.

7-66.
False
p. 210

Government is one of the smallest groups (in sales volume) of customers in the United States.

7-67.
True
p. 210-11

When selling to government customers, both bid buying and negotiated contracts are common.

7-68.
True
p. 211

To share in the government market, it is advantageous to be on the list of approved suppliers.

7-69.
True
p. 212

To compete in the government market, it is very important that marketing mixes are well matched with different bidding procedures.

7-70.
False
p. 212

The Internet is not very useful for firms that want to target government markets.

7-71.
True
p. 212

Although outright influence peddling is common in some international markets, it is not allowed under the Foreign Corrupt Practices Act.

Multiple Choice Questions

7-72.
A
Comp.
Hard
p. 184

Regarding U.S. business and organizational customers,
  A. more goods and services are purchased by business and organizational customers than by final consumers.
  B. there are more business and organizational customers than final consumers.
  C. there are more manufacturers than all other types of business and organizational customers combined.
  D. more goods and services are purchased by government buyers than by all other business and organizational customers.
  E. Both B and D are true.

7-73.
B
Comp.
Med.
p. 184

Concerning consumer and business markets:

A. promotion to consumer markets usually relies more heavily on the use of personal selling.
B. it is often easier to define customer needs in business markets.
C. a marketing mix directed at an organizational customer is usually less precisely adjusted to the needs of the specific customer.
D. All of the above are true.
E. None of the above is true.

7-74.
E
Comp.
Hard
p. 184

Which of the following is NOT true regarding organizational buyers?

A. Buyers for all kinds of organizations (governments, nonprofit groups, middlemen) tend to buy in much the same way as do manufacturers.
B. Business customer buying behavior seems to be similar in the U.S. and international markets.
C. Marketing strategies aimed at them are often tailored to each individual customer.
D. Their purchases are made to help their organizations meet the demands for their products.
E. Their needs are usually harder to define than for final consumers.

7-75.
E
App.
Easy
p. 185

Which of the following is NOT an organizational buyer?

A. the Red Cross buying office supplies.
B. a sporting goods retailer buying skis.
C. a law office buying a background music service.
D. a country club buying tennis balls for a tournament.
E. All of the above are organizational buyers.

7-76.
C
App.
Easy
p. 185

Which of the following is NOT an example of an organizational buyer?

A. a government buyer purchasing a new desk for the mayor's office.
B. a woman buying cookware to sell to her friends and neighbors.
C. a sales rep buying a new necktie to make a good impression.
D. a wholesaler buying a delivery truck.
E. None of the above is a good example.

7-77.
E
Def.
Easy
p. 185

Which of the following are NOT "business and organizational customers?"

A. Wholesalers
B. Manufacturers
C. Financial institutions
D. Government units
E. All of the above ARE business and organizational customers.

7-78.
D
App.
Easy
p. 187

Purchasing specifications may include:

A. the product grade
B. the brand name
C. the part number
D. all of the above
E. none of the above

7-79.
A
Def.
Easy
p. 187

Organizational buying based on a written (or electronic) description of a product is called buying by _____.
   A. purchasing specifications
   B. reciprocity
   C. negotiated contract

7-80.
D
App.
Med.
p. 187

Which of the following products would be bought using purchasing specifications?
   A. 100 gallons of Du Pont brand muriatic acid.
   B. 1,000 double-sided, double-density floppy disks.
   C. 50 pounds of number 10 USX nails.
   D. all of the above.
   E. none of the above.

7-81.
A
App.
Med.
p. 187

Which of the following buying methods would a supermarket buyer be MOST LIKELY to use in the purchase of grade A large eggs?
   A. Purchasing specifications
   B. Competitive bidding
   C. Negotiated contract

7-82.
C
App.
Med.
p. 187

Which of the following buying methods would a purchasing manager be most likely to use on the Internet?
   A. Reciprocity
   B. Negotiated contract
   C. Purchasing specifications

7-83.
D
Comp.
Hard
p. 187

Which of the following statements about ISO 9000 is FALSE?
   A. ISO 9000 is a way for government suppliers to document their quality procedures, but it does not apply to other organizational suppliers.
   B. A supplier that has met the ISO 9000 standard is always better than one that has not.
   C. ISO 9000 applies to international suppliers only.
   D. All of the above are false.
   E. None of the above is false.

7-84.
D
Def.
Easy
p. 187

Buying specialists for organizations are commonly called:
   A. supply agents.
   B. vendor agents.
   C. value analysts.
   D. purchasing managers.
   E. consumer buyers.

7-85.
E
Comp.
Easy
p. 188

A furniture producer has decided to buy its upholstery cloth from new suppliers. The president has given the purchasing manager responsibility to make the final selections and negotiate the terms. The purchasing manager looks through books with samples and specifications, and then calls salespeople to make presentations to the production manager, who is concerned about how easy the cloth will be to cut and sew. In this case, the purchasing manager is
 A. an influencer.
 B. a buyer.
 C. a decider.
 D. a gatekeeper.
 E. all of the above.

7-86.
B
Def.
Hard
p. 188

Regarding organizational buying, the people who have the power to select or approve the supplier--especially for larger purchases--are called:
 A. influencers.
 B. deciders.
 C. buyers.
 D. gatekeepers.
 E. users.

7-87.
A
App.
Med.
p. 188

Cathy Barnwell, director of procurement at Lansing Glass, Inc. must approve every purchase order, and Tom Glendinnig, purchasing manager, must authorize any sales rep who wants to talk to a Lansing employee. Cathy and Tom are acting as _____ and _____, respectively.
 A. decider and gatekeeper
 B. influencer and user
 C. gatekeeper and influencer
 D. buyer and decider
 E. user and gatekeeper

7-88.
B
App.
Easy
p. 188

Multiple buying influence is MOST likely to occur in which of the following purchases?
 A. note pads.
 B. a voice-mail phone system.
 C. a replacement for a broken chair.
 D. gasoline.
 E. paper clips.

7-89.
D
Def.
Easy
p. 188,192

Multiple buying influence should be expected in:
 A. vendor buying.
 B. straight rebuy buying.
 C. modified rebuy buying.
 D. new-task buying.
 E. none of the above.

7-90.
D
Def.
Easy
p. 188,192

If many individuals are involved in a buying decision, this is:
 A. a multiple input situation.
 B. a selective rebuy.
 C. a modified rebuy.
 D. a multiple buying influence situation.
 E. a straight rebuy.

7-91.
A
App.
Easy
p. 188,192

Regarding new-task organizational buying, which of the following persons is LEAST likely to be involved?
A. a competitor's purchasing manager.
B. a purchasing manager.
C. a production line supervisor.
D. the company president.
E. a research assistant.

7-92.
E
App.
Easy
p. 188,192

Regarding new-task organizational buying, which of the following are likely to be involved?
A. top managers.
B. purchasing manager.
C. production process engineers.
D. production line supervisors.
E. all of the above.

7-93.
D
Comp.
Med.
p. 189

When a salesperson calls on a new business prospect,
A. he may have trouble identifying all of the buying center members.
B. he usually must see the purchasing manager first.
C. the probability of encountering a gatekeeper is high.
D. All of the above are true.
E. None of the above is true.

7-94.
A
Comp.
Med.
p. 189

A "buying center"
A. may vary from purchase to purchase.
B. refers to all the purchasing agents in a large firm.
C. is usually identified on a firm's organization chart.
D. is usually controlled by the purchasing manager.
E. is usually located in major wholesale markets.

7-95.
E
Comp.
Easy
p. 189

For new-task buying, a good salesperson will try to contact the potential customer's:
A. deciders.
B. gatekeepers.
C. influencers.
D. buyers (purchasing managers).
E. All of the above.

7-96.
E
Comp.
Med.
p. 189-90

Vendor analysis
A. ensures objectivity by disregarding whether a supplier has been used in the past.
B. emphasizes the emotional factors in a purchase decision.
C. is used less now that multiple buying influence is more common.
D. All of the above are true.
E. None of the above is true.

7-**97.**
D
Comp.
Med.
p. 189

Vendor analysis
A. emphasizes the emotional factors in a purchase decision.
B. is a formal procedure used by a vendor's salespeople to be certain that all members of a buying center have been contacted.
C. is used less now that multiple buying influence is more common.
D. is likely to favor a vendor that offers the customer the lowest total cost associated with the purchase.
E. None of the above is true.

7-**98.**
D
Comp.
Med.
p. 189-90

Most purchasing managers:
A. reject "vendor analysis" as too subjective.
B. want to be "sold" by persuasive salespeople.
C. spend most of their time on new-task buying.
D. stress dependability as well as lower cost and higher quality.
E. dislike the higher risk that is involved in buying from a supplier that meets the ISO 9000 standard.

7-**99.**
C
Comp.
Easy
p. 190

Purchasing managers
A. are, in general, not very well educated.
B. always buy from the lowest price supplier.
C. may be willing to pay more to reduce personal risk.
D. are usually the last ones a salesperson sees, after the order has been approved by the gatekeepers.
E. None of the above is true.

7-**100.**
E
Comp.
Easy
p. 190

Purchasing managers in business markets (compared to buyers in consumer markets) are generally:
A. fewer in number.
B. more technically qualified.
C. less emotional in their buying motives.
D. more insistent on dependability and quality.
E. all of the above.

7-**101.**
B
Comp.
Med.
p. 190

A typical purchasing manager:
A. buys strictly on economic needs.
B. tries to satisfy both individual needs and company needs.
C. seeks the lowest possible cost.
D. has the final decision on all purchases.
E. All of the above.

7-**102.**
D
Comp.
Med.
p. 191

Regarding organizational buying,
A. a "national accounts" sales force often makes sense when firms with many facilities buy from a central location.
B. purchasing managers are more likely to be found in large organizations.
C. a geographically bound salesperson can be at a real disadvantage.
D. All of the above are true.
E. None of the above is true.

7-103.
B
Int.
Med.
p. 190

Organizational buyers:
A. are producers' agents.
B. are problem solvers.
C. base purchasing decisions entirely on company needs.
D. are not affected by emotional needs.
E. All of the above are true.

7-104.
E
Def.
Easy
p. 188-90

Organizational buyers:
A. rely on many sources of information in addition to salespeople when making purchase decisions.
B. may use vendor analysis to make certain that all relevant areas of a purchase decision have been considered.
C. are likely to do little search for additional information if the purchase is unimportant.
D. tend to be more rational--and less emotional--in their buying decisions than final consumers.
E. All of the above are true.

7-105.
C
Int.
Med.
p. 190

Regarding selling to organizational buyers,
A. the buyer's individual needs can be ignored when there is multiple buying influence.
B. purchasing managers are usually more emotional than final consumers.
C. a purchasing manager's emotional needs should be emphasized as well as his economic needs.
D. sellers should try to avoid purchasing managers, since they usually can't make the final buying decision.
E. All of the above are true.

7-106.
B
App.
Easy
p. 191

An office manager needs office supplies, so he fills out a form indicating what he needs and sends it to the purchasing department to be ordered. This form is usually called
A. a purchase order.
B. a requisition.
C. a vendor analysis.
D. a buying center request.
E. the start of the adoption process.

7-107.
E
Comp.
Med.
p. 191

A requisition
A. is only used for nonroutine purchases.
B. is the same as a purchase order.
C. sets the terms under a negotiated contract.
D. is a formal contract between a buyer and a seller.
E. none of the above is true.

7-108.
C
Def.
Easy
p. 191

Which of the following is NOT one of the organizational buying processes discussed in the text?
A. Straight rebuy buying
B. Modified rebuy buying
C. Important task buying
D. New-task buying
E. None of the above, i.e., all are buying processes.

7-109.
A
Def.
Easy
p. 191

Which of the following is NOT one of the organizational buying processes discussed in the text?
A. multiple task buying.
B. modified rebuy buying.
C. new-task buying.
D. straight rebuy buying.
E. None of the above, i.e., all are buying processes.

7-110.
B
Comp.
Hard
p. 192

Straight rebuy
A. decisions, as contrasted with modified rebuys, are more likely to involve multiple buying influence.
B. vendor selections are likely to be made by a purchasing manager--without consulting anyone else.
C. decisions are infrequent, but they typically take longer to make than new-task buying decisions.
D. decisions usually involve getting negotiated bids from suppliers.
E. decisions cannot be influenced by advertising.

7-111.
C
Def.
Easy
p. 192

Organizational buyers:
A. tend to rely almost totally on salespeople as their source of information.
B. prefer formal procedures for rating vendors over informal approaches like vendor analysis.
C. are likely to do little search for additional information if the purchase is unimportant.
D. tend to be more emotional than final consumers--because their jobs are at risk if a problem arises.
E. None of the above is true.

7-112.
A
App.
Med.
p. 192

A vendor is LEAST LIKELY to make a sale if the buyer has not bought from the vendor before and is doing:
A. straight rebuy buying
B. selective buying.
C. new-task buying.
D. selective task buying.
E. modified rebuy buying.

7-113.
C
App.
Med.
p. 192

A buyer who has not purchased from a vendor in the past is MOST LIKELY to buy from that vendor when there is:
A. straight rebuy buying
B. selective buying.
C. new-task buying.
D. selective task buying.
E. modified rebuy buying.

7-114.
C
App.
Easy
p. 192

A straight rebuy is MOST likely to occur for:
A. a new computer network.
B. a pension plan which meets the new government regulations.
C. paper supplies for the copy equipment.
D. electronic components for a new product.
E. executive chairs for a new office building.

7-115.
E
App.
Med.
p. 192

Bart Peterson, purchasing agent for Boswell Plastic Industries, routinely signs purchase orders for office supplies without further consideration. At Boswell, purchases of office supplies are
    A. a modified rebuy.
    B. a necessity.
    C. Somewhat Insignificant Commodity (SIC) items.
    D. swayed by reciprocity.
    E. a straight rebuy.

7-116.
A
App.
Med.
p. 192

A vendor is MOST likely to make a sale if the buyer has bought from the vendor before and is doing:
    A. straight rebuy buying.
    B. selective buying.
    C. multiple task buying.
    D. modified rebuy buying.
    E. new-task buying.

7-117.
B
App.
Hard
p. 192

A modified rebuy would be most likely when:
    A. A railroad plans to change from steel to aluminum rail cars to cut weight.
    B. A car producer is developing a sportier car which will require wider tires.
    C. A bread producer is placing its weekly order for flour.
    D. A computer producer is buying new assembly line equipment.
    E. A shoe factory needs more glue to attach heels to its shoes.

7-118.
D
App.
Easy
p. 192

A modified rebuy is MOST likely to occur for:
    A. file folders.
    B. brooms.
    C. paper clips.
    D. a desk.
    E. copier paper.

7-119.
B
App.
Med.
p. 192

Goforth Corp. is looking for a new vendor for basic chemicals because the present vendor has been inconsistent about meeting delivery schedules. Which of the following buying processes is the firm's purchasing agent MOST LIKELY to use?
    A. Selective buying
    B. Modified rebuy buying
    C. Intensive buying
    D. New-task buying
    E. Straight rebuy buying

7-120.
C
Comp.
Easy
p. 192

Which of the following buying situations gives a seller the most chance for promotion impact?
    A. Selective task buying
    B. Modified rebuy buying
    C. New-task buying
    D. Straight rebuy buying
    E. All of the above are equal.

7-121.
A
Comp.
Hard
p. 193

In business markets, close buyer-seller relationships
A. may improve the profits of both the buyer and the seller.
B. are almost always desirable from the seller's point of view, but not from the buyer's point of view.
C. may have benefits, but they usually increase a firm's uncertainty and risk.
D. None of the above.
E. All of the above.

7-122.
B
Int.
Hard
p. 194

With respect to buyer-seller relationships in business markets,
A. relationships benefit sellers, but not customers.
B. some customers simply are not interested in a close relationship with a supplier.
C. customer firms are better off selecting suppliers with competitive bids rather than establishing a relationship with a single vendor.
D. All of the above are true.
E. None of the above are true.

7-123.
B
Comp.
Easy
p. 194

Which of the following is NOT a key dimension of buyer-seller relationships in business markets?
A. legal bonds
B. new-task sharing
C. cooperation
D. operational linkages
E. information sharing

7-124.
C
Comp.
Easy
p. 194

Which of the following is NOT a key dimension of buyer-seller relationships in business markets?
A. legal bonds
B. relationship-specific adaptations
C. joint inspection
D. operational linkages
E. information sharing

7-125.
B
Comp.
Easy
p. 194

Which of the following is NOT a key dimension of buyer-seller relationships in business markets?
A. legal bonds
B. relationship-specific recycling
C. cooperation
D. operational linkages
E. information sharing

7-126.
E
Comp.
Easy
p. 194

Which of the following is NOT a key dimension of buyer-seller relationships in business markets?
A. legal bonds
B. relationship-specific adaptations
C. cooperation
D. operational linkages
E. bid rigging

7-127.
E
Comp.
Easy
p. 194

Which of the following is NOT a key dimension of buyer-seller relationships in business markets?
A. information sharing
B. legal bonds
C. cooperation
D. operational linkages
E. all of the above are key dimensions

7-128.
D
Comp.
Med.
p. 193-198

Suppliers to business markets often
A. provide information about industry trends.
B. must manage inventory and delivery carefully--to provide customers with just-in-time delivery.
C. serve as technical consultants to their customers.
D. All of the above are true.
E. None of the above is true.

7-129.
E
Comp.
Med.
p. 193-198

In business markets, close buyer-seller relationships
A. often involve a number of people from different areas in both the buyer and supplier firms.
B. may be based on regular, "good-faith" reviews rather than legal contracts.
C. can help reduce uncertainty and risk.
D. usually focus on driving down joint costs.
E. All of the above.

7-130.
E
Comp.
Hard
p. 193-198

A close buyer-seller relationship in a business market:
A. may require relationship-specific adaptations by the seller, the customer, or both.
B. may result in the seller accepting a lower price.
C. may increase the buyer's "switching costs."
D. may not involve a contract that spells out each party's responsibilities.
E. All of the above are true.

7-131.
B
Comp.
Hard
p. 198

Organizational buyers purchase the same product from more than one source
A. if no supplier has a superior marketing mix.
B. to help ensure continuing supplies.
C. because a single vendor usually doesn't want all of the business.
D. if vendor analysis results in a "tie score" for the different suppliers.
E. None of the above is true.

7-132.
A
App.
Med.
p. 197

Which of the following situations would involve negotiated contract buying?
A. design and manufacture a new computer accessory.
B. produce and deliver 1,000 tons of tomatoes.
C. manufacture and ship 500 secretarial chairs.
D. all of the above.
E. none of the above.

7-133.
B
App.
Med.
p. 197

Upbeat Electronics has an idea for a new DVD accessory. Now it is looking for a supplier to design and manufacture the product. It will most likely use _____ buying.
   A. description.
   B. negotiated contract.
   C. reciprocity.

7-134.
A
Def.
Easy
p. 197

When a purchasing manager knows roughly what is needed but can't describe it exactly--or when the purchasing arrangement may change as the job progresses--then buying is likely to be by:
   A. negotiatedcontract.
   B. description.
   C. reciprocity.

7-135.
D
App.
Med.
p. 198

Global Travel Services (GTS) will not buy anything from any seller who will not, in turn, agree to book all of its company travel through GTS. This is an example of:
   A. hardlining.
   B. routinized buying behavior.
   C. negotiated buying.
   D. reciprocity.
   E. conscious parallel action.

7-136.
E
Def.
Easy
p. 198

Regarding organizational buying, "reciprocity" refers to:
   A. several firms pooling their orders.
   B. buying by inspection only.
   C. multiple buying.
   D. refusing to negotiate trading contracts.
   E. the policy of "if you buy from me, I'll buy from you."

7-137.
A
Comp.
Med.
p. 198

Cumming's Steel, a producer, regularly uses a specific railroad to ship its products, since that railroad buys most of the steel for its replacement track from Cumming's.
   A. Reciprocity appears to be involved here.
   B. In this case, the railroad is a part of the buying center.
   C. This is illegal and should be stopped immediately.
   D. All of the above are true.
   E. None of the above is true.

7-138.
E
Comp.
Med.
p. 199-200

Regarding e-commerce website resources:
   A. Collaboration hubs focus on helping firms cooperate on an extended basis.
   B. Catalog and community sites put in digital form information that was already available in other forms.
   C. Exchanges bring buyers and sellers together so they can agree on price.
   D. Procurement hubs direct suppliers to a buyer at one convenient location.
   E. All of the above are true.

7-**139.**
E
Comp.
Med.
p. 199-200

Regarding e-commerce website resources:
A. Purchasing specifications are commonly used online to describe what a firm wants to buy.
B. Online auction sites commonly operate for the benefit of sellers.
C. Competitive bidding systems commonly drive down prices at procurement hubs.
D. Online reverse auction sites commonly operate for the benefit of buyers.
E. All of the above are true.

7-**140.**
C
Comp.
Hard
p. 205

Regarding the size of manufacturing concerns, large firms (with more than 250 employees)
A. outnumber small firms more than two to one.
B. account for about half of all the manufacturing establishments.
C. are few in number but their employees account for about half of all employed people.
D. provide no more "value added" than the many small firms.
E. None of the above is true.

7-**141.**
B
Def.
Hard
p. 205

What percentage of total U.S. "value added" is produced by manufacturers which employ 250 or more employees?
A. 50 percent
B. More than 60 percent
C. 30 percent
D. Less than 5 percent
E. 10 percent

7-**142.**
D
Comp.
Hard
p. 205

Regarding the manufacturers' market, large firms (with more than 250 employees)
A. account for the vast majority of the total "value added" by all manufacturers.
B. are very few compared to the many small firms.
C. employ about half of all people employed in manufacturing.
D. All of the above are true.
E. None of the above is true.

7-**143.**
C
Comp.
Hard
p. 205

Regarding the business (manufacturing) market, small firms (with fewer than 10 employees)
A. are not very numerous compared to the very large firms.
B. account for the vast majority of the total employment provided by all manufacturers.
C. are the majority of all firms, but account for less than 3 percent of "value added" by manufacturing.
D. amount to nearly two million establishments.
E. None of the above is true.

7-**144.**
D
Def.
Med.
p. 205

U.S. business manufacturing markets tend to be concentrated:
A. by industry.
B. with a relatively few large manufacturing plants.
C. by geographical location.
D. All of the above.
E. Only B and C above.

7-145.
C
Def.
Easy
p. 205

U.S. manufacturers:
  A. all employ many workers.
  B. are evenly spread throughout the country.
  C. tend to concentrate by industry.
  D. do not locate close to competitors.
  E. Both C and D.

7-146.
B
Def.
Med.
p. 206

"NAICS" means:
  A. North American Initiative for Competitive Structure.
  B. North American Industry Classification System.
  C. New Auto Industry Classification System.
  D. National Automakers Industry Classification System.
  E. National Apparel Industry Classification System.

7-147.
C
Comp.
Hard
p. 207

You have just been asked by your manager to compile data on firms in California that have a specific 4-digit NAICS code. You should know
  A. that there are no 4-digit NAICS codes.
  B. that there is only one firm to find, since each firm has its own 4-digit NAICS code.
  C. that it is possible that no data will be available, even if there is one large firm in California in that 4-digit industry.
  D. that she is talking about the New Auto Industry Classification Survey.
  E. that none of the above is true.

7-148.
A
App.
Med.
p. 207

Which of the following NAICS codes would be used by a marketing manager who wanted data on the MOST GENERAL breakdown of a particular industry?
  A. 31
  B. 31522
  C. 315
  D. 3152
  E. There is no way to tell from the information provided.

7-149.
B
App.
Med.
p. 207

Which of the following NAICS codes would be used by a marketing manager who wanted data that was the MOST SPECIFIC to a particular type of firm within an industry?
  A. 31
  B. 31522
  C. 315
  D. 3152
  E. There is no way to tell from the information provided.

7-150.
C
Comp.
Hard
p. 207

The U.S. government would NOT publish NAICS data that gives:
  A. the total sales volume of the four steel manufacturers in a Metropolitan Statistical Area.
  B. the number of employees for similar two digit industry groups.
  C. the total sales volume of the only textile equipment manufacturer in a state.
  D. the sales volumes of similar two digit industry groups.
  E. the number of establishments for various industry groups.

7-151.
C
Comp.
Med.
p. 207

If a firm targets business and organizational markets,
- A. the geographic location of the customer is likely to be less important than in segmenting consumer markets.
- B. NAICS codes may help in segmenting manufacturers but not producers of services.
- C. each customer may need to be treated as a different segment.
- D. All of the above are true.
- E. None of the above is true.

7-152.
E
Comp.
Med.
p. 207

If a firm targets business and organizational markets,
- A. NAICS codes may be helpful for segmenting potential customers in Europe but not those in the U.S.
- B. each customer may need to be treated as a different segment.
- C. competing manufacturers are often clustered in geographic locations.
- D. All of the above are true.
- E. Both B and C are true.

7-153.
B
Comp.
Med.
p. 209

When a large wholesaler or retailer uses a buying committee,
- A. the buyer still makes the final purchase decision.
- B. the sales rep may not be able to make a sales presentation to the committee.
- C. the impact of persuasive salespeople is increased.
- D. the middleman is more likely to take a chance on a really new product that hasn't yet proved itself.
- E. All of the above are true.

7-154.
D
Comp.
Med.
p. 209

Committee buying in large retail chains
- A. makes the buyers work as a group and thus lower costs.
- B. allows a sales rep to avoid a difficult buyer.
- C. makes it difficult for the seller to see a buyer personally.
- D. reduces the impact of a persuasive sales rep.
- E. All of the above.

7-155.
B
Int.
Hard
p. 209

Regarding middlemen buying,
- A. computer-controlled inventory systems make buyers more dependent on sales reps.
- B. buying committees are a way for supermarkets to handle the flood of new products.
- C. buyers are seldom influenced by their salespeople.
- D. wholesalers and retailers typically only carry products which they have judged "socially desirable."
- E. all of the above are true.

7-156.
A
Comp.
Hard
p. 209

Because more middlemen are using computer systems to control inventory levels,
- A. they can assess the profitability of each product.
- B. new-task buying is increasing.
- C. they are carrying larger inventories.
- D. negotiated contract buying is increasing.
- E. All of the above are occurring.

7-**157.**
D
Comp.
Med.
p. 209

Large wholesale and retail buyers typically:
A. pay close attention to each of the products they buy.
B. don't trust automatic inventory control methods.
C. see themselves as selling agents for manufacturers.
D. buy most of their products as straight rebuys.
E. None of the above.

7-**158.**
D
Def.
Hard
p. 210

A retail buyer being "open to buy" means that:
A. increases in demand have him back in the market.
B. multiple buying influence will not occur.
C. he will buy only if offered special prices.
D. he has budgeted funds that he can spend during the current period.
E. the sales rep should call during those "open" hours.

7-**159.**
C
Def.
Hard
p. 210

"Open to buy"
A. means that a retail buyer is in the market looking for "good buys."
B. refers to the business hours when the retail buyer is available for sales reps.
C. means that a retail buyer still has budgeted funds to spend during the current period.
D. refers to retail buyers who have shelf space available for new products.
E. means that "new-task" buying is likely.

7-**160.**
A
Comp.
Med.
p. 210

Buyers for retail firms
A. are themselves often involved in selling--or responsible for supervising salespeople.
B. usually want to visit with sales reps from as many suppliers as possible--to make certain that good purchasing opportunities are not missed.
C. usually view themselves as "selling agents" for their suppliers.
D. All of the above are true.
E. None of the above is true.

7-**161.**
E
Def.
Easy
p. 210

Resident buyers
A. are not "resident" in the buying firm, but rather are independent buying agents in central markets.
B. are especially helpful to small producers and middlemen.
C. are frequently used to help select new styles and fashions, as well as fill-in items.
D. are usually paid an annual fee--based on their purchases.
E. All of the above are true.

7-**162.**
B
Def.
Hard
p. 210

Resident buyers:
A. usually work for only one large retailer because of the work involved.
B. are independent buying agents who work for several retailers.
C. frequently travel to central markets to buy new styles.
D. maintain offices in retailers' buying departments.
E. All of the above.

7-163.
E
Def.
Easy
p. 210

Independent buying agents who work in central markets for wholesalers and retailers from outlying areas are called:
  A. buying committees.
  B. buying centers.
  C. buying agents.
  D. brokers.
  E. resident buyers.

7-164.
B
Int.
Hard
p. 210

Regarding the government market,
  A. sales reps generally do not (and should not) write the specifications for government business.
  B. government is the largest customer group in the United States--spending about 35 percent of GNP.
  C. governments buy a lot, but only of certain products and can be safely ignored by most producers.
  D. negotiated contracts are uncommon because of mandatory bidding procedures.
  E. All of the above are true.

7-165.
D
Comp.
Easy
p. 210

The government market
  A. often relies on an "approved supplier list" for routine items that are bought frequently.
  B. is the largest customer group in the United States, accounting for about 35 percent of the gross national product.
  C. usually buys from the lowest price supplier that can meet the written specifications.
  D. All of the above are true.
  E. None of the above are true.

7-166.
A
Comp.
Med.
p. 211

Regarding U.S. government market buying,
  A. a buyer may order from a supplier on the "approved list" at a previously set price--without asking for new bids.
  B. most buyers write specs so that only one brand or supplier qualifies.
  C. it is illegal for a salesperson to try to influence the writing of product specifications.
  D. Both A and C are true.
  E. None of the above is true.

7-167.
E
Def.
Easy
p. 210-11

Government buyers in the U.S. usually buy by:
  A. specification--using a mandatory bidding procedure.
  B. negotiated contracts.
  C. haggling.
  D. reciprocity.
  E. Both A and B.

7-168.
A
Def.
Med.
p. 212

A potential supplier to the government market would probably learn the most about detailed purchase needs of the U.S. federal government by reading or researching the web sites for:
   A. COMMERCE BUSINESS DAILY.
   B. the current STATISTICAL ABSTRACT OF THE U.S.
   C. a trade association.
   D. THE CONGRESSIONAL RECORD.
   E. U.S. PURCHASING, SPECIFICATIONS, AND SALES DIRECTORY.

7-169.
E
Def.
Med.
p. 212

The Foreign Corrupt Practices Act:
   A. allows small "grease money" payments if they are customary in that country.
   B. does not hold a manager responsible if a foreign agent secretly pays a bribe.
   C. allows U.S. firms to pay bribes to foreign officials.
   D. all of the above.
   E. only A and B above.

Chapter 8

Improving Decisions with Marketing Information

True-False Questions:

8-1.
True
p. 218

A marketing information system (MIS) is an organized way of continually gathering, accessing, and analyzing information that marketing managers need to make decisions.

8-2.
False
p. 218

A marketing information system (MIS) is a large computer which allows consumers to determine the prices of food products at grocery stores in any geographic area.

8-3.
False
p. 220

An intranet is useful for numeric data but not for text documents.

8-4.
True
p. 220

An intranet is a system for linking computers within a company.

8-5.
True
p. 220

An intranet works like the Internet but access is limited to a company's employees.

8-6.
False
p. 220

Only large firms have their own intranets.

8-7.
True
p. 220

Access to information on an intranet is usually limited to a firm's own employees.

8-8.
True
p. 220

A decision support system (DSS) is a computer program that makes it easy for a marketing manager to get and use information as he or she is making decisions.

8-9.
False
p. 220

A search engine may make it easier for a marketing manager to get information from the Internet, but it would not be useful on an intranet.

8-10.
True
p. 220

A search engine is a computer program that helps find information.

8-11.
True
p. 220

Search engines use words or phrases to guide the search for information.

8-12.
False
p. 220

A marketing manager who uses a search engine would have little need for a decision support system.

8-13.
True
p. 221

Most marketing managers who see how a marketing information system (MIS) can help their decision-making are eager for more information.

8-14.
True
p. 222

The function of marketing research is to develop and analyze new information to help marketing managers make decisions.

8-15.
True
p. 222

One of the important jobs of marketing researchers is to get the "facts" for marketing managers.

8-16.
False
p. 223

It isn't necessary for marketing managers to be involved with marketing research specialists, since research requires statistical skills which managers usually don't have.

8-17.
True
p. 223

Marketing managers should be able to explain the kinds of problems they are facing and the kinds of marketing research information that will help them make decisions.

8-18.
True
p. 223

Since marketing managers have to be able to evaluate research results, they should be involved in the design of research projects--even though they may not be research specialists.

8-19.
True
p. 223

Use of the scientific method in marketing research helps managers make the best decisions possible.

8-20.
True
p. 223

A marketing researcher using the scientific method develops and tests hypotheses about the relationships between things or about what will happen in the future.

8-21.
False
p. 224

Use of the scientific method in marketing research forces researchers to use an inflexible process.

8-22.
False
p. 224

The scientific method is a research process which consists of five stages: observation, developing hypotheses, predicting the future, collecting data and using statistical methods of analysis.

8-23.
False
p. 224

Defining the problem is the first step in marketing research--and is usually the easiest job for the researcher.

8-24.
True
p. 224

To avoid wasting time working on the wrong problem, marketing researchers can use a logical strategy planning framework to guide their efforts.

8-25.
True
p. 224

Unless the problem is precisely defined, research effort may be wasted on the wrong problem, and may lead to costly mistakes.

8-26.
True
p. 226-29

During the situation analysis, marketing researchers may talk to informed people within the company, study internal records, search libraries for available information, or browse the Internet with a search engine.

8-27.
True
p. 226

Secondary data is information which is already published or collected.

8-28.
False
p. 226

During the situation analysis, a marketing researcher will evaluate primary data rather than secondary data.

8-29.
False
p. 226

The Internet is an excellent source for primary data, but not secondary data.

8-30.
False
p. 228

The government, advertising agencies, newspapers, trade associations, and research subscription services are all major sources of primary data.

8-31.
True
p. 228

The Statistical Abstract of the United States is one of the most useful summaries of secondary data published by the federal government.

8-32.
True
p. 229

A good situation analysis is usually inexpensive compared with more formal research efforts, such as a large scale survey.

8-33.
False
p. 229

In general, a marketing researcher should get some problem-specific data before planning a formal research project.

8-34.
True
p. 229

A formal marketing research project usually involves gathering primary data.

8-35.
True
p. 230

Qualitative research seeks in-depth, open-ended responses.

8-36. Focus group interviews are a form of quantitative research.
False
p. 230

8-37. Electronic focus groups now participate in sessions via the Internet.
True
p. 230

8-38. Open-ended questions are less likely to be asked in quantitative research than in
True qualitative research.
p. 231

8-39. One reason for the popularity of mail surveys is that the response rates are usually very
False high.
p. 233

8-40. Telephone surveys are practical if the information needed is not too personal.
True
p. 233

8-41. Observing--as a method of collecting data--should focus on a well-defined problem.
True
p. 234

8-42. Applying the experimental method in marketing research usually means the responses
True of groups are compared.
p. 236

8-43. A statistical package is likely to be used with quantitative research, but not with
True qualitative research.
p. 239

8-44. Validity concerns the extent to which data measures what it is intended to measure.
True
p. 241

8-45. When a firm is doing similar research projects in different international markets, it
True makes sense for the marketing manager to coordinate the efforts so that comparisons
p. 242 across markets are possible.

8-46. Even though marketing managers might like more information, they must balance the
True high cost of good research against its probable value to management.
p. 243

8-47. A marketing manager should seek help from research only for problems where the risk
True of a decision can be greatly reduced at a reasonable cost.
p. 243

Multiple Choice Questions

8-48.
D
Comp.
Med.
p. 218

When getting information for marketing decisions, the marketing manager:
  A. may need to rely on instincts to make some decisions.
  B. should have access to ongoing information about business performance.
  C. may need to make some decisions based on incomplete information.
  D. All of the above are true.
  E. None of the above is true.

8-49.
B
Comp.
Med.
p. 218

Regarding "marketing research" and "marketing information systems":
  A. marketing information systems gather and analyze data from sources inside the company, while marketing research handles all external sources.
  B. marketing information systems make information more accessible.
  C. marketing information systems tend to increase the quantity of information available for decision making, but with some decrease in quality.
  D. most firms have gone "too far" trying to apply modern decision-making techniques.
  E. All of the above are true.

8-50.
A
Comp.
Med.
p. 218

Setting up a marketing information system can be valuable to marketing managers because
  A. most companies have much useful information available, but it often isn't easy to access when the manager needs it.
  B. most market-oriented companies only need a certain type of information once or twice.
  C. marketing research data is rarely as accurate as data from a marketing information system.
  D. market-oriented managers can always use more data.
  E. a company that can't afford marketing research should at least have a marketing information system.

8-51.
A
Def.
Easy
p. 218

A _____ is an organized way of continually gathering and analyzing data to get information to help marketing managers make decisions.
  A. marketing information system
  B. marketing model
  C. marketing research project
  D. marketing research department
  E. marketing logistics system

8-52.
E
Comp.
Med.
p. 218-20

When getting information for marketing decisions, the marketing manager:
  A. may use both internal and external sources of information.
  B. may need to make some decisions based on incomplete information.
  C. may need to rely on his or her own instincts to make some decisions.
  D. should have access to ongoing information about business performance.
  E. all of the above.

8-53. A complete marketing information system:
C
Comp.
Med.
p. 218-20
A. provides a good overall view on many types of problems, but usually cannot provide answers to specific questions.
B. eliminates the need for "one-shot" marketing research projects.
C. is organized to continually gather data from internal and external sources, including market research studies.
D. is usually too complicated for the marketing manager to use without help from data processing specialists.
E. All of the above are true.

8-54. A complete marketing information system should:
E
Comp.
Med.
p. 218-20
A. provide a good overall view on many types of problems.
B. allows marketing managers to get needed information while they are actually making decisions.
C. provide answers to specific questions.
D. continually gather data from internal and external sources, and from market research studies.
E. All of the above are true.

8-55. Regarding "marketing research" and "marketing information systems":
E
Comp.
Med.
p. 218-22
A. marketing information systems gather, access, and analyze data from intracompany sources, while marketing research handles all external sources.
B. both tend to focus on nonrecurring information needs.
C. marketing information systems tend to increase the quantity of information available for decision making, but with some decrease in quality.
D. most firms have gone "too far" trying to apply modern decision-making techniques.
E. None of the above is true.

8-56. Marketing research:
B
Comp.
Med.
p. 222
A. should be planned by research specialists who understand research techniques better than marketing managers.
B. is needed to keep isolated marketing managers in touch with their markets.
C. consists mainly of survey design and statistical techniques.
D. is only needed by producers who have long channels of distribution.
E. All of the above.

8-57. Procedures to gather and analyze new information to help marketing managers make
A
Def.
Easy
p. 222
decisions are called:
A. marketing research.
B. statistical techniques.
C. operational planning.
D. strategy planning.
E. sample building units (SBUs).

8-58.   Procedures to gather and analyze new information to help marketing managers make
D   decisions are called:
Def.   A. strategy planning.
Easy   B. operational planning.
p. 222   C. analytical research.
                  D. marketing research.
                  E. statistical techniques.

8-59.   Marketing research:
D   A. provides information for use in decision-making.
Comp.   B. must be a joint effort between the researcher and the manager.
Easy   C. may be handled by outside specialists or by people within the firm.
p. 222-23   D. All of the above are true.
                  E. None of the above is true.

8-60.   Marketing research:
E   A. should be planned by research specialists who understand research techniques
Comp.   better than marketing managers.
Med.   B. is only needed by producers who use long channels of distribution.
p. 222   C. should be planned by marketing managers--who understand the problem--not
                     researchers.
                  D. is not needed by business marketers because their needs are different.
                  E. can get the "facts" that are not available in the MIS.

8-61.   Marketing research is concerned with gathering and analyzing new information to help
E   marketing managers do a better job of:
Comp.   A. executing marketing strategies.
Med.   B. planning marketing strategies.
p. 222   C. making operational decisions.
                  D. controlling marketing strategies.
                  E. All of the above.

8-62.   Regarding marketing research,
B   A. when time is short and a decision must be made, it is better not to do a research
Comp.   project that can answer only some of the questions.
Med.   B. a good researcher will understand the marketing problem as well as the technical
p. 223   details of marketing research.
                  C. marketing managers really don't have to know much about how to plan
                     marketing research to use the results effectively.
                  D. most large companies don't use outside research specialists.
                  E. the marketing manager is usually too involved to be objective, so a research
                     specialist should define the problem.

8-**63**.
B
Comp.
Hard.
p. 223

Which of the following statements BEST reflects the point of view of the text with respect to marketing research?
 A. "We don't use computers, surveys and the like because marketing's information needs are usually not that precise anyway."
 B. "When we work with outside marketing research specialists, we expect them to take the time to really understand the problem we are trying to solve."
 C. "As marketing manager, I feel that the marketing researchers should be left alone to do their research--since they often come up with interesting suggestions."
 D. "As marketing research director, I should know the marketing manager's position in advance, so we can prove it is correct if possible."
 E. "Our company is very small, but we should have our own marketing research department anyway--to get the information we need to make good decisions."

8-**64**.
E
Comp.
Med.
p. 223

The scientific method
 A. rejects the idea that marketing managers can make "educated guesses" about marketing relationships.
 B. is an orderly way of presenting your point of view.
 C. assumes that statistical analysis provides the only basis for rejecting an hypothesis.
 D. All of the above are true.
 E. None of the above is true.

8-**65**.
B
Def.
Easy
p. 223

A decision-making approach that focuses on being objective and orderly in testing ideas before accepting them is the:
 A. MIS method.
 B. scientific method.
 C. statistical method.
 D. DSS method.
 E. marketing models method.

8-**66**.
D
Def.
Easy
p. 223

Educated guesses about the relationships between things or about what will happen in the future are:
 A. theories.
 B. laws.
 C. "facts."
 D. hypotheses.
 E. None of the above.

8-**67**.
A
Def.
Easy
p. 223

Educated guesses about the relationships between things or about what will happen in the future are:
 A. hypotheses.
 B. laws.
 C. proposals.
 D. theories.
 E. predictions.

8-**68.**   The scientific method
C   A. rejects the idea that marketing managers can make "educated guesses" about
Comp.   marketing relationships.
Med.   B. shows that every marketing research project should have five steps.
p. 223   C. is an orderly and objective approach to judging how good an idea really is.
             D. recognizes that statistical analysis provides the only basis for rejecting an
                 hypothesis.
             E. None of the above is true.

8-**69.**   Which of the following is NOT part of the five-step marketing research process
A   discussed in the text?
Def.   A. Writing the proposal
Easy   B. Analyzing the situation
p. 224   C. Solving the problem
             D. Interpreting the data
             E. Defining the problem

8-**70.**   Which of the following is NOT part of the five-step marketing research process
B   discussed in the text?
Def.   A. Interpreting the data.
Easy   B. Developing the marketing information system (MIS).
p. 224   C. Analyzing the situation.
             D. Defining the problem.
             E. Solving the problem.

8-**71.**   Which of the following is most consistent with the scientific method approach to
D   marketing research discussed in the text?
Comp.   A. "We continually survey our customers because the results give us good ideas for
Med.   hypotheses."
p. 224   B. "Once we interpret the data, we can define our problem."
             C. "Our research is as precise as possible--because we want to be 100 percent
                 accurate."
             D. "Sometimes the answers from the early stages of the research process are good
                 enough so we stop the research and make our decisions."
             E. None of the above is true.

8-**72.**   The first thing a marketing manager should do if one of his firm's products drops in
B   sales volume is:
App.   A. conduct a survey to see what is wrong.
Med.   B. define the problem.
p. 224   C. set research priorities.
             D. do a situation analysis.
             E. interview representative customers.

8-**73.**   The most difficult step in the marketing research process is:
B   A. interpreting the data.
Def.   B. defining the problem.
Med.   C. gathering primary data.
p. 224   D. gathering secondary data.
             E. both A and C.

8-74.
B
Def.
Med.
p. 224

The most difficult step in the marketing research process is:
- A. analyzing the situation.
- B. defining the problem.
- C. getting problem-specific data.
- D. interpreting the data.
- E. All of the above.

8-75.
B
Comp.
Hard
p. 224

Marketing research:
- A. should be planned by research specialists only, because it requires technical statistical techniques.
- B. is likely to be more effective when guided by the strategy planning framework.
- C. should gather as much information as possible.
- D. is useful for strategy planning but not for operational planning.
- E. All of the above are true.

8-76.
D
Comp.
Easy
p. 224-25

Regarding the marketing research process, defining the problem
- A. is often confused with identifying the symptoms of the problem.
- B. can be guided by the marketing strategy planning framework.
- C. precisely may have to wait until after a situation analysis has been completed.
- D. All of the above are true.
- E. None of the above is true.

8-77.
C
Comp.
Med.
p. 225

Regarding the marketing research process, defining the problem
- A. means identifying the symptoms.
- B. usually requires that problem specific data be collected and interpreted.
- C. may have to wait until after a situation analysis has been completed.
- D. All of the above are true.
- E. None of the above is true.

8-78.
D
Def.
Med.
p. 226

During a "situation analysis," a marketing researcher should:
- A. collect primary data.
- B. talk with competitors facing similar problems.
- C. begin to talk informally to as many customers as possible.
- D. study what information is already available.
- E. All of the above.

8-79.
A
App.
Med.
p. 226

A company that sells equipment through independent wholesalers wants to find out why sales are down in one region. An analyst is asked to interview the wholesaler in that region. This seems to be
- A. part of a situation analysis.
- B. the beginning of a focus group interview.
- C. gathering information that will be analyzed by a statistical package.
- D. bad practice, since the problem has not been defined yet.
- E. None of the above is true.

8-**80.**
A
App.
Med.
p. 226

A marketing manager wants to know why her sales are down. She talks with several sales reps and finds that a competitor has introduced a successful new product. This "research" seems to be part of

    A. the situation analysis.
    B. the problem solution stage.
    C. obtaining problem-specific data.
    D. the data interpretation stage.
    E. the problem definition stage of the research process.

8-**81.**
B
Def.
Med.
p. 226

Data that has already been collected or published is:

    A. useful data.
    B. secondary data.
    C. primary data.
    D. free data.
    E. rarely--if ever--useful for marketing decision making.

8-**82.**
D
Def.
Easy
p. 226

Data that has been collected or published already is:

    A. primary data.
    B. free.
    C. franchised data.
    D. secondary data.
    E. none of the above.

8-**83.**
C
Comp.
Med.
p. 226

Which of the following statements concerning secondary data is correct?

    A. Secondary data usually takes longer to obtain than primary data.
    B. Secondary data is only available within the firm.
    C. Secondary data was originally collected for some other purpose.
    D. All of the above are correct.
    E. None of the above are correct.

8-**84.**
E
Comp.
Easy
p. 226

Secondary data:

    A. may not be specific enough to answer the question under consideration.
    B. should be considered before primary data is collected.
    C. is often all that is needed to solve a problem.
    D. is available both internally and outside the firm.
    E. all of the above.

8-**85.**
B
Comp.
Med.
p. 226

Which of the following statements about doing a situation analysis is correct?

    A. Libraries have good data on specific topics, but it is expensive to find.
    B. It doesn't make sense to start a situation analysis until the problem has begun to surface.
    C. Much good data is available from the government, but most of it is expensive.
    D. A good situation analysis is usually more expensive than collecting primary data.
    E. None of the above is true.

8-86.
D
Comp.
Med.
p. 228

A good place for a marketing analyst to START looking for published statistical data is the:

A. Encyclopedia of Associations.
B. Congressional Record.
C. The Wall Street Journal.
D. Statistical Abstract of the United States.
E. New York Times research files.

8-87.
C
Comp.
Easy
p. 228

Secondary data from federal government sources

A. is readily available, but there is usually not much information at state and local levels.
B. focuses mostly on agriculture.
C. is often very helpful for estimating the size of a market.
D. is only available from the Commerce Department in Washington.
E. None of the above is true.

8-88.
E
Def.
Easy
p. 227-29

Secondary data is often available--at little or no cost--from:

A. both private and government sources.
B. the Internet.
C. trade associations.
D. company files.
E. All of the above.

8-89.
B
Comp.
Med.
p. 229

Which of the following statements about secondary data is correct?

A. Secondary data is obtained only from sources outside of the firm.
B. Secondary data may be available much faster than primary data.
C. Results of "old" surveys are not secondary data.
D. Secondary data is usually more expensive to obtain than primary data.
E. All of the above are true.

8-90.
D
Comp.
Med.
p. 229

Which of the following is most consistent with the marketing research process discussed in the text?

A. "We know that time is always short, so as soon as we define the problem we get on with our data collection."
B. "We pay a lot for marketing research experts, so our managers don't waste time trying to figure out how projects should be conducted."
C. "We always use mail surveys, so that we won't have to worry about nonresponse problems."
D. "Secondary data is often all we need to solve our problems."
E. None of the above is a good answer.

8-91.
B
Comp.
Easy
p. 229

Which of the following statements about doing a situation analysis is correct?

A. There is very little government data on business and commercial markets.
B. Doing a good situation analysis is usually much less expensive than collecting primary data.
C. There is little value to having a marketing researcher involved because a good marketing manager is able to do what is required.
D. All of the above are true.
E. None of the above is true.

8-**92.**
A
App.
Easy
p. 229

A company is considering some opportunities in wholly new industries. A marketing researcher is asked to collect relevant secondary data about the attractiveness of the industries. As a first step, the researcher would be wise to
  A. consult STANDARD AND POOR'S INDUSTRY SURVEYS.
  B. check the STATISTICAL ABSTRACT OF THE UNITED STATES.
  C. check the index for SALES AND MARKETING MANAGEMENT.
  D. look at the ENCYCLOPEDIA OF ASSOCIATIONS.
  E. none of the above would be a good first source.

8-**93.**
B
App.
Med.
p. 229

A marketing manager for a chemical company is seeking some relevant secondary data about his competitors. The following publications are in the firm's library. Which one would be best to look at?
  A. Chain Store Age
  B. Standard and Poor's Industry Surveys
  C. The Index of Business Periodicals
  D. Advertising Age
  E. None of the above is likely to be useful.

8-**94.**
E
App.
Med.
p. 227

Popular Internet search engines for locating secondary data include:
  A. Hotbot
  B. Northern Light
  C. Altavista
  D. Yahoo
  E. All of the above is likely to be useful.

8-**95.**
D
App.
Hard
p. 227-28

Which of the following is likely to be part of a situation analysis?
  A. A marketing analyst looks up data in Advertising Age magazine about expenditures in the firm's market.
  B. A marketing researcher asks a trade association for one of its reports.
  C. A marketing manager searches the computerized database of the Dow Jones interactive news retrieval system.
  D. All of the above.
  E. None of the above.

8-**96.**
D
App.
Hard
p. 229

Which of the following is probably NOT a part of a situation analysis?
  A. a marketing manager asks a radio station for a copy of an audience study.
  B. a marketing analyst determines from a Census publication how many manufacturers are in the Portland area.
  C. a marketing analyst looks in the Index of Business Periodicals for articles about a large retail chain.
  D. a computer company asks ten lawyers to participate in a focus group on how they use computers.
  E. All of the above seem to be part of a situation analysis.

8-**97.**
B
Def.
Med.
p. 229

Which of the following is NOT likely to be included in a research proposal?
  A. how long the research will take.
  B. preliminary recommendations on how to solve the problem.
  C. information about what the research will cost.
  D. a description of what data will be collected.
  E. a description of how data will be collected.

8-98.
A
Def.
Easy
p. 229

Which of the following would NOT be a source of primary data?
A. The Wall Street Journal
B. Market tests
C. Focus groups
D. Observation studies
E. Surveys

8-99.
C
Def.
Easy
p. 229

Which of the following would be a source of primary data?
A. U.S. Census Bureau reports.
B. company records on sales, costs, and advertising.
C. market tests.
D. all of the above.
E. B and C only.

8-100.
B
Def.
Easy
p. 230

"Qualitative research" involves:
A. talks with the firm's own managers.
B. questioning to obtain in-depth open-ended responses.
C. "yes-no" questionnaires.
D. studying secondary data.
E. None of the above.

8-101.
C
Comp.
Med.
p. 230

The big advantage of qualitative research in marketing is:
A. ease of interpretation.
B. it provides a good basis for statistical analysis.
C. the in-depth responses it provides.
D. the analysis can be handled on a personal computer.
E. None of the above.

8-102.
B
Def.
Easy
p. 230

An interview with 6 to 10 people in an informal group setting is called a(an):
A. secondary interview.
B. focus group interview.
C. observation interview.
D. quantitative research interview.
E. informal investigation.

8-103.
D
Comp.
Easy
p. 230

With focus group interviews,
A. consumers talk as a group for about 10 minutes, and then meet individually with an interviewer.
B. it is typical for the researcher to develop quantitative summaries of the results.
C. marketing managers can estimate the size of the market for a new product.
D. the objective is to get the group to interact, so that many ideas are generated.
E. researchers try to select a large sample so they can extend the results to the whole population.

8-104.
B
App.
Easy
p. 230

A consumer products manufacturer wants consumer reaction to its existing products. Interaction is considered important to stimulate thinking. The firm should use:
A. the observation method.
B. focus group interviews.
C. the GSR (galvanic skin response) method.
D. quantitative interviews.
E. telephone interviews.

8-**105.**
B
Comp.
Med.
p. 230

One of the major disadvantages of the focus group interview approach is that
  A. ideas generated by the group can't be tested later with other research.
  B. it is difficult to measure the results objectively.
  C. it is difficult to get in-depth information about the research topic.
  D. there is no interviewer, so the research questions may not be answered.
  E. once the interview is over there is no way for a marketing manager who was not there to evaluate what went on.

8-**106.**
D
Comp.
Med.
p. 230

When focus group interviews are used in marketing,
  A. each person in the group answers the same questionnaire, to focus the discussion.
  B. the typical group size is 15 to 20 typical consumers.
  C. it is primarily as a follow-up to more quantitative research.
  D. the research conclusions will vary depending on who watches the interview.
  E. the consumer in the group who knows the most about the topic is asked to lead the discussion.

8-**107.**
E
Comp.
Easy
p. 231-32

Quantitative marketing research
  A. usually makes it easier and faster for respondents to answer the questions (compared to qualitative research).
  B. can use a large, representative sample.
  C. data can be collected by mail, e-mail, online, telephone, or personal interviews.
  D. makes it easier for the research analyst to summarize answers.
  E. All of the above are true.

8-**108.**
A
Comp.
Med.
p. 231-32

Which of the following is a disadvantage of quantitative research (compared to qualitative research)?
  A. it is harder to get in-depth answers.
  B. the conclusions are likely to vary more from analyst to analyst.
  C. the results are harder to summarize.
  D. it is not as fast for respondents.
  E. None of the above is true.

8-**109.**
B
Def.
Easy
p. 231

Marketing research which seeks structured responses that can be summarized is called:
  A. focus group research.
  B. quantitative research.
  C. qualitative research.
  D. situation analysis research.
  E. open-ended research.

8-**110.**
A
App.
Easy
p. 232-33

A marketing researcher wants to get sensitive information about family spending patterns as part of a survey. He is most likely to get the needed information
  A. with a mail, e-mail, or online survey.
  B. with a VideOcart.
  C. with personal interviews.
  D. with telephone interviews.
  E. Any of the above is about equally effective for getting sensitive information.

8-111.
D
Comp.
Easy
p. 233

Mail surveys:
A. may be more successful than personal interviews for getting personal information.
B. are often limited by low response rates.
C. are popular because they can be a convenient and economical approach.
D. All of the above are true.
E. None of the above is true.

8-112.
E
Comp.
Easy
p. 233

A firm intends to use an online survey questionnaire in a marketing research project. Compared to a mail survey:
A. feedback will likely be faster online.
B. the response rate will likely be lower online.
C. respondents will likely be younger and better educated online.
D. costs will likely be less online.
E. all of the above.

8-113.
D
Def.
Easy
p. 233

The percent of people contacted in a survey who complete a questionnaire is the:
A. qualitative rate.
B. sample rate.
C. population rate.
D. response rate.
E. none of the above.

8-114.
A
Def.
Easy
p. 233

The percent of people contacted who complete a survey questionnaire is the:
A. response rate.
B. sample base unit (SBU) rate.
C. population rate.
D. sample rate.
E. hit rate.

8-115.
C
Comp.
Easy
p. 233

Which of the following is NOT an advantage of telephone surveys?
A. They are effective for getting answers to simple questions.
B. They usually can be conducted quite quickly.
C. They are especially good for getting confidential and personal information.
D. Response rates are high.
E. All of the above are advantage of telephone surveys.

8-116.
A
App.
Med.
p. 233

Which method of quantitative research would probably produce the best results when the questions are simple and require only quick "yes" or "no" answers?
A. telephone interviews.
B. focus group interviews.
C. mail questionnaires.
D. personal interviews.
E. observation.

8-117.
C
App.
Med.
p. 233

Business market researchers commonly use _____ because of their flexibility.
A. mail questionnaires
B. focus group interviews
C. personal interviews
D. telephone interviews
E. none of the above

8-118.
C
Comp.
Med.
p. 234

The observing method in marketing research:
A. uses personal interviews.
B. may require customers to change their normal shopping behavior.
C. is used to gather data without consumers being influenced by the process.
D. is not suitable for obtaining primary data.
E. All of the above.

8-119.
B
App.
Easy
p. 234

What would be the best way for the marketing manager of a supermarket to find out how consumers move through the store?
A. Have an interviewer go through the store with each customer.
B. Observe customers with hidden cameras.
C. Give customers a questionnaire after they have finished shopping.
D. Install checkout counters at the end of each aisle.
E. None of the above would be very good.

8-120.
A
App.
Hard
p. 234

Which of the following is NOT a good example of the observation method of marketing research?
A. The manager of a supermarket occasionally walks through the store to see what customers are doing.
B. A drugstore installs optical scanners at its checkout counters.
C. The owner of a shopping center puts a counting device at the entrance to count how many cars come in.
D. A store manager studies videotapes of consumers shopping in the store.
E. All of the above are good examples of observation research.

8-121.
D
Def.
Easy
p. 235

Ms. Connor-Jennings has agreed to participate in marketing research in which she will provide information about her purchases on an ongoing basis. She is probably part of a:
A. confidence interval.
B. statistical package.
C. contributor group.
D. consumer panel.
E. focus group.

8-122.
B
Def.
Easy
p. 235

Information is obtained on a continuing basis from the same respondents using a:
A. contributor group.
B. consumer panel.
C. responder group.
D. consumer experiment.
E. statistical package.

8-123.
B
App.
Med.
p. 236

A marketing manager wants to know if a "2 for 1" coupon will attract new customers. He will get the most persuasive results if he uses

A. a focus group to ask consumers if they like the idea.
B. an experimental method in which only some consumers get the coupon and the purchases of the two groups (with and without coupons) are compared.
C. personal interviewers to ask consumers how they will react.
D. a mail survey to ask consumers if they use coupons and why.
E. none of the above would allow the manager to determine if the coupon will help get new customers.

8-124.
D
Def.
Easy
p. 236

The _____ method is an information gathering method in which the responses of groups which are similar--except on the characteristic being tested--are compared.

A. focus group
B. random
C. observing
D. experimental
E. qualitative questioning

8-125.
A
App.
Easy
p. 236

Two similar groups of consumers are shown different magazines which include the same ad. Then each consumer is asked questions about the advertised product. This seems to be a description of

A. the experimental method.
B. a set of focus group interviews.
C. a consumer panel research project.
D. a set of personal interviews.
E. None of the above.

8-126.
D
Comp.
Easy
p. 237

Marketing research experiments

A. may be difficult to set up in real world situations.
B. may involve a combination of observing and questioning.
C. are often misunderstood by marketing managers, who don't like the idea of researchers experimenting with the business.
D. All of the above.
E. None of the above.

8-127.
D
Def.
Med.
p. 230-37

To get problem-specific data, a marketing researcher would use:

A. the experimental method.
B. a questioning method.
C. an observing method.
D. Any or all of the above.
E. Either A or B--but not C.

8-128.
A
Def.
Easy
p. 239

Statistical packages are:

A. easy-to-use computer programs that analyze data.
B. subscription research services that do quantitative research.
C. procedures used to be sure that a sample is random.
D. product packages that make it possible to collect data at checkout counters.
E. None of the above.

8-**129.**
A
Def.
Easy
p. 239

The total group a survey researcher is interested in is called the:
A. population.
B. sample.
C. confidence interval group.
D. representative group.
E. None of the above.

8-**130.**
D
Def.
Easy
p. 239

The part of the relevant population that is surveyed by a researcher is called the:
A. representative group.
B. the focal group.
C. target population.
D. sample.
E. confidence interval group.

8-**131.**
B
Def.
Easy
p. 239

The sampling method in which each member of the population has the same chance of being included in the sample is called:
A. representative sampling.
B. random sampling.
C. population sampling.
D. confidence sampling.
E. All of the above.

8-**132.**
C
Comp.
Med.
p. 239

Using a random sample
A. ensures that a representative sample will be obtained.
B. will ensure a good sample, even if the response rate is low.
C. tends to result in responses that are representative of the population.
D. All of the above are true.
E. None of the above is true.

8-**133.**
A
Comp.
Med.
p. 240

Using a random sample
A. makes it possible to calculate confidence intervals.
B. ensures validity of the survey results.
C. ensures that survey responses are representative of the population.
D. All of the above are true.
E. None of the above is true.

8-**134.**
C
Comp.
Med.
p. 240

By computing confidence intervals a researcher can:
A. have just as much confidence in an estimate from a small sample.
B. offset some of the problems of having a nonrandom sample.
C. estimate how precise her research results are likely to be.
D. All of the above are true.
E. None of the above is true.

8-**135.**
C
Def.
Easy
p. 240

Regarding an estimate from a survey, the range on either side of the survey result that is likely to contain the "true" value of the relevant population is called:
A. sample range.
B. accuracy range.
C. confidence interval.
D. validity interval.
E. population estimate.

8-**136.** The response rate to a survey affects
C
Comp.   A. who is in the population for a marketing research study.
Hard   B. whether a statistical package can be used to analyze the data.
p. 240   C. how representative the sample is.
    D. whether the sample is large enough that confidence intervals can be computed.
    E. All of the above are good answers.

8-**137.** The accuracy of quantitative research is affected by
D   A. the sampling procedure.
Comp.   B. the response rate.
Easy   C. the sample size.
p. 240   D. All of the above.
    E. None of the above.

8-**138.** _____ is concerned with whether the research data measures what it is
B   intended to.
Def.   A. Randomness
Easy   B. Validity
p. 241   C. Regularity
    D. Dependability
    E. Confidence

Chapter 9

Elements of Product Planning for Goods and Services

True-False Questions:

9-1.
False
p. 248-49

The "Product" area is concerned with what goods and services are produced, but not with decisions about installation, instructions on use, packaging, a brand name, a warranty, or after-sale service.

9-2.
True
p. 248

A "Product" should be thought of as potential customer satisfactions or benefits.

9-3.
True
p. 248

Product means the need-satisfying offering of a firm.

9-4.
False
p. 248-49

When comparing two similar products, the product with the most features is the higher quality product.

9-5.
True
p. 250

A "Product" might involve a physical good, a service, or a combination of the two.

9-6.
False
p. 250

A service is not a "Product" because services do not include any physical good.

9-7.
False
p. 251

Goods are intangible and services are tangible.

9-8.
True
p. 252

A product assortment is the set of all product lines and individual products that a firm sells.

9-9.
True
p. 253

There are two broad groups of product classes based on the type of customer that will use the product.

9-10.
False
p. 253

According to the text, the consumer product classes are based on why consumers use products.

9-11.
True
p. 253

The four groups of consumer products are: convenience products, shopping products, specialty products, and unsought products.

9-12.
True
p. 253

Products which a consumer needs but isn't willing to spend much time shopping for are convenience products.

9-13.
True
p. 253

Convenience products include staples, impulse products, and emergency products.

9-14.
True
p. 254

Consumer products which are bought often, routinely, and without much thought are staples.

9-15.
False
p. 254

Staples are consumer products which are sold in places like gourmet shops and health food stores, because convenience is not important to the customer.

9-16.
True
p. 254

Consumer products which a customer buys on sight as unplanned purchases, may have bought the same way before, and wants "right now" are impulse products.

9-17.
False
p. 254

Customers usually plan and shop for impulse products.

9-18.
True
p. 254

Emergency products are purchased only when the need is great and urgent, and therefore price is usually not very important.

9-19.
True
p. 254

Consumer products that a customer feels are worth the time and effort to compare with competing products are shopping products.

9-20.
True
p. 254

Shopping products that a customer sees as basically the same and wants at the lowest price are homogeneous shopping products.

9-21.
False
p. 255

Shopping products that a customer sees as basically the same and wants at the lowest price are heterogeneous shopping products.

9-22.
True
p. 255

Shopping products that a customer sees as different and wants to inspect for quality and suitability are heterogeneous shopping products.

9-23.
False
p. 255

Consumer products that a customer really wants and is willing to make a special effort to shop for and compare different possibilities are specialty products.

9-24.
False
p. 255

Shopping for a specialty product involves comparing the special features of different brands.

9-25.
False
p. 255

Specialty products are usually only purchased once-in-a-lifetime, so the customer must search extensively before buying.

9-26.
True
p. 255

Firms should try to show the value of unsought products through promotion because people do not want them or know that they are available.

9-27.
True
p. 255

Without promotion, unsought products will probably stay unsold.

9-28.
True
p. 255

Consumer products which offer really new ideas that potential customers don't know about yet are new unsought products.

9-29.
False
p. 255

Personal selling is important for new unsought products, but it tends not to be important for regularly unsought products.

9-30.
True
p. 256

For different people, the same product might be a convenience product, a shopping product, or a specialty product.

9-31.
False
p. 256

Product class does not vary by country.

9-32.
True
p. 256

The demand for business products derives from the demand for final consumer products.

9-33.
True
p. 256

Although the total industry demand for business products may be inelastic, the demand facing individual sellers may be extremely elastic.

9-34.
False
p. 256-57

Expense items are depreciated over many years, while capital items are charged off as they are used--usually in the year of purchase.

9-35.
False
p. 257

Business product classes are based on the way that buyers shop for and buy products, because there is much more shopping for business products compared to consumer products.

9-36.
True
p. 257

Business product classes are based on how buyers see products and how the products are to be used.

9-37.
True
p. 257

Installations are long-lasting capital items such as buildings and land rights, custom-made equipment, and standard equipment.

9-38.
False
p. 257

Installations are not bought very often, but the number of potential buyers at any particular time is usually quite large.

9-39.
False
p. 257-58

The main difference between installations and accessory equipment is that accessories are capital items while installations are expense items.

9-40.
False
p. 258

Capital items which are more expensive and longer-lived than installations are called accessory equipment.

9-41.
True
p. 258

Raw materials are unprocessed expense items such as farm products and natural products.

9-42.
True
p. 258

One of the important differences between raw materials and other business products is that raw materials usually have to be graded.

9-43.
True
p. 258

An important difference between raw materials and other business products is the need for grading.

9-44.
True
p. 258-59

Expense items which have had more processing than raw materials and become part of a finished product are component parts and materials.

9-45.
False
p. 258

Component parts usually require much processing to get them ready for assembly.

9-46.
True
p. 259

Supplies (business products) are expense items that do not become part of a final product.

9-47.
True
p. 259

The cost of handling a purchase order for operating supplies may be more that the cost of the purchase.

9-48.
True
p. 260

Professional services are usually expense items which support the operation of a firm.

9-49.
False
p. 260

For professional services which are needed only occasionally and require special skills, it is usually better for a firm to have its own employees provide them than to use outsiders.

9-50.
True
p. 260

"Branding" includes the use of trademarks and brand names to identify a product.

9-51.
False
p. 260

A trademark can be a word, but cannot be a symbol.

9-52.
True
p. 260

A service mark is the same as a trademark, except that it refers to a service offering.

9-53.
True
p. 261

Branding is more likely to be successful if the product is the best value for the price, and quality can be consistently maintained.

9-54.
True
p. 261

Branding would be more likely to be successful if dependable and widespread availability of a product is possible.

9-55.
True
p. 262

Brand familiarity means how well customers recognize and accept a company's brand.

9-56.
True
p. 262

Brand preference means customers usually choose the brand over other brands, perhaps out of habit or past experience.

9-57.
False
p. 262

Brand insistence means that customers usually choose one brand over other brands, perhaps out of habit or past experience.

9-58.
True
p. 263

Brand names that convey a positive image in one language may be meaningless in another.

9-59.
False
p. 263

Brand equity is likely to be lower if customers insist on buying a product and retailers are eager to stock it.

9-60.
True
p. 264

The Lanham Act spells out the exact method for protecting registered trademarks, but does not force firms to register their trademarks.

9-61.
True
p. 264

If a trademark is to be used in foreign markets, it is wise to register it under the Lanham Act.

9-62.
True
p. 264

Some nations require that a trademark be registered in its home country before it can be registered in a foreign country.

9-63.
True
p. 264

A marketing manager should make sure the firm's brand names do not become so familiar that they become common descriptive terms for certain kinds of products.

9-64.
True
p. 264

A firm can lose all rights to a brand name if the name becomes a common descriptive term for that kind of product.

9-65.
True
p. 264-65

Family brands may cut promotion costs because the goodwill attached to one or two products may help the others.

9-66.
False
p. 265

A licensed brand can be used by only one company.

9-67.
False
p. 265

There is no real reason for a firm to use individual brands rather than a family brand--except to avoid confusion.

9-68.
False
p. 265

It is usually necessary for a firm to use a family brand rather than individual brands if it plans to offer products at different quality and price levels to different target markets.

9-69.
True
p. 265

A product which has no brand other than the identification of the contents is a generic product.

9-70.
False
p. 265

Generic products account for a large percentage of grocery store sales in the U.S.

9-71.
False
p. 266

Dealer brands are brands created by producers.

9-72.
False
p. 266

Manufacturer brands are always advertised and distributed more widely than dealer brands.

9-73.
True
p. 266

The "battle of the brands" is the competition between dealer brands and manufacturer brands.

9-74.
False
p. 267

The "battle of the brands" hurts consumers by driving up prices.

9-75.
True
p. 268

Because packaged products are regularly seen in retail stores, a good package may give a firm more promotion effect than it could possibly afford with advertising.

9-76.
False
p. 268

Spending money to improve protective packaging may be necessary, but it usually results in higher total distribution costs for a firm's product.

9-77.
True
p. 268

Total distribution costs may increase because of packaging.

9-78.
False
p. 268

The universal product code has been opposed by large supermarket chains because it slows down the checkout process.

9-79.
True
p. 268

The Federal Fair Packaging and Labeling Act of 1966 requires that consumer products be clearly labeled in understandable terms.

9-80.
False
p. 268

The Federal Fair Packaging and Labeling Act of 1966 requires that firms in a product-market reduce the number of package sizes to three or fewer for any product.

9-81.
False
p. 269

It is illegal for a firm to use a package that cannot be recycled.

9-82.
True
p. 269

Unit-pricing means placing the price per ounce, or some other standard measure, on or near the product.

9-83.
True
p. 269

Even consumers who do not pay attention to unit pricing may benefit from the price competition it encourages.

9-84.
True
p. 270

A warranty explains what the seller promises about its product.

9-85.
True
p. 270

A warranty must be available for inspection before a purchase is made.

9-86.
False
p. 271

Customer service guarantees are becoming less common becauase service companies can't live up to their promises.

9-87.
False
p. 271

There's usually less risk in offering a service guarantee than a warranty on a physical product.

9-**88.**
False
p. 271

Most manufacturers would be wise to provide a strong warranty with their products, because customers like them and they are inexpensive to back up.

9-**89.**
True
p. 271

It may be economically impossible for small firms to offer strong warranties.

Multiple Choice Questions

9-**90.**
C
Def.
Med.
p. 248

"Product" means:
A. all the services needed with a physical good.
B. a physical good with all its related services.
C. the need-satisfying offering of a firm.
D. all of a firm's producing and distribution activities.
E. a well-packaged item with a well-advertised brand name.

9-**91.**
C
Def.
Easy
p. 248

According to the text, "product":
A. means a physical good.
B. includes all the elements of a marketing mix.
C. means the need-satisfying offering of a firm.
D. refers to goods but not services.
E. All of the above.

9-**92.**
B
Def.
Easy
p. 249

According to the text, product quality means that:
A. products are designed to meet demanding specifications.
B. a product satisfies a customer's requirements or needs.
C. there are not errors in the production process.
D. the product won't ever break.
E. None of the above is correct.

9-**93.**
D
Comp.
Med
p. 249

From a marketing perspective, product quality primarily depends on,
A. the price of a product.
B. a product working as it is supposed to work.
C. quality control procedures used during manufacturing.
D. the customer's specific requirements and needs.
E. the features of products offered by competitors.

9-**94.**
A
Comp.
Med.
p. 249

From a marketing perspective, a high quality copy machine is one that:
A. does a good job satisfying a customer's requirements or needs.
B. offers the most features.
C. is produced with the best materials.
D. has the longest warranty.
E. is designed and manufactured to last the longest.

9-**95.**
E
App.
Easy
p. 250

According to the text, which of the following is NOT a product?
A. space in Sassy Magazine sold to an advertiser
B. a Sony Discman
C. a Broadway musical play
D. the San Diego Zoo
E. All of the above are products.

9-**96.**
A
Def.
Med.
p. 250

"Product" means:
A. A physical good or service which offers potential customer satisfaction.
B. A physical good with all its related features.
C. The entire physical output of a firm.
D. All of the elements in a firm's marketing mix.
E. Something that has been produced, packaged, branded, and given a warranty.

9-**97.**
E
Comp.
Easy
p. 248-50

A "product" might include:
A. a brand name, a package, and a warranty.
B. instructions.
C. a service which does not include a physical good at all.
D. some physical item and its related features.
E. All of the above.

9-**98.**
E
App.
Easy
p. 248-50

Which of the following is a "product"?
A. a used car
B. a bus ride
C. a haircut
D. a dental exam
E. all of the above

9-**99.**
D
Def.
Easy
p. 252

A product assortment is:
A. something offered by manufacturers but not by retailers.
B. a particular product within a product line.
C. a set of products that are closely related.
D. the set of all product lines and individual products that a firm sells.
E. None of the above.

9-**100.**
D
Def.
Med.
p. 252

A company with a large product assortment might
A. have many product lines with little selection in each.
B. have a single product line.
C. have many individual products.
D. All of the above are true.
E. Only A and C are true.

9-**101.**
B
App.
Med.
p. 252

A large U.S. firm produces potato chips, shortening, dishwashing detergent, laundry detergent, shampoo, disposable diapers, and facial tissues. These are the firm's
A. product classes.
B. product assortment.
C. individual products.
D. marketing mix.
E. product line.

9-**102.**
E
Def.
Easy
p. 252

A product line is a set of individual products that are closely related in which of the following ways?
A. They are sold to the same target market.
B. They are produced and/or operate in a similar manner.
C. They are priced at about the same level.
D. They are sold through the same type of outlets.
E. Any or all of the above.

9-**103.**
E
App.
Easy
p. 252

Which of the following could be an example of a firm's product line?
A. coffees.
B. disposable diapers.
C. snow skis.
D. ski boots.
E. all of the above.

9-**104.**
E
App.
Med.
p. 252

Nike, Inc. markets several types of athletic shoes, along with clothing and fitness equipment. In other words, Nike has
A. product components.
B. a battle of the brands.
C. no product assortment.
D. many product classes.
E. several product lines.

9-**105.**
E
Def.
Med.
p. 252

Individual products:
A. are part of product lines but not product assortments.
B. may require their own marketing mixes.
C. are usually distinguished by brand, size, price, or some other characteristic.
D. All of the above.
E. Both B and C.

9-**106.**
D
App.
Med.
p. 252

Which of the following is the best example of an individual product?
A. 32-ounce boxes of Cheer and Tide.
B. 3 types of pears.
C. six brands of cookies.
D. 12 oz. size of Pert Plus.
E. all of the above.

9-**107.**
E
Comp.
Easy
p. 253

Regarding product classes,
A. Business product classes are based on how buyers think about them and how the products will be used.
B. Consumer product classes are based on how consumers think about and shop for products.
C. Compared to final customers, business customers do less shopping.
D. Products are classified by what type of customer will use them.
E. All of the above are true.

9-**108.**
E
App.
Easy
p. 253

Which of the following is NOT a business product?
A. a roll of sheet metal
B. a metal shelf system for storing inventory
C. a custom-built robot for welding metal
D. a pad of paper.
E. Any of the above could be a business product.

9-**109.** Consumer product classes are based on _____ , while business product
B classes are based on _____ .
Def. A. how the product is to be used, the price for the product
Easy B. how consumers shop for the product, how the product is to be used
p. 253 C. the price of the product, the quality of the product
  D. how the product is produced, how the product is sold
  E. how the product is sold, how the product is produced

9-**110.** According to the text, consumer product classes:
A A. are based on how consumers shop for products.
Comp. B. are interesting, but not helpful for planning marketing strategy.
Easy C. are based on how the products will be used.
p. 253 D. are based on the product features involved.
  E. can be broken down into goods, services, and ideas.

9-**111.** The text's consumer product classes are based on:
B A. each product's price level.
Def. B. the way consumers think about and shop for products.
Med. C. the channel(s) of distribution used for each product.
p. 253 D. the nature of the product and how it will be used.
  E. how the product is produced.

9-**112.** The text's consumer product classes are based on:
B A. the demand elasticity of the products.
Def. B. the way people think about and shop for products.
Easy C. the type of stores that sell the products.
p. 253 D. the quantity in which products will be purchased or used.
  E. how the sellers view the products.

9-**113.** Consumer product classes
D A. are based on how the product will be used.
Comp. B. are based primarily on how much effort is actually involved in making a
Med. purchase.
p. 253 C. suggest the type of marketing mix that should be used, but business product
  classes have little to do with the marketing mix that should be used.
  D. are based on how consumers think about and shop for products.
  E. None of the above is true.

9-**114.** Which of the following is NOT one of the consumer product classes discussed in the
B text?
Int. A. Unsought products
Easy B. Imitation products
p. 253 C. Shopping products
  D. Convenience products
  E. Specialty products

9-115.
B
Int.
Easy
p. 253

Which of the following is NOT one of the consumer product classes discussed in the text?
A. Unsought products
B. Innovative products
C. Shopping products
D. Convenience products
E. Specialty products

9-116.
A
Def.
Med.
p. 253

_____ are products a consumer needs but isn't willing to spend much time and effort shopping for.
A. Convenience products
B. Unsought products
C. Homogeneous shopping products
D. Specialty products
E. Heterogeneous shopping products

9-117.
A
Def.
Med.
p. 253

_____ are products a consumer needs but isn't willing to spend much time and effort shopping for.
A. Convenience products
B. Unsought products
C. Homogeneous shopping products
D. Utility products
E. Heterogeneous shopping products

9-118.
B
App.
Easy
p. 253

Which of the following would be a convenience product for most consumers?
A. Gold jewelry
B. Butter
C. Stereo TVs
D. Dress shoes
E. Bicycles

9-119.
D
Def.
Easy
p. 253

Convenience products include:
A. impulse products.
B. staple products.
C. emergency products.
D. All of the above.
E. Only A and C above.

9-120.
B
Comp.
Hard.
p. 254

Regarding consumer product classes, a convenience product is to an emergency product as
A. a staple is to an emergency product
B. a shopping product is to a heterogeneous shopping product
C. an unsought product is to a specialty product
D. a new unsought product is to a regularly unsought product
E. a specialty product is to a homogeneous shopping product

9-121.
A
Comp.
Hard
p. 254

Regarding the organization of the product classes, an impulse product is to an emergency product as

A. a new unsought product is to a regularly unsought product.
B. an installation is to a homogeneous shopping product.
C. an impulse product is to a convenience product.
D. a consumer product is to a business product.
E. a shopping product is to a specialty product.

9-122.
D
Def.
Med.
p. 254

If a consumer product is used regularly and usually bought frequently and routinely with little thought (although branding may be important), this product is:

A. a routine product.
B. a specialty product.
C. a homogeneous shopping product.
D. a staple product.
E. a casual product.

9-123.
A
Comp.
Hard
p. 254

Staple products:

A. need maximum exposure and widespread distribution at low cost.
B. need adequate representation in major shopping areas.
C. need widespread distribution but with assurance of preferred display.
D. need widespread distribution near probable points of use.
E. can have limited availability as long as display is good.

9-124.
A
Def.
Med.
p. 254

Impulse products:

A. are likely to gain or lose sales depending on where they're sold.
B. require a great deal of advertising.
C. are a specific type of specialty product.
D. are usually high in price.
E. All of the above are correct.

9-125.
D
App.
Med.
p. 254

Which of the following products in a supermarket is MOST likely to be an impulse product?

A. oranges.
B. bread.
C. frozen peas.
D. a child's toy.
E. shampoo.

9-126.
A
App.
Easy
p. 254

Which of the following products in a supermarket is LEAST likely to be an impulse product?

A. bread.
B. local newspaper.
C. camera film.
D. an ice cream cone.
E. flashlight batteries.

9-**127.**
B
Comp.
Med.
p. 254

Impulse products are:
A. products that potential customers do not want yet or know they can buy.
B. bought quickly--as unplanned purchases--because of a strongly felt need.
C. any products that consumers search for because of a strongly felt craving.
D. any convenience products that are bought often and routinely.
E. All of the above.

9-**128.**
A
App.
Med.
p. 254

While shopping in a local supermarket, Mime Abbott came upon an aisle display of cookies and had to have some--immediately. By the time she got to the checkout counter with the rest of her selections, all the cookies were gone. In this case, the cookies were:
A. an impulse product.
B. a staple product.
C. an unsought product.
D. very nutritious.
E. a consumption product.

9-**129.**
B
Comp.
Hard
p. 254

Impulse products:
A. can have limited availability as long as display is good.
B. need widespread distribution with display at point of purchase.
C. need enough exposure to facilitate price comparisons.
D. need adequate representation in major shopping areas.
E. need widespread distribution at low cost.

9-**130.**
B
Comp.
Easy
p. 254

Compared to other consumer products, the major distinguishing characteristic of emergency products is the customer's:
A. desire to negotiate for a "deal."
B. urgency to get the need satisfied.
C. willingness to shop around for a lower price.
D. interest in the brand name.
E. willingness to shop and compare.

9-**131.**
D
App.
Easy
p. 254

During a heavy rainstorm, Avery Battle slipped into a drugstore and bought an umbrella--just like the one he had at home--for $15.00 plus tax. In this case, the umbrella is:
A. a specialty product.
B. a shopping product.
C. an unsought product.
D. an emergency product.
E. an impulse product.

9-**132.**
D
Comp.
Hard
p. 254

Emergency products:
A. need adequate representation in major shopping areas.
B. need widespread distribution but with assurance of preferred display.
C. can have limited availability as long as display is good.
D. need widespread distribution near probable points of use.
E. need widespread distribution at low cost.

9-**133.**
B
Comp.
Hard
p. 254

Homogeneous shopping products:
A. need widespread distribution near probable points of sale.
B. need enough exposure to facilitate price comparison.
C. need widespread distribution with assurance of preferred display.
D. need widespread distribution at low cost.
E. None of the above is true.

9-**134.**
B
Def.
Easy
p. 254

Consumer products which customers see as basically the same and want to buy at the lowest price are called:
A. heterogeneous shopping products.
B. homogeneous shopping products.
C. comparison products.
D. unsought products.
E. convenience products.

9-**135.**
E
Def.
Med.
p. 254

When some customers see all competitors' offerings as basically the same and are willing to spend much time and effort to buy the item at the lowest price, the item is:
A. an analysis product.
B. a specialty product.
C. a staple product.
D. a heterogeneous shopping product.
E. a homogeneous shopping product.

9-**136.**
D
App.
Med.
p. 254

Harry Cronkite wants to buy an electric drill for some jobs around his home. Deciding that all such drills are similar, he reads all the advertisements in his Sunday paper in search of the best price. For Harry, these drills are:
A. a heterogeneous shopping product.
B. a staple product.
C. a specialty product.
D. a homogeneous shopping product.
E. an emergency product.

9-**137.**
A
Int.
Med.
p. 254-55

Having a competitive price is likely to
A. be more important for a homogeneous shopping product than for a specialty product.
B. be more important for a heterogeneous shopping product than for a homogeneous shopping product.
C. be more important for an emergency product than for a staple.
D. keep a product from falling into the "unsought" product class.
E. None of the above is true.

9-**138.**
A
Comp.
Hard
p. 254

Heterogeneous shopping products:
A. need adequate representation in major shopping areas near similar products.
B. need widespread distribution near probable points of sale.
C. need enough exposure to aid price comparison.
D. need widespread distribution at low cost.
E. need widespread distribution but with assurance of preferred display or counter position.

9-**139.**
E
Comp.
Hard
p. 254

Specialty products:
   A. need widespread distribution at low cost.
   B. need enough exposure to facilitate price comparison.
   C. need adequate representation near similar products.
   D. need widespread distribution near probable points of sale.
   E. can have limited availability.

9-**140.**
D
Comp.
Easy
p. 254-55

Which of the following is true regarding shopping products?
   A. Price is less important in the purchase of heterogeneous shopping products than homogeneous shopping products.
   B. Compared to heterogeneous shopping products, homogeneous shopping products are usually more standardized.
   C. Buyers usually expect more sales help or service with heterogeneous shopping products.
   D. All of the above are true.
   E. None of the above.

9-**141.**
B
Def.
Med.
p. 255

When final consumers are willing to spend much time and effort comparing quality and style--with brand and price being less important--the product is:
   A. an inspection product.
   B. a heterogeneous shopping product.
   C. a homogeneous shopping product.
   D. a specialty product.
   E. All of the above are correct.

9-**142.**
D
Comp.
Med.
p. 255

A consumer is most likely to want and expect help from a salesperson when shopping for
   A. a regularly unsought product.
   B. an impulse product.
   C. a staple.
   D. a heterogeneous shopping product.
   E. a homogeneous shopping product.

9-**143.**
B
App.
Med.
p. 255

Gary and Kim want to buy a 27-inch color TV. They look at several brands in several different stores before finally deciding on a Sony. This set was the most expensive model they saw, but they felt it had better colors and would be more reliable. In this case, this TV is:
   A. an impulse product.
   B. a heterogeneous shopping product.
   C. an emergency product.
   D. a specialty product.
   E. a homogeneous shopping product.

9-144.
E
App.
Hard
p. 254-55

Kari Athens was interested in buying a coffee pot to use at college and a cassette player for her sister's birthday present. At the local discount store, she compared prices on coffee pots and chose the cheapest. She read the product information on each cassette player and finally chose one with stereo headphones and a rechargeable battery. For Kari, the coffee pot was

    A. a convenience product, but the cassette player was a specialty product.
    B. a heterogeneous shopping product, but the cassette player was a staple.
    C. an impulse product, but the cassette player was a convenience product.
    D. a specialty product, but the cassette player was a heterogeneous shopping product.
    E. a homogeneous shopping product, but the cassette player was a heterogeneous shopping product.

9-145.
D
Def.
Easy
p. 255

A consumer product that a customer really wants - and is willing to make a special shopping effort to find - is

    A. a staple product.
    B. a convenience product.
    C. a heterogeneous shopping product.
    D. a specialty product.
    E. an emergency product.

9-146.
B
App.
Hard
p. 255

Ms. Templeton had Broyhill brand living room furniture and wanted to buy a particular chair of the same brand. She made a few calls to find a store that had the chair in stock. When she found one, she went there and purchased the chair. For Ms. Templeton, the chair was

    A. a homogeneous shopping product.
    B. a specialty product.
    C. an impulse product.
    D. a heterogeneous shopping product.
    E. an emergency product.

9-147.
B
App.
Med.
p. 255

Larry White won't buy any coffee except "Blue Mountain"--a relatively expensive type that few stores sell. He used to have to drive about 10 miles out of his way to buy it at a small shop--but now he has persuaded his local supermarket manager to handle this coffee. For him, this coffee is

    A. an emergency product.
    B. a specialty product.
    C. a staple product.
    D. an unsought product.
    E. a heterogeneous shopping product.

9-148.
B
App.
Med.
p. 255

Until recently, Larry White wouldn't buy any coffee except "Blue Mountain"--a relatively expensive type that few stores sell. He used to have to drive about 10 miles out of his way to buy it at a small shop. Then he was at a friend's home and tried an inexpensive brand of coffee sold by the local supermarket chain. Now he won't buy anything except that brand. For him, the supermarket coffee is

    A. an emergency product.
    B. a specialty product.
    C. a staple product.
    D. an unsought product.
    E. a heterogeneous shopping product.

9-**149.** Regarding specialty products, which of the following is TRUE?
B   A. Branding does not play an important role in purchasing specialty products.
Comp   B. It is a customer's willingness to search that makes it a specialty product.
Easy   C. Shopping for a specialty product involves much comparing of products.
p. 255 D. It is the extent of searching which the customer has to do that makes it a
           specialty product.
        E. All of the above are true.

9-**150.** Specialty products are consumer products which:
D   A. have elastic demand.
Comp.   B. very few customers want or can afford to buy.
Med.   C. are relatively expensive and purchased only rarely.
p. 255 D. consumers are willing to search for because they really want them.
        E. All of the above.

9-**151.** A specialty product
E   A. may not require much searching to find it, but the customer would be willing to
Def.   search if necessary.
Med.   B. may carry a well-recognized brand.
p. 255 C. may be frequently purchased.
        D. need not be an expensive item.
        E. All of the above.

9-**152.** Specialty products:
B   A. have a number of close substitutes.
Def.   B. are brands customers request by name.
Easy   C. are generally high in price.
p. 255 D. all of the above.
        E. none of the above.

9-**153.** Which of the following orderings suggests the amount of effort (from little to much)
B   that consumers are willing to spend in searching for the "right" product?
Int.   A. Heterogeneous shopping products, specialty products, unsought products
Hard   B. Convenience products, homogeneous shopping products, specialty products
p. 253-55 C. Unsought products, homogeneous shopping products, convenience products
        D. Staples, heterogeneous shopping products, unsought products
        E. Homogeneous shopping products, heterogeneous shopping products, staples

9-**154.** Regarding consumer products,
D   A. All unsought products remain unsought forever.
Int.   B. Convenience products are products which customers want to buy at the lowest
Hard   possible price.
p. 254-55 C. Price is not important for heterogeneous shopping products.
        D. Supermarkets may carry homogeneous shopping products.
        E. Specialty products must be searched for.

9-**155.**
B
Def.
Easy
p. 255

Consumer products which consumers do not yet want or know they can buy - and probably would not buy without special promotion even if they saw them - are called:
A. new brands of well-accepted staples.
B. unsought products.
C. heterogeneous shopping products.
D. emergency products.
E. homogeneous shopping products.

9-**156.**
E
App.
Med.
p. 255

Which of the following is an "unsought product"?
A. Gravestones aimed at "senior citizens."
B. A new type of "health food" produced by a new, small company.
C. Life insurance aimed at college students.
D. Encyclopedias aimed at new parents.
E. All of the above.

9-**157.**
E
Comp.
Med.
p. 255

Unsought products:
A. require wide distribution but little promotion.
B. are generally unprofitable.
C. should not be marketed.
D. All of the above are true.
E. None of the above is true.

9-**158.**
B
Comp.
Med.
p. 255

Personal selling is extremely important for sellers of:
A. specialty products.
B. regularly unsought products.
C. heterogeneous shopping products.
D. new unsought products.
E. homogeneous shopping products.

9-**159.**
E
App.
Med.
p. 256

A $50 consumer product which is purchased infrequently is:
A. an unsought product.
B. a convenience product.
C. a specialty product.
D. a shopping product.
E. It might be any of the above.

9-**160.**
E
App.
Easy
p. 256

If a consumer purchases a new watch, the watch is:
A. a specialty product.
B. a heterogeneous shopping product.
C. a homogeneous shopping product.
D. a convenience product.
E. it is not obvious - the watch could be any of the above.

9-**161.**
B
Int.
Med.
p. 256

Which of the following is usually NOT true about business products?
A. The demand curve for a particular industry is usually inelastic.
B. Demand for consumer products is derived from business products.
C. Suppliers may face almost pure competition.
D. Each product may be only a small part of the cost of a final product.
E. None of the above, i.e., all ARE true.

9-**162.**
B
Def.
Easy
p. 256

The fact that the demand for business products depends a lot on the demand for final consumer products is called:
A. primary demand.
B. derived demand.
C. diminishing demand.
D. elastic demand.
E. secured demand.

9-**163.**
C
Comp.
Hard
p. 256

Why might the demand for business products be INELASTIC, while the demand facing individual sellers of those products is extremely ELASTIC?
A. Because total demand for business products often exceeds supply.
B. Because most business producers use reciprocity in their buying.
C. Because the demand for business products is derived, and some industries have many sellers of essentially homogeneous products.
D. Because the industry demand is rising.
E. None of the above is true.

9-**164.**
D
App.
Hard
p. 256

VoiceSys, Inc. produces voice-mail switchboard systems used in large office buildings, hotels, and other facilities. VoiceSys is short of cash, but its products are so profitable and are selling so well that it has decided to buy more production equipment from one of the many suppliers that serve its industry. This example illustrates:
A. why demand for a particular seller's equipment may be quite elastic.
B. why installations may have to be leased or rented.
C. derived demand.
D. All of the above.
E. None of the above.

9-**165.**
B
App.
Hard
p. 256

VoiceSys, Inc. produces voice-mail switchboard systems used in large office buildings, hotels, and other facilities. VoiceSys's products are selling so well that it has decided to buy new equipment that will increase its production capacity. This example best illustrates
A. why the demand for a particular seller's equipment is inelastic.
B. derived demand.
C. why the industry demand for this kind of equipment is quite elastic.
D. that the market for installations is a "boom or bust" business.
E. All of the above are true.

9-**166.**
A
Int.
Med.
p. 256

Regarding the demand for business products,
A. Demand for business products is derived from the demand for consumer products.
B. The demand facing most individual firms is fairly inelastic.
C. Industry demand is generally highly elastic.
D. All of the above.
E. None of the above.

9-**167.**
B
App.
Med.
p. 256

"Derived demand" is best illustrated by the demand for:
A. tea as a substitute for coffee.
B. brick because of increasing demand for new homes.
C. fresh raspberries during the winter months.
D. CD players because of increasing interest in CD audio discs.
E. all of the above.

9-**168.**
A
App.
Med.
p. 257

Which of the following would probably be treated as a capital item by a large clothing manufacturer?
A. computer-controlled fabric cutting machines.
B. zippers.
C. cloth.
D. buttons.
E. none of the above.

9-**169** .
B
Def.
Easy
p. 256-57

Short-lived goods and services which are charged off as they are used--rather than depreciated over several years--are called:
A. nontaxable items.
B. expense items.
C. derived items.
D. durables.
E. capital items.

9-**170.**
B
Comp.
Med.
p. 257

A local copying service is buying a new kind of high speed color copier.
A. There will probably be more buying influences for the paper for the copier than for the copier.
B. The copier is likely to be purchased with a new-task buying process.
C. The copier will be depreciated as an expense item.
D. A and C are both true.
E. None of the above is true.

9-**171.**
E
App.
Med.
p. 257-58

Which of the following would be treated as an expense item for a children's clothing manufacturer?
A. cloth.
B. sewing needles.
C. buttons.
D. zippers.
E. all of the above.

9-**172.**
A
Comp.
Hard
p. 257

Federal tax rules affect business buying because:
A. capital item purchases can't be fully charged off to the current year's expenses.
B. expense items are depreciated over several years.
C. large purchases must be expensed in one year.
D. capital items are expensed in one year--making them less risky to buy.
E. expense items are very risky since they cannot be depreciated.

9-**173.**
E
Def.
Med.
p. 257

The text's business product classes are based on:
A. how buyers see products.
B. how the products are to be used.
C. the shopping behavior of the buyer.
D. All of the above.
E. Both A and B.

9-**174.**
B
Comp.
Med.
p. 257

Business product classes
A. are based on whether the demand curves are elastic or inelastic.
B. are based on how products will be used.
C. are based on the buying situation--whether the decision is new task, straight rebuy, or modified rebuy.
D. All of the above are true.
E. None of the above is true.

9-**175.**
C
Def.
Easy
p. 257

Which of the following is NOT one of the text's business product classes?
A. Raw materials
B. Component parts and materials
C. Specialty products
D. Professional services
E. Installations

9-**176.**
B
App.
Med.
p. 257

Carrier Corp. manufactures long-lived, custom-made equipment which its customers treat as capital items. Carrier's sales force faces much multiple-buying influence. Carrier's products, which do not become part of the customer's final product, are:
A. accessory equipment.
B. installations.
C. MRO items.
D. component parts.
E. operating supplies.

9-**177.**
A
Def.
Easy
p. 257

Installations:
A. are important long-lived capital items.
B. seldom involve multiple-buying influence.
C. are very large expense items for buyers as soon as they buy.
D. are purchased often.
E. are always custom-made.

9-**178.**
D
App.
Easy
p. 257

Multiple-buying influence would be most likely for:
A. Repair items
B. Accessories
C. Professional services
D. Installations
E. It would be equally likely for all of the above.

9-**179.**
A
Comp.
Med.
p. 257

Regarding installations, which is NOT true?
A. The number of potential customers at any one time is quite large.
B. Leasing installations may be attractive to buyers.
C. It is common for sellers to offer specialized services.
D. The buying needs of potential customers are basically economic.
E. Multiple buying influence is common.

9-**180.**
D
Comp.
Med.
p. 257

"Installation" products:
   A. are hardly ever leased because of the tax disadvantages.
   B. do not include buildings and land rights.
   C. justify multiple buying influence for custom-made equipment but not for standard equipment.
   D. such as custom-made equipment generally require special negotiations for each sale.
   E. All of the above are true.

9-**181.**
B
Comp.
Hard
p. 257

Accessory equipment:
   A. needs fair to widespread distribution for prompt delivery.
   B. needs fairly widespread and numerous contacts by experienced and sometimes technically trained personnel.
   C. needs very widespread distribution for prompt delivery.
   D. needs technical contacts to determine specifications required, but widespread contacts usually are not necessary.
   E. needs fairly widespread contacts with users.

9-**182.**
E
Def.
Easy
p. 258

_____ are capital items that cost less and are shorter-lived than installations.
   A. Supplies
   B. Staples
   C. Component parts
   D. Component materials
   E. Accessory equipment

9-**183.**
A
App.
Med.
p. 258

Sumitomo Bank, a large bank in southern California, has just purchased 120 high-speed telephone fax machines (costing about $1,300 each) to speed communications among its many offices. The purchase was made by the purchasing manager, who expects the machines to last about five years. In this case, the fax machines are:
   A. accessory equipment.
   B. MRO items.
   C. installations.
   D. component parts.
   E. professional services.

9-**184.**
A
Comp.
Med.
p. 258

Regarding accessory equipment, which of the following is NOT true?
   A. Multiple buying influence is less important in the purchase of an installation than with accessory equipment.
   B. There are more customers for accessory equipment than for installations.
   C. Specialized services are more important in the purchase of installations than accessories.
   D. There are more sellers of accessory equipment than of installations.
   E. All of the above ARE true.

9-**185.**
B
Int.
Med.
p. 258

Regarding business products,
A. derived demand has little affect on the market for accessory equipment.
B. sellers of accessory equipment usually must face more competitors than sellers of installations.
C. at any one time there are usually fewer target customers for accessories than for installations.
D. accessory equipment is not treated as a capital item.
E. special services and advice are more important with accessories than with installations.

9-**186.**
D
Comp.
Med.
p. 258

Compared to installations, accessory equipment
A. is usually less standardized.
B. involves more multiple-buying influence.
C. is an expense item instead of a capital item.
D. is sold to more target markets.
E. becomes part of the buyer's final product.

9-**187.**
E
App.
Easy
p. 258

Which of the following is NOT a business raw material?
A. logs.
B. coal.
C. wheat.
D. fish.
E. all of the above are examples.

9-**188.**
B
App.
Easy
p. 258

Which of the following is NOT a business raw material?
A. coal.
B. grease.
C. wheat.
D. fish.
E. logs.

9-**189.**
B
Comp.
Med.
p. 258

Raw materials are different from other business products in that:
A. buyers do not seek sources of supply.
B. they require more grading.
C. each seller's demand curve may be inelastic.
D. they never involve contract production arrangements.
E. pricing decisions for farm products are more complicated.

9-**190.**
B
App.
Easy
p. 258

Logs, fish, cotton, and strawberries can all be:
A. supplies.
B. raw materials.
C. component parts.
D. capital items.
E. accessories.

9-**191.**
E
App.
Easy
p. 258

Procter and Gamble buys unprocessed logs which are handled as little as needed to move them to its plant. Eventually, they become part of P&G's disposable diapers and are considered an expense item on P&G's income statement. For P&G, logs are:
A. farm products
B. supplies
C. component parts
D. component materials
E. raw materials

9-**192.**
D
Def.
Easy
p. 258

Raw materials
A. are treated as expense items.
B. are unprocessed but eventually become part of a final physical good.
C. include both farm products and natural products.
D. All of the above are true.
E. B and C are true.

9-**193.**
C
Def.
Easy
p. 258

A product which becomes part of a buyer's final product and comes finished and ready for assembly is called:
A. a raw material.
B. a component material.
C. a component part.
D. accessory equipment.
E. an installation.

9-**194.**
C
App.
Easy
p. 259

Which of the following is NOT a component material?
A. paper.
B. copper wire.
C. copper ore.
D. copper screens.
E. None of the above, i.e., all are component materials.

9-**195.**
B
App.
Med.
p. 258

Target Electric produces electric motors that power refrigerators, air condition units, washing machines, and many other electric appliances produced by various manufacturers. Target Electric is selling
A. raw materials.
B. component parts.
C. MRO items
D. accessory equipment.
E. installations.

9-**196.**
A
App.
Med.
p. 258

A firm which makes stereo radios and CD players for car manufacturers who install them directly in their new cars is selling:
A. component parts.
B. supplies.
C. component materials.
D. installations.
E. accessory equipment.

9-**197.**
B
App.
Med.
p. 258

A firm which makes special batteries that boat and motorcycle manufacturers buy and install directly in their new boats and cycles is selling:
  A. supplies.
  B. component parts.
  C. component materials.
  D. installations.
  E. accessory equipment.

9-**198.**
B
Def.
Easy
p. 259

A product which becomes part of a buyer's final product, and still requires more processing is called:
  A. a supply.
  B. a component material.
  C. a component part.
  D. a raw material.
  E. an installation.

9-**199.**
D
Comp.
Hard
p. 259

Regarding component parts,
  A. the original equipment market and the replacement market for component parts are typically separate target markets.
  B. a product originally sold as a component part may become a consumer product when sold in the "replacement market."
  C. component buyers want dependable suppliers.
  D. All of the above are true.
  E. None of the above is true.

9-**200.**
E
App.
Med.
p. 259

Bridgestone manufactures tires which truck producers buy and install on their trucks. This company
  A. sells installations for which multiple buying influence is likely to be quite important.
  B. is likely to have good opportunities in the "after market."
  C. is selling to the OEM market.
  D. All of the above are true.
  E. Both B and C are true.

9-**201.**
B
App.
Easy
p. 259

Ray Milano is a purchasing agent for Carson Mfg. Co. He regularly buys items such as nails, light bulbs, brooms, and sweeping compounds. In other words, he buys:
  A. components.
  B. supplies.
  C. installations.
  D. professional services.
  E. accessory equipment.

9-**202.**
A
Def.
Med.
p. 259

"MRO items" are:
  A. supplies.
  B. natural products.
  C. modified rebuy orders.
  D. accessory equipment.
  E. component parts and materials.

9-**203.**
B
Def.
Easy
p. 259

Business products which are expense items, necessary and continually used up, but which do not become part of the buyer's final product are:
  A. component materials.
  B. supplies.
  C. component parts.
  D. raw materials.
  E. accessory equipment.

9-**204.**
B
App.
Med.
p. 259

When business buyers purchase items such as grease, electricity, typing paper, and paper clips, they are buying:
  A. accessory equipment.
  B. operating supplies.
  C. components.
  D. repair supplies.
  E. maintenance supplies.

9-**205.**
D
Comp.
Hard
p. 259

Regarding business supplies, which of the following is NOT true?
  A. Maintenance items are to business buyers as convenience products are to final consumers.
  B. Supplies do not become part of a final product, but they are expense items.
  C. Buyers of important operating supplies are likely to be particularly concerned about dependability.
  D. Operating supplies are frequently called "accessories."
  E. A seller of repair supplies is likely to face fewer competitors than a seller of operating supplies.

9-**206.**
E
Comp.
Med.
p. 259

Regarding supplies,
  A. new-task buying is typical with most purchases.
  B. only one supplier is generally available.
  C. branding is not important for maintenance and small operating supplies.
  D. All of the above are true.
  E. None of the above is true.

9-**207.**
B
Comp.
Hard
p. 257

Operating supplies typically:
  A. need technical and experienced personal contacts, probably at top-management level.
  B. need widespread distribution or prompt delivery.
  C. need technical contacts to determine specifications required, but widespread contacts usually are not necessary.
  D. need skillful personal selling by producer.
  E. None of the above is correct.

9-**208.**
D
Comp.
Med.
p. 259-60

Regarding business products, which of the following is NOT true?
  A. Availability may be more important than low price to a buyer of repair items.
  B. Quality of service may be more important than low price to a buyer of professional services.
  C. A broad product assortment may be more important than low price to a buyer of supply items.
  D. All of the above are true.
  E. None of the above is true.

9-**209.**
E
App.
Easy
p. 260

Anne Walden is a management consultant who helps manufacturers improve their quality-control procedures for new products. Walden is selling:
    A. supplies.
    B. components.
    C. accessories.
    D. MROs.
    E. professional services.

9-**210.**
E
Comp.
Med.
p. 260

Business professional services:
    A. may not be purchased outside the firm if they are needed regularly.
    B. support a firm's operations.
    C. are offered by a growing number of specialists.
    D. are generally treated as expense items.
    E. All of the above are true.

9-**211.**
E
Def.
Easy
p. 258-60

Which of the following business products are usually treated as expense items?
    A. component parts and materials
    B. raw materials
    C. professional services
    D. supplies
    E. all of the above

9-**212.**
D
Int.
Hard
p. 260

Which of the following is(are) TRUE?
    A. "Service mark" refers to all means of product identification.
    B. A "trademark" must be attached to a product to be legally protected.
    C. "Branding" refers to the use of symbols to identify a product--but does not include brand names.
    D. "Brand name" is a word, letter, or group of words or letters.
    E. All of the above are true.

9-**213.**
A
Int.
Hard
p. 260

Which of the following is(are) TRUE?
    A. A "service mark" is to a service what a "trademark" is to a physical good.
    B. "Trademark" refers to all means of product identification.
    C. A "trademark" must be attached to a product to be legally protected.
    D. All of the above are true.
    E. None of the above are true.

9-**214.**
E
Def.
Easy
p. 260

A _____ is a word, letter, or group of words or letters.
    A. UPC
    B. FTC
    C. trademark
    D. SIC
    E. brand name

9-**215.**
D
Comp.
Easy
p. 260

Branding is good for some CONSUMERS because it:
    A. makes shopping easier.
    B. provides dependable guides to product quality.
    C. helps assure regular satisfaction.
    D. All of the above.
    E. None of the above.

9-216.
E
Comp.
Easy
p. 260

Branding can help BRANDERS because it:
A. may lower promotion costs.
B. can improve the company's image.
C. encourages repeat buying.
D. may develop customer loyalty.
E. All of the above.

9-217.
D
Comp.
Med.
p. 261

Branding:
A. is especially helpful with a low quality product.
B. is handled by manufacturers, but not middlemen.
C. helps consumers, but it is bad for the firm because it increases expenses.
D. is more likely to be successful if demand for the general product class is strong enough to allow a profitable price.
E. None of the above is true.

9-218.
B
Comp.
Med.
p. 261

Which of the following is NOT favorable to successful branding?
A. Consistent quality can be maintained.
B. Access to favorable shelf locations is very limited.
C. Economies of scale should be possible.
D. The product is easy to identify by brand or trademark.
E. Dependable and widespread availability should be possible.

9-219.
A
App.
Med.
p. 261

Which of the following would NOT be favorable for successful branding?
A. Product should be hard to identify by brand or trademark.
B. Widespread availability in the market.
C. Economies of scale in production and distribution.
D. The product should offer the best value for the price.
E. Product quality should be easy to maintain.

9-220.
B
App.
Easy
p. 261

Which of the following would NOT be favorable to successful branding?
A. The product offers superior customer value
B. Product quality fluctuates due to variations in raw materials
C. Dependable and widespread availability
D. Economies of scale in production
E. Favorable shelf locations are available

9-221.
B
Comp.
Hard
p. 261

Which of the following statements about branding is TRUE?
A. Brands were originally created by royal decree.
B. Patent medicine manufacturers were the earliest and most aggressive brand promoters in the U.S.
C. Customers are willing to buy by brand only when it assures "top quality."
D. All of the above are true.
E. None of the above is true.

9-222.
C
Comp.
Med.
p. 262

Which of the following statements about branding is TRUE?

A. The earliest and most aggressive brand promoters in America were clothing importers.
B. Branding provides product identification for sellers but usually is not important to consumers.
C. What brand is familiar often varies from one country to another.
D. All of the above.
E. None of the above.

9-223.
B
Def.
Easy
p. 262

_____ means potential customers won't buy a brand--unless its current image is changed.

A. Brand preference
B. Brand rejection
C. Brand insistence
D. Brand recognition
E. Brand nonrecognition

9-224.
D
App.
Med.
p. 262

Dusty Moore has never owned a JVC TV, but his parents owned one and were not at all satisfied. As a result, Dusty won't even consider buying an JVC. As far as Dusty is concerned, JVC has achieved brand _____.

A. preference.
B. recognition.
C. nonrecognition.
D. rejection.
E. insistence.

9-225.
C
App.
Easy
p. 262

Laurie Owens visits the local Healthy Glow spa, but dislikes the dirty dressing area and refuses to go back. This is an example of

A. reciprocity.
B. trademarking.
C. brand rejection.
D. heterogeneous shopping.
E. brand nonrecognition.

9-226.
A
Def.
Easy
p. 262

_____ means a brand is not recognized by final customers at all.

A. Brand nonrecognition
B. Brand rejection
C. Brand insistence
D. Brand recognition
E. Brand preference

9-227.
A
App.
Hard
p. 262

Nonrecognition of the brand name of a firm's product is likely to be LEAST important for:

A. Coal
B. Photographic film
C. Lubricating oils for machinery
D. Cold tablets
E. Replacement auto repair parts

9-**228.**   _____ means potential customers remember a particular brand.
D
Def.   A. Brand preference
Easy   B. Brand non-recognition
p. 262   C. Brand insistence
          D. Brand recognition
          E. Brand rejection

9-**229.**   Connie Seagroves is shopping for a new pair of jeans. She has had good experiences
D   with Chic jeans in the past and is looking for Chic now. She probably will buy Chic if
App.   she finds some that are at least as good-looking as competitive jeans. This is a good
Easy   example of:
p. 262   A. brand rejection.
          B. brand recognition.
          C. brand remembrance.
          D. brand preference.
          E. brand insistence.

9-**230.**   Kaye Dimmig usually buys Prell shampoo because she likes its smell. But this morning
A   her local drugstore was out of Prell, so she decided to buy another highly advertised
App.   brand that was on sale because she really needed to wash her hair that night. For
Med.   Kaye, Prell has probably achieved brand:
p. 262   A. preference.
          B. insistence.
          C. nonrecognition.
          D. rejection.
          E. extinction.

9-**231.**   _____ means target customers will generally choose a particular brand over
B   other brands--perhaps out of habit or past experience.
Def.   A. Brand nonrecognition
Easy   B. Brand preference
p. 262   C. Brand insistence
          D. Brand rejection
          E. Brand recognition

9-**232.**   Steve Joyner read a review about a new computer program that appealed to him very
B   much. He decided to try to find the program. However, the new program was in short
App.   supply--although other brands with similar features were available. Steve had to try
Med.   seven shops before he finally found the program in stock. For Steve, this program
p. 262   achieved brand:
          A. preference.
          B. insistence.
          C. rejection.
          D. nonrecognition.
          E. recognition.

9-**233.** _____ means potential customers insist on a firm's branded product and are
A willing to search for it.
Def. A. Brand insistence
Easy B. Brand preference
p. 262 C. Brand nonrecognition
D. Brand rejection
E. Brand recognition

9-**234.** Which of the characteristics of a good brand name is missing in the following proposed
E name: "Gnucheo" candy?
App. A. Simple
Med. B. Short
p. 263 C. Not offensive
D. Always timely
E. Easy to pronounce

9-**235.** Applying the text's list of characteristics of a good brand name, which of the following
B would be the poorest example of a good brand name?
App. A. Pizza Hut.
Easy B. Jurassic Chewing Gum.
p. 263 C. DieHard flashlights.
D. General Electric TVs.
E. L'eggs hosiery.

9-**236.** Which of the following statements is true?
E A. Consumer demand for a specific brand at a profitable price helps build brand
Comp. equity.
Easy B. Brand equity is likely to be higher if retailers are eager to stock the brand.
p. 263 C. The value of a brand to its current owner is called brand equity.
D. It is usually difficult and expensive to build brand recognition.
E. All of the above are true.

9-**237.** Trademarks
A A. can be legally protected in the U.S. under the Lanham Act.
Comp. B. cannot be registered with a government agency in the U.S.
Easy C. are legally protected in the United States, but not in any other countries.
p. 264 D. and trademark infringement are aggressively policed by a special agency of the
U.S. Government.
E. None of the above is true.

9-**238.** Which of the following statements about trademarks is TRUE?
E A. Trademarks must always be registered in their home country only.
Comp. B. In the U.S., common law protects the rights of the owners of brand names and
Hard trademarks.
p. 264 C. The Lanham Act requires that all trademarks be registered.
D. Registering under the Lanham Act is often a first step to protecting a trademark
to be used in foreign markets.
E. Both B and D are true.

9-**239.**
A
Comp.
Med.
p. 264

The law which focuses on the protection of trademarks and brand names is
A. the Lanham Act.
B. the Magnuson-Moss Act.
C. the Uniform Product Code Act.
D. the Federal Fair Packaging and Labeling Act.
E. None of the above.

9-**240.**
C
Comp.
Hard
p. 264

Registering under the Lanham Act:
A. does not protect a trademark in international markets.
B. is required for all trademarks and brand names.
C. may not stop a brand name from becoming public property.
D. means the federal government will protect the brand name or trademark.
E. All of the above are true.

9-**241.**
B
App.
Med.
p. 264

A trademark or brand name can become public property if:
A. the owner doesn't renew the registration each year.
B. it becomes a common descriptive word for the product.
C. the owner doesn't register it under the Lanham Act.
D. it is sold in international markets.
E. All of the above.

9-**242.**
A
Def.
Easy
p. 264

A producer that is selling all its products under one brand name is using
_____ brand.
A. a family
B. a generic
C. a licensed
D. a national
E. an individual

9-**243.**
D
App.
Med.
p. 264

A producer of high quality stereo component equipment has developed a new line of very inexpensive, low quality "rack systems" to sell through discount stores. It probably should not use its current _____ brand for the new line.
A. dealer
B. licensed
C. middleman
D. family
E. generic

9-**244.**
E
Comp.
Med.
p. 264-65

Use of family brands
A. may involve several firms--if one licenses its brand.
B. is common among both producers and middlemen.
C. can provide customers with cues about the quality of new products.
D. can be efficient, since the brand name will carry over in the firm's advertising.
E. All of the above are true.

9-**245.**
E
App.
Easy
p. 264-65

Sears uses a _____ brand when it uses the same brand name for several products. In contrast, General Motors, by using different brands for each car line, uses _____ brands.
   A. individual, generic
   B. generic, family
   C. manufacturer, dealer
   D. national, local
   E. family, individual

9-**246.**
B
App.
Easy
p. 265

Which of the following would be MOST LIKELY to use individual brands rather than a family brand for its products?
   A. Manufacturer of knives and scissors for "top quality" market
   B. Manufacturer of canned pet food and sandwich spread for final consumers
   C. Manufacturer of sweeping compounds, brooms, and mops for business firms
   D. Manufacturer of flour for the "mass market"
   E. Manufacturer of packaged potato chips and crackers.

9-**247.**
A
App.
Easy
p. 264-66

Sears' Kenmore brand of appliances sold in all Sears stores illustrates two kinds of brands.
   A. dealer and family brands.
   B. local and national brands.
   C. generic and family brands.
   D. licensed and dealer brands.
   E. manufacturer and family brands.

9-**248.**
A
Def.
Easy
p. 265

Products which have no brand other than the identification of their contents are called
   A. generic products.
   B. local brands.
   C. regional brands.
   D. licensed products.
   E. dealer brands.

9-**249.**
E
Def.
Easy
p. 266

"Manufacturer brands" are:
   A. also called family brands.
   B. often called private brands.
   C. called licensed brands.
   D. those having national distribution.
   E. sometimes called national brands.

9-**250.**
C
Int.
Hard
p. 266

Which of the following is true?
   A. Manufacturer brands usually have national distribution while dealer brands are only distributed locally.
   B. Dealer brands are always priced lower than manufacturer brands.
   C. Dealer brands may be distributed as widely or more widely than many manufacturer brands.
   D. Dealer brands are distributed only by chain-store retailers.
   E. All of the above are true.

9-**251.**   A "dealer brand" is sometimes called a _____ brand.
D   A. national
Def.   B. local
Easy   C. manufacturer
p. 266   D. private
                        E. regional

9-**252.**   Dealer brands, compared to manufacturer brands, usually offer wholesalers and
B   retailers:
Comp.   A. less risk.
Hard   B. higher gross margins.
p. 266   C. faster turnover at reduced selling costs.
                        D. products which are presold to target customers.
                        E. more prestige.

9-**253.**   Food Lion (a large supermarket chain that emphasizes "low prices") sells a dealer
C   brand of frozen green beans. Here,
App.   A. the producer of the green beans probably does a lot of advertising.
Med.   B. a trademark cannot be used.
p. 266   C. a similar manufacturer brand is likely to be given less shelf space.
                        D. the price to the consumer will probably be higher than for competing
                             manufacturer brands.
                        E. None of the above.

9-**254.**   The current status of the "battle of the brands" is that:
E   A. dealer brands will seek narrower distribution in the future.
Comp.   B. retailers now control the marketplace.
Med.   C. the vast majority of consumers clearly prefer manufacturer brands over dealer
p. 267   brands.
                        D. manufacturers are gaining on middlemen.
                        E. competition has reduced the gap in prices.

9-**255.**   The "battle of the brands" refers to competition between:
A   A. manufacturers and middlemen.
Def.   B. retailers and wholesalers.
Easy   C. retailers and other retailers.
p. 266   D. wholesalers and other wholesalers.
                        E. manufacturers and other manufacturers.

9-**256.**   A carefully designed package may:
E   A. raise total distribution cost.
Comp.   B. provide more "promotion" effect--and at a lower cost--than advertising.
Med.   C. enhance the product by making it easier or safer to use.
p. 267-68   D. help middlemen by using a universal product code on the label.
                        E. All of the above are true.

9-**257.**
E
Comp.
Med.
p. 267-68

Packaging
A. can serve as a useful enhancement tool.
B. can increase costs to the consumer.
C. can serve as a useful promotional tool.
D. is concerned with protecting the product in shipping and on the shelf.
E. All of the above are true.

9-**258.**
E
Comp.
Easy
p. 267-68

Packaging
A. objectives should primarily focus on promoting the product at the point of purchase.
B. costs as a percentage of selling price vary little.
C. decisions should be based on what package will result in the lowest possible cost to the consumer.
D. All of the above are true.
E. None of the above is true.

9-**259.**
D
Comp.
Med.
p. 268

A good marketing manager knows that:
A. packaging suppliers are often a poor source of information.
B. underpackaging generally costs less than overpackaging.
C. packaging costs should be kept to a minimum.
D. good packaging can tie the product to the rest of a marketing strategy.
E. All of the above are true.

9-**260.**
B
Comp.
Hard
p. 267-68

Which of the following statements about packaging is TRUE?
A. Better packaging almost always increases total distribution cost.
B. A package should satisfy not only the needs of consumers but also those of middlemen customers.
C. A package doesn't have much promotion impact at retail stores.
D. Packaging can increase sales--but it cannot create a new product.
E. All of the above are true.

9-**261.**
C
Int.
Hard
p. 268

Which of the following statements about packaging is TRUE?
A. The number of package sizes for similar products from different manufacturers is increasing dramatically, because most firms realize that this makes direct comparisons among brands harder.
B. There is very little government regulation of packaging, except for drug products.
C. Putting universal product codes on packages helps retailers more than producers.
D. All of the above are true.
E. None of the above is true.

9-**262.**
A
Comp.
Med.
p. 268

A "universal product code" (UPC):
A. identifies a product with a mark which can be "read" by electronic scanners.
B. was required by the Federal Fair Packaging and Labeling Act.
C. slows down the retail checkout process.
D. involves placing the price per ounce on or near the product.
E. All of the above are true.

9-**263.**
D
Def.
Easy
p. 268

The Federal Fair Packaging and Labeling Act:
- A. was created due to consumer criticism of packaging and labeling.
- B. calls on government agencies and industry to try to reduce the number of packaging sizes.
- C. requires that consumer goods be clearly labeled in understandable terms.
- D. all of the above.
- E. A and B only.

9-**264.**
A
Comp.
Hard
p. 268

The Federal Fair Packaging and Labeling Act:
- A. requires that consumer goods be clearly labeled in understandable terms--to give more information.
- B. requires informative labeling of food products regarding nutrients, taste and texture.
- C. requires "unit-pricing."
- D. requires the use of universal product codes.
- E. All of the above.

9-**265.**
B
Comp.
Med.
p. 270

The national law which is primarily concerned with regulating product warranties is
- A. the Lanham Act.
- B. the Magnuson-Moss Act.
- C. the Uniform Product Code Act.
- D. the Federal Fair Packaging and Labeling Act.
- E. None of the above.

9-**266.**
D
Def.
Med.
p. 270

The Magnuson-Moss Act:
- A. requires that all warranties be "full."
- B. says that all firms must offer written warranties for all products.
- C. requires that all warranties cover at least a one-year period.
- D. says that producers must provide a clearly written warranty if they choose to offer any warranty.
- E. All of the above.

9-**267.**
E
Comp.
Easy
p. 270

If a firm offers a written warranty, it
- A. must be labeled either "full" or "limited."
- B. must be available to buyers before the sale.
- C. shouldn't be "deceptive" or "unfair" per FTC guidelines.
- D. may help create a new strategy.
- E. All of the above are true.

9-**268.**
D
Comp.
Easy
p. 271

If a firm offers a service guarantee, it
- A. can be effective in creating repeat customers.
- B. takes on more risk than offering a warranty on a physical product.
- C. can be expensive if its employees are apathetic.
- D. All of the above are true.
- E. Only A and C are true.

Chapter 10

Product Management and New-Product Development

True-False Questions:

10-1.
False
p. 276
The product life cycle concept is concerned with planning for product recycling to protect the environment.

10-2.
True
p. 276
The product life cycle is the four stages a new product idea goes through from beginning to end.

10-3.
True
p. 276
Market introduction, market growth, market maturity, and sales decline are the four stages of the product life cycle.

10-4.
False
p. 276
During the various stages of the product life cycle, the attitudes and needs of target customers do not change.

10-5.
False
p. 276
Sales and profits generally decrease continually throughout the product life cycle.

10-6.
True
p. 277
The market introduction stage of the product life cycle is usually marked by losses, as money is being invested in the hope of future profits.

10-7.
False
p. 277
In the market growth stage of the product life cycle, firms usually earn smaller profits than they did in the market introduction stage because new competitors enter the market.

10-8.
True
p. 277
During the market growth stage of the product life cycle, industry profits usually reach their peak and begin to decline.

10-9.
False
p. 277
The market maturity stage of the product life cycle has very low promotion expenditures, little price competition, and rising industry profits.

10-10.
True
p. 277
Industry profits usually decline steadily during the market maturity stage of the product life cycle.

10-**11.**
False
p. 278

The market maturity stage of the product life cycle rarely lasts more than one or two months.

10-**12.**
False
p. 278

During the sales decline stage of the product life cycle, no firm can earn a profit.

10-**13.**
True
p. 278

Product life cycles describe industry sales and profits within a particular product-market, and not the sales and profits of individual products or brands.

10-**14.**
False
p. 278

The product life cycle shows that sales of an individual firm's product follows a general pattern--which is very useful for marketing strategy planning.

10-**15.**
True
p. 278

The sales and profits of an individual brand may or may not follow the life cycle pattern of the product idea.

10-**16.**
True
p. 278

A product idea may be in different life-cycle stages in different markets.

10-**17.**
True
p. 278

A firm may introduce or withdraw a product during any stage of the product life cycle.

10-**18.**
True
p. 279

It's possible for a firm with a mature product in the U.S. to experience new growth with the same product in international markets.

10-**19.**
True
p. 279

To fully understand the nature of competition and the speed of the relevant product life cycle, it is important not to define a market too narrowly.

10-**20.**
True
p. 280

The more narrowly we define a product-market, the shorter the product life cycle because improved product ideas come along to replace the old.

10-**21.**
False
p. 280

The length of each stage in the product life cycle is set.

10-**22.**
False
p. 280

The product life cycle concept tells a manager how long each stage of the cycle will last.

10-**23.**
False
p. 280

The smaller the comparative advantage of a new product over those already on the market, the faster its sales will grow.

10-24.
True
p. 280

Sales growth is faster when a new product is easy to use and its advantages are easy to communicate.

10-25.
True
p. 280

Sales growth is faster when the product can be used on a trial basis.

10-26.
False
p. 280

Sales growth is usually faster when the product is incompatible with the past values and experience of the target market.

10-27.
False
p. 281

In general, product life cycles appear to be getting longer in recent years.

10-28.
False
p. 281

Having a patent on a new product provides very strong protection in slowing down competitors.

10-29.
True
p. 281

Firms should try to develop marketing mixes that make the most of the market growth stage of the product life cycle--when profits are highest.

10-30.
True
p. 281

The stage of the product life cycle in which competitors are most likely to introduce product improvements is the market growth stage.

10-31.
True
p. 282

Fashion changes are a luxury that most people in less-developed economies can't afford.

10-32.
True
p. 283

A fad cycle is shorter than a fashion cycle.

10-33.
False
p. 283

The probable length of the product life cycle has little effect on strategy planning.

10-34.
True
p. 283

Marketing strategy planning for a product depends on where the product is in its life cycle and how fast it is moving to the next stage.

10-35.
False
p. 284

When introducing a really new product, the marketer should be concerned about building channels of distribution, but not about promotion.

10-36.
True
p. 284

How quickly a new product will be accepted by customers and how quickly competitors will follow with their own version of a product are important factors when planning the best strategy for a new product.

10-**37.**
False
p. 287

The strategies for all stages of the product life cycle should be growth strategies.

10-**38.**
True
p. 287

If the prospects in some product-market are poor, a firm may need a "phase out" strategy.

10-**39.**
True
p. 288

A product that is new in any way for the company concerned is a new product, according to the text.

10-**40.**
False
p. 288

The FTC places no restriction on the length of time a product can be called "new."

10-**41.**
True
p. 288

To be called "new" according to the FTC, a product must be entirely new or changed in a functionally significant or substantial respect.

10-**42.**
False
p. 289

The risks and costs of failure in new-product development are minor when one considers the likely rewards.

10-**43.**
True
p. 289

Experts estimate that 70-80 percent of all new consumer packaged goods brands fail.

10-**44.**
True
p. 290

A new-product development process helps make sure that new ideas for products are carefully studied and good ideas are marketed profitably.

10-**45.**
False
p. 290

The first step in new-product development is evaluating ideas.

10-**46.**
True
p. 290

In the new-product development process discussed in the text, the burden is on the new-product idea to prove itself or be rejected.

10-**47.**
True
p. 291-92

A "deficient" product is one which provides low immediate satisfaction and low long-run welfare for consumers.

10-**48.**
False
p. 292

When planning new products, managers need not be too concerned about safe design because it is each consumer's responsibility to decide what products are safe to buy and use.

10-**49.**
True
p. 292

If an individual is injured by a defective or unsafely designed product, the seller's legal obligation to pay damages is called product liability.

10-50.
True
p. 292

Relative to most other countries, the U.S. has very strict product liability standards.

10-51.
False
p. 293

Compared to the U.S., Japan makes it even easier for consumers (and their lawyers) to bring product liability suits against a producer.

10-52.
False
p. 295

Even in a full-scale market test, the firm is testing only the product, not the whole marketing mix.

10-53.
True
p. 295

Test marketing can be risky because it gives information to competitors, but not testing may be even riskier.

10-54.
False
p. 296

New-product development usually fits into the old routines of a firm, so it is not necessary for top management to support new-product development in any special way.

10-55.
False
p. 298

Product managers or brand managers are most often found in firms with only one or a few related products.

10-56.
True
p. 298

When a large firm has several different kinds of products, product managers or brand managers may be put in charge of each one.

Multiple Choice Questions

10-57.
B
Def.
Easy
p. 276

Which of the following is NOT one of the text's product life cycle stages?
A. Market maturity
B. Market penetration
C. Market introduction
D. Sales decline
E. Market growth

10-58.
A
Comp.
Hard
p. 276

Regarding product life cycles, a good marketing manager knows that
A. entirely different target markets may be involved at different stages of the product life cycle.
B. a product that doesn't get beyond the introduction stage is still likely to be very profitable.
C. industry profits are increasing well after sales start to decline.
D. once a market goes into sales decline, oligopoly conditions set in.
E. All of the above are true.

10-**59.**
D
Comp.
Hard
p. 276

As a product moves through its product life cycle:
A. a firm should change its target market--but not its marketing mix.
B. the competitive situation moves toward monopoly.
C. industry profits keep increasing along with industry sales.
D. customers' needs and attitudes may change.
E. All of the above are true.

10-**60.**
E
Comp.
Med.
p. 276-78

As a product moves through its product life cycle:
A. industry profits may decrease while industry sales increase.
B. the nature of competition moves toward pure competition or oligopoly.
C. entirely different target markets may be aimed at.
D. customers' attitudes and needs may change.
E. All of the above are true.

10-**61.**
D
Comp.
Med.
p. 277

During the MARKET INTRODUCTION stage of the product life cycle:
A. large profits are typical--until competition arrives.
B. Price and Promotion are more important than Place and Product.
C. much money is spent on Promotion, while spending on Place is left until later.
D. money is invested--in the hope of FUTURE profits.
E. most customers will try really new products.

10-**62.**
A
App.
Med.
p. 277

Pfizer Corp. is introducing a really new product idea. Pfizer is spending a lot of money to inform potential customers and middlemen about the availability and advantages of the new product. Although sales are rising slowly, Pfizer doesn't expect the product to become profitable for at least another year. Pfizer's new product is in which stage of the product life cycle?
A. Market introduction
B. Sales decline
C. Market development
D. Market growth
E. Market maturity

10-**63.**
D
App.
Hard
p. 277

In which of the following situations is the new product entering the MARKET INTRODUCTION stage of the product life cycle?
A. Mercedes just introduced a new luxury sport-ute to compete against sport-utes made by others.
B. Colgate-Palmolive just introduced a "new and improved" chemical formula for its "Total" toothpaste.
C. Home Depot (a home improvement chain) just introduced its own dealer brand of paint.
D. Toshiba just introduced a computer program that is so "user-friendly" it responds to spoken commands.
E. All of the above.

10-64.
A
App.
Med.
p. 277

Cargill, Inc. is finally earning a profit on the unique product it introduced six months ago. Cargill's advertising is both informative and persuasive. Much money is being spent on Place development. There is little price competition, although several competitors have come out with reasonable imitations. Total industry sales and profits are both rising. In which stage of the product life cycle is Cargill operating?

    A. Market growth
    B. Market introduction
    C. Sales decline
    D. Market maturity
    E. Market development

10-65.
B
Def.
Med.
p. 277

Industry profits are largest in which of the following product life cycle stages?

    A. market introduction.
    B. market growth.
    C. market maturity.
    D. sales decline.
    E. any of the above.

10-66.
E
Comp.
Med.
p. 277

Total industry profits reach their maximum during the _____ stage of the product life cycle.

    A. market maturity
    B. sales decline
    C. market development
    D. market introduction
    E. market growth

10-67.
E
Comp.
Med.
p. 277

In the MARKET GROWTH stage of the product life cycle:

    A. competing products become almost the same in the minds of potential consumers.
    B. distribution moves from intensive to selective.
    C. many competitors drop out of the market.
    D. total industry sales increase very slowly.
    E. total industry profits reach their peak and begin to decline.

10-68.
C
Def.
Easy
p. 277

Industry sales are highest in which of the following product life cycle stages?

    A. market growth.
    B. market development.
    C. market maturity.
    D. sales decline.
    E. market introduction.

10-69.
C
Def.
Med.
p. 277

Competition is toughest in which of the following product life cycle stages?

    A. market introduction.
    B. market growth.
    C. market maturity.
    D. market development.

10-**70.**
A
Def.
Med.
p. 278

Persuasive promotion is especially important in which of the following product life cycle stages?
  A. market maturity.
  B. sales decline.
  C. market introduction.
  D. market growth.

10-**71.**
B
Int.
Hard
p. 278

Regarding product life cycles, which of the following is NOT true?
  A. Industry profits are likely to level off or decline before sales level off.
  B. The level of promotion usually decreases in market maturity since there is less revenue to cover the cost.
  C. Many close substitutes are usually competing in the market maturity stage.
  D. It is usually expensive for a new firm to enter in the market maturity stage.
  E. There is a downward pressure on prices over time.

10-**72.**
B
Comp.
Hard
p. 278

During the MARKET MATURITY stage of the product life cycle:
  A. some competitors drop out of the market--and no new firms enter.
  B. persuasive promotion becomes more important.
  C. promotion emphasizes the advantages of the basic product concept.
  D. total industry sales and profits reach their maximum levels.
  E. All of the above.

10-**73.**
B
App.
Med.
p. 278

An industry's sales have leveled off and profits are declining in oligopolistic competition. Consumers see competing products as "homogeneous." Several firms have dropped out of the industry, but a new one entered recently. Firms in the industry are trying to avoid price-cutting by spending on persuasive advertising. These firms are competing in which stage of the product life cycle?
  A. Market growth
  B. Market maturity
  C. Market development
  D. Market introduction
  E. Sales decline

10-**74.**
A
Int.
Hard
p. 278-79

Regarding product life cycle planning, good marketing managers know that:
  A. a "me-too" new brand may immediately enter during market growth or market maturity.
  B. every brand must go through the sales decline stage.
  C. market introduction is usually profitable for the innovator.
  D. any change in an existing product results in a new product life cycle.
  E. All of the above are true.

10-**75.**
A
Comp.
Med.
p. 278

During the SALES DECLINE stage of the product life cycle:
  A. firms with strong brands may make profits almost until the end.
  B. no profits are earned.
  C. price competition usually declines.
  D. brand loyalty declines.
  E. monopoly is typical.

10-76.
E
App.
Easy
p. 278

LusterWare, Inc. has seen most of its competitors drop out of its product-market due to declining industry sales and profits. But LusterWare still has much demand for its product from a small group of loyal customers. This product-market is in which product life cycle stage?
  A. Market introduction
  B. Market maturity
  C. Market development
  D. Market growth
  E. Sales decline

10-77.
B
App.
Easy
p. 278

Product life cycles refer to the life of:
  A. a firm's individual product.
  B. a product idea.
  C. a firm's brand.
  D. fads.
  E. all of the above.

10-78.
D
Comp.
Med.
p. 278

"Product life cycles" are concerned with sales and profits:
  A. in generic markets--not individual product-markets.
  B. of a firm's individual products or brands.
  C. of goods but not services.
  D. in a product-market.
  E. Both A and C.

10-79.
B
Int.
Hard
p. 278

Regarding product life cycles, which is TRUE?
  A. Industry sales and profits tend to reach their maximum during the market maturity stage.
  B. Product life cycles describe industry sales and profits within some product-market.
  C. Product life cycles are generally getting shorter and cannot be extended.
  D. Every new brand must pass through all four stages of the product life cycle.
  E. All of the above are true.

10-80.
D
Comp.
Med.
p. 280

The shape, length, and current stage of a product life cycle may vary depending:
  A. on how the market is defined.
  B. on the nature of the competition.
  C. on the nature of the products involved.
  D. All of the above.
  E. None of the above.

10-81.
C
Comp.
Med.
p. 280

Concerning product life cycles:
  A. each of a producer's individual products follows the life cycle pattern.
  B. in the early part of market maturity, new products begin to replace the old.
  C. the stages usually have varying lengths.
  D. in general, life cycles are getting longer.
  E. None of the above is true.

10-**82.**
E
Comp.
Med.
p. 280

A new product idea is more likely to move quickly through the early stages of the product life cycle when:
- A. the product is easy to use.
- B. the product is compatible with the values and experiences of target customers.
- C. the product can be given a trial.
- D. the product's advantages are easy to communicate.
- E. All of the above are correct.

10-**83.**
D
Comp.
Med.
p. 281

According to the text, product life cycles are:
- A. getting longer
- B. speeding up in the later stages.
- C. now about the same length as 100 years ago.
- D. getting shorter.
- E. slowing down in the early stages.

10-**84.**
A
Comp.
Easy
p. 281

Regarding product life cycles, which of the following statements is NOT true?
- A. Patents offer strong protection for most new product ideas.
- B. Fashion-related products tend to have short life cycles.
- C. Rapid changes in technology often lead to shorter product life cycles.
- D. Product life cycles seem to be getting shorter in both consumer and business product markets.
- E. All of the above are true.

10-**85.**
E
Def.
Easy
p. 282

"Fashion" is the currently accepted or popular _____:
- A. trend.
- B. idea.
- C. fad.
- D. assortment.
- E. style.

10-**86.**
B
Comp.
Hard
p. 282

A good marketing manager knows that:
- A. modern communication does not affect the speed of fashion change.
- B. the faster fashions change, the harder marketing strategy planning is.
- C. the speed of fashion cycles decreases the cost of marketing.
- D. how a fashion gets started is well understood by marketers.
- E. a higher standard of living discourages fashion buying.

10-**87.**
D
Def.
Med.
p. 282-83

Regarding fashions and fads, which is TRUE?
- A. A fashion is the currently accepted or popular style.
- B. The cycle for a style may go up and down as it comes back into fashion.
- C. A fad is an idea that is fashionable only to certain enthusiastic--but perhaps fickle--groups.
- D. All of the above are true.
- E. None of the above is true.

10-**88.**
D
Comp.
Hard
p. 284

During the introduction stage of the product life cycle,
- A. "me-too" products quickly take market share away from the innovator.
- B. most products achieve intensive distribution.
- C. industry profits are at their highest.
- D. promotion is likely to be needed to build primary demand.
- E. None of the above is true.

10-**89.**
C
Comp.
Hard
p. 283

As a product moves into the market maturity stage of its life cycle, the marketing manager should:
  A. try to build primary demand.
  B. move toward exclusive distribution.
  C. expect the market to move toward pure competition.
  D. All of the above are true.
  E. None of the above is true.

10-**90.**
D
Comp.
Med.
p. 284

When moving into the market maturity stage of the product life cycle, a firm might be able to obtain a competitive advantage:
  A. with lower production costs.
  B. by being more successful at promotion.
  C. by having a slightly better product than competitors.
  D. all of the above.
  E. none of the above.

10-**91.**
D
Int.
Med.
p. 285

Regarding product life cycles, good marketing managers know that:
  A. any new brand must start off in the market introduction stage.
  B. any product modification results in a new product life cycle.
  C. product life cycles cannot be extended.
  D. a firm's product can be withdrawn before its related product life cycle is over.
  E. All of the above are true.

10-**92.**
B
Comp.
Med.
p. 285

Concerning the product life cycle:
  A. profits and sales begin to decline in the maturity stage.
  B. individual products may enter and leave the market at any stage.
  C. a successful introduction almost guarantees that the product will remain a success over the life cycle.
  D. All of the above are true.
  E. None of the above is true.

10-**93.**
B
Int.
Med.
p. 285

Regarding product life cycles, good marketing managers know that:
  A. all new brands start off in the market introduction stage.
  B. product life cycles can be extended through product modifications.
  C. a product must pass through all the product life cycle stages.
  D. no strategy planning is needed during the sales decline stage.
  E. a firm should use penetration pricing during market introduction, especially if the cycle is expected to move slowly.

10-**94.**
E
App.
Med.
p. 288

According to your text, which of the following is an example of a "new product"?
  A. An existing product that has been modified in some way.
  B. An existing product for which new uses have been found in other product-markets.
  C. A wholly new product idea.
  D. An existing product being offered to new markets.
  E. All of the above.

10-**95.**
A
Comp.
Med.
p. 288

Regarding what a "new product" is, your text says:
A. a product should be considered "new" if it is new in any way for the company concerned.
B. that the FTC would not call an existing product new, even if it were changed in a functionally significant way.
C. there is no legal limit on how long a product can be called "new."
D. a new product must be totally different before it can be called a "new product."
E. All of the above.

10-**96.**
C
Def.
Easy
p. 288

According to the text, a "new product" is one that is:
A. physically changed.
B. unique.
C. new in any way for the company concerned.
D. completely new physically and conceptually.
E. None of the above.

10-**97.**
C
App.
Med.
p. 288

Seeking to stop declining sales for an established mouthwash, a sales manager suggests that new coloring be added to the product and a major promotion effort be started for the "new" product. The Federal Trade Commission would:
A. be concerned about the possibility of the firm getting a monopoly.
B. allow the company to call the product "new" for only six months.
C. probably not approve of this at all because the product doesn't meet the FTC's definition of "new."
D. allow the promotion effort if it felt that consumers would think the coloring made it "new."
E. none of the above is true.

10-**98.**
B
App.
Med.
p. 288

Sales of a producer's wax paper food-wrap are declining fast. The advertising manager--looking for a way to attract attention to the brand--suggests changing the package somewhat and promoting it as a "new" product. The Federal Trade Commission
A. would allow the company to call the product "new" for only six months.
B. probably would not approve of this at all.
C. would allow the advertising campaign if it concluded that consumers thought the different package made it new.
D. does not regulate advertising, so it would not pay any attention to this firm.
E. None of the above is true.

10-**99.**
C
Def.
Hard
p. 288

According to the FTC, for a producer to call a product "new," the product:
A. must be no more than two months old.
B. must have achieved brand insistence.
C. must be entirely new or changed in a functionally significant or substantial respect.
D. must have been changed in some way during the last year.
E. Both A and C.

10-100.
A
Comp.
Med.
p. 289

Which of the following is a common cause of new product failures?
A. The product fails to offer the customer a unique benefit.
B. The company tries to follow an organized new-product development process--rather than using a faster and more spontaneous, "race-to-market" approach.
C. The managers worry too much about the competition.
D. The company delays putting the product on the market until it has developed a complete marketing plan.
E. all of the above.

10-101.
A
Comp.
Med.
p. 290

The new-product development process discussed in the text
A. is based on the idea that a firm should eliminate potentially unprofitable product ideas as early as possible.
B. seeks to take as many ideas to market as possible, hoping to find a breakthrough opportunity.
C. relies solely on test marketing to decide whether to drop an idea or take it to market.
D. is especially important since it increases the number of new product ideas that get to the commercialization stage.
E. None of the above is true.

10-102.
B
Def.
Hard
p. 290

Which of the following gives the correct order of the steps in the new-product development process?
A. Screening, idea generation, idea evaluation, development, commercialization
B. Idea generation, screening, idea evaluation, development, commercialization
C. Idea generation, idea evaluation, development, screening, commercialization
D. Development, idea generation, screening, commercialization, idea evaluation
E. Commercialization, idea generation, idea evaluation, screening, development

10-103.
B
Def.
Easy
p. 290

The last step in the new-product development process is:
A. idea generation.
B. commercialization.
C. idea evaluation.
D. development.
E. screening.

10-104.
E
App.
Easy
p. 290

When looking for new product ideas, which of the following would be good sources?
A. your salespeople.
B. your middlemen.
C. your competitors.
D. your production people.
E. all of the above.

10-105.
E
App.
Easy
p. 290

If you are seeking new product ideas for your business, a good source is:
A. Middlemen
B. Customers
C. Your production people
D. Your salespeople
E. All of the above.

10-**106.**
E
Comp.
Med.
p. 290

Which of the following is an effective source of ideas at the idea generation stage of the new-product development process?

A. customer complaints.
B. lead-users of the product.
C. competitors' products.
D. products found in overseas markets.
E. all of the above.

10-**107.**
A
Comp.
Med.
p. 290

Ideas about potential new products should

A. be encouraged from any and all sources, since only a few ideas will develop into successful products.
B. not be eliminated from consideration until they have been tested in the commercialization stage.
C. come primarily from employees of the firm--so that time won't be wasted evaluating product ideas that are inconsistent with the firm's objectives and resources.
D. come from outside the firm, since studies show that really new ideas require a fresh perspective.
E. None of the above is correct.

10-**108.**
A
Comp.
Med.
p. 291

Regarding the idea generation stage of the new-product development process, which of the following is TRUE?

A. Business firms often approach their suppliers with new product ideas.
B. It is best to focus on only a few good ideas at this stage.
C. Studying customers' ideas is not very helpful, since they tend to focus on minor technical changes in existing products.
D. Most companies don't need a special procedure for seeking new product ideas because so many ideas are coming from so many different sources.
E. None of the above is true.

10-**109.**
C
App.
Med.
p. 291

Many small cars get better gas mileage than the old "gas-guzzlers." This was achieved by using lighter (and less protective) materials. Using less gas while being less safe makes such a car a:

A. desirable product.
B. salutary product.
C. pleasing product.
D. deficient product.
E. There is not enough information to tell.

10-**110.**
B
App.
Med.
p. 291

Many people like to drive motorcycles. But motorcycles have a high death rate in even minor accidents. These motorcycles should probably be thought of as

A. desirable products.
B. pleasing products.
C. salutary products.
D. deficient products.
E. There is not enough information to tell.

10-**111.**
B
App.
Med.
p. 291

Pressure from consumer groups is encouraging some producers to develop more
_____ products.
   A. deficient.
   B. desirable.
   C. acceptable.
   D. pleasing.
   E. salutary.

10-**112.**
D
App.
Med.
p. 291

From a "social responsibility" viewpoint, marketers should try to design and sell:
   A. deficient products.
   B. salutary products.
   C. pleasing products.
   D. desirable products.

10-**113.**
A
Def.
Med.
p. 291

Low immediate satisfaction but high long-run consumer welfare is provided by:
   A. salutary products.
   B. desirable products.
   C. deficient products.
   D. pleasing products.

10-**114.**
B
Def.
Med.
p. 291

Which of the following provides low immediate satisfaction and low long-run consumer welfare?
   A. Pleasing products
   B. Deficient products
   C. Desirable products
   D. Salutary products

10-**115.**
C
Def.
Med.
p. 291

Low immediate satisfaction and low long-run consumer welfare is provided by:
   A. pleasing products.
   B. salutary products.
   C. deficient products.
   D. desirable products.

10-**116.**
D
Def.
Med.
p. 291

Which of the following provides low immediate satisfaction but high long-run consumer welfare?
   A. Pleasing products
   B. Desirable products
   C. Deficient products
   D. Salutary products

10-**117.**
B
App.
Med.
p. 291

A drug company has developed a new diet pill that helps people lose weight easily. Research shows a high level of consumer immediate satisfaction. However, their effect on long-term consumer welfare is low because they permanently increase the consumer's blood pressure. In this (hypothetical) situation, the product should be thought of as a

    A. desirable product.
    B. pleasing product.
    C. salutary product.
    D. deficient product.
    E. There is not enough information to tell.

10-**118.**
B
Def.
Med.
p. 291

Low long-run consumer welfare but high immediate satisfaction is provided by:
    A. deficient products.
    B. pleasing products.
    C. desirable products.
    D. salutary products.

10-**119.**
A
Def.
Med.
p. 291

Which of the following provides high immediate satisfaction but low long-run consumer welfare?
    A. Pleasing products
    B. Salutary products
    C. Deficient products
    D. Desirable products

10-**120.**
C
Def.
Med.
p. 291

High immediate satisfaction and high long-run consumer welfare is provided by:
    A. salutary products.
    B. pleasing products.
    C. desirable products.
    D. deficient products.

10-**121.**
C
Def.
Med.
p. 291

Which of the following provides high immediate satisfaction and high long-run consumer welfare?
    A. Salutary products
    B. Deficient products
    C. Desirable products
    D. Pleasing products

10-**122.**
B
App.
Easy
p. 291

Even though safety helmets offer protection while riding a bike, many Americans don't use them because they are uncomfortable or restricting. For all these people, safety helmets are a:
    A. pleasing product.
    B. salutary product.
    C. deficient product.
    D. desirable product.
    E. There is not enough information to tell.

10-**123.**
E
Def.
Easy
p. 292

The Consumer Product Safety Commission can:
A. back up its orders with jail sentences.
B. set safety standards for products.
C. back up its orders with fines.
D. order return of "unsafe products."
E. All of the above.

10-**124.**
D
Def.
Med.
p. 292

The Consumer Product Safety Commission can:
A. order costly repairs of "unsafe products."
B. back up its orders with fines or jail sentences.
C. set safety standards for products.
D. All of the above.
E. Both A and C--but NOT B.

10-**125.**
A
Comp.
Hard
p. 292

Passage of the Consumer Product Safety Act means that:
A. some business people may go to jail if they offer unsafe products.
B. consumers will be more willing to pay for safer products in the future.
C. product-related injuries will be eliminated in the future.
D. producers are no longer liable for an injury if it is the consumer's fault.
E. All of the above.

10-**126.**
D
Comp.
Hard
p. 292

The Consumer Product Safety Commission
A. sets safety standards for new products, but has little power until after a consumer accident occurs.
B. must approve every new product (including foods and drugs) before it can be sold.
C. provides product liability insurance.
D. can order costly returns of products it considers unsafe.
E. has very little power.

10-**127.**
D
Def.
Easy
p. 292

The legal obligation of sellers to pay damages to individuals who are injured by defective or unsafely designed products is called:
A. product responsibility.
B. breach of warranty.
C. rule of reason.
D. product liability.
E. design enforcement.

10-**128.**
B
Def.
Easy
p. 292

The legal obligation of sellers to pay damages to individuals who are injured by defective or unsafely designed products is called:
A. breach of warranty.
B. product liability.
C. deficit accountability.
D. the rule of reason.
E. salutary responsibility.

10-**129.**
C
Comp.
Hard
p. 293

Concept testing:
A. takes place during the screening step of the new-product development process.
B. involves usage tests by potential customers.
C. seeks potential customers' reactions and attitudes toward new product ideas--before actual models are developed.
D. is the last step before commercialization of a new product idea.
E. Both A and D.

10-**130.**
C
Comp.
Hard
p. 295

Regarding new-product development, market tests:
A. are used mostly for durable products because of their high production costs and risks.
B. seek customer reactions to ideas--not actual products.
C. should test specific marketing mix variables.
D. are especially important for high fashion products.
E. should always be run because testing does not involve any risk--but NOT TESTING does.

10-**131.**
E
Comp.
Hard
p. 295

An ROI estimate is needed during the _____ step of the new-product development process.
A. commercialization
B. development
C. idea evaluation
D. screening
E. All of the above.

10-**132.**
C
Int.
Hard
p. 295

Regarding the new-product development process:
A. a gradual "roll-out" should be used to cut promotion costs.
B. the ROI screen may have to be lowered to get enough good ideas through.
C. screening criteria should be both qualitative and quantitative.
D. all product ideas should go through market testing before being accepted or killed.
E. All of the above are true.

10-**133.**
E
Int.
Med.
p. 293-96

Regarding the new-product development process:
A. market tests may not be practical for fashion products.
B. a gradual "roll-out" of the product--region by region--allows for more market testing.
C. concept tests are done before any physical models are produced.
D. likely ROI should be estimated throughout the process to force the new idea to prove itself.
E. All of the above are true.

10-**134.**
A
Comp.
Med.
p. 296

The new-product development process
A. should have ongoing support from top management.
B. should avoid applying quantitative screening criteria--since applying such criteria tends to eliminate most of the "really new" ideas.
C. should be informal--to encourage creativity.
D. should start whenever the majority of current products are in the market maturity stage of the product life cycle.
E. All of the above are correct.

10-**135.**
C

Comp.
Med.
p. 297

Which of the following statements about organizing for new-product development is TRUE?

A. New-product development departments or committees usually cause delays and should be avoided.
B. Few new-product ideas fail when product managers control the new-product development process.
C. The specific organization arrangement may not be too important--as long as there is top-level support.
D. Marketing managers should control new-product development.
E. All of the above are true.

10-**136.**
E

Comp.
Easy
p. 298

The job of product or brand manager is often created when a firm:

A. has many different kinds of products or brands.
B. wants to eliminate the job of the research and development department.
C. wants to eliminate the job of sales manager.
D. wants each product or brand to have a "champion."
E. Both A and D.

Chapter 11

Place and Development of Channel Systems

True-False Questions:

11-1.
True
p. 304-305

Place is concerned with the selection and use of marketing specialists--middlemen and facilitators--to provide target customers with time, place, and possession utilities.

11-2.
True
p. 307

The Internet is making it possible for firms to reach customers that were impossible to reach before.

11-3.
True
p. 307

With the Internet, even very small specialized firms can draw customers from all over the world.

11-4.
False
p. 307

The Internet gives large firms access to repeat customers, but it does little for small firms trying to develop an initial base of customers.

11-5.
True
p. 307

Firms that use direct distribution can usually adjust their marketing mixes faster than firms that use indirect distribution.

11-6.
False
p. 308

Aggressive, market-oriented middlemen are almost always available and eager to handle the distribution of innovative, new products.

11-7.
True
p. 308

Some firms are forced to use direct distribution when they can't find middlemen willing to carry innovative, new products.

11-8.
True
p. 308

Selling direct-to-customer is more common with business products than consumer products.

11-9.
False
p. 308

Direct-to-customer channels are rarely used in business markets because they are much more expensive and less efficient than using middlemen.

11-10.
False
p. 308

Many business products are sold direct, but hardly any services are.

11-**11.**
False
p. 309

The terms "direct marketing" and "direct distribution" mean the same thing.

11-**12.**
True
p. 309

Consumer product companies such as Tupperware that appear to be selling direct may not be because their salespeople are independent middlemen, not company employees.

11-**13.**
True
p. 309

Firms that use direct marketing promotion may or may not use direct distribution.

11-**14.**
False
p. 309

Direct marketing and direct distribution are the same thing.

11-**15.**
True
p. 309

Direct marketing is primarily concerned with Promotion, not Place.

11-**16.**
True
p. 309

A producer who wants to reach certain customers may have no choice about which wholesaler to use.

11-**17.**
True
p. 309

A wholesaler might help a producer by reducing the producer's need to carry large inventory stocks.

11-**18.**
True
p. 309

A wholesaler might help a producer by reducing the producer's need for market research.

11-**19.**
True
p. 310

The most important reason to use indirect channels is if middlemen can help serve customers better and at lower cost.

11-**20.**
True
p. 310

Discrepancies of quantity occur because individual producers want to produce large quantities of products while individual consumers prefer to buy products in small quantities.

11-**21.**
False
p. 310

Discrepancies of assortment occur because individual producers tend to specialize in producing a large assortment of products while individual consumers prefer to buy a small assortment of products.

11-**22.**
False
p. 310

Discrepancies of quantity and assortment occur because individual producers find it economical to produce and sell small quantities of a large assortment of products while individual consumers prefer to buy large quantities of a small assortment of products.

11-**23.**
True
p. 311

"Regrouping activities" involve adjusting the quantities and/or assortments of products handled at each level in a channel of distribution.

11-**24.**
True
p. 311

Accumulating involves collecting products from many small producers--often as a way to get lower transportation rates.

11-**25.**
False
p. 312

Bulk-breaking means separating products into grades and qualities desired by different target markets.

11-**26.**
False
p. 312

When a warehouse is rearranged to speed up order processing, "regrouping activities" are being performed.

11-**27.**
True
p. 312

Assorting activities involve putting together a variety of products to give a target market what it wants.

11-**28.**
True
p. 314

In an indirect channel of distribution, both vertical conflict and horizontal conflict may arise.

11-**29.**
True
p. 314

A "channel captain" is a manager who helps direct the activities of a whole channel.

11-**30.**
True
p. 314

Most traditional channel systems don't have a channel captain.

11-**31.**
False
p. 315-16

According to the text, it's best for the "channel captain" to be a producer rather than a wholesaler or retailer.

11-**32.**
True
p. 316

In Japan, large, wholesale "trading companies" often serve as the channel captain.

11-**33.**
True
p. 317

Because middlemen are closer to the final user, they are in an ideal position to assume the channel captain role.

11-**34.**
False
p. 317

Traditional channel systems are growing faster than vertical marketing systems.

11-**35.**
False
p. 318

In administered channel systems, vertical cooperation is achieved by acquiring firms at different levels of activity.

11-**36.**
True
p. 318

Administered and contractual channel systems are vertical marketing systems which depend on informal agreements--or contracts between channel members--to cooperate.

11-**37.**
True
p. 318

Any contractual channel system--by definition--is also an administered channel system.

11-**38.**
True
p. 319

Vertical marketing systems account for more than 60 percent of U.S. retail sales.

11-**39.**
False
p. 319

Vertical marketing systems are growing in the U.S., but declining in the rest of the world.

11-**40.**
True
p. 319

"Ideal market exposure" should make a product widely enough available to satisfy target customers' needs, but not exceed them.

11-**41.**
True
p. 319

Intensive distribution is selling a product through all responsible and suitable wholesalers or retailers who will stock and/or sell the product.

11-**42.**
False
p. 319

Intensive distribution is selling through only those middlemen who will give the product special attention.

11-**43.**
False
p. 321

Selective distribution is growing in popularity because it provides 100 percent coverage of the market.

11-**44.**
True
p. 321

Exclusive distribution is selling through only one middleman in each geographic area.

11-**45.**
True
p. 321

The "80/20 rule" is more likely to apply to a firm that uses intensive distribution than a firm that uses selective distribution.

11-**46.**
False
p. 321

Compared to intensive distribution, selective distribution gives a producer a greater opportunity for profit but usually makes it more difficult for middlemen to make a profit.

11-**47.**
True
p. 321

Exclusive distribution is more likely to involve a written agreement than is selective or intensive distribution.

11-**48.**
True
p. 322

Horizontal agreements to limit sales by territory or customer are always illegal according to the Supreme Court.

11-**49.**
False
p. 322

Vertical agreements to limit sales by customer or territory are always illegal, while horizontal agreements may be legal sometimes.

11-**50.**
True
p. 323

A manufacturer that uses several competing channels to reach the same target market is using "dual distribution."

11-**51.**
True
p. 323

A manufacturer may be forced to use dual distribution because a big retail chain wants to deal directly with it instead of wholesalers.

11-**52.**
True
p. 323

Manufacturers are sometimes forced to use "dual distribution" because their present channels are doing a poor job or are not reaching some potential customers.

11-**53.**
False
p. 324

Reverse channels are used when dual distribution fails.

11-**54.**
True
p. 324

Reverse channels may provide a way to retrieve unwanted products from middlemen, business customers, or final consumers.

Multiple Choice Questions

11-**55.**
A
Def.
Easy
p. 305

Strategy "Place" decisions would NOT include:
A. geographic pricing policy.
B. type of channel of distribution.
C. type of middlemen/facilitators.
D. type of physical distribution facilities.
E. degree of market exposure desired.

11-**56.**
E
Def.
Med.
p. 305

Strategy "Place" decisions would NOT include:
A. type of physical distribution facilities.
B. type of channel of distribution.
C. degree of market exposure desired.
D. distribution customer service level.
E. how to train wholesalers' salespeople.

11-**57.**
A
Def.
Easy
p. 305

A channel of distribution:
A. is any series of firms or individuals who participate in the flow of goods and services from producer to consumer or final user.
B. is only needed when products must be stored.
C. must include one or more middlemen.
D. helps create possession utility but not time utility.
E. Both B and C.

11-**58.**
C
Comp.
Med.
p. 306

Which of the following statements about Place is NOT true?
A. Most consumer products move from producer to middlemen to final customer.
B. A series of participants in the flow of goods and services from producer to final customer is called a channel of distribution.
C. There is always one Place arrangement that is "best" for a product.
D. Middlemen develop to adjust discrepancies in quantity and assortment.
E. All of the above are true.

11-**59.**
B
Comp.
Med.
p. 306

Which of the following statements about Place is true?
A. Most consumer products and most business products are sold to middlemen who then sell them to final customers.
B. Place decisions are usually harder to change than other marketing mix decisions.
C. There is always one Place arrangement that is "best" for a product.
D. A series of individuals who aid in the flow of goods and services from producer to final customer is called a distribution network.
E. None of the above is true.

11-**60.**
E
Comp.
Easy
p. 305-306

"Place" decisions:
A. may focus on the location of retail stores and wholesale facilities.
B. may focus on the selection and use of middlemen and facilitators.
C. can be aided by knowing about the product classes.
D. are harder to change than Product, Promotion, or Price decisions.
E. All of the above are true.

11-**61.**
B
Comp.
Med.
p. 306

Because of long-run effects, decisions about one of the four Ps is often harder to change than the others. This P is:
A. product.
B. place.
C. promotion.
D. price.

11-**62.**
B
Comp.
Med.
p. 307

A direct-to-customer channel
A. includes a retailer but not a wholesaler.
B. usually helps the producer to be more aware of changes in final customer attitudes.
C. eliminates some of the marketing functions.
D. is typical to reach final consumer markets.
E. is most suitable when a large number of transactions are required in the channel or when orders are smaller.

11-**63.**
B
Comp.
Med.
p. 307

Which of the following statements about direct channel systems is NOT true?
A. There is no reliance on independent middlemen whose objectives may be different from the producer's objectives.
B. A product's marketing mix is harder to adjust without the help of middlemen.
C. The producer can be more aware of changes in customer attitudes.
D. Direct channels are more typical with business products than with consumer products.
E. All of the above are true.

11-**64.**
E
Comp.
Hard
p. 307

A disadvantage of direct-to-customer channels is that they
A. are not suitable when the number of transactions is small or when orders are large.
B. are illegal in business and organizational markets.
C. make it more difficult to serve buyers who want to lease rather than buy products.
D. require the producer to coordinate with many retailers.
E. None of the above is a disadvantage.

11-**65.**
E
Comp.
Hard
p. 307

A disadvantage of direct-to-customer channels is that
A. most organizational buyers are used to relying on middlemen to serve as their purchasing advisors.
B. they require producers to shift many marketing functions to others.
C. this approach makes is hard to achieve coordination among the required marketing activities.
D. they make it more difficult to get information about changing needs of the market.
E. None of the above is a disadvantage.

11-**66.**
E
Comp.
Med.
p. 309

Choosing an INDIRECT channel probably will be better than a direct channel if a producer wants to:
A. provide special technical service.
B. make it easier to do marketing research.
C. be more sensitive to coming changes in customer needs and attitudes.
D. obtain a very aggressive selling effort.
E. adjust large discrepancies of quantity and assortment.

11-**67.**
E
Comp.
Med.
p. 309

INDIRECT channels are probably a better choice than direct channels when:
A. the firm has limited financial resources.
B. the product is a consumer product instead of a business product.
C. target customers already have established buying patterns for where to search for the product.
D. retailers are already conveniently located where consumers shop.
E. all of the above.

11-**68.**
E
Comp.
Hard
p. 309-10

Which of the following is a function that a middleman is likely to provide for customers?
A. reduce inventory costs
B. regroup products
C. provide delivery
D. grant credit
E. All of the above are functions provided for customers.

11-**69.**
E
Comp.
Med.
p. 309-10

Which of the following is NOT a benefit that a middleman is likely to provide for producer-suppliers?
A. reduce credit risk
B. reduce the need to store inventory
C. reduce the need for marketing research
D. reduce the need for working capital
E. All of the above are likely benefits provided to suppliers.

11-**70.**
E
App.
Hard
p. 310

Which of the following best illustrates "discrepancies of quantity"?
A. Firestone makes tires, but most consumers also want a large selection of car-care services.
B. Some stores sell large quantities of Firestone tires, but only small quantities of tires made by other companies.
C. There are 270 million consumers in the U.S. but only a small portion buy tires in any given year.
D. Four firms make over 90 percent of all the tires sold in the United States.
E. Firestone made millions of tires last year--but most customers bought only one set.

11-**71.**
A
Comp.
Med.
p. 310

"Discrepancies of quantity" occur because
A. producers seek economies of scale.
B. most middlemen specialize in selected product lines and buy in large enough quantities to get a good price.
C. adding middlemen in a channel of distribution increases the cost of getting products to consumers.
D. consumers want the convenience of buying many different types of products at one time.
E. all of the above.

11-**72.**
D
Def.
Easy
p. 310

"Discrepancies of quantity" means:
A. some consumers buy more products than others.
B. there are more consumers than producers.
C. some manufacturers can produce more products than others.
D. the difference between the quantity of products it is economical for an individual producer to make and the quantity normally wanted by individual consumers or users.
E. that demand is greater than what a company can supply.

11-**73.**
E
Def.
Med.
p. 310

"Discrepancies of quantity" means:
A. there are more producers than consumers.
B. there are more consumers than producers.
C. the difference between the product lines the typical producer makes and the assortment wanted by consumers or final users.
D. consumers want more products than producers can make.
E. the difference between the quantity of products it is economical for an individual producer to make and the quantity normally wanted by individual consumers or users.

11-**74.**
E
Def.
Easy
p. 311

"Discrepancies of assortment" means:
A. some producers can produce more products than others.
B. some consumers buy more products than others.
C. consumers want more output than producers can make.
D. there are more producers than wholesalers.
E. the difference between the product lines the typical producer makes and the assortment wanted by final consumers or users.

11-**75.**
C
Def.
Med.
p. 311

"Discrepancies of assortment" means:
A.   there are more producers than consumers.
B.   consumers want more output than producers make.
C.   the difference between the product lines the typical producer makes and the assortment wanted by final consumers or users.
D.   there are more consumers than producers.
E.   the difference between the quantity of products the typical producer makes and the quantity wanted by individual consumers.

11-**76.**
B
App.
Hard
p. 311

Which of the following best illustrates adjusting "discrepancies of assortment?"
A.   General Motors makes Buick for one product-market and Chevrolet for another product-market.
B.   A hardware store sells all the hardware items wanted by most people.
C.   Over 270 million U.S. consumers are served by over 350,000 manufacturers.
D.   Magnavox sold more than 2,000,000 TVs last year.
E.   Three firms produce over 90 percent of all the VCRs made in the United States.

11-**77.**
B
App.
Med.
p. 311

A publisher of photography books finds that it is cost-effective to print 10,000 or more at a time. But a bookstore orders only a few copies of each book since its customers want to select from a wide variety. This example shows
A.   why discrepancies of quantity occur.
B.   why both discrepancies of quantity and assortment occur.
C.   neither discrepancies of assortment or quantity.
D.   why discrepancies of assortment occur.
E.   dual distribution.

11-**78.**
B
Def.
Med.
p. 311

Which of the following is NOT one of the "regrouping activities?"
A.   Assorting
B.   Ranking
C.   Sorting
D.   Bulk-breaking
E.   Accumulating

11-**79.**
E
App.
Med.
p. 311

Specialty Produce, Inc. buys artichokes from many small farmers, assembles them into larger quantities, and ships in carload quantities to a central market where they are sold to large food processors. This "regrouping activity" is called:
A.   bulk-breaking.
B.   assorting.
C.   sorting.
D.   wholesaling.
E.   accumulating.

11-**80.**
E
App.
Easy
p. 311

Small farmers in the mountains of Colombia pick coffee beans by hand, obtaining only a bucket a day. Then they sell them to buyers who put the beans in large bags to be shipped to processors. This regrouping activity is called:
A.   Assorting
B.   Wholesaling
C.   Bulk-breaking
D.   Sorting
E.   Accumulating

11-**81.**
C
Def.
Easy
p. 311

The regrouping activity which involves collecting products from many small producers so that the products can be handled more economically further along in the channel is called:
- A. sorting.
- B. wholesaling.
- C. accumulating.
- D. assorting.
- E. bulk-breaking.

11-**82.**
E
App.
Med.
p. 311-12

Every morning, Sycamore Dairy picks up milk which farmers have "milked" that morning. The dairy processes the milk and separates the cream from the milk. Some of the cream is made into butter and packaged in various sizes. The milk and remaining cream are blended into various products, sealed in pint, quart, and half-gallon containers, and delivered to supermarkets in the quantities and assortments they want. The dairy is providing what regrouping activity?
- A. Assorting
- B. Accumulating
- C. Sorting
- D. Bulk-breaking
- E. All of the above.

11-**83.**
E
Def.
Easy
p. 312

The "regrouping activity" which involves breaking carload or truckload shipments into smaller quantities as products get closer to final customers is called:
- A. sorting.
- B. retailing.
- C. assorting.
- D. accumulating.
- E. bulk-breaking.

11-**84.**
D
App.
Med.
p. 312

International Hardware Co. buys carload quantities of bolts, screws, nuts, washers, and other hardware from a large producer in Germany, breaks these shipments into smaller quantities, and sells them to other wholesalers and retail chains. This "regrouping activity" is called:
- A. assorting.
- B. wholesaling.
- C. accumulating.
- D. bulk-breaking.
- E. sorting.

11-**85.**
C
App.
Med.
p. 312

Mount Airy Apple Co. buys fresh apples in truckload quantities, regroups the heterogeneous commodities into homogeneous lots according to grade and quality, and then sells them to retailers. This "regrouping activity" is called:
- A. accumulating.
- B. bulk-breaking.
- C. sorting.
- D. wholesaling.
- E. assorting.

11-**86.**
B
Def.
Easy
p. 312

The regrouping activity which involves grading or sorting products into the grades and qualities desired by different target markets is called:
A. assorting.
B. sorting.
C. wholesaling.
D. accumulating.
E. allocation.

11-**87.**
C
App.
Easy
p. 312

Recently, retail stores that sell "seconds" and "irregular" products at discount prices have opened all over the country. These stores are needed because of what regrouping activity?
A. Accumulating
B. Bulk-breaking
C. Sorting
D. Assorting
E. None of the above

11-**88.**
B
App.
Med.
p. 312

Some sporting goods manufacturers do not make a "full line" of equipment. So the Sports World retain chain carefully selects the brands of several manufacturers to sell. This regrouping activity is called:
A. accumulating.
B. assorting.
C. retailing.
D. bulk-breaking.
E. sorting.

11-**89.**
A
Def.
Easy
p. 312

The regrouping activity which involves putting together a variety of products to give a target market what it wants is called:
A. assorting.
B. bulk-breaking.
C. wholesaling.
D. accumulating.
E. sorting.

11-**90.**
B
Comp.
Med.
p. 313

The desirability of a common "product-market commitment" is based on the idea that:
A. each member of the channel should focus on a different target market.
B. the whole channel is competing with other channel systems.
C. the producer should always be the "channel captain."
D. a channel can eliminate the marketing functions.
E. All of the above are true.

11-**91.**
B
Comp.
Med.
p. 313

A common "product-market commitment" in a channel system helps to eliminate:
A. the need for a channel captain.
B. unnecessary and costly duplication of marketing functions.
C. all production-oriented channel members.
D. competition among different channel systems.
E. the need for marketing managers in individual firms.

11-**92.**
D
Comp.
Med.
p. 306-13

Channels of distribution:
A. that include middlemen result in higher distribution costs than for channels without middlemen.
B. should be designed to increase discrepancies of quantity between producers and consumers.
C. usually do not involve conflicts as long as each channel member has profit as a goal.
D. usually require longer-term planning than other market mix elements because channel decisions are more difficult to change quickly.
E. none of the above.

11-**93.**
E
Comp.
Med.
p. 313

A good "channel captain" knows that:
A. direct-to-customer channels usually cost less and perform more efficiently than indirect channels.
B. marketing functions can be shifted and shared within a channel--but they cannot be completely eliminated.
C. a channel system works best when all its members have a shared product-market commitment.
D. some marketing functions can usually be completely eliminated by using short channels instead of long channels.
E. Both B and C are true.

11-**94.**
D
Comp.
Hard
p. 314

Traditional channels of distribution
A. do not perform bulk-breaking activities.
B. are usually preferred to other distribution arrangements.
C. are easier to control than corporate channel systems.
D. may involve little or no cooperation among channel members.
E. are usually controlled through strong legal contracts.

11-**95.**
D
Def.
Easy
p. 314

In "traditional channel systems," the channel members:
A. consider traditional values--like cooperation and respect--as central to their relationship.
B. have franchise contracts.
C. usually have a common product-market commitment.
D. make little or no effort to cooperate with each other.
E. are integrated.

11-**96.**
A
Def.
Easy
p. 314

Channel systems in which the various channel members make little or no effort to cooperate with each other are called _____ systems.
A. traditional channel
B. vertically integrated
C. direct-to-customer channel
D. franchising
E. administered channel

11-**97.**
E
Comp.
Med.
p. 314

The role of "channel captain":
A. should be taken by producers because they have more power.
B. is to force other channel members to accept the channel captain's plan.
C. should be taken by retailers because they are closer to consumers.
D. may not be necessary if the channel members are satisfied with the "status-quo."
E. is to help a channel system compete more effectively with other channel systems.

11-**98.**
D
Def.
Easy
p. 315-17

The text suggests that a "channel captain" should be:
A. a strong wholesaler.
B. a market-oriented producer.
C. a large retailer.
D. any of the above--i.e. whoever can provide leadership.

11-**99.**
D
Comp.
Med.
p. 314-17

A "channel captain"
A. might be any member of the channel (that is, at any level in the channel)
B. views the members of the channel as a unit.
C. should help to make the channel more efficient by reducing conflict.
D. all of the above.
E. none of the above.

11-**100.**
A
Int.
Hard
p. 317

A good reason for developing or joining a vertical marketing system
A. is that the whole channel focuses on the same target market at the end of the channel and seems to be more effective.
B. market competition at each level of the channel eliminates inefficient firms and serves consumers' needs better.
C. is that no member of the channel has to bear the costs of the regrouping activities.
D. is that no member of the channel has to plan for the whole channel since good decisions at each level run the channel.
E. All of the above.

11-**101.**
B
App.
Easy
p. 317

A large food retailer acquiring a cheese factory is an example of:
A. dual distribution.
B. vertical integration.
C. a tying contract.
D. horizontal integration.
E. internal expansion.

11-**102.**
D
App.
Med.
p. 317

If a large furniture retailer were to purchase Drexel (a manufacturer of sofas and chairs), this would be an example of:
A. a tying contract.
B. an administered channel system.
C. internal expansion.
D. vertical integration.
E. horizontal integration.

11-**103.**
D
App.
Med.
p. 317

Lake Wobegon Mills, a manufacturer of textile products, bought out the wholesaler that had been handling its distribution in Canada. This is an example of:
A. dual distribution.
B. reverse distribution.
C. a contractual channel system.
D. vertical integration.
E. accumulating.

11-**104.**
A
Def.
Easy
p. 317

A firm acquiring another firm at a different level of activity within a channel of distribution is called:
A. vertical integration.
B. a tying contract.
C. dual distribution.
D. horizontal integration.
E. a regrouping activity.

11-**105.**
A
Comp.
Med.
p. 318

Which of the following is NOT a likely advantage of vertical integration?
A. Lower capital requirements.
B. Opportunities for reducing costs through shared overhead.
C. Better coordination of inventories at different channel levels.
D. Better quality control
E. Better assurance of material availability

11-**106.**
C
Comp.
Med.
p. 318

Which of the following is NOT an advantage of vertical integration?
A. Lower overhead
B. Better control of the whole production-distribution system
C. Easier adjustment of discrepancies of quantity and assortment.
D. Greater buying power
E. Assurance of materials and supplies

11-**107.**
D
Int.
Hard
p. 318

Which of the following statements about channel systems is TRUE?
A. Traditional channel systems are more efficient because of their greater freedom.
B. Vertical integration works best when discrepancies of quantity are large.
C. Most corporate channel systems use dual distribution.
D. Some administered channel systems obtain the advantages of vertically integrated systems while still retaining flexibility.
E. All of the above are true.

11-**108.**
A
App.
Med.
p. 318

A computer manufacturer runs training programs for its "cooperating" retailers' salespeople, as well as providing newspaper advertising layouts, point-of-purchase materials, and sales manuals. This is an example of:
A. an administered channel system.
B. a contractual channel system.
C. a traditional channel system
D. a vertically integrated corporate channel system.
E. a franchising system.

11-**109.**
D
Def.
Easy
p. 318

A channel system in which the various members informally agree to cooperate with each other is called a(an) _____ system.
A. contractual channel
B. dual distribution
C. traditional channel
D. administered channel
E. franchising

11-**110.**
B
Def.
Easy
p. 318

A channel system in which the various members agree by contract to cooperate with each other is called a(an) _____ system.
A. dual distribution
B. contractual channel
C. traditional channel
D. administered channel
E. vertically integrated channel

11-**111.**
B
Comp.
Med.
p. 318

When planning channels of distribution, a marketing manager should know that
A. vertically integrated systems are seldom used--because of the difficulty of maintaining control.
B. a contractual system offers both flexibility and stability for its members.
C. the disadvantage of a corporate channel system is reduced control over distribution activities.
D. all of the above.
E. none of the above.

11-**112.**
B
Def.
Hard
p. 319

Vertical marketing systems now account for _____ percent of all retail sales in the United States.
A. 40
B. More than 60
C. 30
D. 10
E. 20

11-**113.**
B
Comp.
Easy
p. 319

With respect to consumer products, which of the following is the most common system for distributing consumer products in the U.S.?
A. direct channel systems.
B. vertical marketing systems.
C. traditional channel systems.
D. horizontal marketing systems.
E. none of the above.

11-**114.**
B
Def.
Easy
p. 319

Which of the following is NOT one of the degrees of market exposure?
A. Selective distribution
B. Dual distribution
C. Intensive distribution
D. Exclusive distribution
E. None of the above, i.e. all are degrees of market exposure.

11-**115.**
B
App.
Easy
p. 319

Middlemen are needed MOST when the desired degree of market exposure is:
A. selective.
B. intensive.
C. exclusive.
D. administered.
E. none of the above.

11-**116.**   Middlemen are needed LEAST when the desired degree of market exposure is:
D
App.
Easy
p. 319
A. intensive.
B. ideal.
C. selective.
D. exclusive.
E. none of the above.

11-**117.**   "Intensive distribution" means selling through:
B
Def.
Med.
p. 319
A. only one channel of distribution.
B. all responsible and suitable retailers or wholesalers.
C. only one middleman in a particular geographic area.
D. only those middlemen who give the product special attention.
E. all retail outlets.

11-**118.**   _____ means selling a product through all responsible and suitable
D
wholesalers or retailers who will stock and/or sell the product.
Def.
Easy
p. 319
A. Selective distribution
B. Dual distribution
C. Exclusive distribution
D. Intensive distribution
E. Aggressive distribution

11-**119.**   "Selective distribution" means selling through:
D
Def.
Med.
p. 319
A. retailers but not wholesalers.
B. dual channels of distribution.
C. all responsible and suitable wholesalers.
D. only those middlemen who give the product special attention.
E. only one middleman in each geographic area.

11-**120.**   _____ means selling a product only through those middlemen who will give
B
the product special attention.
Def.
Easy
p. 319
A. Dual distribution
B. Selective distribution
C. Administered distribution
D. Exclusive distribution
E. Intensive distribution

11-**121.**   "Exclusive distribution" means selling through:
B
Def.
Med.
p. 319
A. the most prestigious retail outlets.
B. only one middlemen in a particular geographic area.
C. only responsible and suitable retailers or wholesalers.
D. retailers that handle specialty products.
E. only those middlemen who will give the product special attention.

11-**122.**   _____ means selling a product through only one middleman in a particular
A
geographic area.
Def.
Easy
p. 319
A. Exclusive distribution
B. Direct distribution
C. Intensive distribution
D. Dual distribution
E. Selective distribution

11-**123.**
B
Comp.
Med.
p. 320

Intensive distribution is often very appropriate for:
A. shopping products and convenience products.
B. convenience products and business supplies.
C. business products of all classes.
D. unsought products and specialty products.
E. shopping, specialty, and unsought products.

11-**124.**
D
Comp.
Med.
p. 320

Intensive distribution:
A. gives a retailer more incentive to promote a product than he would have with exclusive distribution.
B. is not very likely to be used in combination with dual distribution.
C. is more likely to be used with relatively high priced products than with low priced products.
D. is often used for convenience products.
E. none of the above.

11-**125.**
B
App.
Easy
p. 320

Intensive distribution at the retail level would probably be most appropriate for:
A. Sports coats
B. Batteries
C. 10 speed bicycles
D. Tennis rackets
E. 35mm cameras

11-**126.**
B
Int.
Hard
p. 320

From a producer's viewpoint, which of the following is an advantage of INTENSIVE DISTRIBUTION over selective distribution?
A. Middlemen price-cutting may be reduced.
B. Middlemen facilities will be more convenient for customers.
C. Middlemen can be required to carry larger stocks.
D. More aggressive selling can be expected from middlemen.
E. Better service can be required from middlemen.

11-**127.**
B
App.
Med.
p. 320

Which degree of market exposure would probably be most suitable for a heterogeneous shopping product which has achieved brand preference and sells for about $300?
A. Concentrated distribution
B. Selective distribution
C. Administered distribution
D. Intensive distribution
E. Exclusive distribution

11-**128.**
A
Comp.
Med.
p. 320

Selective distribution is particularly useful for:
A. business, specialty, and shopping products.
B. specialty and unsought products.
C. convenience and shopping products.
D. specialty, shopping, and unsought products.
E. unsought and business products.

11-**129.**
E
Comp.
Med.
p. 320-21

Selective distribution:
A. is likely to reduce high administrative expenses caused by a large proportion of small orders.
B. is especially sensible for shopping and specialty products.
C. is becoming more popular.
D. is a good idea if some of the available middlemen are not financially solid.
E. All of the above are true.

11-**130.**
A
Comp.
Hard
p. 321

If a producer's marketing manager wants middlemen to take over all responsibility for promoting his product he probably should use
A. exclusive distribution.
B. any of the above, since every channel member must support a product with promotion.
C. intensive distribution.
D. a vertically integrated distribution system.
E. selective distribution.

11-**131.**
B
App.
Med.
p. 321

If a producer has a technically superior and expensive product--which has achieved brand preference--and wants retailers to provide aggressive promotion and maximum customer service, this producer should seek:
A. Dual distribution.
B. Exclusive distribution.
C. Administered distribution.
D. Intensive distribution.
E. Selective distribution.

11-**132.**
D
Comp.
Hard
p. 321

Exclusive distribution
A. should generally be used only if it is not possible to generate middleman interest in intensive distribution.
B. is legal as long as it does not involve vertical channel arrangements.
C. arrangements between a producer and middleman are illegal for most types of products, and thus they are not very common in the U.S.
D. usually involves some type of formal (contractual) arrangement among channel members.
E. None of the above is true.

11-**133.**
A
Int.
Hard
p. 319-22

Which of the following statements about ideal market exposure is TRUE?
A. As a firm goes from exclusive to intensive distribution, it loses progressively more control over price and service offered by retailers.
B. A producer usually should seek maximum market exposure.
C. Intensive distribution means trying to sell through all retail stores.
D. It is necessary to get almost 100 percent market exposure to justify national promotion.
E. All of the above are true.

11-**134.**
B
Comp.
Med.
p. 322

Legal concerns about channel of distribution arrangements are most likely to arise when:

A. a traditional channel system is involved.
B. there are horizontal arrangements between firms at the same level of the channel.
C. the firm is using intensive distribution.
D. a firm uses dual distribution to reach its target markets.
E. a corporate channel system is involved.

11-**135.**
E
Comp.
Hard
p. 322

Distribution agreements which limit sales by customer or territory:

A. are always illegal.
B. may be legal if they are vertical agreements between producers and middlemen.
C. are definitely illegal if they are horizontal agreements among competing producers or middlemen.
D. are definitely illegal if they are vertical agreements between producers and middlemen.
E. Both B and C are true.

11-**136.**
C
Comp.
Hard
p. 322

When selecting the degree of market exposure for a firm's products, it's important to remember that:

A. vertical arrangements between producers and middlemen which limit sales by customer or territory are definitely illegal.
B. The Federal Trade Commission prohibits exclusive distribution.
C. vertical arrangements between producers and middlemen which limit sales by customer or territory may be legal according to a recent Supreme Court ruling.
D. horizontal arrangements among competing producers or middlemen which limit sales by customer or territory are generally considered legal.
E. Both B and D are true.

11-**137.**
B
App.
Hard
p. 322

If Apex Mfg. Corp. gives the Atlantic Distributing Co. the exclusive right to distribute Apex's products in Virginia--with the understanding that Atlantic can't sell Apex's products outside Virginia or to other wholesalers in Virginia, this arrangement:

A. WOULD DEFINITELY BE ILLEGAL because the courts have ruled that all vertical arrangements between producers and middlemen are illegal.
B. MAY OR MAY NOT BE LEGAL--the courts would weigh the possible good effects of this vertical arrangement against possible restrictions on competition.
C. WOULD DEFINITELY BE LEGAL because the courts have ruled that all vertical arrangements between producers and middlemen are legal.
D. WOULD DEFINITELY BE ILLEGAL because the courts have ruled that all horizontal arrangements between competitors are illegal.
E. WOULD DEFINITELY BE LEGAL because the courts have ruled that all horizontal arrangements between competitors are legal.

11-**138.**
D
Comp.
Med.
p. 323

Producers often have to use "dual distribution":

A. because their present channel is doing a poor job.
B. because big retail chains want to deal directly with producers.
C. to reach all their target customers.
D. All of the above.
E. None of the above.

11-**139.**   A producer using several competing channels to distribute its products to its target
A   market is using _____ distribution.
Def.   A.   dual
Easy   B.   intensive
p. 322   C.   administered
                    D.   horizontal
                    E.   selective

11-**140.**   Reverse channels may be used to retrieve products from:
D   A.   business customers
Def.   B.   final consumers
Easy   C.   middlemen
p. 324-25   D.   all of the above
                    E.   only A and C above

Chapter 12

Distribution Customer Service and Logistics

True-False Questions:

12-1.
True
p. 330

For many physical goods, firms spend half or more of their total marketing dollars on physical distribution activities.

12-2.
False
p. 332-33

A marketing manager should never increase the total cost of distribution--even if this would result in a better customer service level for his target market.

12-3.
True
p. 333

The physical distribution concept seeks to minimize the cost of distribution for a given customer service level.

12-4.
False
p. 333

The physical distribution concept is based on the idea that selecting the lowest cost transporting alternative and the lowest cost storing alternative will result in the lowest total distribution cost.

12-5.
True
p. 333

With the PD concept, firms decide what specific service level to provide to their customers.

12-6.
True
p. 334

The "total cost approach" to physical distribution management involves evaluating all the costs of alternative physical distribution systems, including transporting, storing, and handling costs.

12-7.
False
p. 336

Most marketing functions can be shared in a channel, but the storing function is almost always handled by the producer.

12-8.
True
p. 337

Just-in-time delivery reduces storing and handling costs for business customers.

12-9.
False
p. 338

Just-in-time delivery systems typically shift more responsibility for PD activities to the customer rather than the supplier.

12-10.
False
p. 338

Every firm should try to use the just-in-time approach to physical distribution.

12-11.
True
p. 338

A channel of distribution is part of a broader network of relationships called a chain of supply.

12-12.
True
p. 338

A channel of distribution is part of a chain of supply.

12-13.
False
p. 338

The term "chain of supply" can be misleading because the chain typically involves only two firms: a vendor (selling firm) and a customer (buying firm).

12-14.
True
p. 338

A chain of supply includes all the activities involved in procuring materials, transforming them into products, and distributing them to customers.

12-15.
False
p. 338

A channel of distribution for a product involves more firms than a chain of supply for the same product.

12-16.
False
p. 338

The "chain of supply" concept refers to the idea that distribution can usually be reduced if the firm that is the "weakest link" in the channel of distribution is eliminated.

12-17.
True
p. 338

In both a chain of supply and a channel of distribution, the primary aim should be to create maximum value for the customer.

12-18.
False
p. 338

In both chains of supply and channels of distribution, the primary aim should be for each firm to keep its own costs as low as possible.

12-19.
True
p. 338

The challenges of coordinating logistics functions in a chain of supply has led to increased use of outside experts and computer models.

12-20.
False
p. 339

Electronic data interchange is important in business markets in the U.S., but it plays little role in international trade.

12-21.
True
p. 341

Transporting costs usually add relatively little to the cost of valuable products.

12-22.
False
p. 341

In the U.S., there is little competition among transporting firms for shipping business because government regulations control most transporting rates, routes, and schedules.

12-23.
True
p. 342

The best transporting mode is the one that provides the required level of service at the lowest cost.

12-24.
True
p. 342

Low transporting cost is not the only criterion for selecting the best mode of transportation.

12-25.
False
p. 342

In the U.S., trucks carry more freight over more miles than any other mode of transportation.

12-26.
True
p. 343

Heavy, bulky goods requiring long distance movement are usually carried by railroads.

12-27.
True
p. 343

About 75 percent of all U.S. freight moves, at least part of the way, by trucks.

12-28.
False
p. 343

For short distances and higher-value products, trucks may charge rates that are much higher than railroad rates and yet provide slower service.

12-29.
False
p. 343

Trucking rates are roughly one half of railroad rates.

12-30.
True
p. 343

Although ships and barges are slow, they are the lowest cost method of freight transporting, and are useful when speed is not critical.

12-31.
False
p. 344

Airfreight generally increases both transporting cost and the total cost of distribution because it tends to add to inventory costs, spoilage, theft, and damage.

12-32.
True
p. 345

Loading truck trailers on railcars for shipment closer to the trucks' destination points is called "piggyback service."

12-33.
True
p. 345

Efforts to reduce the environmental efforts of transporting usually increase the firm's distribution costs.

12-34.
True
p. 346

A freight forwarder is basically a wholesaler of space on transport facilities owned by others.

12-35.
False
p. 347

Storing provides place, possession, and form utility.

12-36.
True
p. 349

Private warehouses (compared to public warehouses) are most appropriate when a firm has a regular need to store a large quantity of goods.

12-**37.**
False
p. 349

Public warehouses (compared to private warehouses) provide greater economy and flexibility when a firm does not have a regular need to store a large volume of goods, but they provide fewer services than a firm's own warehouse could.

12-**38.**
True
p. 350

The main function of a "distribution center" is to speed the flow of goods and avoid unnecessary storage.

12-**39.**
False
p. 350

A "distribution center" is a special kind of public warehouse designed specifically for storing perishable products.

12-**40.**
False
p. 350

When both regrouping and storing are needed, a firm should add a distribution center.

Multiple Choice Questions

12-**41.**
E
Comp.
Easy
p. 330

"Logistics" is concerned with:
  A. creating time and place utility.
  B. transporting, storing, and handling of physical goods along channel systems.
  C. transporting, storing, and handling of physical goods within individual firms.
  D. logistics.
  E. All of the above.

12-**42.**
C
Def.
Easy
p. 330

The "logistics" functions create:
  A. possession utility.
  B. form utility.
  C. time and place utility.
  D. spatial separations between producers and consumers.
  E. Only B and C above.

12-**43.**
E
Comp.
Easy
p. 330

Physical distribution decisions may impact
  A. location decisions.
  B. target market selection.
  C. price decisions.
  D. channel of distribution decisions.
  E. all of the above.

12-**44.**
B
Comp.
Med.
p. 331-33

When planning physical distribution, the marketing manager should:
  A. set the customer service level so that every customer can get the product exactly when he wants it.
  B. minimize the cost of distribution for a given customer service level.
  C. minimize the cost of transportation.
  D. maximize the speed of delivery.
  E. make use of a distribution center.

12-**45**.   The right physical distribution system should be based primarily on
A   A. the desired customer service level.
Comp.   B. how customers store the product.
Med.   C. the physical characteristics of the product.
p. 331-33   D. what is the lowest cost method of transportation for the product.
                  E. the inventory level that allows the smoothest production runs.

12-**46**.   The physical distribution concept says (or implies) that:
C   A. transporting, storing, and product-handling are unrelated activities for cost
Comp.   control.
Med.   B. the best distribution system is the lowest cost one.
p. 333   C. a firm should seek to minimize the total cost of transporting, storing, and
                          product-handling--for a given level of customer service.
                  D. if the transporting department minimizes its costs and the storing department
                          minimizes its costs and the product-handling department minimizes its costs--then
                          the total cost of physical distribution will be minimized.
                  E. Both A and D.

12-**47**.   The _____ concept says that all transporting, storing, and product-handling
D   activities of a business and a channel system should be thought of as part of one system
Def.   which should seek to minimize the cost of distribution for a given customer service
Easy   level.
p. 333   A. PERT
                  B. product-market
                  C. distribution center
                  D. physical distribution
                  E. marketing

12-**48**.   The "physical distribution concept" is probably being used in a firm if:
D   A. inventories are set based on just-in-time delivery policies.
Comp.   B. the total cost of distribution is as low as possible.
Med.   C. storing costs have been minimized.
p. 333   D. transporting, storing, and product-handling are seen as interrelated parts of one
                          PD system.
                  E. transporting costs have been minimized.

12-**49.**
E
App.
Easy
p. 333-34

A merchant wholesaler is considering four physical distribution systems and estimates the total cost and customer service level for each as follows:

	TOTAL COST	CUSTOMER SERVICE LEVEL
Airfreight	$1,000,000	90%
Inland waterways	250,000	50%
Truck	300,000	60%
Rail and warehouse	425,000	70%

The best alternative is:
A. truck.
B. airfreight.
C. rail and warehouse.
D. inland waterways.
E. Cannot be determined without knowing how the target customers feel about the customer service level.

12-**50.**
A
Comp.
Easy
p. 333

A good marketing manager will try to:
A. set the desired customer service level before trying to minimize physical distribution costs.
B. minimize the total cost of physical distribution.
C. maximize the level of customer service provided by his firm.
D. minimize storing time and costs.
E. provide customers with just-in-time delivery service.

12-**51.**
C
Comp.
Med.
p. 334

The "total cost approach" to physical distribution management:
A. seeks to eliminate the storing function.
B. seeks to minimize the cost of transportation.
C. might suggest a high-cost transporting mode if storing costs could be reduced enough to lower total distribution costs.
D. ignores inventory carrying costs.
E. All of the above.

12-**52.**
B
Comp.
Med.
p. 337-38

Which of the following statements about just-in-time delivery is FALSE?
A. Just-in-time shifts greater responsibility for physical distribution backward in the channel.
B. Just-in-time reduces storing and handling costs for everyone in the channel.
C. Just-in-time increases the coordination needed among channel members.
D. Just-in-time reduces storing and handling costs for business customers.
E. None of the above are false.

12-**53.**
C
Comp.
Easy
p. 338

A chain of supply:

    A. focuses on making services available whereas a channel of distribution focuses on making goods available.

    B. may involve many firms, but only one manufacturer.

    C. includes all the activities involved in procuring materials, transforming them into products, and distributing them to customers.

    D. is easier to coordinate than a channel of distribution.

    E. all of the above.

12-**54.**
D
Comp.
Med.
p. 338

Which of the following statements about chains of supply is FALSE?

    A. A chain of supply includes all the activities involved in procuring materials, transforming them into products, and distributing them to customers.

    B. A chain of supply includes one or more channels of distribution.

    C. The primary aim of any firm in a chain of supply is to contribute to customer value by minimizing its own distribution costs.

    D. Few firms are willing to give "outsiders" access to information in their computer systems, so it is likely to be quite some time before computers have the impact on managing a chain of supply that they have had in other areas of business.

    E. None of the above is false.

12-**55.**
C
Comp.
Med.
p. 338

A chain of supply:

    A. is part of a broader network of relationships called a channel of distribution.

    B. is most effective when the objectives of the manufacturer at the beginning of the chain guide the activities of all other firms in the chain.

    C. requires skill in coordinating activities among different firms, and this has prompted many firms to seek help from outside experts.

    D. focuses on procuring materials needed for production, so its main weakness is that it ignores customer needs.

    E. A chain of supply concerns only direct relationships between producers, but a channel of distribution may involve middlemen.

12-**56.**
B
Comp.
Med.
p. 339

Which of the following statements about electronic data interchange is FALSE?

    A. Inventory information is automatically updated.

    B. EDI has not yet spread to international markets.

    C. A customer transmits its order information directly to the supplier's computer.

    D. EDI is very common in the United States.

    E. EDI puts information into a standardized format.

12-**57.**
E
Comp.
Hard
p. 341

The transporting function provides:

    A. place utility.

    B. possession utility.

    C. time utility.

    D. form utility.

    E. Both A and C.

12-**58.**
E
Comp.
Med.
p. 341

Good marketing strategy planners know that:
A. transporting costs may limit a marketing manager's possible target markets.
B. the transporting costs for some bulky or low-value products may be greater than their manufacturing costs.
C. transporting is vital for mass distribution and modern urban life.
D. the cost of shipping some "high-value" products to users is less than 5 percent of their selling prices.
E. All of the above are true.

12-**59.**
A
Comp.
Med.
p. 343

Regarding railroads,
A. full carload rates are lower than less-than-carload rates.
B. rail shipments usually move much faster than truck shipments.
C. they transport the same products in less-than-carload lots faster than full carload shipments.
D. they handle products only if they are shipped in full carload lots.
E. All of the above are true.

12-**60.**
B
Def.
Hard
p. 343

At least _____ percent of all freight shipped in the United States moves by trucks--at least part of the way--from producer to user.
A. 20
B. 75
C. 15
D. 5
E. 10

12-**61.**
D
App.
Easy
p. 343

A marketing manager who wants to ship small quantities (1,500 pounds) of relatively high-value products short distances at an economical cost should use:
A. inland waterways.
B. pipelines.
C. railroads.
D. trucks.
E. airways.

12-**62.**
A
Def.
Med.
p. 342-44

Regarding alternative transporting modes:
A. trucks are good for speed, frequency, dependability, and number of locations served.
B. pipelines are slower and less dependable than water transport, but also less expensive and able to serve more locations.
C. airways are faster, cheaper, and more dependable than railways.
D. waterways are slow, costly, and unable to handle a variety of shipments.

12-**63.**
D
Comp.
Med.
p. 343

Trucks
A. offer diversion in transit services to compete with trains for agricultural shipments.
B. are the most expensive of any of the modes.
C. are very slow compared to railroads, and this makes it hard to compete effectively.
D. compete aggressively with railroads for high-value shipments.
E. All of the above are true.

12-**64.**
E
Def.
Med.
p. 342-44

Regarding alternative transporting modes, which of the following statements is TRUE?
A. Waterways usually provide the lowest cost way of shipping heavy freight.
B. Airways are quickest.
C. Pipelines offer reliability in moving oil and natural gas.
D. Trucks serve the most locations.
E. All of the above are true.

12-**65.**
A
Comp.
Med.
p. 343

It is usually most economical to ship bulky nonperishable items, such as coal and iron ore, by
A. water.
B. pipeline.
C. truck.
D. air.
E. None of the above is a good answer, since the cost of shipping a product usually does not vary from one mode to another.

12-**66.**
A
Def.
Med.
p. 343

Considering weight, which one of the following transporting modes usually has the LOWEST cost?
A. Waterways
B. Airways
C. Trucks
D. Railroads
E. Pipelines

12-**67.**
B
Comp.
Easy
p. 343

The slowest transportation is typically by
A. rail.
B. water.
C. truck.
D. air.

12-**68.**
B
Comp.
Med.
p. 344

Regarding transportation modes, which of the following statements is NOT true?
A. The majority of the pipelines in the U.S. are in the Southwest.
B. Airfreight costs about the same as trucks for long distances, not counting the cost of transporting to and from the airport.
C. Water transportation is the slowest shipping mode.
D. Most cities in the United States are less than 200 miles from a major petroleum pipeline.

12-**69.**
E
Def.
Easy
p. 344

Considering weight, the most expensive transporting mode is:
A. pipelines.
B. railroads.
C. trucks.
D. inland waterways.
E. airfreight.

12-**70.**
B
Def.
Hard
p. 344

Regarding alternative transporting modes, which of the following statements is TRUE?
A. Waterways serve the most locations.
B. Airways offer the most expensive transporting mode.
C. Railways provide the lowest cost considering weight.
D. Trucks offer the fastest speed.
E. Pipelines in the U.S. are located mostly in the Northeast.

12-**71.**
E
Comp.
Easy
p. 344-45

Using airfreight instead of some other mode of transporting may result in:
A. lower packing costs.
B. lower total cost of distribution.
C. less damage in transit.
D. higher transporting costs.
E. All of the above.

12-**72.**
A
Comp.
Easy
p. 344-45

Shipping by air
A. is most useful for smaller, high-value items.
B. generally increases handling costs.
C. is generally the most economical transportation method.
D. all of the above.
E. none of the above.

12-**73.**
D
Comp.
Easy
p. 344-45

Shipping by air
A. is most useful for smaller, high-value items.
B. may reduce handling costs.
C. generally involves higher transportation costs than other modes of transportation.
D. All of the above are true.
E. None of the above is true.

12-**74.**
B
Comp.
Med.
p. 344-45

Regarding airfreight, which of the following statements is NOT true?
A. Airfreight may reduce the total cost of distribution.
B. Inventory costs usually increase, since only small quantities can be shipped at a time.
C. Very bulky items cannot be shipped economically.
D. Airfreight is opening up new markets for many perishable items.
E. There are usually fewer problems from theft and damage with airfreight.

12-**75.**
D
Comp.
Med.
p. 345

Containerization:
A. is widely used by railroads, but has not caught on with other modes.
B. makes it easier to load and unload products, but it increases the risk of damage.
C. has increased competition between railroads and water shippers since both offer this service.
D. is commonly used for international shipments from Japan.
E. None of the above is true.

12-76.
D
Def.
Easy
p. 345

The railroad service which picks up truck trailers at a producer's location, loads them onto rail flatcars, hauls them close to the customer, and then delivers them to the buyer's door is:
  A. truck service.
  B. fast freight.
  C. diversion in transit.
  D. piggyback service.
  E. pool car service.

12-77.
C
Comp.
Med.
p. 346

Transportation rates usually reflect the idea that
  A. different modes of transportation do not compete with each other.
  B. customers won't pay for faster, more reliable service.
  C. there are economies of scale in transportation.
  D. small quantities can be shipped at a lower cost per pound than large quantities.
  E. All of the above are true.

12-78.
D
Comp.
Hard
p. 346

The way transportation rates are arranged:
  A. offers much lower rates for larger quantities that make efficient use of transport facilities.
  B. suggests that there are economies of scale in transportation.
  C. helps explain why wholesalers may develop in a channel.
  D. All of the above are true.
  E. None of the above is true.

12-79.
C
Def.
Easy
p. 346

Freight forwarders can often charge shippers lower rates than the basic carriers because they:
  A. will only deliver to selected locations.
  B. only handle large shipments.
  C. combine the small shipments of many shippers into more economical shipping quantities.
  D. reserve the right to decide on the destination to which products will be shipped.
  E. Both A and C.

12-80.
E
Comp.
Med.
p. 346

Freight forwarders:
  A. handle about 75 percent of the general cargo exported.
  B. generally own their own transporting facilities.
  C. can be especially helpful to marketing mangers who ship large quantities of products.
  D. combine the small shipments of many shippers into larger quantities to obtain lower transporting rates.
  E. Both A and D.

12-81.
A
Comp.
Med.
p. 346

Freight forwarders:
  A. make a profit by using transporting facilities more efficiently.
  B. are primarily involved in arranging transfers of freight from one transporting mode to another in distant cities.
  C. do not deal with international shipments.
  D. usually own the transporting facilities they use.
  E. All of the above are true.

12-**82.**
D
App.
Med.
p. 346

National Power Tool Co. does not own its own transport facilities, but it regularly ships small orders to the wholesalers that handle its products. Tools that are going across the country are usually shipped by rail. Regional shipments usually go by truck. It probably makes sense for National to use
A. diversion in transit.
B. containerization.
C. piggyback service.
D. a freight forwarder.
E. None of the above makes sense.

12-**83.**
A
Comp.
Med.
p. 346

Which of the regrouping activities is the main work of a freight forwarder?
A. Accumulating
B. Assorting
C. Bulk-breaking
D. Sorting
E. None of the above is closely related.

12-**84.**
B
Comp.
Med.
p. 347

Storing:
A. must be provided by all channel members.
B. is necessary when production does not match consumption.
C. is related to Place--but not to Price.
D. creates form utility.
E. All of the above.

12-**85.**
C
Def.
Easy
p. 347

The storing function provides:
A. place utility.
B. form utility.
C. time utility.
D. possession utility.
E. None of the above.

12-**86.**
E
Comp.
Easy
p. 347-49

A marketing manager might greatly improve his marketing mix by:
A. shifting the storing job to a specialized storage facility.
B. adjusting the time products will be held by channel members.
C. encouraging final consumers to store some products for future consumption.
D. sharing the storage function (and costs) with middlemen.
E. All of the above.

12-**87.**
E
Comp.
Easy
p. 347-49

Storing:
A. costs include the costs of damage, theft, and reduced value if products get out-of-date.
B. costs can be reduced in the channel if suppliers are reliable about meeting delivery schedules.
C. too few products is likely to reduce a firm's costs, sales, and profits.
D. decisions are more difficult to make when demand is irregular.
E. All of the above are true.

12-**88.**
B
Def.
Hard
p. 348

The cost of carrying inventory is estimated to run as high as _____ percent of the value of the average inventory a year.
  A. 22
  B. 40
  C. 15
  D. 3
  E. 8

12-**89.**
B
App.
Med.
p. 349

A cheese processor having regular need for regional storage of a large quantity of cheese probably should use _____ warehouses.
  A. public
  B. private
  C. general merchandise
  D. commodity

12-**90.**
A
Comp.
Med.
p. 349

Compared to public warehouses, PRIVATE warehouses:
  A. may have low unit costs if the volume is high.
  B. are better if space will only be needed infrequently.
  C. offer low fixed investments.
  D. increase managerial flexibility.
  E. All of the above.

12-**91.**
C
Comp.
Med.
p. 349

Public warehouses:
  A. generally do not provide all the services that could be obtained in a company's own branch warehouse.
  B. are not usually responsible for the risk of damage in the warehouse.
  C. provide flexibility because the user pays only for the space used.
  D. are not very useful to manufacturers who must maintain stocks in many locations, including foreign countries.
  E. All of the above.

12-**92.**
B
Comp.
Med.
p. 349

Compared to private warehouses, PUBLIC warehouses:
  A. are not any more flexible because long-term leases are usually required.
  B. may not always be conveniently available.
  C. require no fixed investment but per unit storing costs are usually higher.
  D. reduce managerial flexibility.
  E. All of the above.

12-**93.**
D
Comp.
Med.
p. 349

There are big shifts in demand from season to season for the lawn mowers produced by Grow Green Co.--and its need for storage facilities also varies. Grow Green should think about using:
  A. piggyback service.
  B. diversion in transit.
  C. distribution centers.
  D. public warehousing facilities.
  E. None of the above is a good answer.

12-**94.**
E
Comp.
Med.
p. 350

Modern warehouses typically do NOT have:
A. power-operated lift trucks.
B. electric hoists.
C. battery-operated motor scooters.
D. roller-skating order pickers.
E. freight elevators.

12-**95.**
D
Comp.
Med.
p. 350

Compared to a warehouse, a DISTRIBUTION CENTER is:
A. designed to provide more efficient use of storage space.
B. concerned with eliminating the need for bulk-breaking.
C. designed to eliminate all storage.
D. set up to speed the flow of products toward the consumer.
E. a storage facility used by several middlemen--to share costs.

12-**96.**
B
Def.
Easy
p. 350

The primary function of a _____ is to speed the flow of products and avoid unnecessary storing costs.
A. commodity warehouse
B. distribution center
C. merchant wholesaler
D. public warehouse
E. private warehouse

12-**97.**
A
Comp.
Hard
p. 350

Which of the following statements about inventory and storage is TRUE?
A. A distribution center is used to avoid unnecessary storing costs.
B. Only government agencies can store products in public warehouses.
C. Decisions about inventory levels are usually not of concern to marketing managers--since inventory levels are best determined based on the amount of the product produced.
D. Achieving customer service goals makes a large inventory almost inevitable.
E. Minimizing storage costs will lead to lower total distribution costs.

Chapter 13

Retailers, Wholesalers, and Their Strategy Planning

True-False Questions:

13-1.
False
p. 357

Retailing includes all of the activities involved in reselling goods to final consumers, but it does not include the sale of services to final consumers since services must be produced.

13-2.
True
p. 358-59

Social class appeal is one of the emotional needs that seems to affect a consumer's choice of a retail store.

13-3.
False
p. 358

A consumer's choice of a retail store appears to be based almost entirely on economic needs.

13-4.
False
p. 358-59

Retailers and their strategies can easily be classified based on the type of merchandise they sell.

13-5.
False
p. 360

Most "conventional" retailers are single-line or limited-line stores that have very low expenses relative to sales.

13-6.
True
p. 360

Most single-line and limited-line stores apply the retailing philosophy of buying low and selling high.

13-7.
True
p. 360

In most countries, small limited-line retailers account for the majority of all retailers.

13-8.
True
p. 360

Specialty shops are limited-line stores which aim at a carefully defined target market with a unique product assortment, good service, and knowledgeable salespeople.

13-9.
False
p. 361

Department stores are stores which usually try to serve customers seeking a variety of convenience products.

13-10.
False
p. 361

Department stores keep growing in numbers, sales, and market share.

13-11.
True
p. 361

Mass-merchandisers have proved to be effective competitors in taking away department store customers.

13-12.
False
p. 361

Retailers who follow a policy of "buy low and sell high" are practicing the "mass-merchandising concept."

13-13.
False
p. 362

Warehouse clubs started the move to mass-merchandising.

13-14.
False
p. 362

The basic idea for supermarkets developed in the U.S. in the 1960s when consumers started to move from the cities to the suburbs.

13-15.
True
p. 362

Large sales volume and efficient operation are usually very important for supermarkets, since net profits usually run 1 percent of sales or less.

13-16.
False
p. 363

Super warehouse stores charge higher prices than supermarkets and focus on attracting customers who want better selections of perishables like meat and produce.

13-17.
False
p. 363

Catalog showroom retailers tend to sell brands which are not well known, because their main selling point is low price.

13-18.
False
p. 364

Today, discount houses are found in low-rent facilities, have poor images with customers, and offer few services and no guarantees.

13-19.
False
p. 364

Mass-merchandisers emphasize "hard goods" while discount houses emphasize "soft goods."

13-20.
True
p. 364

Mass-merchandisers may have reached the market maturity stage of their life cycle since industry profits are declining.

13-21.
False
p. 364

"Supercenters" are very large stores that specialize in selling a big variety of infrequently purchased products that would otherwise be hard for consumers to find.

13-22.
True
p. 364

A consumer who went to shop at a "supercenter" would probably expect not only to be able to buy food and health care products, but also to leave dry-cleaning or have shoes repaired.

13-23.
True
p. 365

In addition to food, warehouse clubs carry homogeneous shopping goods.

13-24.
False
p. 365

In addition to food, warehouse clubs emphasize heterogeneous shopping goods.

13-25.
True
p. 365

Category killers is another name for single-line mass-merchandisers.

13-26.
True
p. 365

Because of their higher margins, faster turnover, and narrower assortments, convenience food stores generally are more profitable than supermarkets.

13-27.
True
p. 365

Convenience food stores now compete with grocery stores, gas stations, and fast-food outlets.

13-28.
False
p. 365

The sale of candy from a vending machine at a bus station is not considered retailing since no store is involved.

13-29.
False
p. 365

The major advantage of vending machine retailing is that the costs are low relative to the volume they sell.

13-30.
False
p. 365

Automatic vending accounts for 15 percent of total U.S. retail sales.

13-31.
False
p. 365-66

Door-to-door selling is an important method for selling new or unsought products and it accounts for more than 15 percent of all retail sales.

13-32.
True
p. 366

Telephone and direct-mail retailers typically earn after-tax profit margins that are much higher than the profit margins of other types of retailers.

13-33.
False
p. 366

After-tax profits for mail-order retailers average about 30 percent of sales--and in the future they are expected to grow even larger.

13-34.
True
p. 366

Electronic shopping, which puts catalogs on cable TV or Internet websites, got off to a slow start but is making headway now.

13-35.
False
p. 366

It's best to think of retailing on the Internet as just another example of how low-margin mass-merchandisers appel to large target marktes with discount prices.

13-36.
True
p. 367

All types of retailers are now establishing a presence on the Internet.

13-37.
True
p. 367

In total, the economic impact of the Internet on our current retail system has been fairly limited so far.

13-38.
False
p. 367

Retailing on the Internet already accounts for about 25 percent of all retail sales.

13-39.
False
p. 367

Retail sales on the Internet grew very rapidly at first, but now are expected to grow slowly.

13-40.
False
p. 368

It's usually possible for a consumer to get much more information about a product in a retail store than on the Web.

13-41.
True
p. 369

Shopping on the Internet is easier when you know exactly what you're looking for.

13-42.
True
p. 369

The Internet makes it easy to do comparison shopping of products and prices.

13-43.
True
p. 369

A consumer's total cost of shopping on the Internet includes delivery costs in addition to purchase price.

13-44.
False
p. 371

The "wheel of retailing" theory says that new retailers enter the market as high-status, high-margin, high-price operators and then evolve into discount stores as competition becomes more intense.

13-45.
True
p. 371

The "wheel of retailing" theory fails to explain some major retailing developments, such as vending machines and convenience food stores, which did not enter the market with a low-price emphasis.

13-46.
True
p. 371

The development of vending machines and convenience food stores is not explained by the "Wheel of Retailing" theory.

13-47.
False
p. 371

"Scrambled merchandising" refers to the practice of conventional retailers handling many products within a limited-line, even though many of these products have to be sold at a low profit.

13-48.
True
p. 371

Retailers who carry any product line that will sell profitably are practicing "scrambled merchandising."

13-49.
True
p. 371

Scrambled merchandising means mixing product lines for higher profits.

13-**50.**
True
p. 372

The product life cycle concept applies to retailers as well as products.

13-**51.**
False
p. 372

Application of the product life cycle concept to retailing suggests that all types of retailers are in early market growth due to continually increasing family income.

13-**52.**
True
p. 373

The majority of all retailers in the U.S. have annual average sales of less than $1 million.

13-**53.**
True
p. 373

Less than 10 percent of retail stores in the U.S. account for more than half of the nation's retail sales.

13-**54.**
True
p. 373

The average retail store is too small to gain economies of scale.

13-**55.**
False
p. 373

Corporate chains are taking a smaller percentage of retail sales now that consumers are demanding lower prices.

13-**56.**
True
p. 373

The growth of cooperative chains of retail stores is due to the desire of small retailers to achieve some of the benefits of large-scale corporate chains.

13-**57.**
True
p. 373

"Cooperative chains" are retailer-sponsored groups formed by independent retailers to run their own buying organizations.

13-**58.**
False
p. 373-74

"Voluntary chains" are retailer-sponsored groups--and "cooperative chains" are wholesaler-sponsored groups--which work together to better compete with corporate chains.

13-**59.**
False
p. 374

Unlike franchise operations which tend to focus on newcomers to retailing, voluntary chains tend to work with existing retailers.

13-**60.**
True
p. 373-74

Unlike franchise operations which tend to focus on newcomers to retailing, cooperative chains tend to work with existing retailers.

13-**61.**
True
p. 374

Only 5 percent of new franchise operations fail in the first few years, compared to about 70 percent for other new retailers.

13-**62.**
False
p. 375

The supercenter retailing format began in the U.S. and then was exported to other countries.

13-63.
True
p. 375

Small limited-line shops still dominate retailing in Asia, Europe, and South America because of the political and legal environments in those regions.

13-64.
False
p. 376

Retailing is likely to see a continuation of past trends--and especially growth in the profits of "conventional" retailers.

13-65.
False
p. 376

According to the U.S. Bureau of Census, wholesaling is defined as the activities of firms which sell to retailers, but do not sell in large amounts to final consumers, manufacturers, or other institutional users.

13-66.
False
p. 376

Wholesalers are more likely to dominate distribution channels in more advanced economies than in less-developed ones.

13-67.
True
p. 376

Wholesaling has adopted new strategies and big changes are underway even though they may be invisible to consumers.

13-68.
True
p. 376-77

Although wholesalers no longer dominate channels in the U.S., they do provide a necessary function and have survived because of new management and new techniques.

13-69.
False
p. 377

Modern wholesalers want to sell to as many retailer-customers as possible, since cost analysis shows that even very small customers are usually very profitable.

13-70.
False
p. 378

When considering cost as a percent of sales, agent middlemen are more expensive than manufacturers' sales branches.

13-71.
False
p. 378

Agent middlemen usually have higher operating expenses (as a percentage of sales) than merchant wholesalers.

13-72.
True
p. 378

Merchant wholesalers account for over 50 percent of all wholesalers.

13-73.
False
p. 379

Manufacturers' sales branches operate like wholesalers, but the U. S. Census Bureau does not consider them wholesaling establishments because they do not involve a separate warehouse.

13-74.
True
p. 379

One reason manufacturers' sales branches handle over 30 percent of wholesale sales is that they are located in the best market areas.

13-75.
False
p. 379

Manufacturers usually operate sales branches in areas where sales potential is very low--because middlemen are not interested in serving such markets.

13-**76.**
True
p. 379

A hardware wholesaler that buys nails from a manufacturer and then sells them to retail hardware stores is a merchant wholesaler.

13-**77.**
True
p. 380

Merchant wholesalers in Africa are often smaller, carry narrower product lines, and deal with fewer customers than their counterparts in North America.

13-**78.**
True
p. 380

"Merchant wholesalers"--who take title to the products they sell--are the most common type of wholesaling establishment.

13-**79.**
True
p. 380

Service wholesalers may be either general merchandise, single-line, or specialty wholesalers.

13-**80.**
True
p. 380

General merchandise wholesalers handle a wide variety of nonperishable items--and usually serve many different kinds of retail stores.

13-**81.**
True
p. 380

In consumer products, single-line wholesalers serve single-line and limited-line retail stores.

13-**82.**
True
p. 380

Specialty wholesalers usually sell a very narrow range of products and compete with other wholesalers who have a broader range of products by offering expert technical help and/or service to their customers.

13-**83.**
True
p. 380

Of all service wholesalers, specialty wholesalers carry the narrowest range of products and offer the most service.

13-**84.**
True
p. 381

Limited-function wholesalers provide only some of the wholesaling functions.

13-**85.**
False
p. 381

Limited-function wholesalers provide all of the basic wholesaling functions, except that they do not take title to the products they sell.

13-**86.**
False
p. 381

Cash-and-carry wholesalers do not deliver products or grant credit, but their costs are high relative to other types of wholesalers because of all of the other services they provide to small retailers.

13-**87.**
True
p. 381

Cash-and-carry wholesalers are more common in underdeveloped nations than in the U.S.--where big warehouse clubs have taken much of the business.

13-**88.**
True
p. 381

Drop-shippers have low operating costs because they do not actually handle the products they sell.

13-89.
False
p. 381

Drop-shippers keep adequate quantities of every product they carry in their own warehouses so that they can ship them out quickly.

13-90.
True
p. 381-82

Truck wholesalers may provide almost the same services as full service wholesalers, but they usually specialize in perishable products that regular wholesalers prefer not to carry.

13-91.
False
p. 382

A retailer that buys from a rack jobber needs to have an employee who is a specialist in the products the rack jobber handles.

13-92.
True
p. 382

Catalog wholesalers usually sell to business customers who don't have a local wholesaler or otherwise are not called on by other middlemen.

13-93.
False
p. 382

Agent middlemen do not own the products they sell, but they usually perform even more functions than a service wholesaler.

13-94.
False
p. 382

Agent middlemen typically provide even more functions than full service merchant wholesalers.

13-95.
True
p. 382

Agent middlemen are very common in international marketing.

13-96.
False
p. 382

Manufacturers' agents sell related products for several competing manufacturers.

13-97.
False
p. 382

Manufacturers' agents try to work for one producer at a time so they can devote all their energies to that producer's products.

13-98.
True
p. 383

Manufacturers' agents are usually much less expensive than a company's own sales force in market areas where sales potential is low.

13-99.
True
p. 383

Manufacturers' agents do not take title to the products they sell--and are paid a commission on sales.

13-100.
False
p. 383

Manufacturers' agents are mainly used as an inexpensive way to continue getting sales for a product--once a company's own sales force has successfully introduced it to the market.

13-101.
True
p. 383

Export and import agents are basically manufacturers' agents who specialize in international trade.

13-**102.**
True
p. 383

The "Product" that brokers sell is information about what buyers need and what supplies are available.

13-**103.**
True
p. 383

A broker's "product" is market information.

13-**104.**
True
p. 383

Brokers usually have a temporary relationship with the buyer and seller.

13-**105.**
False
p. 384

Over time, use of the Internet will result in a larger number of brokers.

13-**106.**
True
p. 384

A selling agent takes over the whole marketing job of producers, not just the selling function.

13-**107.**
True
p. 384

A manufacturers' agent represents a manufacturer in some specified geographic area, while selling agents usually handle the entire output of one or more producers.

13-**108.**
False
p. 384

Selling agents avoid working for a manufacturer that is having financial trouble because of the high risk.

13-**109.**
True
p. 384

A combination export manager is a blend of manufacturers' agent and selling agent.

13-**110.**
True
p. 384

Auction companies are used for products which require inspection by the buyer and for which demand and supply conditions change rapidly.

13-**111.**
True
p. 384

With auction companies, demand and supply interact to determine the price.

13-**112.**
True
p. 384

The Internet has expanded the number of auction companies in lines of business where auctions have previously not been common.

Multiple Choice Questions

13-113.
A
Def.
Med.
p. 357

"Retailing" refers to:
A. the sale of products to final consumers.
B. the sale of both business and consumer products.
C. the sale of consumer products to wholesalers, retailers, or final consumers.
D. the performance of regrouping activities.
E. All of the above.

13-114.
A
Def.
Easy
p. 357

"Retailing" covers all the activities involved in the sale of products to:
A. final consumers.
B. organizational and business customers.
C. producer/suppliers.
D. middlemen.
E. All of the above.

13-115.
E
App.
Med.
p. 357

Which of the following is NOT retailing?
A. A vacuum cleaner manufacturer hires its own sales force to sell door to door.
B. A private ambulance service takes an accident victim to a hospital and charges him $100.
C. A group of students sell donuts to people passing by their dorm.
D. A book wholesaler has a mail-order catalog which offers discounts to final consumers who buy by mail.
E. All of the above are retailing.

13-116.
E
Comp.
Easy
p. 358

Which of the following could be considered part of a retailer's "Product"?
A. location of store.
B. width and depth of product assortment.
C. reputation for fairness.
D. helpfulness of salespeople.
E. all of the above.

13-117.
E
Comp.
Easy
p. 358

Which of the following could be considered a part of a retailer's "Product"?
A. advice from salespeople.
B. assortment of services.
C. convenient parking.
D. width and depth of product assortment.
E. all of the above.

13-118.
E
Comp.
Easy
p. 358

A retailer's "Product" may include:
A. a particular assortment of goods and services.
B. location.
C. advice from salesclerks.
D. convenience.
E. all of the above.

13-119.
B
Comp.
Med.
p. 358

The percentage of new retailing ventures which fail during their first year is:
A. two-thirds.
B. three-fourths.
C. one-half.
D. one-fourth.
E. one-third.

13-120.
B
App.
Med.
p. 358

A "good" retail strategy planner knows that:
A. its a mistake to try to develop a strategy that isn't equally appealing to all social class groups.
B. the failure rate among beginning small retailers is quite high.
C. emotional needs are more important than economic needs in choosing a retailer.
D. All of the above are true.
E. None of the above are true.

13-121.
E
Comp.
Easy
p. 358

Which of the following is NOT relevant regarding why some consumers prefer one retailer over another?
A. convenience.
B. social class.
C. assortment carried.
D. service.
E. All of the above can be relevant.

13-122.
D
Comp.
Med.
p. 358

A good marketing manager for a retailer knows that:
A. economic needs are more important than emotional needs in choosing a store.
B. no store can serve more than one social class.
C. consumers only go to stores that offer the lowest possible prices.
D. individual consumers have different economic and emotional needs.
E. All of the above are true.

13-123.
D
Def.
Easy
p. 358

Which of the following is an economic need which helps explain why consumers choose a particular retailer?
A. Prestige
B. Status
C. Comfort
D. Value
E. Safety

13-124.
D
Def.
Easy
p. 358

Which of the following is NOT an economic need which helps explain why consumers choose a particular retailer?
A. Helpful information
B. Product selection
C. Prices
D. Social image
E. Fairness in dealings

13-**125.**
B
Def.
Easy
p. 358

Which of the following is NOT an economic need which helps explain why consumers choose a particular retailer?
A. Information
B. Shopping atmosphere
C. Special services
D. Convenience
E. Quality

13-**126.**
C
Comp.
Easy
p. 360

Most conventional retailers in the U.S. are:
A. supermarkets.
B. mass-merchandisers.
C. limited-line stores.
D. specialty stores.
E. department stores.

13-**127.**
A
Comp.
Easy
p. 360

Which of the following is the best example of a conventional retailer?
A. A limited-line store.
B. A department store.
C. A supermarket.
D. A convenience (food) store.
E. None of the above.

13-**128.**
A
App.
Med.
p. 360

A limited-line store is to a single-line store as
A. a tennis shop is to a sporting goods store.
B. a paint store is to a drugstore.
C. quality is to price.
D. a CD and tape store is to a movie theater.
E. full service is to self-service.

13-**129.**
D
Comp.
Med.
p. 360

A typical problem for limited-line retailers is that:
A. it is almost impossible for them to satisfy any particular target markets better than other types of retailers.
B. their marketing strategy usually relies only on low price.
C. they usually cannot carry enough items in a line for any customers to find what they want.
D. many of the items they carry are slow moving.
E. All of the above are problems.

13-**130.**
E
Comp.
Med.
p. 360

Which of the following statements about single- and limited-line stores is TRUE?
A. Many are small, with high expenses relative to sales.
B. They usually believe in a "buy low and sell high" philosophy.
C. Such stores face the costly problem of having to stock some slow-moving items in order to satisfy their target markets.
D. Most conventional retailers are single- or limited-line stores.
E. All of the above are true.

13-**131.**
C
Def.
Easy
p. 361-62

Which of the following are NOT "conventional retailers"?
A. Single-line stores
B. General stores
C. Supermarkets
D. Limited-line stores
E. None of the above, i.e., all are "conventional retailers."

13-**132.**
B
App.
Med.
p. 360

The "Fashion Place" carries a carefully selected and distinctive assortment of traditional women's business clothing and accessories for upper-class executives in Boston. It emphasizes customer service with its well-trained salesclerks. The store is probably a:
A. small department store.
B. specialty shop.
C. convenience store.
D. single-line store.
E. specialty store.

13-**133.**
D
Comp.
Easy
p. 360

Compared to more conventional retailers, which of the following retailers offer both expanded assortment and service?
A. mass-merchandisers.
B. door-to-door salespeople.
C. mail order.
D. specialty shops.
E. supermarkets.

13-**134.**
C
Comp.
Hard
p. 360

Specialty shops:
A. offer fewer services than the typical limited-line store.
B. have trouble deciding what to carry because it's hard for them to get to know what their customers want.
C. rely heavily on knowledgeable salesclerks.
D. All of the above.
E. None of the above.

13-**135.**
A
Def.
Easy
p. 360

Specialty shops generally:
A. want to be known for the distinctiveness of their product assortment and the special services they offer.
B. sell homogeneous shopping products.
C. are very good at speeding turnover.
D. carry complete lines--like department stores.
E. All of the above.

13-**136.**
D
Def.
Easy
p. 361

Department stores:
A. usually aim at customers seeking convenience products.
B. have accounted for a larger share of retail sales every year since 1950.
C. have no trouble holding their own against mass-merchandisers.
D. are organized into separate departments.
E. All of the above are true.

13-**137.**
D
Comp.
Hard
p. 361

Department stores:
A. are basically a group of limited-line stores under one roof.
B. are decreasing in number, average sales per store, and share of retail business.
C. usually aim at customers seeking shopping products.
D. All of the above are true.
E. Only B and C are true.

13-**138.**
B
Comp.
Hard
p. 361

Department stores:
A. are large stores which emphasize depth and distinctiveness rather than variety.
B. have declined since the 1970s because of competition from well-run limited-line stores and mass-merchandisers.
C. are usually weak in customer service.
D. usually emphasize specialty products.
E. All of the above are true.

13-**139.**
B
Comp.
Med.
p. 361

The "mass-merchandising" concept:
A. suggests aiming at small but profitable target markets.
B. focuses on increasing sales and speeding turnover by lowering prices.
C. supports the conventional retailer's "buy-low and sell-high" philosophy.
D. stresses the need for conventional stores.
E. All of the above.

13-**140.**
B
Comp.
Easy
p. 362

The first retailers to really show the importance of the mass-merchandising concept were the operators of:
A. general stores.
B. supermarkets.
C. catalog showroom retailers.
D. department stores.
E. limited-line stores.

13-**141.**
C
Comp.
Easy
p. 362

Which of the following retailers was the first to adopt the mass-merchandising concept?
A. department stores.
B. discount houses.
C. supermarkets.
D. general stores.
E. supercenters.

13-**142.**
B
Comp.
Easy
p. 362

Compared to conventional retailers, which of the following types of retailers offer a wider product assortment but less service?
A. convenience stores.
B. supermarkets.
C. telephone order retailers.
D. department stores.
E. limited-line stores.

13-**143.**
B
Comp.
Med.
p. 363

Regarding supermarkets, which of the following statements is TRUE?
A. It's best to think of supermarkets as "conventional retailers."
B. Supermarket net profits after taxes usually are about 1 percent of sales--or less.
C. Worldwide, supermarkets make up the majority of food stores.
D. The early supermarkets were based on the premise that consumers would pay more for better selection and service.
E. All of the above are true.

13-**144.**
B
Comp.
Hard
p. 362-63

Regarding supermarkets, which of the following is NOT true?
A. They introduced self-service to reduce their costs.
B. After-tax profits are very good--averaging 10 to 15 percent of sales.
C. The newer ones carry 40,000 product items.
D. They average about $17 million a year in sales.
E. They got their start as an experiment during the Depression.

13-**145.**
E
Comp.
Easy
p. 362-63

Regarding supermarkets, which of the following statements is TRUE?
A. They average less than $5 million a year in sales.
B. Net profits after taxes usually amount to about 3 percent of sales.
C. Compared to super warehouse stores, they offer lower prices and more service.
D. All of the above are true.
E. None of the above is true.

13-**146.**
E
Def.
Easy
p. 362

A retail store that averages about $17 million in sales annually and specializes in groceries--with self-service and large assortments is a:
A. mass-merchandiser.
B. specialty shop.
C. convenience food store.
D. discount house.
E. supermarket.

13-**147.**
D
Def.
Med.
p. 363

Catalog showroom retailers:
A. are mainly mail-order retailers.
B. usually stress convenience and avoid price competition.
C. usually charge above-average prices to cover the costs of printing and distributing catalogs to consumers.
D. sell several lines out of a catalog and display showroom--with backup inventories.
E. All of the above are true.

13-**148.**
E
Comp.
Med.
p. 363-64

Regarding discount houses, which of the following statements is TRUE?
A. The early discount houses emphasized nationally advertised hard goods.
B. While some conventional retailers cut price on competitive items, discount houses regularly sell all of their products at smaller markups.
C. As early discounters were able to offer full assortments, they also sought "respectability" and moved to better locations.
D. Discount houses are fast-turnover, price-cutting operations.
E. All of the above are true.

13-149.
B
Comp.
Med.
p. 364

Mass-merchandisers:
A. locate only in large downtown areas with large sales potential.
B. are large, self-service stores which stress low price to get faster turnover.
C. emphasize nationally-advertised "hard goods."
D. usually have about as much floor space as the average supermarket.
E. Both A and D are true.

13-150.
A
Def.
Easy
p. 364

Large self-service retail stores that emphasize lower margins to get faster turnover--especially on "soft goods"--are called:
A. mass-merchandisers.
B. convenience food stores.
C. department stores.
D. specialty shops.
E. single-line stores.

13-151.
B
Comp.
Hard
p. 364

Mass-merchandisers:
A. face a bright future and increasing profits--because of decreasing competition.
B. usually operate with low margins on individual items.
C. operate on the "buy low, sell high" philosophy.
D. try to reduce costs by reducing inventory turnover.
E. All of the above are true.

13-152.
E
Comp.
Med.
p. 364

Mass-merchandisers:
A. usually operated with low margins on individual items.
B. are facing declining profits--because of the intense competition.
C. generally run a self service operation.
D. are concerned with maintaining high inventory turnover.
E. All of the above are true.

13-153.
A
Comp.
Med.
p. 364

A "supercenter":
A. tries to provide all of a customer's routine needs--at a low price.
B. probably would not affect nearby supermarkets.
C. is just another name for a mass-merchandiser.
D. is a large department store which uses supermarket methods.
E. All of the above are true.

13-154.
A
App.
Med.
p. 364

Which of the following is LEAST likely to be sold by a supercenter?
A. trash compactor
B. Photo finishing
C. Lawn care materials
D. Aspirin
E. Milk

13-155.
A
Def.
Easy
p. 364

Very large retail stores that carry not only foods--but all goods and services which consumers purchase ROUTINELY--are called:
A. supercenters.
B. general stores.
C. supermarkets.
D. mass-merchandisers.
E. department stores.

13-**156.**
E
Def.
Med.
p. 365

Warehouse clubs such as Sam's Club and Costco
  A. usually operate in large, no-frills facilities.
  B. have been successful targeting small-business customers.
  C. emphasize homogeneous shopping products.
  D. usually charge consumers an annual membership fee.
  E. All of the above are true.

13-**157.**
B
Comp.
Med.
p. 365

Regarding retailing, which of the following statements is NOT true?
  A. Supermarkets average about $17 million in sales per year.
  B. Single-line mass-merchandisers have not been successful--probably because their assortments are so limited.
  C. Mass-merchandisers put less emphasis on knowledgeable salespeople than more conventional retailers.
  D. Discount houses got their start selling "hard goods" at lower prices.
  E. Catalog showroom retailers offer few services and tend to focus on well-known manufacturers' brands.

13-**158.**
E
Def.
Easy
p. 365

Which of the following would be considered a retailing "category killer"?
  A. Toys "R" Us (toys)
  B. Circuit City (electronics)
  C. Home Depot (home improvements)
  D. Ikea (furniture)
  E. all of the above

13-**159.**
E
Def.
Easy
p. 365

Which of the following would be considered a retailing "category killer"?
  A. Office Deport (office supplies)
  B. PayLess (drugstores)
  C. Lowe's (home improvements)
  D. B. Dalton (books)
  E. all of the above

13-**160.**
D
Def.
Easy
p. 365

Convenience (food) stores offer:
  A. wide assortments.
  B. low prices.
  C. more customer service than supermarkets.
  D. a limited assortment of "fill-in" items.
  E. All of the above.

13-**161.**
C
Comp.
Med.
p. 365

Convenience (food) stores:
  A. have enjoyed higher profits as more gas stations have converted and made this approach more popular.
  B. None of the above are true.
  C. try to earn better profits by high margins on a narrow assortment which turns over quickly.
  D. offer greater width of assortment but less depth than most supermarkets.
  E. charge about the same prices as nearby supermarkets.

13-162.
E
Comp.
Easy
p. 365

Regarding automatic vending, which of the following statements is TRUE?
A. It is important for cigarettes, soft drinks, and candy.
B. Costs are relatively high because the machines are expensive to stock and repair.
C. Although its growth has been spectacular, automatic vending still accounts for less than 2 percent of total U.S. retail sales.
D. A major advantage is customer convenience.
E. All of the above are true.

13-163.
D
Comp.
Med.
p. 365

Vending machine
A. sales now account for almost 20 percent of consumer spending.
B. retailing requires a lower margin to cover costs than for comparable products sold in stores.
C. retailing has been declining--because of high margin requirements.
D. operating expenses are high relative to the sales volume involved.
E. None of the above is true.

13-164.
A
Comp.
Easy
p. 365

Compared to conventional retailers, which of the following types of retailers added more convenient service while reducing product assortment?
A. door-to-door salespeople.
B. department stores.
C. specialty shops.
D. single-line stores.
E. superstores.

13-165.
A
Comp.
Med.
p. 365-66

Door-to-door selling at consumers' homes:
A. meets some consumers' needs for convenience.
B. can be very useful for selling convenience products.
C. accounts for more than 5 percent of total U.S. retail sales.
D. All of the above are true.
E. None of the above are true.

13-166.
B
App.
Med.
p. 365-66

In recent years, changes in the social and cultural environment have had a significant effect on door-to-door selling. Which of the following is MOST likely given the changes that have occurred:
A. Fuller Brush has seen a dramatic increase in profits from its door-to-door selling operations.
B. Sarah Coventry Jewelry has started distributing its products through jewelry stores because of the difficulties of finding someone at home during the day.
C. Avon Cosmetics has found that it needs a larger door-to-door sales force because dual career families have more income and more demand.
D. None of the above is likely.

13-167.
C
Comp.
Hard
p. 366

Telephone and direct-mail retailers:
A. have profits margins that are similar to those of other types of retailers.
B. have real trouble reaching their target markets, since their customers are so dispersed geographically.
C. can do well with products that would be unprofitable for a local retailer to carry.
D. All of the above are true.
E. None of the above is true.

13-**168.**
A
Comp.
Med.
p. 366

Telephone and direct-mail retailing:
    A. profit margins have been falling because of increased competition.
    B. have not had much success with expensive items, but do well with low prices on general merchandise.
    C. was once popular, but the Internet put all these firms out of business.
    D. is generally a mass marketing approach.
    E. All of the above are true.

13-**169.**
D
Comp.
Hard
p. 366

Regarding direct-mail retailers, which of the following statements is TRUE?
    A. They emphasize low-price "commodities" that can be found in local stores
    B. Their profit margins are typically less than for other types of retailers.
    C. They have higher operating costs than most conventional retailers.
    D. Some aim at very narrow target markets.
    E. All of the above are true.

13-**170.**
C
Comp.
Med.
p. 367

Retailing on the Internet:
    A. makes it hard for consumers to compare products or prices.
    B. is limited to only a few mass-merchandisers.
    C. makes shopping very convenient for some consumers.
    D. is not expected to grow very fast.
    E. all of the above.

13-**171.**
E
Def.
Easy
p. 367

Internet retailers include:
    A. limited-line retailers.
    B. service providers.
    C. mass-merchandisers.
    D. department stores.
    E. all of the above.

13-**172.**
E
Comp.
Med.
p. 367

Some differences between online and in-store customers include:
    A. In-store customers can usually inspect and immediately use the product.
    B. Online customers are usually younger, better educated, and more upscale.
    C. In-store customers usually get better customer service.
    D. Online customers usually have better access to comparative information about products.
    E. All of the above.

13-**173.**
E
Comp.
Med.
p. 368-69

Which of the following statements about retailing on the Internet is(are) true?
    A. More product information is readily available.
    B. Computer-related products have been the biggest sellers so far.
    C. Product assortments available are not limited by the customer's location.
    D. Price comparisons are easy.
    E. All of the above are true.

13-**174.**
C
Def.
Hard
p. 371

The "wheel of retailing" theory says that:
    A. retailers go through cycles from high costs and prices to lower costs and profits.
    B. general stores will dominate U.S. retailing in the next century.
    C. new types of retailers enter as low-status, low-margin, low-price operators and eventually offer more services and charge higher prices.
    D. all of the above are true.
    E. none of the above are true.

13-**175.**
A
Def.
Easy
p. 371

The idea that new types of retailers begin as low-status, low-margin, low-price operators and then--if successful--evolve into more conventional retailers offering more services is called the:
   A. wheel of retailing theory.
   B. pyramid concept.
   C. scrambled merchandising concept.
   D. superstore concept.
   E. mass-merchandising concept.

13-**176.**
A
Comp.
Med.
p. 371

The wheel of retailing concept
   A. is consistent with the emergence of supermarkets in the 1930s.
   B. explains the early success of convenience (food) stores.
   C. explains the early success of vending machines.
   D. suggests that new types of retailers usually emerge as high-price, high-cost operations, and then cut their prices as competitors enter the market.
   E. None of the above is true.

13-**177.**
B
App.
Med.
p. 371

Which of the following is best illustrated by a supermarket that carries Nintendo video games?
   A. The "superstore" concept
   B. Scrambled merchandising
   C. The "wheel of retailing"
   D. Target marketing
   E. Mass merchandising

13-**178.**
C
Def.
Med.
p. 371

"Scrambled merchandising" refers to:
   A. retailers shifting from one product-market to another (e.g., a food retailer shifting to clothing).
   B. limited-line retailers carrying wide assortments.
   C. retailers carrying any product lines they can sell profitably.
   D. displays of impulse products in supermarkets.
   E. incompatible price and promotion policies.

13-**179.**
D
Def.
Med.
p. 371

The idea that retailers will start to sell a new product that offers a profit margin higher than what they achieve on their traditional product line is consistent with the
   A. marketing concept.
   B. operating philosophy of most limited-line retailers.
   C. wheel of retailing concept.
   D. scrambled merchandising concept.
   E. none of the above.

13-**180.**
D
Comp.
Med.
p. 371

The trend toward scrambled merchandising can be explained by:
   A. the "Wheel of Retailing" Theory.
   B. the fact that cities are getting larger and larger, and it is harder for a retailer to segment the market.
   C. growing consumer demand for more service in retail stores.
   D. the fact that some retailers have traditionally used markups which seem "too high" to other retailers.
   E. the growth of telephone and direct-mail retailers.

13-181.
B
Comp.
Hard
p. 372

The development of new types of retailers can be best explained by applying:
A. the rule of franchising.
B. target marketing and product life cycle concepts.
C. the corporate chain hypothesis.
D. the wheel of retailing theory.
E. the law of retail gravitation.

13-182.
B
Def.
Easy
p. 372

Retailer life cycles (from introduction to maturity) seem to be:
A. getting longer.
B. getting shorter.
C. staying about the same.
D. changing erratically.
E. none of the above.

13-183.
B
Comp.
Hard
p. 373

Regarding retailer store size, it is true that:
A. more than 90 percent of all retail stores have annual sales of $50,000 or less--barely enough to support one person after expenses.
B. over half of all retail sales are made by the largest stores--those with sales over $5 million a year.
C. small retailers are unimportant and can safely be ignored by most manufacturers and wholesalers.
D. All of the above are true.
E. None of the above is true.

13-184.
D
Def.
Hard
p. 373

U.S. Census data show that:
A. about half of all retailers account for less than 10 percent of all sales.
B. very large retailers account for a small percentage of total retail sales.
C. manufacturers and wholesalers are more numerous than retailers in the United States.
D. less than 10 percent of all retailers have annual sales over $5 million.
E. All of the above.

13-185.
D
Def.
Hard
p. 373

U.S. Census data show that:
A. retailers are more numerous than manufacturers and wholesalers combined.
B. less than 10 percent of all retailers have annual sales over $5 million.
C. over 60 percent of all retailers have annual sales less than $1 million.
D. all of the above.
E. none of the above.

13-186.
A
Comp.
Med.
p. 373

Corporate chains:
A. can get a cost advantage over independent stores by spreading management costs to many stores.
B. account for nearly 10 percent of retail sales.
C. usually cannot obtain economies of scale in distribution.
D. are declining in importance.
E. All of the above are true.

13-**187.**
D
Comp.
Med.
p. 373

Corporate chains
A. have continued to grow--and now account for about half of all retail sales.
B. have an advantage relative to independent stores when it comes to promotion and use of dealer brands.
C. increase their buying power by centralizing at least some of the buying for different stores.
D. all of the above.
E. none of the above.

13-**188.**
C
Comp.
Med.
p. 373

Cooperative chains:
A. are sponsored by wholesalers to try to compete with corporate chains.
B. are experiencing declining sales.
C. are formed by independent retailers to run their own buying organizations and conduct joint promotion efforts.
D. are consumer groups who run nonprofit buying associations.
E. All of the above are true.

13-**189.**
A
Def.
Easy
p. 373

Chains formed by independent retailers to run their own buying organizations and conduct joint promotion efforts are called:
A. cooperative chains.
B. IGAs.
C. voluntary chains.
D. retailer chains.
E. franchise operations.

13-**190.**
D
Def.
Easy
p. 374

A wholesaler-sponsored retail chain is called a:
A. consumer cooperative.
B. corporate chain.
C. franchise chain.
D. voluntary chain.
E. cooperative chain.

13-**191.**
B
App.
Med.
p. 373

A number of independent drugstores are working with a wholesaler to obtain economies of scale in buying. They were organized by this wholesaler after a recent meeting to discuss ways of competing with corporate chains. These drugstores are now part of a:
A. corporate chain.
B. voluntary chain.
C. consumer cooperative.
D. cooperative chain.
E. franchise chain.

13-**192.**
B
Int.
Hard
p. 374

Franchise operations provide a good example of:
A. vertical integration.
B. contractual vertical marketing systems.
C. administered channels in which the retailers are the channel captains.
D. direct-to-buyer channels.
E. None of the above.

13-**193.**
D
App.
Hard
p. 374

Which of the following is NOT a franchise operation?
A. Midas Muffler
B. Kinko's Copy Center.
C. Computerland
D. Ace Hardware
E. Subway Sandwiches and Salads

13-**194.**
A
App.
Med.
p. 374

Which of the following is NOT a franchise operation?
A. Super Valu (food).
B. H & R Block (tax work).
C. Midas Mufflers (auto repair).
D. 7-Eleven (convenience store).
E. Subway (food).

13-**195.**
C
Comp.
Med.
p. 374

Franchise operations:
A. generally have very loose ties between the franchisor and franchise holders.
B. are organized very differently than voluntary chains.
C. often like to work with newcomers to retailing--whom they train and get started.
D. are very similar to cooperative chains.
E. All of the above are true.

13-**196.**
A
Comp.
Med.
p. 375

Which of the following statements about retailing in different nations in NOT true?
A. Mass-merchandisers are especially popular in less-developed nations.
B. Consumer cooperatives are important in Switzerland.
C. Supermarkets started in the U.S.
D. Supercenters started in Europe.
E. New retailing formats that succeed in one country are quickly adapted to other countries.

13-**197.**
B
Int.
Med.
p. 365-75

Regarding retailing, which of the following is LEAST LIKELY to occur in the future?
A. Vertical integration will increase in importance in the channels.
B. In-home shopping will become less popular.
C. More manufacturers will go into retailing.
D. Along with larger stores, there will also be more smaller stores.
E. Scrambled merchandising will continue to increase.

13-**198.**
D
Def.
Med.
p. 376

Business firms that sell to retailers and other merchants, and/or to industrial, institutional, and commercial users--but which do not sell in large amounts to final consumers--are:
A. retailers.
B. facilitators.
C. middlemen.
D. wholesalers.
E. intermediaries.

13-199.
D
Def.
Hard
p. 376

Wholesaling is concerned with the activities of:
A. manufacturers who set up branch warehouses at separate locations.
B. persons or establishments that sell to industrial, institutional, and commercial users.
C. persons or establishments that sell to retailers.
D. All of the above.
E. Only A and B above.

13-200.
E
Comp.
Med.
p. 377-78

Regarding modern wholesaling, which of the following statements is TRUE?
A. More careful selection of retailer customers has increased profitability.
B. Wholesalers are now more "retailer-minded."
C. Greater attention is being given to management advisory services.
D. Many wholesalers are using the Internet to reach new customers and improve profits.
E. All of the above are true.

13-201.
C
Comp.
Med.
p. 377-78

Regarding the future of wholesalers, which of the following statements is TRUE?
A. Most high-cost wholesalers will disappear in the near future.
B. Modern wholesalers are seeing that vertical integration with producers provides their only assurance of long-run survival.
C. Some small high-cost wholesalers will probably survive due to the specialized services they offer some market segments.
D. Net profit margins in wholesaling have been increasing in recent years.
E. All of the above are true.

13-202.
A
Comp.
Hard
p. 378

Regarding wholesaling, which of the following is (are) true?
A. Merchant wholesalers have higher sales than agent middlemen, but their costs (as a percent of sales) are over three times as high.
B. There are many more manufacturers' sales branches than merchant wholesalers.
C. Manufacturers' sales branches have higher costs than agent middlemen and account for a small part of total sales.
D. Good marketing managers select the type of wholesaler with the lowest cost when planning channels of distribution.
E. All of the above are true.

13-203.
B
Def.
Hard
p. 378

Regarding types of wholesalers, which of the following has the HIGHEST operating expenses as a percent of sales?
A. Manufacturers' sales branches (with stock)
B. Merchant wholesalers
C. Brokers
D. Manufacturers' agents
E. Agent middlemen

13-204.
E
Def.
Easy
p. 378

Regarding wholesalers, which of the following is the most numerous?
A. Service wholesalers
B. Agent middlemen
C. Limited-function wholesalers.
D. Manufacturers' sales branches
E. Merchant wholesalers

13-**205.**
D
Def.
Hard
p. 378

Regarding wholesalers, which of the following types has the LOWEST operating expenses as a percent of sales?
A. Specialty wholesalers
B. Merchant wholesalers
C. Manufacturers' sales branches
D. Agent middlemen
E. Service wholesalers

13-**206.**
D
App.
Hard
p. 379

A producer has a few territories where many big customers are concentrated, but most of its target customers are spread all over the country.
A. The company should use manufacturers' agents in the best territories and sales branches in the others, since good agents won't work the smaller territories.
B. The company should use sales branches everywhere, since it will cost more to use manufacturers' agents.
C. The company will probably have to rely only on manufacturers' agents, since they will only be willing to take the widely scattered markets if they can have the good territories too.
D. The company should use sales branches in the concentrated territories and agents in the others--assuming the concentrated territories are large enough to support sales branches.
E. All of the above are good alternatives.

13-**207.**
B
Comp.
Med.
p. 379

A good share of total U.S. wholesale sales are made by manufacturers' sales branches because:
A. they are well-managed.
B. branches are usually placed in the best market areas.
C. costs are lower because some marketing functions are eliminated.
D. about half of all wholesale businesses are owned by manufacturers.
E. All of the above.

13-**208.**
D
Def.
Easy
p. 379

The main difference between merchant wholesalers and other wholesalers is that they:
A. are more aggressive at selling than agent middlemen.
B. offer fewer wholesaling functions.
C. have the lowest operating expenses as a percent of sales.
D. own (take title to) the products they handle.
E. are willing to perform retailing functions also.

13-**209.**
D
Def.
Easy
p. 379

The two basic types of merchant wholesalers are:
A. single-line and limited function.
B. agents and merchants.
C. service and general line.
D. service and limited function.
E. single-line and general line.

13-**210.**
A
Def.
Med.
p. 380

Which of the following is NOT a full-service merchant wholesaler?
A. Broker
B. Single-line wholesaler
C. General-line wholesaler
D. General merchandise wholesaler
E. Specialty wholesaler

13-**211.**
B
App.
Med.
p. 380

Midway Plumbing, Inc. buys plumbing supplies, pipes, and tools from different manufacturers and resells them to construction companies. Midway is MOST LIKELY:
A. a rack jobber.
B. a service (merchant) wholesaler.
C. a drop-shipper.
D. an agent middleman.
E. a manufacturers' agent.

13-**212.**
E
App.
Med.
p. 380

A full-service wholesaler in Dallas takes title to the products it stocks--a full line of home repair products for independent hardware stores. This wholesaler is a:
A. selling agent.
B. broker.
C. specialty wholesaler.
D. rack jobber.
E. single-line wholesaler.

13-**213.**
A
App.
Hard
p. 380

Milt's Supply stocks electronic repair parts and related supplies and tools from various producers. Milt's sells primarily to small TV and electronic repair shops throughout the country that only want to order one or two items at a time. Orders are usually shipped out on UPS trucks. It appears that Milt's is a
A. single-line wholesaler.
B. manufacturers' agent.
C. drop-shipper.
D. truck wholesaler.
E. rack jobber.

13-**214.**
E
Def.
Easy
p. 380

Compared to specialty wholesalers, general merchandise wholesalers handle:
A. a narrower line--or perhaps only a specific line of merchandise.
B. almost no physical products.
C. a very narrow assortment of products.
D. products they do not own, while specialty wholesalers do own them.
E. a broader variety of products.

13-**215.**
B
App.
Med.
p. 380

A full-service wholesaler in London takes title to the "oriental foods" she sells to supermarkets, gourmet shops, and restaurants. This wholesaler is a:
A. manufacturers' agent.
B. specialty wholesaler.
C. selling agent.
D. single-line wholesaler.
E. general merchandise wholesaler.

13-**216.**
D
App.
Hard
p. 380

A manufacturer of which of the following product lines would be most likely to use a specialty wholesaler?
A. Electric appliances
B. Hardware items
C. Lumber
D. Plastic materials
E. Industrial cleaning supplies

13-**217.**
B
Comp.
Med.
p. 380

Which of the following is NOT a limited function merchant wholesaler?
A. A truck wholesaler
B. A general-line wholesaler
C. A rack jobber
D. A drop-shipper
E. A catalog wholesaler

13-**218.**
A
Def.
Easy
p. 380

Which of the following is NOT a type of limited-function wholesaler?
A. Specialty wholesalers
B. Catalog wholesalers
C. Truck wholesalers
D. Drop-shippers
E. Cash-and-carry wholesalers

13-**219.**
E
Comp.
Med.
p. 382

Which of the following is a limited-function merchant wholesaler?
A. An auction company
B. A broker
C. A manufacturers' agent
D. A general-line wholesaler
E. A rack jobber

13-**220.**
C
Def.
Easy
p. 381

Limited-function wholesalers:
A. are counted separately by the U.S. Census.
B. include manufacturers' agents.
C. own (take title to) the products they sell.
D. usually cost more than service wholesalers.
E. All of the above.

13-**221.**
D
Def.
Easy
p. 381

A cash-and-carry wholesaler does NOT:
A. store inventory.
B. anticipate his customers' needs.
C. take title to the products he sells.
D. grant credit.
E. both C and D.

13-**222.**
B
Comp.
Med.
p. 381

Drop-shippers:
A. have high operating costs because they do transporting and storing.
B. do not stock the products they sell.
C. do not take title to the products they sell.
D. do not emphasize selling.
E. Both C and D.

13-**223.**
B
Def.
Easy
p. 381

Which of the following wholesalers do NOT carry stocks for their customers?
A. Specialty wholesalers
B. Drop-shippers
C. Cash-and-carry wholesalers
D. Single-line wholesalers
E. Catalog wholesalers

13-**224.**
E
App.
Med.
p. 381

Cole Smithers sells fiberglass resins and fiberglass wire to the many small sailboat manufacturers in southern California. He takes title to the products but does not handle them. Instead, the resins are shipped in 50 gallon barrels directly from the producer to the sailboat manufacturers. Cole is a:
  A. selling agent.
  B. cash-and-carry wholesaler.
  C. manufacturers' agent.
  D. specialty wholesaler.
  E. drop-shipper.

13-**225.**
E
App.
Med.
p. 381

Which of the following products is most likely to be sold by a drop-shipper?
  A. Skis
  B. Toothpaste
  C. Greeting cards
  D. Printing supplies
  E. Coal

13-**226.**
C
Comp.
Med.
p. 381

Drop-shippers:
  A. are used because it is cheaper for producers to ship to them by rail and let the drop-shipper drop the products off at local retailers with small trucks.
  B. never take title to the products they sell.
  C. typically sell large shipments, e.g., rail carloads.
  D. have very high operating expenses.
  E. are full-service merchant wholesalers.

13-**227.**
A
Comp.
Hard
p. 381-82

Truck wholesalers:
  A. usually sell perishable products that other wholesalers prefer not to carry.
  B. don't own the products they sell.
  C. usually sell in large quantities, e.g., truckloads.
  D. have relatively low operating costs because of low overhead.
  E. All of the above.

13-**228.**
E
Int.
Med.
p. 381-82

Which of the following statements about limited-function wholesalers is TRUE?
  A. Cash-and-carry wholesalers serve small retailers who must perform some wholesaling functions themselves.
  B. Truck wholesalers sell perishable products which other wholesalers prefer not to carry.
  C. Rack jobbers specialize in nonfood products that sell in small quantities.
  D. Catalog wholesalers sell hardware, jewelry, sporting goods, and general merchandise--often catering to small industrial or retailer customers.
  E. All of the above are true.

13-**229.**
B
Comp.
Med.
p. 382

Rack jobbers:
  A. don't own the products they sell.
  B. apply their knowledge of the local market to many stores.
  C. are full service merchant wholesalers.
  D. are different from most wholesalers because they specialize in giving small retailers long-term credit.
  E. All of the above.

13-**230.**
A
Comp.
Med.
p. 382

Kristen Triplett is just starting as a rack jobber. She will:
- A. do what a lot of grocery store managers don't want to do.
- B. need a lot of money to get started, since all her customers will expect 30 days to pay their bills.
- C. not have to know very much about the preferences of the consumers who buy the products she handles.
- D. never actually handle or deliver the products in her line.
- E. probably get tired of visiting farmers' markets.

13-**231.**
C
App.
Med.
p. 382

Saul Monehan sells a wide assortment (in small quantities) of "emergency" home repair items (fuses, electrical tape, small packets of nails) to grocery and convenience stores. He owns the products he handles, and displays them for his customers. Saul is a:
- A. manufacturers' agent.
- B. selling agent.
- C. rack jobber.
- D. cash-and-carry wholesaler.
- E. truck wholesaler.

13-**232.**
D
App.
Med.
p. 382

A grocery store chain has decided to sell a small assortment of fast moving auto repair items--but is not certain what stock to carry in which stores and does not want to leave the decision to the local store manager. The chain should probably get help from a
- A. broker.
- B. cash-and-carry wholesaler.
- C. specialty wholesaler.
- D. rack jobber.
- E. manufacturers' agent.

13-**233.**
D
App.
Med.
p. 382

A national grocery store chain has decided to sell an assortment of hobby, gardening, and cook books. Buyers in the chain's main office are not certain what to stock because they think that consumers in different areas of the country will probably be interested in different books. The store managers have said they don't know what to order either. The chain should probably get help from a
- A. broker.
- B. cash-and-carry wholesaler.
- C. specialty wholesaler.
- D. rack jobber.
- E. manufacturers' agent.

13-**234.**
D
Def.
Easy
p. 382

_____ sell hardware, jewelry, and sporting goods out of a catalog to small industrial or retail customers who other middlemen may not call on.
- A. Specialty wholesalers
- B. Cash-and-carry wholesalers
- C. Selling agents
- D. Catalog wholesalers
- E. Truck wholesalers

13-**235.**
A
Comp.
Easy
p. 382

Agent middlemen are:
- A. mainly concerned with buying and selling.
- B. used by small companies that want a wholesaler to assume all of the risk of carrying inventory.
- C. specialists in certain geographic areas, rather than specializing by product or customer type.
- D. at a disadvantage because manufacturers expect them to pay for products before they are shipped.
- E. None of the above is true.

13-**236.**
B
Comp.
Easy
p. 382

The main difference between agent middlemen and merchant wholesalers is:
- A. the kind of selling they do.
- B. that agent middlemen do not own the products they sell--while merchant wholesalers do.
- C. that no agent middlemen physically handle products--while all merchant wholesalers do.
- D. their attitudes regarding the marketing concept.
- E. There is no difference--an agent middleman IS a merchant wholesaler.

13-**237.**
D
Comp.
Med.
p. 383

Which of the following statements about agent middlemen is FALSE?
- A. Agent middlemen based in a foreign market can be helpful in working through government red tape because they know the local business customs.
- B. Export and import brokers bring together buyers and sellers from different countries.
- C. Sometimes a manufacturers' agent takes on responsibility for a whole country or region.
- D. Export and import agents are basically selling agents who specialize in international trade.
- E. Agent middlemen are common in international trade.

13-**238.**
A
App.
Med.
p. 382-83

Debbie Wood sells food products to grocery wholesalers and large retail grocery chains in Tallahassee. She sells for several manufacturers with noncompeting lines of food products--earning a 5 percent sales commission. She neither handles nor owns the products she sells. Debbie is a:
- A. manufacturers' agent.
- B. rack jobber.
- C. broker.
- D. truck wholesaler.
- E. selling agent.

13-**239.**
E
App.
Med.
p. 382-83

Amanda Cloves calls on the many gift shops at Martha's Vineyard and sells a variety of unique decorative glass items, wind chimes, and picture frames produced by the companies that he represents. The store owners can order from Amanda rather than from the three different producers she represents. Apparently, Amanda is a
- A. selling agent.
- B. rack jobber.
- C. drop-shipper.
- D. broker.
- E. manufacturers' agent.

13-**240.**
A
Comp.
Med.
p. 382-83

Manufacturers' agents:
A. are often used to sell products whose limited sales potential discourages manufacturers from using their own sales forces.
B. can sell at a lower price than a manufacturer's own salespeople because agents are free to sell in any geographic territory.
C. usually perform storing and transporting functions.
D. usually handle the competing lines of several manufacturers.
E. All of the above.

13-**241.**
D
Def.
Easy
p. 382-83

Manufacturers' agents usually work for:
A. manufacturers' sales branches.
B. only one manufacturer.
C. selling agents.
D. several manufacturers of noncompeting lines.
E. service wholesalers.

13-**242.**
E
Comp.
Med.
p. 382-83

A manufacturers' agent:
A. sells noncompeting products for several manufacturers in a limited territory.
B. is often replaced by a manufacturer's own sales force when sales rise.
C. is paid a commission on sales.
D. can be especially useful to a small manufacturer with a narrow line of new products.
E. All of the above.

13-**243.**
A
App.
Med.
p. 382-83

Which of the following middlemen would be most helpful to a small manufacturer of computer components who wants to obtain distribution in several major markets and still retain control of the marketing of its products?
A. Manufacturers' agents
B. Rack jobbers
C. Selling agents
D. Brokers
E. Manufacturers' sales branches

13-**244.**
A
Comp.
Med.
p. 382-83

Manufacturers' agents:
A. are frequently used by manufacturers to help introduce a new product.
B. typically have a temporary relationship with a manufacturer, until a specific item is sold.
C. usually handle products for only a few companies since the cost of adding additional lines is quite high.
D. usually handle a full assortment of products from competing manufacturers.
E. buy large inventories from small manufacturers--helping them acquire working capital.

13-**245.**
A
Comp.
Med.
p. 382-84

Which of the following is NOT an agent middleman?
A. A drop-shipper
B. An auction company
C. A selling agent
D. A broker
E. A manufacturers' agent

13-246. Which of the following wholesalers own (take title to) the products they sell?
E
Def.   A. Selling agents
Med.   B. Combination export managers
p. 382-84   C. Brokers
               D. Manufacturers' agents
               E. None of the above.

13-247. A broker's "Product" is:
C
Def.   A. financial skills--and perhaps credit.
Easy   B. market contacts for new products.
p. 383   C. information about what buyers need and what suppliers are available.
               D. good storage and transportation facilities.
               E. All of the above.

13-248. David and Jan Meisenheimer bought a tire recapping facility from a man who had
B
App.   decided to retire. They were going to convert the building to a studio for dance
Hard   lessons--so they wanted to sell off the inventory of recapped tires and equipment for
p. 383   whatever they could get. The Meisenheimers don't know any buyers who might be
               interested in these products. Which of the following types of wholesalers would be
               most helpful?
               A. Rack jobbers
               B. Brokers
               C. Specialty wholesalers
               D. Selling agents
               E. Manufacturers' agents

13-249. Until recently, Triad Equipment, Inc. took trade-ins when it sold new equipment to
B
App.   manufacturers. Now, Triad has a new owner who wants to sell the inventory of used
Med.   equipment quickly to the best available buyer. He should look for:
p. 383   A. a manufacturers' sales branch.
               B. a broker.
               C. a selling agent.
               D. a manufacturers' agent.
               E. sales finance company.

13-250. A wholesaler who takes over the whole marketing job NATIONALLY for one or a few
E
Def.   manufacturers is called a:
Easy   A. merchant wholesaler.
p. 384   B. manufacturers' agent.
               C. broker.
               D. specialty wholesaler.
               E. selling agent.

13-**251.**
B
App.
Med.
p. 384

Stephanie Johansson sells the entire output of several small companies based in Silicon Valley. Each of the companies designs and produces remote control devices. Stephanie has almost complete control of pricing and selling--because the engineers who started the companies are mainly interested in inventing things. In addition, Stephanie often provides working capital to the producers, who have very limited financial resources. Stephanie is paid a substantial commission on all sales. Stephanie is a:

   A. broker.
   B. selling agent.
   C. field warehouser.
   D. manufacturers' agent.
   E. factor.

13-**252.**
A
Comp.
Med.
p. 384

A producer is most likely to use a "selling agent" if:
   A. he lacks marketing know-how and working capital.
   B. he produces a broad product line.
   C. he mainly needs aggressive selling.
   D. his target customers are concentrated in a small geographic area.
   E. he sells a technical product that needs a lot of follow-up service.

13-**253.**
D
Int.
Hard
p. 384

Regarding wholesalers, which of the following descriptions is TRUE?
   A. MANUFACTURERS' AGENT: does not own the products, usually carries stocks, represents several competing manufacturers within a geographic area.
   B. MERCHANT WHOLESALER: does not take title to products, takes possession, provides full service, and usually handles a broad variety of products.
   C. BROKER: does not own the products, does not take possession, major function is selling, and does not anticipate customer needs.
   D. SELLING AGENT: does not own the products, does the whole marketing job nationally, and may handle competing lines.
   E. All of the above are true.

13-**254.**
D
App.
Hard
p. 384

If a small U.S. producer with limited financial resources and little marketing know-how wants to sell its products in international markets, it should use:
   A. an export commission house.
   B. a factor.
   C. an export agent.
   D. a combination export manager.
   E. an export broker.

13-**255.**
D
Def.
Easy
p. 384

The major function of auction companies is to:
   A. deliver the products they handle.
   B. help finance by owning products.
   C. take title to the products they sell.
   D. provide a place where buyers and sellers can complete a transaction.
   E. All of the above.

13-**256.**   Traditionally, auction companies would MOST likely be used for:
C   A. children's clothing.
App.   B. sports equipment.
Med.   C. antique furniture.
p. 384   D. small appliances.
                  E. industrial chemicals.

Chapter 14

Promotion--Introduction to Integrated Marketing Communications

True-False Questions:

14-**1.**
True
p. 392

Promotion is communicating information between seller and buyer to influence buyer attitudes and behavior.

14-**2.**
True
p. 392

The marketing manager's promotion job is to tell target customers that the right Product is available at the right Place at the right Price.

14-**3.**
False
p. 392

A marketing manager can choose from only two promotion methods--personal selling and mass selling.

14-**4.**
True
p. 393

Direct spoken communication between sellers and potential customers is personal selling.

14-**5.**
True
p. 393

Personal selling involves direct spoken communication between sellers and potential customers.

14-**6.**
True
p. 393

With personal selling, the company's marketing mix can be adapted to the needs of each target market, but personal selling is usually quite expensive.

14-**7.**
False
p. 393

Face-to-face communication with large numbers of customers at the same time is mass selling.

14-**8.**
False
p. 393

Spoken communication with large numbers of customers at the same time is mass selling.

14-**9.**
True
p. 393

When the target market is large and spread out, mass selling may be less expensive than personal selling.

14-**10.**
True
p. 393

Advertising is any paid form of nonpersonal presentation of ideas, goods or services by an identified sponsor.

14-**11.**
False
p. 393

A major advantage of mass selling is that the source can receive immediate feedback from the receiver.

14-**12.**
True
p. 393

Mass selling includes both advertising and publicity.

14-**13.**
False
p. 393

Publicity is the nonpersonal presentation of ideas, goods, or services which is paid for by an identified sponsor.

14-**14.**
False
p. 393-94

Because publicity is "free," it is usually far less effective than advertising if the firm has a new message.

14-**15.**
False
p. 393

More money is spent on media costs for publicity each year than is spent on media costs for advertising.

14-**16.**
True
p. 393

Publicity allows a firm to avoid media costs.

14-**17.**
False
p. 394

Sales promotion is special advertising or personal selling that is aimed at middlemen in the channel.

14-**18.**
True
p. 394

Sales promotion can be aimed at middlemen, at final consumers, or even at a firm's own employees.

14-**19.**
True
p. 394

Sales promotion may be aimed at final consumers, retailers, wholesalers, or a company's own employees.

14-**20.**
True
p. 394

A point-of-purchase sample given to consumers is a good example of sales promotion.

14-**21.**
True
p. 395

In total, firms spend less money on advertising than on personal selling or sales promotion.

14-**22.**
True
p. 396

It is the job of the marketing manager to come up with an effective promotion blend.

14-**23.**
False
p. 396

It is the job of a sales promotion specialist to come up with an effective promotion blend.

14-**24.**
False
p. 397

Because the advertising, sales, and sales promotion managers all have similar outlooks and experiences, they usually work together very well to develop the right promotion blend.

14-**25.**
False
p. 397

Deciding on the right promotion blend should be the job of the advertising manager.

14-**26.**
False
p. 397

The basic idea behind integrated marketing communications is that it is critical for all of the different firms in a channel of distribution for a product to have an input in developing the advertising campaign for the product.

14-**27.**
True
p. 397

A firm that adopts the integrated marketing communications concept tries to coordinate all of its promotion communications to a target customer to convey a consistent and complete message.

14-**28.**
True
p. 397

Developing integrated marketing communications is more difficult when different firms at different levels in the distribution channel handle different promotion jobs.

14-**29.**
True
p. 397

The general objective of promotion is to affect buyer behavior.

14-**30.**
True
p. 398

The three general promotion objectives of informing, persuading, and reminding are all concerned with providing more information.

14-**31.**
True
p. 398

The informing objective in Promotion is simply a matter of educating the consumer about the firm's product.

14-**32.**
True
p. 399

The four promotion jobs of the AIDA model are to get Attention, to hold Interest, to arouse Desire, and to obtain Action.

14-**33.**
False
p. 399

The four promotion jobs of the AIDA model are to get Attention, to Inform, to eliminate Doubt, and to change Attitudes.

14-**34.**
False
p. 399

According to the AIDA model, promotion should try to change Attitudes, shape Intentions, arouse Desire, and cause Activity.

14-**35.**
False
p. 399

The AIDA model focuses on markets as a whole while the adoption curve model focuses on individuals.

14-36.
False
p. 400

In the traditional communication process, a receiver tries to deliver a message to a source through a message channel.

14-37.
True
p. 400

"Noise" in the traditional communication process is any distraction that reduces the effectiveness of the communication process.

14-38.
True
p. 400

Communication often breaks down because the receiver's decoded message is different than the message the source encoded.

14-39.
False
p. 400

During the traditional communication process, a source does decoding and a receiver does encoding.

14-40.
True
p. 400

For communication to be effective, there must be a common frame of reference between the source and the receiver.

14-41.
True
p. 401

The message channel may be as important as the message itself in influencing the receiver.

14-42.
True
p. 402

Most direct marketing communications are designed to prompt immediate feedback.

14-43.
True
p. 402

Achieving a measurable, direct response from specific target customers is the heart of direct marketing.

14-44.
False
p. 402

The main problem with integrated direct-response promotion is that it's nearly impossible to determine if it's effective.

14-45.
True
p. 402

Integrated direct-response promotion has expanded beyond direct-mail advertising to include other media.

14-46.
True
p. 402

In addition to mail, direct-response promotion may include telephone, print, e-mail, and the Internet.

14-47.
True
p. 402

In addition to mail, direct-response promotion may include websites, broadcast, e-mail, and interactive media.

14-48.
True
p. 403

Direct-response promotion targets specific individuals who respond directly.

14-**49.**
False
p. 403

Direct-response promotion targets groups instead of individuals.

14-**50.**
True
p. 404

Direct-response promotion usually relies on a computerized database.

14-**51.**
True
p. 404

The traditional view of promotion has focused on communication initiated by the seller.

14-**52.**
False
p. 404

The traditional view of promotion has focused on communication initiated by the buyer.

14-**53.**
True
p. 405

With new types of interactive promotion, the communication process is often initiated by the buyer.

14-**54.**
False
p. 406

In customer-initiated interactive communication, noise is no longer a factor.

14-**55.**
False
p. 406

In customer-initiated interactive communication, action is usually less immediate than in the traditional communication process.

14-**56.**
True
p. 407

A complete promotion blend may need to consider channel members (along the channel) as well as customers (at the end of the channel).

14-**57.**
True
p. 407

Pushing (a product through a channel) means using normal promotion effort to help sell the whole marketing mix to middlemen.

14-**58.**
False
p. 407

"Pushing" a product through a channel relies on very aggressive promotion to final consumers to try to get them to ask middlemen for the product.

14-**59.**
True
p. 407

The pushing approach recognizes the value of cooperation among firms in a distribution channel.

14-**60.**
True
p. 408

A pushing effort might include sales promotion as well as personal selling.

14-**61.**
True
p. 409

The idea behind a pulling policy is that customer demand helps to pull the product through the channel.

14-62.
False
p. 409

"Pulling" a product through a channel of distribution focuses promotion effort on wholesalers and retailers to get them interested in a producer's marketing mix.

14-63.
False
p. 409

Producers with well-branded consumer products and well-established channels typically emphasize personal selling--rather than advertising--in their promotion blends.

14-64.
True
p. 410

Promotion to business customers emphasizes personal selling.

14-65.
True
p. 410

It is usually too expensive for personal selling to do the whole promotion job for business products, so mass selling is useful too.

14-66.
False
p. 411

The adoption curve shows when different groups will accept new ideas, assuming that the promotion effort should stay the same for all groups.

14-67.
False
p. 411

The adoption curve shows that it is important to keep the promotion effort the same as time passes--so consumers won't be confused.

14-68.
True
p. 411

The adoption curve concept suggests that some groups within a market tend to be leaders in accepting new ideas.

14-69.
True
p. 411

Consumers who are innovators tend to be young and well educated.

14-70.
True
p. 411

A innovator is more likely to rely on information from an impersonal source (such as an article in a scientific magazine) than from a company's salesperson.

14-71.
True
p. 412

Early adopters are respected by their peers--and often are opinion leaders--so what they think about a product is especially important for reaching later adopter groups.

14-72.
True
p. 412

Personal selling is likely to be an effective method of promotion for reaching the opinion leaders in the early adopter group.

14-73.
False
p. 412

Favorable word-of-mouth information from opinion leaders can help a new product, but a negative reaction by opinion leaders tends to have no effect.

14-74.
True
p. 412

The early majority avoids risk by waiting until many early adopters have tried a product--to see if they liked it.

14-75.
True
p. 413

The late majority are less likely to follow opinion leaders and may need some pressure from their own group before they try a new product.

14-76.
False
p. 413

The adoption curve concept suggests that it is essential to stimulate early adoption by the laggards--or the product will never get beyond introduction.

14-77.
True
p. 414

During the market introduction stage of the product life cycle, the basic promotion objective is informing.

14-78.
True
p. 414

During the market maturity stage of the product life cycle, the basic promotion objective is persuading.

14-79.
True
p. 415

Firms in monopolistic competition may favor mass selling because they have differentiated their marketing mixes and have something to talk about.

14-80.
True
p. 416

The total cost of mass media may force a small firm to use promotion alternatives that are more expensive on a per contact basis.

14-81.
True
p. 417

The task method of budgeting bases the budget on the job to be done now, not on what was spent in the past.

14-82.
False
p. 417

The task method of budgeting focuses on the amount being spent by competitors.

Multiple Choice Questions

14-83.
B
Comp.
Med.
p. 392

"Promotion" is MAINLY concerned with:
  A. obtaining a favorable corporate image.
  B. telling the target market that the right Product is available in the right Place at the right Price.
  C. obtaining maximum publicity--at the lowest cost.
  D. informing the public about the firm's offerings to maximize sales.
  E. getting people to buy a firm's product--even when it isn't needed.

14-84.
E
Comp.
Easy
p. 392

"Promotion" is concerned with:
  A. how suitable messages are communicated to target customers.
  B. communicating information between seller and buyer to influence attitudes and behavior.
  C. informing customers that the right Product is available at the right Place at the right Price.
  D. blending personal selling, mass selling, and sales promotion.
  E. All of the above.

14-**85.**
D
Def.
Easy
p. 393

"Promotion" includes:
A. personal selling.
B. mass selling.
C. sales promotion.
D. All of the above.
E. only A and B above.

14-**86.**
D
Def.
Easy
p. 393

Which of the following is NOT a promotion method?
A. mass selling
B. personal selling
C. sales promotion
D. All of the above are promotion methods.
E. None of the above are promotion methods.

14-**87.**
D
Def.
Med.
p. 393

"Promotion" does NOT include:
A. personal selling.
B. sales promotion.
C. advertising.
D. introductory price dealing.
E. publicity.

14-**88.**
A
Int.
Med.
p. 393

Regarding promotion methods, which of the following statements is TRUE?
A. Personal selling can provide immediate feedback.
B. Publicity is "free," but usually is ineffective for really new products.
C. Advertising is usually more tailored to the individual needs and attitudes of target customers than personal selling.
D. Sales promotion activities produce results very slowly compared to advertising.
E. All of the above are true.

14-**89.**
A
Comp.
Easy
p. 393

"Personal selling:"
A. involves direct spoken communication between sellers and potential customers.
B. costs less than advertising for reaching a large, widespread market.
C. tries to communicate with many customers at the same time.
D. refers to "promoting" at trade shows, demonstrations, and contests.
E. All of the above.

14-**90.**
D
Comp.
Med.
p. 393

Compared with other promotion methods, PERSONAL SELLING:
A. is less expensive when the target customers are numerous and widespread.
B. is less effective in overcoming sales resistance.
C. is less flexible in adapting to customers' needs and attitudes.
D. provides more immediate feedback.
E. All of the above.

14-**91.**
D
Comp.
Med.
p. 393

MASS SELLING, in contrast to personal selling:
A. is less expensive when the target customers are numerous and scattered.
B. doesn't provide immediate feedback.
C. is less flexible in adapting to customers' needs and attitudes.
D. All of the above.

14-**92.**
E
Comp.
Med.
p. 393

"Advertising":
A. is less expensive than personal selling for reaching large and widespread target markets.
B. is any paid form of nonpersonal presentation of ideas, goods, or services by an identified seller.
C. is not the same as publicity.
D. is less flexible than personal selling.
E. All of the above are true.

14-**93.**
E
Def.
Easy
p. 393

"Advertising":
A. is the only form of mass selling.
B. is also called "sales promotion."
C. is concerned with "promotion" using samples, coupons, and contests.
D. involves direct spoken communication between sellers and potential customers.
E. is any paid form of nonpersonal presentation of ideas, goods, or services by an identified sponsor.

14-**94.**
C
App.
Easy
p. 393

A car company sent three automobile magazines some technical information and explanations about the features of its innovative new model. One of the magazines later printed a story about the car. This is an example of:
A. personal selling.
B. advertising.
C. publicity.
D. sales promotion.
E. None of the above.

14-**95.**
C
App.
Easy
p. 393

A computer software company sent three computer magazines some information about the latest release of its popular software program. One of the magazines printed a story about the new version. This is an example of:
A. personal selling.
B. advertising.
C. publicity.
D. sales promotion.
E. None of the above.

14-**96.**
B
Comp.
Med.
p. 393

"Publicity":
A. is generally less effective than advertising for promoting a really new product.
B. is mass selling that avoids paying media costs.
C. is any paid form of nonpersonal presentation of ideas, goods, or services by an identified sponsor.
D. is more expensive than all other promotion methods.
E. Both A and B are true.

14-**97.**
A
Def.
Easy
p. 394

"Sales promotion":
A. can complement a firm's personal selling and mass selling efforts.
B. involves direct spoken communication between sellers and potential customers.
C. is any paid form of nonpersonal presentation of goods or services by an identified sponsor.
D. is "free" like publicity.
E. consists of personal selling and mass selling.

14-**98.**
D
Def.
Easy
p. 394

"Sales promotion" can be aimed at:
A. middlemen.
B. a company's own sales force.
C. final consumers or users.
D. Any or all of the above.

14-**99.**
D
Def.
Med.
p. 394

Point-of-purchase materials, coupons, trade shows, calendars, merchandising aids, and sales training materials are all examples of:
A. publicity.
B. advertising.
C. mass selling.
D. sales promotion.
E. personal selling.

14-**100.**
E
App.
Med.
p. 394

Which of the following is NOT an example of sales promotion?
A. A "10 cents off" coupon promotion.
B. Point-of-purchase displays.
C. Trade show exhibits.
D. Free samples.
E. A wholly new kind of ad.

14-**101.**
B
App.
Med.
p. 394

Which of the following is NOT an example of sales promotion?
A. a small toy in "kids' packs" at a Wendy's fast-food restaurant.
B. a half-page ad in the telephone Yellow Pages for a security service.
C. an auto bumper sticker that says "Buy American."
D. samples of a new brand of cheese given away at a supermarket.
E. a display of fishing equipment by a sporting goods store in a shopping mall.

14-**102.**
A
App.
Med.
p. 394

Which of the following is NOT an example of sales promotion?
A. a banner ad on AOL's stock page.
B. a bumper sticker that says, "Drink more milk."
C. samples of a new low-fat snack cracker given away at a supermarket.
D. a display of fishing equipment by a sporting goods store in a shopping mall.
E. a small toy in a kid's "happy meal" at McDonald's.

14-**103.**
E
App.
Easy
p. 394

Which of the following is NOT an example of sales promotion?
A. A contest to motivate a company's own sales force.
B. Point-of-purchase displays at the checkout counters of a retail store.
C. Price-off coupons distributed to consumers' homes.
D. A trade show for wholesalers.
E. All of the above ARE examples.

14-**104.**
D
Int.
Easy
p. 396

Developing and selecting the "best" PROMOTION BLEND should be done by a producer's:
A. sales manager.
B. advertising agency.
C. sales promotion manager.
D. marketing manager.
E. advertising manager.

14-**105.**
D
Comp.
Easy
p. 397-98

A firm's promotion efforts may seek to:
A. make its demand curve more inelastic.
B. change the attitudes and behavior of its target market.
C. shift its demand curve to the right.
D. All of the above.

14-**106.**
E
Comp.
Med.
p. 397-98

When a firm uses Promotion, its BASIC objective is to:
A. make its demand curve more inelastic.
B. shift its demand curve to the right.
C. make its demand curve more elastic.
D. shift its demand curve to the left.
E. Both A and B.

14-**107.**
C
Def.
Easy
p. 398

Which of the following is NOT one of the basic promotion objectives discussed in the text?
A. to inform
B. to remind
C. to manipulate
D. to persuade
E. All of the above are promotion objectives.

14-**108.**
D
Def.
Easy
p. 398

A retailer's promotion objective might be to _____ its target market about its marketing mix.
A. inform
B. persuade
C. remind
D. All of the above.
E. Only A and C above.

14-**109.**
D
Comp.
Easy
p. 398-99

The various Promotion methods:
A. are all intended to lead to customer decisions favorable to the firm.
B. are all different forms of communication.
C. have a difficult task--since it is not easy to affect buying behavior.
D. All of the above are true.
E. None of the above is true.

14-**110.**
D
App.
Easy
p. 398

What basic promotion objective should be emphasized by a producer introducing a really new product which satisfies customer needs better than any existing product?
A. Persuading
B. Reminding
C. Maximizing
D. Informing
E. Communicating

14-**111.**
A
App.
Easy
p. 398

What basic promotion objective should be sought by a producer whose Product is very similar to its many competitors' Products?
  A. Persuading
  B. Promoting
  C. Communicating
  D. Informing
  E. Reminding

14-**112.**
B
App.
Easy
p. 398

What basic promotion objective can be sought by a producer who has won brand insistence among its target customers?
  A. Persuading
  B. Reminding
  C. Informing
  D. Communicating
  E. Promoting

14-**113.**
A
App.
Med.
p. 398

Office Distributing Co. sells frequently purchased office supplies to businesses in a metropolitan area. It is a well established company with a large share of the market. Its promotion should probably focus on
  A. reminding.
  B. stimulating primary demand.
  C. informing.
  D. innovators.
  E. making the demand curve less elastic.

14-**114.**
A
Def.
Easy
p. 399

The AIDA model includes all of the following promotion jobs EXCEPT:
  A. increasing demand.
  B. obtaining action.
  C. arousing desire.
  D. getting attention.
  E. holding interest.

14-**115.**
C
Comp.
Med.
p. 399

The AIDA model:
  A. focuses on what happens after the adoption process is complete.
  B. shows that the promotion effort is done once desire is aroused.
  C. consists of four basic promotion jobs.
  D. suggests that mass media can get consumers' attention only if that is what consumers desire.
  E. All of the above are true.

14-**116.**
D
Def.
Hard
p. 399

The AIDA model consists of four promotion jobs:
  A. getting Attention, building Intrigue, arousing Desire, and obtaining Action
  B. becoming Aware, holding Interest, arousing Desire, and providing Assistance
  C. getting Attention, holding Interest, creating Demand, and obtaining Action
  D. getting Attention, holding Interest, arousing Desire, and obtaining Action
  E. becoming Aware, holding Interest, arousing Desire, and obtaining Action

14-117.
A
Def.
Med.
p. 399

The AIDA model's four basic promotion jobs are concerned with:
A. attention, interest, desire, action.
B. action, interest, desire, acceptance.
C. awareness, interest, demand, action.
D. attention, internalization, decision, action.
E. awareness, interest, decision, acceptance.

14-118.
A
Def.
Easy
p. 400

The traditional communication process does NOT include:
A. response.
B. receiver.
C. encoding.
D. feedback.
E. source.

14-119.
A
Def.
Med.
p. 400

"Noise" (in the traditional communication process) refers to:
A. any distractions that reduce the effectiveness of the communication process.
B. radio advertising interference only.
C. messages which are too loud or bold.
D. efforts by a firm's competitors to block its message channel.
E. the encoded message before it is decoded.

14-120.
B
App.
Med.
p. 400

Which of the following best illustrates communication "noise"?
A. A TV ad is recorded at a higher volume than is used for most TV shows.
B. A motorist doesn't hear a radio ad because she is being stopped by a police officer for speeding.
C. A political candidate rides through town in a car with a loud speaker--asking pedestrians to vote for her.
D. Magazine sales reps telephone consumers to offer low-price subscriptions.

14-121.
E
App.
Med.
p. 400

Which of the following best illustrates communication "noise"?
A. Magazine sales reps telephone consumers to offer low-price subscriptions.
B. A TV ad is recorded at a higher volume than is used for most TV shows.
C. A political candidate rides through town in a car with a loud speaker--asking pedestrians to vote for her.
D. All of the above illustrate "noise."
E. None of the above clearly illustrates "noise."

14-122.
A
Int.
Med.
p. 400

The "communication process" shows that:
A. sources and receivers should have a common frame of reference.
B. the receiver is usually not influenced by the nature of the message channel.
C. sources decode messages and receivers encode them.
D. all media appear to be equally effective as message channels.
E. None of the above is true.

14-123.
B
App.
Med.
p. 400

Poor communication is likely if:
A. there is no "noise" in the message channel.
B. the source and the receiver do not have a common frame of reference.
C. the encoder and the decoder are not the same person.
D. immediate feedback is not possible.
E. the source and the receiver don't have personal contact.

14-**124.**
D
Comp.
Hard
p. 401

Good marketing managers know that:
A. a major advantage of personal selling is that noise can be eliminated.
B. noise in the communication process improves promotion effectiveness.
C. the trustworthiness of the source does not affect how receivers evaluate a message.
D. different audiences may see the same message in different ways.
E. All of the above are true.

14-**125.**
E
App.
Med.
p. 401

Producers that advertise in GOOD HOUSEKEEPING magazine sometimes show that they have the Good Housekeeping "seal of approval." This illustrates their recognition of the importance of the _____ in the communication process?
A. feedback
B. noise
C. decoding
D. encoding
E. message channel

14-**126.**
E
Comp.
Med.
p. 402

What medium is appropriate for integrated direct-response promotion:
A. telephone
B. interactive video
C. print
D. mail
E. any of the above might be appropriate

14-**127.**
E
Def.
Med.
p. 402

In addition to snail mail, direct-response promotion may include:
A. print
B. telephone
C. e-mail
D. the Internet
E. any of the above

14-**128.**
E
Def.
Med.
p. 402

Direct-response promotion may include:
A. interactive video
B. mail
C. website
D. broadcast
E. all of the above

14-**129.**
C
Comp.
Med.
p. 402

Integrated direct-response promotion:
A. isn't necessary or useful when the channel of distribution involves middlemen.
B. is usually part of a pushing effort rather than part of a pulling approach.
C. focuses on achieving a measurable, direct response from specific target customers.
D. All of the above are true.
E. None of the above are true.

14-**130.**
D
Comp.
Med.
p. 402-403

Integrated direct-response promotion:
A. got its start in the area of direct-mail advertising.
B. is often part of an integrated marketing communications program.
C. focuses on achieving feedback from a target customer that is immediate and measurable.
D. All of the above are true.
E. None of the above are true.

14-**131.**
D
Comp.
Med.
p. 404

An integrated direct-response promotion is most likely to be effective if:
A. it is used by a nonprofit organization rather than a firm.
B. other elements of the promotion blend are not integrated.
C. it involves one-way communications between a firm and its target customer.
D. it relies on a database to target specific individuals.
E. None of the above is a good answer.

14-**132.**
E
Comp.
Med.
p. 402-404

Integrated direct-response promotion:
A. got it's start when the introduction of TV made it possible for firms to use broadcast advertising to reach mass markets.
B. is an alternative to integrated marketing communications, which are used when direct-response is not required.
C. takes many forms, but it always involves the use of mail advertising.
D. all of the above are true.
E. none of the above are true.

14-**133.**
D
Comp.
Med.
p. 405

In customer-initiated interactive communication:
A. the message channel has no impact.
B. noise is no longer a factor.
C. the source initiates the communication.
D. information technology plays a big role.
E. action is less immediate.

14-**134.**
E
Comp.
Med.
p. 405-406

Which of the following statements about communication processes is(are) true?
A. Action is more immediate in customer-initiated interactive communication.
B. The seller starts the communication in the traditional communication process.
C. Noise can distract the process in traditional and customer-initiated interactive communication.
D. The buyer starts the communication in the customer-initiated interactive communication process.
E. All of the above are true.

14-**135.**
D
Comp.
Med.
p. 405

In the customer-initiated interactive communication process:
A. the message channel is no longer a factor.
B. noise is no longer a factor.
C. messages typically must be very short and simple.
D. the buyer starts the process.
E. none of the above are true.

14-**136.**
B
Comp.
Med.
p. 407-10

When developing a good promotion blend, a marketing manager should:
A. be more concerned with persuading the target customers than informing or reminding.
B. determine who the firm is trying to influence.
C. realize that the right blend depends more on what customers expect than on what the firm wants to accomplish.
D. All of the above are true.
E. None of the above is true.

14-**137.**
D
Def.
Easy
p. 407

A producer using normal promotion efforts--personal selling, sales promotion, and advertising--to help sell a whole marketing mix to possible channel members has:
A. a selective distribution policy.
B. a target marketing policy.
C. an intensive distribution policy.
D. a pushing policy.
E. a pulling policy.

14-**138.**
E
App.
Med.
p. 408

McPherson's, Inc. uses dealer incentives, discounts, and sales contests in order to encourage retailers to give special attention to selling its products. McPherson's is using
A. exclusive distribution.
B. a corporate channel system.
C. dual distribution.
D. an administered channel system.
E. pushing.

14-**139.**
D
App.
Med.
p. 408

American Tourister, Inc.--a producer of luggage--is planning to introduce a new product line. The marketing manager is having her sales force call on retailers to explain American Tourister's consumer advertising plans, the unique features of the new luggage, how the distributors can best promote it, and what sales volume and profit margins they can reasonably expect. This is an example of:
A. a "pulling" policy.
B. intensive distribution.
C. selective distribution.
D. a "pushing" policy.
E. exclusive distribution.

14-**140.**
E
Comp.
Med.
p. 408

In promotion to middlemen:
A. personal selling is the dominant promotion method.
B. trade ads are used to inform middlemen about new offerings.
C. promotion must be both informative and persuasive.
D. sales promotions are used to boost the middleman's profits on a short-term basis.
E. all of the above.

14-141.
E
Comp.
Med.
p. 407-408

Which of the following is NOT true about the relation between promotion blends and the promotion target?
 A. Pushing in the channel means using normal promotion to middlemen.
 B. Service-oriented companies often try to design ads targeted at customers that also communicate to their own employees.
 C. Promotion to middlemen emphasizes personal selling.
 D. Pushing within the firm involves promotion to employees, especially salespeople.
 E. All of the above are true.

14-142.
B
App.
Med.
p. 409

Soft Sheen Corp. is introducing a new brand of shampoo in a highly competitive market. Wholesalers might be willing to handle the new product, except that retailers are already complaining about overcrowded shelf space. Therefore, Soft Sheen has decided to spend $10 million on TV advertising and send free samples to 3,000,000 households to convince consumers of the new product's superiority--and to get them to ask for it at their retail store. Soft Sheen is using:
 A. dual distribution.
 B. a "pulling" policy.
 C. direct marketing.
 D. a "pushing" policy.
 E. a sampling distribution.

14-143.
A
Comp.
Med.
p. 409

A producer might use a "pulling policy" rather than a "pushing policy" if:
 A. middlemen are reluctant to handle a new product.
 B. it is offering a very "high-tech" product to a small product-market.
 C. its sales force has been very successful getting wholesalers and retailers to handle its product.
 D. it has a very limited promotion budget.
 E. All of the above.

14-144.
A
Def.
Easy
p. 409

A producer using very aggressive promotion to get final consumers to ask middlemen for a new product has:
 A. a pulling policy.
 B. a target marketing policy.
 C. a selective distribution policy.
 D. a pushing policy.
 E. an intensive distribution policy.

14-145.
E
Comp.
Med.
p. 409

In promotion to final consumers:
 A. mass selling and sales promotion are the dominant promotion methods.
 B. aggressive personal selling is usually found only in expensive channel systems.
 C. reminder ads may be all the promotion that is needed for products that have won brand preference or insistence.
 D. personal selling is effective for technical products and services.
 E. all of the above.

14-**146.**
A
App.
Easy
p. 410

Personal selling is MOST LIKELY to dominate a producer's promotion blend when the target customers are:
A. organizational and business buyers
B. young married couples
C. teenagers
D. working wives
E. senior citizens

14-**147.**
E
Comp.
Med.
p. 410

In promotion to business customers, personal selling is often the dominant promotion method because:
A. there are fewer business customers than final consumers.
B. the sales message may need to be adjusted to the needs of different people in the firm.
C. purchases are typically large and thus justify the effort.
D. buyers are more likely to have technical questions.
E. all of the above.

14-**148.**
A
Def.
Med.
p. 410

Wholesalers spend the largest share of their promotion money on:
A. personal selling.
B. direct-mail advertising.
C. advertising.
D. sales promotion.
E. publicity.

14-**149.**
A
Def.
Easy
p. 411

The "adoption curve" shows:
A. when different groups accept ideas.
B. how quickly a firm should drop current products.
C. the relationship between promotion spending and sales.
D. when a firm should introduce a new product.
E. All of the above.

14-**150.**
C
Comp.
Med.
p. 411

The adoption curve concept is most closely related to which of the following?
A. "noise" in the communication process
B. sales promotion aimed at a company's own sales force
C. the product life cycle
D. selective demand
E. the AIDA model

14-**151.**
C
Comp.
Med.
p. 411

The "adoption curve" shows that:
A. most new products are introduced too slowly.
B. the marketing plan for a new product should schedule most of the promotion spending right when the product is first introduced.
C. some groups accept a new idea before others.
D. a firm should stick to the same promotion effort as time passes.
E. All of the above.

14-**152.**
C
Comp.
Med.
p. 411

A marketing manager should realize that the adoption curve concept implies
A. that the firm's promotion target should be the innovators.
B. that the laggards are cautious, but that they are willing to adopt a new product quickly if advertising gets their attention.
C. using different promotional mixes for different adopter groups.
D. All of the above are true.
E. None of the above is true.

14-**153.**
B
Comp.
Easy
p. 411

Which of the following groups is likely to be the first to adopt a new product?
A. early majority
B. innovators
C. late majority
D. early adopters
E. laggards

14-**154.**
A
App.
Med.
p. 411

A retailer's target customers are young, well educated, and mobile--with many contacts outside their local social group and community. They are eager to try new ideas and are willing to take risks. These target customers are:
A. innovators.
B. laggards.
C. early adopters.
D. the late majority.
E. the early majority.

14-**155.**
D
Def.
Med.
p. 411

The best way to reach INNOVATORS is through:
A. the mass media.
B. salespeople.
C. local opinion leaders.
D. impersonal and scientific information sources.
E. salespeople and the mass media.

14-**156.**
B
Def.
Med.
p. 412

Early adopters
A. tend to rely on information sources that are not controlled by marketers.
B. tend to be opinion leaders.
C. are the first adoption curve group to buy a product.
D. all of the above.
E. none of the above.

14-**157.**
B
Def.
Med.
p. 412

The best way to reach EARLY adopters is through:
A. impersonal and scientific information media.
B. salespeople and mass media.
C. innovators.
D. the mass media.
E. opinion leaders.

14-158.
D
App.
Med.
p. 412

A research report shows that a magazine's readers are well respected by their peers and high in opinion leadership. They tend to be younger, more mobile, and more creative than later adopters. But they have fewer contacts outside their own social group or community than innovators. A firm might advertise to the readers of this magazine if it is targeting:
   A. laggards.
   B. innovators.
   C. the early majority.
   D. early adopters.
   E. the late majority.

14-159.
D
Comp.
Med.
p. 411-12

When marketing a truly new product, a marketing manager should:
   A. use an informing promotional objective.
   B. target communication towards innovators and early adopters.
   C. attempt to obtain publicity.
   D. All of the above are true.
   E. None of the above is true.

14-160.
E
App.
Med.
p. 412

Which of the following adopter groups is most important to "sell"--given the importance of opinion leaders?
   A. Late majority
   B. Early majority
   C. Laggards
   D. Innovators
   E. Early adopters

14-161.
E
Int.
Hard
p. 412

Regarding opinion leadership, which of the following statements is TRUE?
   A. Opinion leaders are easy to identify because people seek them out for advice on all kinds of topics.
   B. It is very important to reach the innovators--because this adopter group is the highest in opinion leadership.
   C. "Word of mouth" always does the real selling job--so Promotion is not necessary.
   D. All of the above are true.
   E. None of the above is true.

14-162.
D
App.
Med.
p. 412

A retailer's target market consists of people who usually will not consider a new idea until others have tried it--and liked it. These potential customers have a lot of contact with mass media and salespeople, but usually are not opinion leaders. These target customers are:
   A. early adopters.
   B. laggards.
   C. innovators.
   D. the early majority.
   E. the late majority.

14-**163.** The EARLY MAJORITY have a lot of contact with:
C
Def. A. innovators.
Med. B. the mass media only.
p. 412 C. the mass media, salespeople, and early adopter opinion leaders.
D. impersonal and scientific information sources.
E. salespeople only.

14-**164.** The LATE MAJORITY:
B
Def. A. make a lot of use of mass media.
Med. B. respond more to social pressure from other late adopters than to salespeople.
p. 413 C. make a lot of use of salespeople.
D. use salespeople and have much contact with the early majority.
E. have a lot of contact with early adopters.

14-**165.** A retailer's target customers are skeptical and cautious about new ideas. Strong social
E pressure from their own peer group may be needed before they adopt a new product.
App. These target customers are:
Med. A. the early majority.
p. 413 B. laggards.
C. innovators.
D. early adopters.
E. the late majority.

14-**166.** LAGGARDS or NON-ADOPTERS:
E
Comp. A. seem to have the lowest social status and income.
Easy B. tend to be older and less well educated.
p. 413 C. rely mainly on other laggards for information.
D. are suspicious of new ideas.
E. All of the above.

14-**167.** Regarding adopter groups, which of the following statements is TRUE?
B
Int. A. Innovators rely on the mass media and salespeople.
Med. B. The early majority usually aren't opinion leaders.
p. 411-13 C. Laggards rely primarily on opinion leaders.
D. Early adopters make little use of salespeople.
E. The late majority make the most use of salespeople.

14-**168.** Which of the following adopter groups is described correctly?
B
Int. A. Laggards--respectable
Easy B. Innovators--willing to take risks
p. 411-13 C. The late majority--follow the innovators
D. The early majority--opinion leaders
E. Early adopters--traditional

14-**169.** Which of the following is NOT true concerning adoption curve groups?
B
Comp. A. The early adopter group tends to have the greatest contact with salespeople.
Med. B. Early adopters are often unusual people who are not seen as opinion leaders.
p. 411-12 C. Innovators rely more on impersonal sources of information than on salespeople.
D. Business firms in the innovator group are usually large and rather specialized.
E. The early majority group have a lot of contact with mass media, salespeople, and opinion leaders.

14-**170.**
C
Comp.
Med.
p. 411-13

Regarding adoption curve groups, which of the following is TRUE?
A. By the time the early majority buy a product it is usually in the market maturity stage of the product life cycle.
B. The early adopters have many contacts outside their own social group, and are important in spreading information to laggards.
C. Business firms in the late majority group tend to be conservative, smaller-sized firms with little specialization.
D. The laggard group may be slow to adopt, but it is so large that it is very important to reach them.
E. None of the above is true.

14-**171.**
A
Comp.
Med.
p. 414

A producer is likely to focus its promotion effort on stimulating primary demand at what stage in the product life cycle?
A. Market introduction
B. Market growth
C. Market maturity
D. Sales decline
E. When selective demand is over.

14-**172.**
B
Comp.
Med.
p. 414

A producer is likely to focus its promotion effort on stimulating selective demand at what stage in the product life cycle?
A. Market introduction
B. Market growth
C. Market maturity
D. Sales decline
E. When primary demand is exhausted.

14-**173.**
C
Comp.
Med.
p. 414

Regarding PRODUCT LIFE CYCLES and PROMOTION:
A. During market introduction, the basic promotion objective is to remind.
B. In sales decline, the amount spent on promotion usually increases as firms use reminder promotion to increase demand.
C. Persuading becomes important in the market growth stage.
D. In market maturity, more competitors enter the market and the promotion emphasis must now shift to building selective demand for the firm's own brand.
E. All of the above are true.

14-**174.**
E
Comp.
Hard
p. 414

A firm with a product in the maturity stage of the product life cycle is likely to focus on which basic promotion objective?
A. pioneering
B. publicizing
C. informing
D. lagging
E. persuading

14-**175.**
C
Int.
Hard
p. 415

Regarding promotion blends, which of the following statements is TRUE?
A. Consumer products producers in monopolistic competition should rely almost completely on personal selling.
B. Reminding becomes important in the market introduction stage.
C. More targeted promotion is needed during the sales decline stage of the product life cycle.
D. Informing becomes important in the market growth stage.
E. Persuading becomes important in the market maturity stage.

14-**176.**
D
Comp.
Hard
p. 415

Good marketing managers in monopolistic competition situations:
A. favor personal selling, so they can adjust prices on the spot.
B. use promotion in the same way as they would in pure competition.
C. promote price cutting to increase total revenue.
D. may use mass selling to promote their differentiated marketing mixes.
E. None of the above is true.

14-**177.**
D
Def.
Easy
p. 413-17

Selecting an effective promotion blend to reach a firm's promotion objectives requires careful consideration of the:
A. nature of competition.
B. promotion budget available.
C. product life cycle stage.
D. All of the above.
E. Only A and B.

14-**178.**
E
Comp.
Med.
p. 415-16

Regarding PROMOTION BUDGETS and PROMOTION BLENDS:
A. A national TV ad might cost less per person reached than a local TV ad.
B. The total cost of mass media may force small firms to use promotion alternatives that are more expensive per person.
C. A city-wide newspaper ad might cost less per person reached than a neighborhood newspaper ad.
D. There are some economies of scale in promotion.
E. All of the above are true.

14-**179.**
E
Comp.
Med.
p. 416

The MOST COMMON method of setting the marketing budget is to
A. use PERT approaches.
B. estimate what competitors are spending.
C. determine the cost of the tasks to be accomplished.
D. use all uncommitted revenue.
E. use some predetermined percentage of past or forecast sales.

14-**180.**
E
Comp.
Easy
p. 416

The most COMMON method of budgeting for marketing expenses is to:
A. match competitors' spending.
B. allocate any funds not already allocated to other functions.
C. allocate enough to completely eliminate the cost of lost customers.
D. allocate for the job that needs to be done.
E. allow a percentage of either past or forecasted sales.

14-**181.**
D
Comp.
Med.
p. 416

Budgeting for marketing expenses by computing a percentage of forecasted sales:

A. is especially suitable for new products.
B. always results in increased expenditure levels from year to year.
C. is very complicated--and thus this method is not used very often.
D. may lead to a drop in marketing expenses at a time when the firm wants to maintain or expand sales.
E. tends to result in large changes in marketing expenses from year to year.

14-**182.**
C
Comp.
Easy
p. 417

According to the text discussion on setting a marketing budget,

A. the most objective approach is to use Pareto approaches.
B. the only practical alternative is to match what competitors are spending.
C. the most sensible approach is to determine the cost of the tasks to be accomplished.
D. the task method is likely to result in too low a budget when sales are going well.
E. it is generally best to simply use some predetermined percentage of past or forecast sales.

14-**183.**
C
Comp.
Med.
p. 417

The task method for budgeting marketing expenses:

A. means that a company budgets roughly what competitors budget for each item.
B. budgets last year's marketing expense ratio times FORECASTED sales.
C. might result in very different marketing expenses from year to year.
D. is the most commonly used method of setting budgets.
E. None of the above is true.

14-**184.**
E
Comp.
Easy
p. 417

According to the text, the most sensible method for budgeting marketing expenses is to:

A. allocate some fixed percentage of net sales.
B. allocate all available funds.
C. allocate money for direct-response promotion first and then use money that's left for integrated marketing communications.
D. match expenditures with competitors.
E. use the "task method."

Chapter 15

Personal Selling

True-False Questions:

15-1.
True
p. 422

While face-to-face with prospects, a salesperson can adjust what he or she says or does to take into consideration culture and other behavioral influences.

15-2.
True
p. 422

It is the sales manager's job to implement the personal selling part of a marketing strategy.

15-3.
False
p. 422-23

Personal selling techniques vary very little from country to country.

15-4.
True
p. 423

About 10 percent of the total U.S. labor force is in sales work.

15-5.
False
p. 423

In the U.S., almost as many people are employed in sales work as in advertising.

15-6.
True
p. 423

About 20 times more people are employed in selling than in advertising.

15-7.
True
p. 423

Good salespeople try to help customers buy by presenting both the advantages and disadvantages of a product--and showing how it will satisfy the customer's needs.

15-8.
True
p. 423

Salespeople often are responsible for representing the customer inside their own company as well as representing their company to the customer.

15-9.
True
p. 423

Salespeople may represent their company to customers and, in turn, represent their customers within the company.

15-10.
True
p. 424

Sales reps often must plan whole marketing strategies for their own geographic territories.

15-11.
True
p. 425

Although the salesperson's job may change constantly, there are three basic sales tasks.

15-12.
True
p. 425

A salesperson's main task might be order getting, order taking, or supporting, but sometimes one salesperson does all three tasks.

15-13.
False
p. 425

A salesperson who aggressively seeks out possible buyers with a well-organized sales presentation designed to sell a product is a missionary sales rep.

15-14.
True
p. 425

Order getters are concerned with finding new opportunities for the company.

15-15.
True
p. 425

Order getters are even more important for business products than for consumer products.

15-16.
True
p. 425

A good order getter tries to sell solutions to the customer's problems--not just physical products.

15-17.
True
p. 426

Agent middlemen--particularly manufacturers' agents and brokers--are often order getters.

15-18.
True
p. 426

Retail order getters are usually needed for unsought products, and are desirable for some shopping products.

15-19.
False
p. 426

Homogeneous shopping products need order getters more than heterogeneous shopping products.

15-20.
False
p. 427

Order getters complete most sales transactions.

15-21.
True
p. 427

A salesperson who completes routine sales made regularly to target customers is an order taker.

15-22.
True
p. 427

A producer's order taker may explain details, handle complaints, and train the customer's employees.

15-23.
True
p. 427

Order takers should work on improving the whole relationship with the customer, not just on completing a single transaction.

15-24.
True
p. 428

A wholesaler's order-getting salespeople are likely to be paid more than its order takers.

15-25.
False
p. 429

Missionary salespeople usually work for wholesalers and provide special promotion help to producers whose products are widely distributed.

15-26.
True
p. 429

Developing goodwill and stimulating demand are tasks performed by missionary salespeople.

15-27.
True
p. 429

Scientists or engineers--who may have little interest in sales but do provide technical assistance to order getters--are called technical specialists.

15-28.
True
p. 430

Team selling might involve a technical specialist and an order getter working together on a specific account.

15-29.
True
p. 431

A major accounts sales force is used when a company wants to be certain that its most important customers get a special selling effort.

15-30.
True
p. 431

Telemarketing can help a firm extend its personal selling efforts to new target markets without investing a lot of time and money.

15-31.
False
p. 431

Although telemarketing saves time and money, it has been declining in recent years.

15-32.
False
p. 432

When deciding how many salespeople are needed, the first step is to determine how many sales reps are used by competing companies.

15-33.
True
p. 434

It is primarily the sales manager's job to decide what types of information technology tools salespeople need and how they will be used.

15-34.
True
p. 434-36

Some firms are adopting new software and hardware technologies to get a competitive advantage in personal selling.

15-35.
False
p. 435

The availability of new information technologies usually changes the basic nature of the sales tasks to be accomplished.

15-36.
False
p. 434-36

A company that provides its sales reps with information technology tools should expect that reps will do a better job with administrative tasks but that they will be less effective in their actual sales calls.

15-**37.**
False
p. 436

Using psychological tests to select "born salespeople" works so well that it almost guarantees success.

15-**38.**
True
p. 436

The job description should provide clear guidelines concerning (1) who should be selected, (2) how they are trained, (3) how well they are performing, and (4) how they should be paid.

15-**39.**
False
p. 436-37

Job descriptions are not necessary for personal selling because all salespeople are expected to do the same task--sell products.

15-**40.**
True
p. 437

A firm's initial sales training program should cover company policies, product information, building relationships with customers, and selling skills.

15-**41.**
False
p. 438

Salespeople usually earn more than top management.

15-**42.**
True
p. 438

A company's salespeople are usually paid more than its office help or production workers, but less than top management.

15-**43.**
True
p. 438

Regarding sales force compensation, straight salary gives the most security for a salesperson, while straight commission gives the most incentive.

15-**44.**
True
p. 438

Most sales managers offer their salespeople a "combination plan" because this method of compensation provides a balance between incentive and security.

15-**45.**
True
p. 438

A sales manager who wishes to supervise and control his salespeople's activities closely should pay them a straight salary instead of a straight commission.

15-**46.**
True
p. 441

Prospecting involves following all the "leads" in the target market.

15-**47.**
False
p. 442

Telephone selling is becoming less common because it is too hard to tell if a customer might be a good prospect on the telephone.

15-**48.**
True
p. 443

Personal computers--and specially developed software--can help salespeople do a better job with prospecting.

15-**49.**
True
p. 443

A salesperson's request for an order during a sales presentation is called a "close."

15-50.
False
p. 443

A customer's effort to keep a salesperson from completing a sales presentation is called a "close."

15-51.
False
p. 443

The main advantage of the prepared sales presentation approach is that it tends to work equally well with different types of customers.

15-52.
True
p. 444

The most suitable sales presentation for prospective customers whose needs are very different is the "consultative selling approach."

15-53.
False
p. 444

The "consultative selling" sales presentation is fast and requires little skill.

15-54.
True
p. 444

The "selling formula approach" to sales presentations assumes that something is known about the target customer's needs and attitudes.

15-55.
True
p. 444

The "selling formula" approach to making a sales presentation is really a combination of the "prepared sales presentation" approach and the "consultative selling" approach.

15-56.
True
p. 444

The AIDA sequence can help a sales manager evaluate a possible sales presentation.

Multiple Choice Questions

15-57.
E
Def.
Easy
p. 422

Marketing managers should make specific strategy decisions about:
A. how many and what kind of salespeople are needed.
B. how salespeople should be supervised and motivated.
C. what kind of sales presentation should be used.
D. how salespeople should be selected and trained.
E. All of the above.

15-58.
B
Comp.
Easy
p. 423

Personal selling
A. is important to business firms, but only about 1 percent of the U.S. labor force does personal selling work.
B. is often a company's largest single operating expense.
C. requires only that the sales rep have an engaging smile, a big expense account, and the ability to get along well with people.
D. All of the above are true.
E. None of the above is true.

15-59.   At least _____ percent of the total U.S. labor force do sales work.
B
Def.
Hard
p. 423
   A. 20
   B. 10
   C. 30
   D. 50
   E. 40

15-60.   Good marketing managers know that:
B
Comp.
Easy
p. 423
   A. most salespeople are "bags of wind."
   B. good salespeople try to help customers buy.
   C. the role of the salesperson has been down-graded in business marketing.
   D. organizational buyers have little use for salespeople.
   E. the salesperson's job is to "get rid of the product."

15-61.   A professional salesperson:
E
Comp.
Med.
p. 423-24
   A. may negotiate prices or diagnose technical problems when a product doesn't work well.
   B. doesn't try to "sell" customers, but rather tries to help them satisfy their needs.
   C. is a representative of the whole company.
   D. is responsible for feeding back information about customers and competitors.
   E. All of the above.

15-62.   A professional salesperson:
C
Comp.
Med.
p. 424
   A. is only expected to "get rid of the product."
   B. has only one basic job--to communicate the company's story to customers.
   C. may be given a title such as field manager or market specialist.
   D. is expected to overcome the customer's objection--whatever it may be.
   E. All of the above.

15-63.   Some salespeople are expected to act as "marketing managers" in their own geographic territories and decide:
E
Comp.
Easy
p. 424
   A. how they will allocate their promotion money and their own time.
   B. which customers they will aim at.
   C. which middlemen they will call on or work with.
   D. which products in the company's line they will push aggressively.
   E. All of the above.

15-64.   A salesperson may have to make choices about
E
Comp.
Med.
p. 424
   A. which particular products in the whole line to push most aggressively.
   B. what specific target customers to aim at.
   C. how to adjust prices.
   D. which middlemen to call on or work with the hardest.
   E. All of the above.

15-65.   Salespeople are likely to be responsible for:
E
Comp.
Easy
p. 424-25
   A. providing market information to the firm.
   B. providing technical support.
   C. attaining sales goals.
   D. maintaining customer relations.
   E. Any of the above.

15-**66.**
C
Int.
Med.
p. 425

Which of the following descriptions of the three basic sales tasks is CORRECT?
A. ORDER-TAKING: various activities aimed at getting sales in the long run.
B. SUPPORTING: routine completion of sales made regularly to target customers.
C. ORDER-GETTING: seeking possible buyers with a well-organized sales presentation designed to sell a good, service, or idea.
D. All of the above are correct.
E. None of the above are correct.

15-**67.**
C
Def.
Easy
p. 425

Which of the following is NOT one of the basic sales tasks?
A. Order-taking
B. Supporting
C. Sales-promoting
D. Order-getting
E. None of the above, i.e. all are basic sales tasks

15-**68.**
C
Def.
Easy
p. 425

A salesperson who seeks possible buyers with a well-organized sales presentation designed to get new business is:
A. a technical specialist.
B. a supporting salesperson.
C. an order getter.
D. a missionary salesperson.
E. an order taker.

15-**69.**
D
App.
Easy
p. 425

Ms. Applegate works for a cable TV company in a large city. She makes telephone calls during the early evening and tries to sell cable services to nonsubscribers. Ms. Applegate is
A. a technical specialist.
B. a sales promotion specialist.
C. an order taker.
D. an order getter.
E. none of the above.

15-**70.**
D
Comp.
Med.
p. 425

Which of the following types of salespeople is essential for selling installations and accessory equipment?
A. Order takers
B. Missionary salespeople
C. Merchandisers
D. Order getters
E. Technical specialists

15-**71.**
D
Comp.
Easy
p. 425-26

A good order getter:
A. is likely to use a high level of personal persuasion.
B. is especially important for selling installations and accessory equipment.
C. needs "know how" to help solve customers' problems.
D. All of the above are true.
E. None of the above is true.

15-72.
D
App.
Med.
p. 425-26

Alan Thompson works for a producer of industrial elevators. He knows all the technical details of the many different ways they are used by business customers. He makes presentations to new prospects and eventually gets a share of their business. Alan is:

A. a member of the firm's major accounts sales force.
B. a missionary salesperson.
C. a technical specialist.
D. a producer's order getter.
E. None of the above is true.

15-73.
B
App.
Easy
p. 426

Scott Moody is a sales rep for a producer of fiberglass roofing shingles. He tries to persuade building materials wholesalers to switch from competing producers. Scott is:

A. an order taker.
B. an order getter.
C. a supporting salesperson.

15-74.
D
Comp.
Med.
p. 425-26

Customers for complicated installations and accessories usually expect a sales rep

A. to know all the technical details of the product.
B. to be able to discuss general business conditions with their top executives.
C. to know the details of their particular applications of the product.
D. All of the above are likely to be expected.
E. None of the above is likely to be expected.

15-75.
A
Comp.
Med.
p. 425-26

Order getters:

A. may make a sale by helping a customer solve a problem.
B. are more likely to be used with homogeneous shopping products than heterogeneous shopping products.
C. are used in business markets but not in consumer markets.
D. generally rely on a routine "canned" sales presentation.
E. All of the above are true.

15-76.
A
App.
Med.
p. 426

Allison Tate is an order getter for a modern wholesaler. Ms. Tate is LEAST likely to be involved with:

A. repairing products returned to retailers by customers.
B. conducting demonstrations for retailers' salespeople and customers.
C. checking stock to determine what retailers should order.
D. helping to plan special promotions and advertising for retailers.
E. serving as a marketing advisor to her retailers.

15-77.
E
App.
Easy
p. 426

Jamie Locklear is a manufacturers' agent. Jamie is most likely to have responsibilities like those of

A. a wholesaler's order taker.
B. a producer's order taker.
C. a producer's supporting salesperson.
D. a retail order taker.
E. a producer's order getter.

15-**78.**
B
App.
Med.
p. 426

A producer of business supplies is using manufacturers' agents to do:
 A. merchandising.
 B. order-getting.
 C. order-taking.
 D. technical advising.
 E. supporting activities.

15-**79.**
E
Comp.
Easy
p. 426

Retail order getters are usually required for:
 A. unsought products.
 B. heterogeneous shopping products.
 C. impulse products.
 D. All of the above.
 E. A and B only.

15-**80.**
D
App.
Med.
p. 426

Retailers of expensive heterogeneous shopping products usually have a strong need for:
 A. order takers.
 B. technical specialists.
 C. merchandisers.
 D. order getters.
 E. supporting salespeople.

15-**81.**
A
Def.
Easy
p. 427

Routine completion of sales made regularly to target customers is done by:
 A. an order taker.
 B. a merchandiser.
 C. a detailer.
 D. an order getter.
 E. a supporting salesperson.

15-**82.**
A
Comp.
Med.
p. 427

A good sales manager knows that:
 A. order takers usually do very little aggressive selling.
 B. order takers can be used by middlemen--but not by producers.
 C. order getters complete almost all sales in our country.
 D. whenever possible, order takers should be replaced by order getters.
 E. All of the above.

15-**83.**
B
App.
Easy
p. 427

A Taco Bell's fast-food restaurant needs _____ to serve its customers.
 A. merchandisers
 B. order takers
 C. order getters
 D. hucksters
 E. supporting salespeople

15-**84.**
A
Comp.
Med.
p. 427

Regarding personal selling, good sales managers know that:
 A. many orders are lost simply because the salesperson didn't ask for the order.
 B. salespeople should spend the same amount of time with each prospect.
 C. the sales rep has very little influence on a prospect's response.
 D. good salespeople are born--not taught.
 E. All of the above.

15-85.
B
Comp.
Med.
p. 427

Order takers:
  A. are not necessary if the firm has good order getters.
  B. are the routine contact people in the sales force.
  C. usually don't call on customers.
  D. do not require any specialized training.
  E. All of the above are correct.

15-86.
B
Comp.
Med.
p. 428

A producer's order taker
  A. usually has little opportunity to increase sales in a territory.
  B. is expected to help customers when something goes wrong with the marketing mix.
  C. doesn't have to make sales presentations or keep customers informed about new developments--order getters do these tasks.
  D. All of the above are true.
  E. None of the above is true.

15-87.
A
App.
Med.
p. 428

An order-taking sales rep would be MOST appropriate for a producer of:
  A. cleaning materials for maintenance--calling on regular customers.
  B. designer clothing--calling on possible new retailers.
  C. laptop computers--selling to manufacturers who don't yet have any computers.
  D. airplanes--calling on possible corporate jet customers.
  E. a new brand of DVD system--calling on wholesalers.

15-88.
B
App.
Med.
p. 428

Andrea Mercer is tired of being a manufacturers' agent of accessories sold through merchant wholesalers. She is willing to accept a lower income for less travel and stress. She also wants to continue selling in the same industry so that her experience and business degree will not be wasted. Andrea should look for a job as a:
  A. producer's order getter.
  B. wholesaler's order taker.
  C. retail order taker.
  D. technical specialist for a manufacturer.
  E. None of the above fits her needs.

15-89.
C
App.
Hard
p. 428

Mark Johnson's business card says he is a "Customer Service Representative" for OceanView Metal Industries--a wholesaler of standardized steel components used in construction. Mark answers customer questions about the firm's products and arranges for routine orders to be sent to the customer's construction site. It appears that Mark is primarily:
  A. a missionary salesperson.
  B. a technical specialist.
  C. an order taker.
  D. an order getter.
  E. none of the above.

15-90.
B
Comp.
Med.
p. 428

An established merchant wholesaler of business supplies would rely mainly on:
  A. merchandisers.
  B. order takers.
  C. order getters.
  D. supporting salespeople.
  E. missionary salespeople.

15-91.
D
Def.
Easy
p. 429-30

People who help order-oriented salespeople--but don't try for orders themselves are:
A. technical specialists.
B. missionary salespeople.
C. supporting salespeople.
D. All of the above.
E. None of the above.

15-92.
A
App.
Med.
p. 429

_____ would be LEAST LIKELY to use supporting salespeople.
A. Supermarkets
B. Producers of prescription drugs
C. Producers of business accessories
D. Producers of consumer staples
E. Merchant wholesalers of installations

15-93.
D
Comp.
Med.
p. 429

Missionary sales reps:
A. are order takers.
B. are sales reps in training.
C. are used mainly for religious products.
D. help train middlemen's salespeople and set up retail displays.
E. do a lot of aggressive selling.

15-94.
B
Int.
Med.
p. 429

The sales manager for a producer of consumer convenience products should recognize that the company may need:
A. order getters to sell its established line to regular wholesaler customers.
B. missionary salespeople to support its wholesalers.
C. order takers to open up new territories.
D. technical specialists to sell to purchasing agents.
E. All of the above.

15-95.
E
App.
Med.
p. 429

Gloria Highnote works for CD Wholesale. She helps CD's retailer-customers set up their cooperative advertising, helps train the retailer's salespeople, and gives CD feedback on how sales promotion ideas are working. Gloria is:
A. a technical specialist.
B. a scrambled merchandiser.
C. an order getter.
D. an order taker.
E. a missionary salesperson.

15-96.
B
App.
Med.
p. 429

Jose Montenegro has been working for a producer of video games that sell through toy wholesalers to retailers. He knows all about the games sold by his company and by competitors. He goes into his wholesalers' territories and tries to get local retailer customers interested in the company's line--and even trains retailers to demonstrate the games. When a retailer is ready to buy, Jose turns the business over to the wholesaler's sales rep. Jose is a:
A. member of the firm's major accounts sales force.
B. missionary salesperson.
C. technical specialist.
D. manufacturers' agent.
E. None of the above is correct.

15-97.
E
App.
Med.
p. 429

Megan Rivers works for a large cosmetics company. She calls on retailers to tell them about her firm's new products, to train the retailers' salespeople, and to set up promotion displays. Her boss actually handles the order-related activities. Megan is:
    A. an order getter.
    B. a manufacturers' agent.
    C. a technical specialist.
    D. an order taker.
    E. a missionary sales rep.

15-98.
A
App.
Med.
p. 429

A large producer of snack foods feels that retailers do not promote its products aggressively enough--because they also sell competitors' products. The producer should use some:
    A. missionary sales reps.
    B. more aggressive sales reps.
    C. order takers.
    D. order getters.
    E. manufacturers' agents.

15-99.
D
Comp.
Med.
p. 429

Missionary selling:
    A. is another name for major accounts selling.
    B. is the performance of personal selling activities for a nonprofit organization.
    C. is the same as prospecting.
    D. is often an entry position for higher level sales and marketing jobs.
    E. is typically only used with a firm's largest or most important customers.

15-100.
B
Comp.
Easy
p. 429

"Technical specialists":
    A. are usually paid a straight commission on sales.
    B. help explain technical details as needed.
    C. usually work with business purchasing agents.
    D. usually install emergency products.
    E. are technical order getters.

15-101.
D
Comp.
Med.
p. 429-30

A technical specialist:
    A. often has a background in product applications rather than sales.
    B. may call on the customer both before and after a purchase.
    C. may work in conjunction with an order getter to persuade new clients.
    D. All of the above are true.
    E. None of the above is true.

15-102.
D
App.
Med.
p. 429

IBM's customers often need help installing its mini computer systems, so IBM should support the efforts of its order getters with:
    A. sales promotion specialists.
    B. selling aids.
    C. missionary salespeople.
    D. technical specialists.
    E. order takers.

15-**103.**
E
App.
Med.
p. 429

Unisys sells custom-made computer systems. Besides order getters, Unisys probably uses:
A.   order takers.
B.   missionary salespeople.
C.   merchandisers.
D.   manufacturers' agents.
E.   technical specialists.

15-**104.**
C
Comp.
Med.
p. 430

A good marketing manager organizing a new sales force knows that:
A.   new sales reps should start out on the major accounts sales force so they can learn the business from the bottom up.
B.   the most profitable approach is to start with a small number of salespeople, and then quickly add more if they can't do the job.
C.   it may be necessary to have more than one rep call on a single customer if different skills are needed.
D.   All of the above are true.
E.   None of the above is true.

15-**105.**
E
App.
Med.
p. 431

Jeffrey O'Donnell works for a producer of dairy products and knows all about these products. He is responsible for only two very large chain customers. Other sales reps, like Jeffrey, call on other large chains for this producer. They regularly call on the central offices of these big retail chains and encourage them to buy the company's full line. Jeffrey is:
A.   a missionary salesperson.
B.   a retail order taker.
C.   a technical specialist.
D.   a manufacturers' agent.
E.   a member of his company's major accounts sales force.

15-**106.**
D
Math
Hard
p. 432

Allied Corp. has found that an effective salesperson should call on each account about six times a year and spend about two hours per sales call. Every salesperson works a 40-hour week and takes off two weeks for vacation each year. A salesperson must spend half of his time on travel and administration. Approximately how many salespeople does Allied need to service 500 accounts?
A.   12
B.   30
C.   2
D.   6
E.   There is not enough information to determine the answer.

15-**107.**
E
App.
Easy
p. 435

A sales rep might use new software for _____ to provide a competitive advantage:
A.   sales forecasting.
B.   shelf-space management.
C.   customer contact management.
D.   time management.
E.   all of the above.

15-**108.** A sales rep might use new software for _____ to provide a competitive
E advantage:
App. A. sales forecasting.
Easy B. spreadsheet analysis.
p. 435 C. electronic presentations.
  D. customer contacts.
  E. all of the above.

15-**109.** Selecting "good, well-qualified" salespeople can be aided by:
E A. multiple interviews with company executives.
Comp. B. systematic selection procedures.
Easy C. good job descriptions.
p. 436 D. psychological tests.
  E. All of the above.

15-**110.** A job description for a sales position
A A. should be detailed enough that it lists the specific tasks to be performed.
Comp. B. should be in writing, but should be quite general so that it doesn't reduce the
Med.   sales manager's flexibility in assigning jobs.
p. 436 C. should look pretty much the same from one company to another.
  D. is not very useful, since the job is always changing.
  E. all of the above.

15-**111.** A good job description will help a new sales manager see:
E A. the kind of training needed.
Def. B. the kind of salespeople to be selected.
Easy C. what selling tasks are needed.
p. 436 D. how salespeople should be paid.
  E. All of the above.

15-**112.** Which of the following statements by a sales manager suggests a problem?
D A. "Taking a successful sales rep out of a territory for sales training is like spending
Comp.   money to teach a fish to swim."
Med. B. "I was a sales rep before becoming manager, so I don't need a job description to
p. 436-37   help me look for new salespeople."
  C. "I select new salespeople all by myself, because I am the one responsible for the
    performance of the sales force."
  D. Each of the above indicates a problem.
  E. None of the above indicates a problem.

15-**113.** Sales force training is needed for anyone:
E A. with prior selling experience with the firm's type of products.
Def. B. with knowledge of the company's products--but no selling experience.
Easy C. with some selling experience--but no knowledge of the company or its products.
p. 437 D. who is new to sales and/or the company's products.
  E. All of the above.

15-114.
E
Comp.
Med.
p. 437

Regarding sales force training,
  A. it is rarely necessary to take a successful and experienced sales rep out of the field for a training program.
  B. every new sales rep should go through all parts of a firm's training program, so that nothing is missed.
  C. training programs should focus on company policies and product information, since sales presentation skills are best learned in the field.
  D. All of the above are true.
  E. None of the above is true.

15-115.
E
Comp.
Easy
p. 437

Sales training:
  A. usually isn't necessary if a new salesperson has had similar selling experience calling on the same customers for a competing company.
  B. programs should focus on product and company information--since research shows that training is not effective in developing selling skills.
  C. is usually needed only for new salespeople.
  D. All of the above are true.
  E. None of the above is true.

15-116.
E
Def.
Easy
p. 437

A firm's sales training should cover:
  A. professional selling skills.
  B. building relationships with customers.
  C. company policies and practices.
  D. product information.
  E. all of the above.

15-117.
D
Comp.
Med.
p. 438

When setting salespeople's compensation level,
  A. a company should pay everyone at least the going market wage for order getters.
  B. salespeople should be the highest-paid employees in the company.
  C. order takers should be paid more than order getters.
  D. the first step is to write job descriptions.
  E. All of the above.

15-118.
E
Comp.
Easy
p. 438

A firm's sales compensation plan should consider
  A. the pay for other jobs in the firm.
  B. the amount of direct control desired by the firm.
  C. the amount of selling versus nonselling time.
  D. what competitors pay salespeople.
  E. all of the above.

15-119.
B
App.
Med.
p. 438

A producer wants to increase the amount of time its sales reps spend on supporting activities. It also wishes to keep its sales reps motivated and aggressive, and also provide some security. Which payment plan should the firm use?
  A. Straight salary
  B. Combination plan
  C. Straight commission

15-**120.**
C
App.
Med.
p. 438

A producer wants to reduce sales force turnover AND obtain a more aggressive sales effort for its accessories. Which of the following sales force payment methods should it use?
  A. Straight salary
  B. Selling formula plan
  C. Combination plan
  D. Straight commission

15-**121.**
A
Def.
Med.
p. 438

The most popular sales force payment method is:
  A. a combination plan.
  B. the consultative selling method.
  C. straight salary.
  D. straight commission.

15-**122.**
A
Int.
Med.
p. 438

Regarding sales force compensation methods:
  A. combination plans provide some security and some incentive.
  B. straight commission avoids the need to consider a sales quota.
  C. straight salary provides the most incentive.
  D. combination plans provide both simplicity and flexibility.
  E. All of the above.

15-**123.**
B
App.
Easy
p. 438-39

A merchant wholesaler who wants to provide the most INCENTIVE in his sales force payment plan should use:
  A. salary plus commission.
  B. straight commission.
  C. the same level of pay for all salespeople.
  D. salary plus bonus.
  E. straight salary.

15-**124.**
C
Comp.
Med.
p. 438-39

A sales manager's CONTROL over his salespeople:
  A. is strongest with order getters who are paid on straight commission.
  B. cannot be obtained with combination plans.
  C. can be the strongest with a straight salary plan.
  D. is small, it's the responsibility of the marketing manager.
  E. is not too important if the salespeople regularly meet their sales quotas.

15-**125.**
E
Def.
Easy
p. 438-40

Once the compensation level for a producer's salespeople has been set, the particular METHOD of payment depends on the:
  A. need for incentive.
  B. desire for flexibility.
  C. desire for simplicity.
  D. need for control.
  E. All of the above.

15-**126.**
E
Int.
Med.
p. 438-40

Regarding sales force payment methods:
A. it is common to sacrifice some simplicity to gain more flexibility, incentive, or control.
B. combination plans offer some degree of security, incentive, and control.
C. straight commission offers the most incentive.
D. straight salary provides the most security and control.
E. All of the above are true.

15-**127.**
E
Comp.
Easy
p. 439-40

A sales force payment plan may have to be developed to provide for flexibility:
A. among products.
B. among people.
C. among territories.
D. in selling costs.
E. All of the above.

15-**128.**
B
Comp.
Easy
p. 440

Which of the following statements relating to sales quotas is FALSE?
A. Sales potential usually differs from one sales territory to another.
B. A salesperson's sales quota is the specific level of sales he or she achieved in the previous sales period.
C. Unless the pay plan allows for territory differences, some sales reps may be overworked and others may be underworked.
D. Unless the pay plan allows for territory differences, some sales reps may be underpaid for the same amount of effort.

15-**129.**
A
Comp.
Easy
p. 440

A sales compensation plan should:
A. be easy for salespeople to understand.
B. use the same commission rates on all products--if commissions are used at all.
C. be based on salary or commission, but not a combination of the two.
D. All of the above are true.
E. None of the above is true.

15-**130.**
D
Def.
Easy
p. 440

Which of the following sales force payment methods is best for SIMPLICITY?
A. Salary plus bonus plan
B. Value plan
C. Combination plan
D. Straight salary
E. None of the above, i.e., all are equal.

15-**131.**
D
Def.
Easy
p. 441

Personal selling techniques include all of the following EXCEPT:
A. searching for prospects.
B. making sales presentations.
C. planning sales presentations.
D. preparing job descriptions.
E. following up after the sale.

15-**132.**   "Prospecting:"
E   A. involves following all the leads in the target market.
Comp.   B. should require a sales rep to spend the same amount of time with each prospect.
Med.   C. refers to selection of the firm's target market.
p. 441-43   D. should use a system for allocating time to potential customers based on their
                 potential.
             E. Both A and D.

15-**133.**   A salesperson's use of the telephone:
D   A. can sell "hot prospects" immediately.
Comp.   B. is a common aid in sales prospecting.
Easy   C. can provide information which can be used in follow-up visits.
p. 441-42   D. All of the above are true.
             E. None of the above is true.

15-**134.**   Which of the following is NOT one of the sales presentation approaches discussed in
D   the text?
Def.   A. Prepared sales presentation
Easy   B. Selling formula approach
p. 443   C. Consultative selling approach
             D. Target market approach
             E. None of the above, i.e., all are discussed in the text.

15-**135.**   A prepared sales presentation:
E   A. is the best approach for most selling situations--since the company can control
Comp.   what the sales rep says.
Med.   B. usually involves many questions, to be sure each customer's needs are fully
p. 443   understood.
             C. is common with high value items--to be sure the customer learns about all of the
                 technical details.
             D. is best when a lot of time is available for a sales presentation.
             E. None of the above is true.

15-**136.**   Which sales presentation would be "best" for convenience (food) store clerks?
B   A. Selling formula approach
App.   B. Prepared sales presentation
Med.   C. Target market presentation
p. 443   D. Consultative selling approach
             E. None of the above.

15-**137.**   A lawn care firm selling by phone to people listed in the telephone directory should use
C   which of the following sales presentations?
App.   A. consultative selling approach.
Med.   B. selling formula approach.
p. 443   C. prepared sales presentation.
             D. target market presentation.
             E. None of the above.

15-**138.**
A
Def.
Easy
p. 443

A sales presentation in which the sales rep does most of the talking, using a "canned" presentation to obtain a "yes" answer to a "trial close" is a:
  A. prepared sales presentation.
  B. target market presentation.
  C. consultative selling presentation.
  D. selling formula presentation.
  E. None of the above.

15-**139.**
D
App.
Med.
p. 443-44

Vernon Sorensson sells a diverse line of conveyor systems to small manufacturers. He has found that he is most successful when he uses the sales call to help the customer solve some problem using one of his products. Vernon probably relies on
  A. the missionary approach.
  B. the prepared presentation approach.
  C. the selling formula approach.
  D. the consultative selling approach.
  E. Any of the above is equally likely.

15-**140.**
D
App.
Med.
p. 443-44

Clara St. James sells women's clothing and gets most of her business from regular customers who have bought from her before. Clara never tries to sell anything before first trying to determine each customer's specific needs. Once she understands the customer's needs, Clara helps the customer understand her own needs and then shows how some product will fill those needs. Clara's sales presentation uses the:
  A. "canned" approach.
  B. target market presentation.
  C. selling formula approach.
  D. consultative selling approach.
  E. None of the above.

15-**141.**
A
App.
Med.
p. 443-44

A sales rep for installations probably should use a _____ sales presentation.
  A. consultative selling approach
  B. target market
  C. prepared
  D. selling formula approach
  E. any of the above

15-**142.**
C
Def.
Med.
p. 443-44

Some sales reps try to get a prospect to do most of the talking at first--to help pinpoint the potential customer's needs. After the sales rep feels that he understands the customer's needs, he begins to enter more into the discussion, helping the customer understand his own needs, showing how his product satisfies the customer's needs, and then trying to close the sale. This type of sales presentation uses the:
  A. selling formula approach.
  B. target market presentation.
  C. consultative selling approach.
  D. prepared sales presentation.
  E. None of the above.

15-**143.**
A
Comp.
Med.
p. 444

The selling formula approach:
A. starts with a prepared presentation outline, discovers each customer's specific needs, and then leads the customer through some logical steps to a final close.
B. uses the same sales presentation with every potential customer.
C. usually requires a more skilled salesperson than the consultative selling approach.
D. All of the above are true.
E. None of the above is true.

15-**144.**
A
App.
Med.
p. 444

Progressive Insurance Company uses relatively untrained people to sell its life insurance. The sales reps learn prepared sales presentations which help them describe the firm's policies to potential customers, discover each customer's specific needs, and then lead them through some logical steps to a final close. They are using a:
A. selling formula approach.
B. missionary presentation.
C. target market presentation.
D. consultative selling approach.
E. prepared sales presentation.

15-**145.**
D
Def.
Med.
p. 444

Producers who know something about their target customers' needs and attitudes often supply their relatively untrained salespeople with a sales presentation in which (1) the salesperson does most of the talking at the beginning, (2) then brings the customer into the discussion to clarify the customer's needs, and (3) tries to close the sale. They are using a:
A. consultative selling approach.
B. quota system.
C. prepared sales presentation.
D. selling formula approach.
E. target market presentation.

Chapter 16

Advertising and Sales Promotion

True-False Questions:

16-1.
True
p. 450

Mass selling is not as pinpointed as personal selling, but it can be a lower cost way to reach large numbers of potential customers at the same time.

16-2.
True
p. 450

Most promotion blends contain advertising and publicity as well as personal selling and sales promotion.

16-3.
True
p. 452

The amount of money spent on advertising in the United States grew continuously in the last half of the twentieth century.

16-4.
True
p. 452

By 2001, advertising expenditures in the United States were about $250 billion.

16-5.
True
p. 452

Total advertising spending in other countries is much lower than in the U.S.

16-6.
True
p. 452

Advertising in the U.S. accounts for roughly one-half of worldwide advertising spending.

16-7.
False
p. 452

In the last decade, total advertising spending has increased in the U.S., but it has decreased in the rest of the world.

16-8.
False
p. 452

The main problem with advertising is that it costs so much--on average about one third of sales dollars for U.S. companies.

16-9.
True
p. 452

On average, U.S. corporations spend only about 2.5 percent of their sales on advertising.

16-10.
False
p. 452

Producers of business products generally spend a larger percent on advertising than do producers of consumer products.

16-11.
True
p. 453

Games and toys producers spend a higher percentage of their sales on advertising than do footwear producers.

16-12.
False
p. 453

Motor vehicles producers spend a higher percentage of their sales on advertising than do perfumes and cosmetics producers.

16-13.
True
p. 453

Furniture stores spend a higher percentage of their sales on advertising than do grocery stores.

16-14.
False
p. 453

Videotape rental stores spend a higher percentage of their sales on advertising than do amusement parks.

16-15.
True
p. 453

The three top global ad spenders are all consumer packaged goods producers.

16-16.
True
p. 453

In total, advertising costs much less than personal selling and sales promotion.

16-17.
False
p. 453

More money (in the U.S.) is spent on advertising than on personal selling and sales promotion combined.

16-18.
True
p. 453

The largest share of total advertising expenditures in the United States goes for TV (including cable) advertising.

16-19.
False
p. 453

The largest share of total advertising expenditures in the United States goes for newspaper advertising.

16-20.
True
p. 453

The U.S. has about 500,000 people working directly in the advertising industry, and half of them work for advertising agencies.

16-21.
False
p. 453

On average, the 500,000 advertising agencies in the United States are large, employing about 200 people each.

16-22.
True
p. 453

Although advertising expenditures in the United States by 2001 were around $250 billion, the major expense was for media time and space--not payroll expense to people who worked in the advertising industry.

16-23.
True
p. 454

Advertising objectives should be very specific, even more specific than personal selling objectives.

16-24.
True
p. 454

Marketing managers should set overall advertising objectives, but then it's usually the advertising manager's job to set specific objectives for each ad.

16-25.
True
p. 455

Product advertising tries to sell a specific product, while institutional advertising tries to develop goodwill or improve an organization's relations with various groups.

16-26.
False
p. 455

Product advertising is aimed at final consumers; institutional advertising is aimed at middlemen.

16-27.
False
p. 455

Institutional advertising is advertising aimed at business customers and middlemen.

16-28.
False
p. 455

The basic job of pioneering advertising is to persuade, not inform.

16-29.
False
p. 456

Competitive advertising is typically used in the market introduction stage of the product life cycle--to develop primary demand.

16-30.
True
p. 456

Competitive advertising tries to develop selective demand for a specific brand.

16-31.
True
p. 456

When a firm's advertising says "our motorcycles will outperform any other brand," it is using competitive advertising to develop selective demand.

16-32.
True
p. 456

The direct type of competitive advertising tries to obtain immediate buying action.

16-33.
False
p. 456

Indirect competitive advertising aims for immediate buying action while direct competitive advertising aims for future buying action.

16-34.
True
p. 456

When a retailer advertises a "special 24-hour sale on GE brand air conditioners," direct competitive advertising is being used.

16-35.
True
p. 456

Comparative advertising makes specific brand comparisons using actual product names.

16-36.
False
p. 456

Comparative advertising has been banned by the Federal Trade Commission because it was so effective in winning sales from competing products named in ads.

16-37.
True
p. 456

Many countries forbid comparative advertising, but it is now legal in both the U.S. and Japan.

16-38.
True
p. 457

Reminder advertising is most likely to be useful in the market maturity or sales decline stages of the product life cycle--especially when the product has achieved brand insistence or brand preference.

16-39.
False
p. 457

Reminder advertising is likely to be most useful in the market growth stage of the product life cycle.

16-40.
True
p. 457

Institutional advertising may try to inform, persuade, or remind, but it usually focuses on the name and prestige of an organization or industry.

16-41.
False
p. 457

Institutional advertising emphasizes a particular product and plays down the name of the company.

16-42.
True
p. 457

A chemical company might use institutional ads to highlight its concern for the environment.

16-43.
True
p. 458

Advertising allowances are price reductions given to firms further along in the channel to encourage them to advertise or otherwise promote a producer's products locally.

16-44.
False
p. 458

Cooperative advertising is not very economical--because media rate structures usually require local firms to pay more for local advertising than the same ad would cost a national advertiser.

16-45.
True
p. 458

A cooperative advertising program can help a producer achieve coordination and integration of ad messages in the channel of distribution.

16-46.
True
p. 458

Producers can help prevent misuse of advertising allowances by setting the allowance amount as a percent of the retailer's actual purchases and insisting on proof that the advertising was really done.

16-47.
True
p. 458

Manufacturers who use cooperative advertising should insist on proof that allowances have been used for advertising purposes.

16-48.
True
p. 458

The effectiveness of an advertising medium depends on how well it fits with the rest of a particular marketing strategy.

16-49.
False
p. 459

The best advertising medium is television, but some advertisers must use other media because they do not have enough money for TV.

16-**50.**
True
p. 459

To guarantee good media selection, the advertiser must specify its target market and then choose media that will reach these target customers.

16-**51.**
False
p. 460

One advantage of the major mass media is that the advertiser does not have to pay for the whole audience the media delivers, but instead just pays based on the number of potential customers in the audience.

16-**52.**
False
p. 461

The medium with the lowest "cost per 1,000 people" has the greatest potential to reach the advertiser's target market at the lowest cost.

16-**53.**
True
p. 461

Even though the cost per person may be higher and the number of persons reached may be smaller, specialized media is sometimes more effective than mass media.

16-**54.**
True
p. 461-62

Even with specialized media, consumers may selectively tune out ads that don't interest them.

16-**55.**
True
p. 463

Some advertising media are "must buys" because they are obvious choices to reach the target audience.

16-**56.**
True
p. 463

An Internet banner ad is a headline that appears on a web page.

16-**57.**
True
p. 463

The purpose of an Internet banner ad is to encourage the target market to visit the advertiser's website for more information.

16-**58.**
True
p. 463-64

Although there are millions of websites on the Internet, a small subset account for a large percent of the potential audience.

16-**59.**
True
p. 464

Some websites are better than others for reaching target customers.

16-**60.**
True
p. 464

With Internet advertising, noncompeting firms that share a similar target market can post ads on each other's website.

16-**61.**
True
p. 464-65

Both context advertising and pointcasting are approaches for targeting customers on the Internet.

16-**62.**
True
p. 465

Pointcasting displays an Internet ad only to those individuals who meet certain qualifications.

16-63.
True
p. 465

Juno is a firm that provides free e-mail service to those people who provide detailed information for its database and who also agree to look at ads that Juno selects to match their interests.

16-64.
True
p. 465

Some Internet users get free benefits if they agree to look at Internet ads.

16-65.
True
p. 465

At some websites, Internet ads are free if the ads don't get results.

16-66.
True
p. 466

"Clickthrough" is the number of people who actually click on the Internet ad and link to the advertiser's website.

16-67.
False
p. 466

"Copy thrust" refers to the choice of media to deliver a message to the target audience.

16-68.
True
p. 466

The AIDA model can help plan messages for advertisements.

16-69.
True
p. 467-69

Advertising can be useful in a marketing strategy for getting attention, holding interest, arousing desire, and obtaining action.

16-70.
False
p. 469

One of the big problems with using an advertising agency is that the advertiser must stick with the agency for a long time--at least two years--even if the agency's work is not satisfactory.

16-71.
False
p. 469

The vast majority of advertising agencies are large (20 or more employees), but the smaller, more creative agencies account for most of the billings.

16-72.
True
p. 469-70

The growth of mega-agencies has been prompted by large corporations who need to advertise worldwide.

16-73.
False
p. 470

Advertising agencies usually earn a 15 percent commission on all the media they buy for local advertisers.

16-74.
True
p. 470

Local retailers seldom use advertising agencies because the agencies don't get discounts from the rates charged to local advertisers.

16-75.
False
p. 470

The fixed commission system of advertising agency compensation is more favored by local consumer products firms who do a lot of advertising than by business firms who do little advertising.

16-76.
False
p. 470-71

The American Association of Advertising Agencies requires that all agencies be compensated based on a standard 15 percent commission system.

16-77.
False
p. 470

Some firms would like to base advertising agency compensation on results achieved, but that would be illegal.

16-78.
True
p. 471

Advertising effectiveness is usually very difficult to measure because sales result from the total marketing mix, not just promotion.

16-79.
True
p. 471

Except with direct-response advertising, we usually can't measure advertising success just by looking at sales.

16-80.
False
p. 472

The effectiveness of advertising is best measured by relying on the judgment of creative people and advertising "experts."

16-81.
False
p. 472

To evaluate the effectiveness of advertising, it's better to rely on the judgment of the creative people in ad agencies than to rely on the results of advertising research.

16-82.
False
p. 472

The U.S. is one of only a few countries in the world where the government takes an active role in deciding what kinds of advertising are allowable, fair, or appropriate.

16-83.
True
p. 473

Because of different advertising rules in different countries, it's best for a marketing manager to get help from local advertising experts.

16-84.
True
p. 473

In the U.S., the regulation of "deceptive" and "unfair" advertising is the responsibility of the Federal Trade Commission.

16-85.
True
p. 473

The Federal Trade Commission can require firms to use "corrective advertising" or "affirmative disclosures," if it decides a particular advertisement is unfair or deceptive.

16-86.
True
p. 474

In general, sales promotion tries to spark immediate interest, trial, or purchase.

16-87.
True
p. 474

Sales promotions can usually get sales results sooner than advertising.

16-88.
False
p. 474

Advertising can usually get sales results sooner than sales promotion.

16-89.
True
p. 475

Spending on sales promotion exceeds spending on advertising.

16-90.
False
p. 476

Producers of consumer packaged goods typically stop using sales promotion when their product-markets mature.

16-91.
False
p. 476

Because consumers are becoming less and less price-sensitive, the use of sales promotion is increasing.

16-92.
False
p. 476-77

Procter & Gamble is an example of a consumer packaged goods firm that has dramatically increased its use of trade promotion in the promotion blend.

16-93.
True
p. 477

Sales promotion problems are likely to be greater when an advertising or sales manager, instead of a sales promotion manager, has responsibility for sales promotion.

16-94.
True
p. 478

A sales promotion can cost more than it adds in sales.

16-95.
True
p. 479

Trade promotion usually stresses price-related matters.

16-96.
False
p. 479

It is against the law for industrial buyers to accept promotion items from suppliers.

16-97.
True
p. 479

Sales promotion directed at employees is especially popular with service-oriented firms.

Multiple Choice Questions

16-98.
A
Comp.
Easy
p. 450

Mass selling:
  A. makes widespread distribution possible--by reaching many potential customers at the same time.
  B. alternatives do not vary much in cost (and results) when target market preferences are considered.
  C. is usually more expensive than personal selling on a per contact basis.
  D. All of the above are true.
  E. None of the above is true.

16-**99.**
E
Def.
Easy
p. 450

Planning for mass selling involves strategy decisions about:
A. what is to be said to the target customers.
B. how target customers are to be reached.
C. who is the target audience.
D. what kind of advertising is to be used.
E. All of the above.

16-**100.**
B
Def.
Med.
p. 452

By 2001, advertising spending in the United States was about:
A. $150 billion.
B. $250 billion.
C. $ 3 billion.
D. $ 33 billion.
E. $103 billion.

16-**101.**
D
Comp.
Med.
p. 452

Total advertising expenditures by 2001:
A. were about 15 percent of all firms' sales.
B. were larger in Europe than in the U.S.
C. declined to the level of the early 1960s.
D. were about $250 billion.
E. were under $25 billion.

16-**102.**
C
Comp.
Med.
p. 452

Advertising spending
A. by U.S. corporations averages about 25 percent of their sales dollars.
B. exceeded $1.5 trillion in 2001.
C. represents only a small portion of what people pay for products.
D. in the U.S. exceeds the amount spent on any other element of promotion.
E. All of the above are true.

16-**103.**
D
Def.
Med.
p. 452

U.S. corporations spend about _____ percent of their sales on advertising.
A. 25.0
B. 35.0
C. 15.0
D. 2.5
E. 7.5

16-**104.**
A
Comp.
Hard
p. 452

Advertising expenditures by U.S. corporations:
A. average only about 2.5 percent of sales.
B. must be approved by an advertising agency that is registered with the Federal Trade Commission.
C. are higher for newspaper advertising than television advertising.
D. are much higher than either personal selling or sales promotion expenditures.
E. are highest for business product companies (as a percent of sales).

16-**105.**
A
Def.
Hard
p. 453

Advertising spending as a percent of sales dollars is largest for:
A. soaps and detergents.
B. greeting cards.
C. sporting and athletic goods.
D. soft drinks and water.
E. motor vehicles.

16-**106.**
C
Def.
Hard
p. 453

Advertising spending as a percent of sales dollars is largest for:
A. computers.
B. business services.
C. toys.
D. motor vehicles.
E. malt beverages.

16-**107.**
D
Def.
Hard
p. 453

Advertising spending as a percent of sales dollars is lowest for:
A. shoes.
B. investment advice.
C. plastics.
D. computers.
E. perfume.

16-**108.**
D
Def.
Hard
p. 453

Which of the following retailers spend more on advertising as a percent of sales?
A. Grocery stores.
B. Hotels and motels.
C. Women's clothing stores.
D. Furniture stores.

16-**109.**
C
Comp.
Med.
p. 453

The largest share of total U.S. advertising expenditures is for:
A. advertising agency personnel costs.
B. creating and producing ads.
C. media time and space.
D. advertising to business customers.
E. None of the above is true.

16-**110.**
E
Def.
Med.
p. 453

The largest share of U.S. advertising money goes for:
A. radio.
B. newspapers.
C. magazines.
D. direct mail.
E. television (including cable).

16-**111.**
C
Comp.
Med.
p. 453

In the U.S., the largest share of advertising expenditures is spent on:
A. direct mail.
B. radio.
C. TV (including cable).
D. billboards.
E. newspapers.

16-**112.**
A
Comp.
Med.
p. 453

Regarding mass selling and other elements of promotion,
A. less money is spent on advertising than on personal selling.
B. many more people work in advertising than in personal selling.
C. more dollars are spent on advertising than on the rest of promotion.
D. All of the above are true.
E. None of the above is true.

16-**113.**
A
Comp.
Easy
p. 454

Advertising objectives should be:
A. more specific than personal selling objectives.
B. decided by the creative experts who work with advertising agencies.
C. quite general to allow for creativity.
D. set by the advertising manager--not the marketing manager.
E. determined by the kind of advertising that is required.

16-**114.**
B
App.
Med.
p. 454

Which of the following is the LEAST appropriate advertising objective?
A. To increase sales by 20 percent this year.
B. To improve consumer goodwill and help sell the product.
C. To increase target customers' brand awareness by 50 percent this year.
D. To increase a brand's market share by 10 percent.
E. To obtain 20 new accounts in the Oakland Bay area.

16-**115.**
A
App.
Easy
p. 454

Which of the following advertising objectives is the BEST example of a specific advertising objective?
A. To increase a firm's market share by 20 percent--this year.
B. To increase consumer awareness of the product.
C. To help attract new retailers on the West Coast.
D. To sell the company "image" to senior citizens.
E. To increase store traffic.

16-**116.**
A
App.
Hard
p. 454

Which of the following is the BEST example of an advertising objective?
A. "We want 35 percent of our target customers to be aware of our new product within the next two months."
B. "We want to generate enough interest in our product that middlemen will be willing to stock it."
C. "We want to make older consumers aware of our product--since they have the greatest need."
D. "We want to increase profits--and that will require significantly expanding sales of our product."
E. "We want to win an advertising industry artistic award for the creative effort on the ad."

16-**117.**
B
App.
Med.
p. 454

Which of the following is the LEAST appropriate advertising objective?
A. "We want our ads to increase traffic in our retail outlets by 10%.
B. "We want our TV ads to really promote the product."
C. "We want the ad campaign to increase our market share by 3 percent."
D. "We want distribution in 30 percent of the desirable retail outlets."
E. None of the above, i.e., all are equally appropriate.

16-**118.**
D
Comp.
Med.
p. 454

Advertising objectives should
A. be specific, but not as specific as the objectives for the personal selling effort.
B. be set by the specialists--the creative people at the advertising agency.
C. be quite general so that ads will appeal to the largest possible audience.
D. determine the kinds of advertising needed.
E. be more specific for institutional advertising than for direct type competitive advertising.

16-**119.**
C
Def.
Med.
p. 455

Institutional advertising:
A. tries to stimulate primary demand rather than selective demand.
B. involves no media costs.
C. tries to develop goodwill for a company or even an industry.
D. tries to keep a product's name before the public.
E. is always aimed at final consumers or users.

16-**120.**
C
Def.
Easy
p. 455

_____ advertising tries to develop goodwill for a company or even an industry--instead of a specific product.
A. Primary demand
B. Selective demand
C. Institutional
D. Persuading
E. Pioneering

16-**121.**
C
Def.
Easy
p. 455

Focusing a company's advertising on its name and prestige is called _____ advertising.
A. reminder
B. primary
C. institutional
D. competitive
E. pioneering

16-**122.**
A
App.
Easy
p. 455

When a firm's president appears in TV testimonial ads to assure customers, employees and stockholders that the firm is making a fast recovery from some problem, this is:
A. institutional advertising.
B. reminder advertising.
C. competitive advertising.
D. comparative advertising.
E. pioneering advertising.

16-**123.**
E
App.
Med.
p. 455

Which of the following is the BEST example of "institutional advertising?"
A. "I'd walk a mile for a Pepsi"
B. "IBM is THE standard for personal computers"
C. "Mobil gas makes your car perform better"
D. "Promise her anything but give her Obsession"
E. "Better living through research"

16-**124.**
A
App.
Med.
p. 455

The National Cheese Association's ad theme "We are making better cheese for you" is an example of:
A. institutional advertising.
B. cooperative advertising.
C. pioneering advertising.
D. competitive advertising.
E. reminder advertising.

16-**125.**
E
Comp.
Med.
p. 455

Institutional advertising:
A. may try to improve a firm's image with shareholders.
B. may seek to inform, persuade, or remind.
C. may try to improve a firm's image with the general public.
D. focuses on the name and prestige of a company or industry.
E. All of the above.

16-**126.**
B
Def.
Med.
p. 455

"Pioneering advertising" tries to:
A. develop goodwill toward a company.
B. develop primary demand.
C. build a brand image.
D. develop selective demand.
E. build demand for a specific brand.

16-**127.**
A
App.
Hard
p. 455

Which of the following advertising headlines is MOST oriented toward stimulating PRIMARY demand?
A. "See your Hewlett Packard dealer to learn how an affordable portable printer can make business travel easier."
B. "Panasonic is the value leader."
C. "IBM printers set the quality standard."
D. "Buy Quality. Buy from an authorized Epson dealer."
E. "Canon portable computers are lighter to carry than any other brand.

16-**128.**
A
App.
Med.
p. 455

Kodak has developed a revolutionary new kind of electronic color camera that does not require film. People will need to adjust their thinking about how a camera works. The "camera" will cut the cost of color pictures by 50 percent--if the market accepts the idea. Kodak is about to advertise this product to inform potential customers about what it does and how it works. The campaign should emphasize:
A. pioneering advertising.
B. institutional advertising.
C. competitive advertising.
D. reminder advertising.
E. None of the above.

16-**129.**
D
Def.
Easy
p. 455

Advertising which tries to develop primary demand for a product category rather than a specific brand is called _____ advertising.
A. comparative
B. institutional
C. competitive
D. pioneering
E. persuading

16-**130.**
B
App.
Med.
p. 455

A farmer's cooperative in California is sponsoring TV ads aimed at getting Americans to eat more garlic. The ads don't mention any brand names. This is an example of _____ advertising.
A. competitive
B. pioneering
C. indirect competitive
D. reminder
E. comparative

16-131.
E
App.
Med.
p. 455

Faced with a decline in red meat consumption, the American Beef Association is sponsoring an advertising campaign to increase consumption of beef by stressing new research results about beef's nutritional benefits. This is an example of:
  A. competitive advertising.
  B. reminder advertising.
  C. comparative advertising.
  D. indirect action advertising.
  E. pioneering advertising.

16-132.
D
App.
Med.
p. 455

Boomerang, Inc. has created a really new product and the firm's marketing manager is worried that consumers may not buy the product because it is such a different way of satisfying the basic need. The promotion blend for the new product probably should emphasize _____ during market introduction.
  A. comparative advertising
  B. institutional advertising
  C. reminder advertising
  D. pioneering advertising
  E. competitive advertising

16-133.
E
Comp.
Easy
p. 455

Pioneering advertising is often needed during the _____ stage of the product life cycle.
  A. Sales decline
  B. Turbulence
  C. Market maturity
  D. Market growth
  E. Market introduction

16-134.
A
Comp.
Med.
p. 456

Using advertising to develop selective demand:
  A. may become necessary as a firm's product moves through its product life cycle.
  B. should only be tried with selective distribution.
  C. is needed when consumers do not know a new product is available.
  D. is intended to produce immediate buying action.
  E. is needed when a firm has a monopoly.

16-135.
A
Def.
Med.
p. 456

"Competitive advertising" tries to:
  A. develop selective demand rather than primary demand.
  B. keep a product's name before the public.
  C. promote the competitive products of an industry rather than a particular firm.
  D. build demand for a product category.
  E. create goodwill for a firm.

16-136.
B
Def.
Easy
p. 456

Advertising which tries to develop selective demand for a specific brand rather than a product category is called _____ advertising.
  A. institutional
  B. competitive
  C. indirect reminder
  D. direct pioneering
  E. primary

16-**137.**
E
App.
Med.
p. 456

An ad stressing the advantages of one brand of cookware--compared to similar (but unnamed) competitive products--is an example of _____ advertising.
   A. institutional
   B. comparative
   C. pioneering
   D. primary
   E. competitive

16-**138.**
B
App.
Med.
p. 456

Which kind of advertising should a manufacturer of paper towels (that are basically similar to competitive products) use if it wants to increase its market share?
   A. Reminder
   B. Competitive
   C. Institutional
   D. Primary demand
   E. Pioneering

16-**139.**
A
Comp.
Easy
p. 456

DIRECT competitive advertising:
   A. aims for immediate buying action.
   B. tries to develop primary demand.
   C. is only seen in newspapers.
   D. only uses direct mail.
   E. stresses specific product advantages--so the target customers will buy the advertised brand when they are ready to buy.

16-**140.**
B
App.
Med.
p. 456

A typical retailer's newspaper ad stressing "today's" sale prices on "regular" stock is an example of _____ advertising.
   A. reminder
   B. direct competitive
   C. pioneering
   D. institutional
   E. indirect competitive

16-**141.**
E
App.
Med.
p. 456

A supermarket manager should use _____ advertising to increase store traffic during the middle of the week.
   A. institutional
   B. indirect competitive
   C. pioneering
   D. reminder
   E. direct competitive

16-**142.**
A
App.
Med.
p. 456

Glitter, Inc. advertises its "gold-tone" jewelry on TV, along with a toll free number and the message that "operators are standing by now to take your credit card order." This is an example of:
   A. direct type competitive advertising.
   B. pioneering advertising.
   C. primary advertising.
   D. comparative advertising.
   E. indirect type competitive advertising.

16-**143.**   INDIRECT competitive advertising seeks:
D
Def.   A. to develop primary demand.
Easy   B. immediate buying action.
p. 456   C. to develop goodwill for a company--so target customers will eventually buy one
                      or more of its products.
                 D. to develop selective demand--to affect future buying decisions.
                 E. None of the above.

16-**144.**   A manufacturer of computer printers has decided to add scanners to its line. Which
E   kind of advertising should it stress if it wants to persuade consumers to buy its brand of
App.   more or less similar scanners?
Hard   A. Reminder
p. 456   B. Direct competitive
                 C. Pioneering
                 D. Institutional
                 E. Indirect competitive

16-**145.**   Best Sound, Inc. placed a full-page color ad in Car Talk magazine--stressing the better
E   sound available with its car stereo product as compared to similarly priced products--to
App.   try to affect its target market's future buying decisions. This is an example of:
Med.   A. reminder advertising.
p. 456   B. pioneering advertising.
                 C. direct competitive advertising.
                 D. institutional advertising.
                 E. indirect competitive advertising.

16-**146.**   Sears advertises its "DieHard" auto batteries as "even better than your original
B   battery." The ads tell possible customers to get a DieHard at their Sears auto center the
App.   next time they need one. This is an example of
Med.   A. institutional advertising.
p. 456   B. the indirect type of competitive advertising.
                 C. the direct type of competitive advertising.
                 D. comparative advertising.
                 E. reminder advertising.

16-**147.**   Competitive advertising which makes specific brand comparisons--using actual
C   names--is _____ advertising.
Def.   A. direct competitive
Easy   B. cooperative
p. 456   C. comparative
                 D. pioneering
                 E. institutional

16-**148.**   Nissan's Altima advertises the performance of its new luxury sedan by showing it
D   side-by-side with competing brands, like Lexus and BMW. This is:
App.   A. primary advertising.
Easy   B. institutional advertising.
p. 456   C. reminder advertising.
                 D. comparative advertising.
                 E. selective advertising.

16-**149.**
B
App.
Med.
p. 456

An ad for Toyota's lowest priced truck claimed that it "is tougher, gives better mileage, and costs less that any other truck"--and specifically named the directly competitive trucks. This is:
   A. institutional advertising.
   B. comparative advertising.
   C. cooperative advertising.
   D. direct competitive advertising.
   E. pioneering advertising.

16-**150.**
C
Comp.
Hard
p. 457

"Comparative advertising":
   A. is usually ignored by consumers.
   B. is illegal--according to the FTC.
   C. may benefit the competitive brand more than the advertiser's brand.
   D. must focus on major consumer benefits to be legal.
   E. None of the above.

16-**151.**
A
Comp.
Med.
p. 457

A major difference between reminder advertising and pioneering advertising is that:
   A. reminder advertising focuses on selective demand, while pioneering advertising tries to develop primary demand.
   B. reminder advertising is less likely to use "soft sell" ads.
   C. reminder advertising is emphasized in the early stages of the product life cycle and pioneering advertising is emphasized later.
   D. All of the above are true.
   E. None of the above is true.

16-**152.**
D
App.
Med.
p. 457

When a producer has won brand preference for its product--but is entering the sales decline stage of its life cycle--it probably should use:
   A. pioneering advertising.
   B. competitive advertising.
   C. primary advertising.
   D. reminder advertising.
   E. institutional advertising.

16-**153.**
A
Def.
Easy
p. 457

When a producer has won brand insistence in its target market--and just wants to keep the product's name before the public--it can use:
   A. reminder advertising.
   B. pioneering advertising.
   C. direct-action advertising.
   D. comparative advertising.
   E. institutional advertising.

16-**154.**
D
Def.
Easy
p. 458

Price reductions given to channel members to encourage them to advertise or otherwise promote a firm's products locally are:
   A. quantity discounts.
   B. brokerage allowances.
   C. push money allowances.
   D. advertising allowances.
   E. trade incentives.

16-**155**.
D
App.
Easy
p. 458

A producer of country music CDs pays a share of local retailers' costs--to get them to promote its new releases. This is an example of:
  A. pioneering advertising.
  B. institutional advertising.
  C. comparative advertising.
  D. cooperative advertising.
  E. selective advertising.

16-**156**.
D
Int.
Med.
p. 458

Cooperative advertising is:
  A. advertising by several producers of the same product type--to stimulate primary demand.
  B. encouraged by the Federal Trade Commission.
  C. the opposite of competitive advertising.
  D. a way for a producer to get more promotion for its advertising dollar.
  E. None of the above is true.

16-**157**.
E
Comp.
Hard
p. 458

Producers do cooperative advertising with retailers because:
  A. media rate structures give local firms lower rates than national firms.
  B. the FTC requires it.
  C. retailers create better ads than producers.
  D. retailers are more likely to follow through when they are paying a share of the cost.
  E. Both A and D.

16-**158**.
E
Def.
Med.
p. 458

"Cooperative advertising" involves producers:
  A. paying for middlemen's total advertising costs.
  B. agreeing with competitors to limit advertising spending.
  C. doing some advertising and expecting their middlemen to provide the rest of the promotion blend.
  D. and middlemen sharing in the cost of advertising placed in national media.
  E. and middlemen sharing in the cost of local advertising.

16-**159**.
B
Def.
Easy
p. 458

A producer and middlemen sharing the cost of ads in local media is called:
  A. comparative advertising.
  B. cooperative advertising.
  C. pioneering advertising.
  D. campaign advertising.
  E. institutional advertising.

16-**160**.
D
Comp.
Easy
p. 458

Which of the following is NOT a concern in selecting the advertising media to use?
  A. the advertising budget.
  B. the nature of the media.
  C. the target market.
  D. All of the above are relevant concerns.

16-**161.**
E
Def.
Easy
p. 458

Selecting the most effective advertising media depends on the:
A. nature of the media--i.e. reach, frequency, impact and cost.
B. firm's target market.
C. funds available for advertising.
D. firm's promotion objectives.
E. All of the above.

16-**162.**
E
Comp.
Easy
p. 459-61

To choose the best advertising medium, you have to:
A. decide what target market(s) should be reached.
B. decide on promotion objectives.
C. know the cost of alternative media.
D. decide what must be said.
E. all of the above.

16-**163.**
B
App.
Med.
p. 459

Regarding advertising media selection, which of the following is the best advice?
A. "There is no such thing as a `must buy'."
B. "Be sure the media match your target market."
C. "Avoid the local media."
D. "Make sure your first media choice reaches the whole target market."
E. "Set very general promotion objectives to stay flexible."

16-**164.**
A
Int.
Med.
p. 459-60

Regarding media selection:
A. the major broadcasting media usually cannot be definite about who actually sees or hears each show.
B. "must buys" usually consume a manager's total advertising budget.
C. the use of "mass market magazines" is growing in popularity--to cut costs.
D. the only advertising medium available for direct-response ads is mail.
E. All of the above.

16-**165.**
A
Int.
Med.
p. 459-60

Good media buyers know that:
A. the major media gather audience information, but it is not as specific as the segmenting dimensions which potential advertisers want to use.
B. the most targeted medium is newspapers.
C. media costs generally have little relation to audience size or circulation.
D. television is superior to newspapers or radio.
E. All of the above.

16-**166.**
E
Comp.
Med.
p. 461

When selecting advertising media, a good advertising manager knows that:
A. TV typically reaches more targeted markets than radio.
B. direct-response ads are not a good alternative unless you already have your own mailing list.
C. big national magazines, like TIME, may have wide circulation, but are not practical for reaching regional markets.
D. Magazines can't be used for reaching specific business or trade audiences.
E. objective measures--like "cost per thousand"--can be misleading.

16-**167.**
E
Comp.
Med.
p. 463-66

Regarding Internet advertising:
A. At some web sites, ads are free if they don't get results.
B. Internet banner ads encourage viewers to visit the advertiser's web site for more information.
C. Some web sites are better than others for reaching target customers.
D. Both context advertising and pointcasting are approaches for targeting customers.
E. All of the above.

16-**168.**
E
Comp.
Med.
p. 463-65

Which of the following statements about advertising on the Internet is(are) true?
A. When a web site sets fees based on actual sales, it is setting fees in the same manner as traditional media.
B. Content on a web site is similar to traditional advertising.
C. There are very good measures of how many people are exposed to Internet ads.
D. All of the above are true.
E. None of the above is true.

16-**169.**
D
Def.
Easy
p. 466

"Copy thrust" refers to:
A. competitors who make similar claims in their ads.
B. an FTC challenge to the claims made by an advertiser.
C. all the advertising copy prepared for a particular brand.
D. what is to be communicated by the words and illustrations.
E. how much the audience believes what the advertiser says.

16-**170.**
B
Comp.
Med.
p. 466

Regarding message planning:
A. a specific message usually can be used for several target markets.
B. communication may be poor if there is not a common frame of reference.
C. behavioral research shows that most consumers cannot "tune out" advertising messages.
D. advertising is more suitable for changing behavior than attitudes.
E. All of the above.

16-**171.**
B
Int.
Hard
p. 468

Regarding message planning and the AIDA model:
A. "getting action" is the final and easiest step in the process.
B. focusing on one unique selling proposition is one way to arouse desire.
C. a successful attention-getting device assures "holding interest."
D. "arousing desire" is the first and hardest step in the process.
E. All of the above are true.

16-**172.**
C
App.
Med.
p. 468

Regarding advertising and the AIDA model, which of the following is the best example of advertising aimed at obtaining action?
A. A TV ad at 10:00 PM for the luncheon buffet at a local restaurant.
B. A car at an auto junk yard--with the operating hours painted on the side.
C. An ad for a restaurant in the Yellow Pages.
D. A classified ad in a newspaper with the word "SEX" in bold print and then the name and telephone number of a dry cleaner.
E. None of the above.

16-173.
B
App.
Hard
p. 468

An ad which offers the consumer $1.00 off on his next grocery store visit is most likely aimed at:
  A. arousing desire
  B. obtaining action.
  C. getting attention.
  D. holding interest.
  E. none of the above.

16-174.
A
Def.
Easy
p. 469

An advertising manager's job is to:
  A. manage the firm's advertising effort.
  B. plan creative marketing strategies.
  C. develop the firm's marketing mix.
  D. develop the firm's promotion blend.
  E. both A and D.

16-175.
E
Comp.
Easy
p. 469

"Advertising agencies":
  A. usually require advertisers to sign long-term contracts.
  B. prefer to work with local advertisers rather than national advertisers.
  C. compete against the national media for the business of big advertisers.
  D. do little more than sell media time or space to advertisers.
  E. are specialists in planning and handling mass selling details.

16-176.
A
Comp.
Med.
p. 469

Advertising agencies:
  A. may do a better job at less cost than firms' own advertising departments because they are specialists with an outside viewpoint.
  B. earn a mandatory 15 percent commission on all local media buys.
  C. usually do marketing strategy planning for their clients.
  D. obtain most of their income from advertisers--as service fees.
  E. All of the above.

16-177.
E
Comp.
Med.
p. 469

Natalie St. John, brand manager for a cookie producer, says that she is looking for a "full service" advertising agency. Apparently, in addition to having the agency purchase media, she wants an agency to help
  A. plan package development.
  B. develop sales promotions.
  C. provide market research.
  D. create the actual advertisements.
  E. A full service agency might help with any of the above.

16-178.
C
Comp.
Med.
p. 470

Advertising agencies
  A. can be helpful, but they are always more expensive than a firm doing its own advertising work.
  B. must be selected very carefully since most agencies require long-term contracts.
  C. that are smaller in size will probably continue to play an important role despite the creation of mega-agencies.
  D. usually don't cost local retailers anything to use, since the media commission is usually all the compensation the agency expects.
  E. None of the above is true.

16-**179.**
C
Comp.
Med.
p. 470-71

The "traditional" commission approach for paying advertising agencies:
A. encouraged agencies to minimize media time and space purchases.
B. resulted in more local advertisers than national advertisers using ad agencies.
C. made it difficult for agencies to be completely objective in designing advertising campaigns.
D. encouraged agencies to do research on the effect of the ads they created.
E. All of the above.

16-**180.**
B
Int.
Med.
p. 470-71

In recent years,
A. specialists in media buying have disappeared.
B. there has been growing interest in paying agencies based on the results they actually produce.
C. almost all advertising agencies have switched to the full-service approach.
D. conflicts between creative and business-oriented advertising people have almost disappeared due to acceptance of the marketing concept.
E. more ad agencies have been adopting the 15 percent commission system.

16-**181.**
C
App.
Hard
p. 470

The "traditional" approach for compensating ad agencies was most favored by:
A. large producers of consumer products.
B. not-for-profit organizations.
C. business products producers.
D. small local retailers.
E. the Federal Trade Commission.

16-**182.**
C
Comp.
Hard
p. 470-71

Regarding ad agencies, a good marketing manager knows that:
A. a 15 percent commission system can be a real bargain for firms that need little service but buy a lot of media time and space.
B. ad agencies earn commissions from media only when they buy at local rates.
C. the traditional 15 percent commission system is no longer required.
D. it is hard to end an agency relationship.
E. All of the above.

16-**183.**
A
App.
Med.
p. 471

Trion, Inc. recently spent $1,000,000 on newspaper advertising and obtained a 30 percent increase in sales. Which of the following is TRUE regarding Trion's advertising effectiveness?
A. It's hard to evaluate the ad's effectiveness because the sales increase was the result of Trion's whole marketing mix--not just its advertising.
B. It is not possible to measure the effectiveness of Trion's advertising.
C. Trion's advertising effectiveness should be evaluated by how many potential customers were exposed to the ads.
D. Trying to measure the effectiveness of Trion's advertising is not possible unless the ads were pretested.

16-**184.**
A
App.
Easy
p. 471

Analysis of sales increases for measuring the effectiveness of a firm's advertising makes the most sense with _____ advertising.
A. direct-response
B. comparative
C. broadcast (radio and television)
D. billboard
E. institutional

16-**185.**
C
Comp.
Med.
p. 472

Research to evaluate advertising effectiveness:
- A. is especially difficult with direct-response promotion.
- B. should focus primarily on measuring increases in sales.
- C. includes experiments conducted using split runs on cable TV systems.
- D. is a problem because nothing can be done until after the ad has actually run.
- E. All of the above are true.

16-**186.**
A
Comp.
Med.
p. 472

Regarding measuring advertising effectiveness, which of the following statements is FALSE?
- A. The most reliable approach is to check the size and composition of media audiences.
- B. Managers probably should pretest advertising rather than relying only on the judgment of advertising "experts."
- C. If specific advertising objectives are set, then marketing research can help evaluate the effectiveness of ads.
- D. Some advertisers are now demanding laboratory or market tests to evaluate effectiveness.
- E. No single research technique has proven most effective.

16-**187.**
E
Def.
Hard
p. 472-73

Which of the following statements are TRUE regarding government's role in regulating advertising?
- A. Canada and Sweden ban any advertising targeted directly at children.
- B. Italy severely limits the number of times a specific ad can be shown on TV.
- C. Switzerland does not allow an actor to represent a consumer in an ad.
- D. New Zealand limits political ads on TV.
- E. All of the above are true.

16-**188.**
B
App.
Med.
p. 474

Which of the following might the FTC consider as UNFAIR advertising--rather than DECEPTIVE advertising?
- A. Having a top rock star say that he prefers Coke--when he actually prefers Pepsi.
- B. Aiming ads for high-calorie foods at children.
- C. Making a claim that cannot be supported.
- D. Claiming that your brand of ice cream is the "best-tasting."
- E. Making a factual claim that is partially true--and partially false.

16-**189.**
E
Comp.
Easy
p. 473-74

Regarding advertising, the Federal Trade Commission:
- A. can require firms to run corrective ads.
- B. can regulate deceptive advertising.
- C. can require firms to support ad claims.
- D. can police ads it considers to be "unfair"--but cannot use "unfairness" in a rule affecting a whole industry.
- E. All of the above.

16-**190.**
D
Comp.
Med.
p. 473-74

A firm has run a comparative ad, and a competitor immediately complained that the claims made by the ad are deceptive. In such a case,

A. the ad agency that created the ad could share responsibility in any action brought by the FTC.
B. the firm that sponsored the ad might need to provide research proof that its claims are accurate.
C. the Federal Trade Commission has the power to require corrective advertising--if the ad was really deceptive.
D. All of the above are true.
E. A and C are true, but not B.

16-**191.**
E
Comp.
Med.
p. 474-77

Sales promotion activities:

A. can usually be implemented quickly and get results sooner than advertising.
B. may be aimed at final consumers, middlemen, and/or a firm's own sales force.
C. cost more than the total expenditures on advertising.
D. are currently a weak spot in many firms' marketing strategies.
E. All of the above.

16-**192.**
B
Comp.
Med.
p. 475

Sales promotion:

A. is not likely to be used in the market maturity stage of the product life cycle.
B. objectives and situation should determine what specific type of sales promotion is best.
C. should not be needed if a firm has a good mass selling program.
D. objectives should be developed after the other promotion decisions have been made--so the manager knows how much is left in the budget.
E. None of the above is true.

16-**193.**
D
Comp.
Med.
p. 477

Sales promotion:

A. should not be needed if a firm has a good mass selling program.
B. is not likely to be used in the market maturity stage of the product life cycle.
C. objectives should be developed after the other promotion decisions have been made--so the manager knows how much is left in the budget.
D. activities are often handled by outside specialists.
E. All of the above are true.

16-**194.**
E
Comp.
Easy
p. 477-79

Sales promotion should be targeted toward

A. wholesalers.
B. business customers.
C. final consumers.
D. retailers.
E. Any of the above could be an appropriate target.

Chapter 17

Pricing Objectives and Policies

True-False Questions:

17-1.
True
p. 485

Any business transaction can be thought of as an exchange of "something of value" for money--where the money is the price.

17-2.
True
p. 486

Pricing objectives and policies should flow from company-level objectives.

17-3.
True
p. 487

A target return pricing objective seeks to obtain a specific level of profit--often stated as a percentage of sales or return on investment.

17-4.
True
p. 487

A target return pricing objective has administrative advantages in a large company where there are many divisions to compare.

17-5.
True
p. 487

Many nonprofit organizations try to set a price level that will earn a target return figure of zero.

17-6.
True
p. 487

A target return objective and a profit maximization objective are both profit-oriented objectives.

17-7.
False
p. 488

Profit maximization objectives lead to high prices and monopolies--and are generally not in the public interest.

17-8.
True
p. 488

A profit maximization pricing objective may lead to relatively low prices, especially if demand is very elastic.

17-9.
True
p. 488

Sales-oriented pricing objectives don't refer to profit.

17-10.
True
p. 488

A sales-oriented pricing objective seeks some level of unit sales, dollar sales, or share of market--without referring to profit.

17-11.
False
p. 488

Sales-oriented pricing objectives are sensible because sales growth almost guarantees higher profits.

17-12.
False
p. 489

A marketing manager who sets prices to achieve a given level of market share is using a profit-oriented pricing objective.

17-13.
False
p. 489

Sales-oriented pricing objectives--such as maintaining or increasing market share--are unpopular because it is so difficult to measure results.

17-14.
True
p. 489

A firm should not simply assume that its profits will grow if its sales grow.

17-15.
True
p. 489

Status quo pricing objectives might focus on meeting competition, avoiding competition, or stabilizing prices.

17-16.
True
p. 489-90

Meeting competition and nonprice competition are both status-quo objectives.

17-17.
True
p. 490

Status quo pricing objectives suggest avoiding price competition, but may lead to very aggressive competition with Promotion, Place, or Product.

17-18.
False
p. 490

Administered prices are prices agreed to by competing firms in a market.

17-19.
False
p. 490

When a firm sells through middlemen, there is little reason to try to administer the price middlemen charge final consumers.

17-20.
False
p. 490

Most firms avoid administered prices because they may be illegal under the Robinson-Patman Act.

17-21.
False
p. 491

Most firms in the U.S. avoid using a one-price policy because it is so inconvenient to administer and leads to more negotiation and higher selling costs.

17-22.
True
p. 491-92

Flexible-price policies are most common in the channels and in direct sales to business customers because sales reps may need to make adjustments for market conditions.

17-23.
False
p. 491-92

A flexible-price policy is illegal in the U.S.

17-24.
True
p. 492

A flexible-price policy is most often used where products are not standardized and where bargaining is common.

17-25.
True
p. 492

The haggling that often occurs when a consumer buys a new car is a direct result of the flexible pricing most auto dealers use.

17-26.
True
p. 493

A skimming pricing policy tries to sell to customers who are at the top of the demand curve first, before aiming for more price sensitive customers.

17-27.
False
p. 493

In the market introduction stage of the product life cycle, if a firm has economies of scale and expects competitors to enter the market soon, it would be wise to adopt a skimming pricing policy.

17-28.
True
p. 494

A skimming price policy usually involves a slow reduction in price over time.

17-29.
True
p. 494

If a firm's demand curve is fairly elastic, a penetration pricing policy would be more suitable than a skimming pricing policy.

17-30.
True
p. 494

A low penetration price discourages competitors from entering the market.

17-31.
False
p. 495

Introductory price dealing means setting a low "penetration" price early in the product life cycle to discourage competitors from entering the market.

17-32.
False
p. 495

Introductory price dealing involves setting high initial prices on a product when it is introduced--to see how much consumers are willing to pay.

17-33.
True
p. 496

How much a nation's money is worth in some other nation's currency can impact the price level in both local and international markets.

17-34.
False
p. 496

The exchange rate affects what is a competitive price for products sold in international markets, but not local markets.

17-35.
True
p. 497

Basic list prices are the prices that final consumers or users are normally asked to pay.

17-36.
True
p. 497

Quantity discounts encourage customers to buy in larger amounts.

17-37.
True
p. 498

Cumulative quantity discounts encourage repeat buying from the same seller, while noncumulative quantity discounts encourage large individual orders.

17-38.
False
p. 498

Noncumulative quantity discounts are intended to encourage customers to make more of their on-going purchases from the same seller.

17-39.
True
p. 498

A seasonal discount encourages buyers to stock products earlier than present demand requires.

17-40.
True
p. 498-99

Seasonal discounts tend to smooth out sales during the year and therefore permit year-round operation.

17-41.
False
p. 499

The term "3/10, net 30" means that thirty percent of the face value of the invoice is due immediately, and that the rest must be paid within 30 days.

17-42.
True
p. 499

The term "3/10, net 30" means that a 3 percent discount off the face value of the invoice is allowed if the invoice is paid within 10 days, and that otherwise the full face value is due within 30 days.

17-43.
True
p. 499

Not taking advantage of cash discounts may have the same effect as paying a fairly large "interest charge."

17-44.
True
p. 501

Many middlemen seek advertising allowances from manufacturers to help them pay the cost of advertising the products they sell.

17-45.
True
p. 501

Stocking allowances are given to a middleman to get shelf space for a product.

17-46.
True
p. 501

Push money allowances are intended to make the retailers' salespeople sell particular products very aggressively.

17-47.
True
p. 503

F.O.B. "shipping point" pricing simplifies the seller's pricing, but tends to reduce the size of the seller's market.

17-48.
True
p. 503

If a seller wanted to pay the delivery charges and keep title to the products until delivered to a buyer, the seller could use "F.O.B. buyer's factory" geographic pricing terms.

17-49.
False
p. 503

When a seller uses "zone pricing," the actual freight charge for delivering each order is included in the price the buyer pays for the product.

17-50.
True
p. 503

When a seller uses "zone pricing," all customers who are in the same zone are charged the same freight charge--even if the actual shipping cost varies.

17-51.
True
p. 503

Uniform delivered pricing is most commonly used when transportation costs are relatively low.

17-52.
True
p. 503

Freight-absorption pricing basically amounts to cutting list price on sales to distant customers.

17-53.
False
p. 504

Value pricing involves developing a "bare bones" marketing mix and a cheap price.

17-54.
False
p. 504

A value pricer tries to offer a target market the same marketing mix as competitors but with a below-the-market price.

17-55.
False
p. 505

There are more pricing options in pure competition than in monopolistic competition.

17-56.
True
p. 505

Most firms operate in monopolistic competition instead of pure competition.

17-57.
True
p. 507

In both pure competition and oligopoly situations, the only sensible policy is meeting competition.

17-58.
True
p. 507

Meeting the competitive price often makes sense for a firm in an oligopoly situation, because setting a price above the market will usually result in a large loss of sales it might have gotten at the competitive price.

17-59.
False
p. 507

The unfair trade practices acts are intended to prevent middlemen from using "outrageously" high markups that would cheat consumers.

17-60.
True
p. 507

In states which have unfair trade practice acts, wholesalers and retailers are usually required to mark up merchandise a certain minimum percentage above cost.

17-61.
True
p. 508

Pricing a product sold in a foreign market lower than the cost of producing it is called dumping.

17-62.
False
p. 508

Pricing a product sold in a foreign market higher than in its domestic market is referred to as dumping.

17-63.
False
p. 508

Unfortunately, no laws prevent a retailer from using a phony list price--to make a consumer think that the price being charged offers a really big discount.

17-64.
False
p. 509

Price fixing is not illegal unless it hurts a competitor.

17-65.
True
p. 509

Price discrimination is illegal according to the provisions of the Robinson-Patman Act.

17-66.
False
p. 509

In the "Borden case," the U.S. Supreme Court ruled that a well-known label alone makes a product different from a physically similar product with an unknown label.

17-67.
False
p. 509

It is always illegal to sell the same products to different buyers at different prices, even if the price differences are based on cost differences.

17-68.
True
p. 509

"Meeting competition" in "good faith" is allowed as a defense in price discrimination situations.

17-69.
True
p. 509

The Robinson-Patman Act permits promotion allowances only if they are made available to all customers on "proportionately equal terms."

Multiple Choice Questions

17-70.
E
Def.
Easy
p. 485

Strategy planning for Price is concerned with:
A. to whom and when discounts and allowances will be given.
B. how transportation costs will be handled.
C. how flexible prices will be.
D. at what level prices will be set over the product life cycle.
E. All of the above.

17-71.
C
Def.
Easy
p. 485

Any business transaction in a modern economy involves:
A. an exchange at a list price.
B. "dumping."
C. an exchange of money--the money being the Price--for something of value.
D. a loss of consumer surplus.
E. an exchange in which price serves as a measure of quality.

17-72.
E
Def.
Easy
p. 485

Which of the following is not an example of price?
A. college tuition.
B. doctor's fee.
C. apartment rent.
D. interest on a loan.
E. all of the above are examples of price.

17-73.
A
Def.
Med.
p. 486

Which of the following is NOT a "Something of Value" which might be offered to CONSUMERS in the "price equation"?
A. Stocking allowance
B. Service
C. Repair facilities
D. Credit
E. Packaging

17-74.
B
Def.
Med.
p. 486

Which of the following is LEAST LIKELY to be in the "Something of Value" part of the "price equation" for CHANNEL MEMBERS?
A. Repair facilities
B. Rebates
C. Price-level guarantees
D. Promotion aimed at customers
E. Convenient packaging for handling

17-75.
D
Def.
Easy
p. 487

A marketing manager may choose a pricing objective that is:
A. sales oriented.
B. status-quo oriented.
C. profit oriented.
D. any of the above--depending on the situation.
E. None of the above.

17-76.
D
Comp.
Med.
p. 487

A pricing objective that seeks a specific level of profit is a:
A. profit maximization objective.
B. value objective.
C. sales-oriented objective.
D. target return objective.
E. status-quo objective.

17-77.
D
Def.
Easy
p. 487

Which of the following pricing objectives is a producer seeking when the producer tries to obtain some percent return on his investment?
A. Status quo
B. Meeting competition
C. Profit maximization
D. Target return
E. Growth in market share

17-78.
C
Def.
Easy
p. 487

Which of the following is a PROFIT-ORIENTED pricing objective?
A. Meeting competition
B. Sales growth
C. Target return
D. Nonprice competition
E. Growth in market share

17-79.
A
App.
Med.
p. 487

Fidelity Corp. earned a 6 percent return on investment last year and wants to increase it to 10 percent this year. Which of the following pricing objectives is Fidelity seeking?
A. Target return
B. Growth in sales
C. Growth in market share
D. Maximize profits
E. Nonprice competition

17-80.
D
Comp.
Med.
p. 487

Target return pricing objectives:
A. usually are very high for firms facing heavy competition.
B. aren't used by industry leaders because they can maximize profits.
C. would never make sense for a nonprofit organization.
D. may simplify the management of large producers with many divisions or departments.
E. All of the above.

17-81.
A
Def.
Hard
p. 487

Some top managers seek only enough profits to convince stockholders that they are "doing a good job." The pricing objective of such managers is:
A. satisfactory profits.
B. status quo.
C. nonprice competition.
D. profit maximization.
E. meeting competition.

17-82.
E
App.
Hard
p. 487

Caught between the threat of antitrust action, stockholder demands, and public interest groups, some large corporations set a(an) _____ pricing objective.
A. increasing target return
B. "aggressive" competition
C. profit maximization
D. increasing market share
E. satisfactory long-run target return

17-83.
A
App.
Med.
p. 488

Genetech Corp. has invested heavily to develop a patented new product. Genetech wants to achieve a rapid return on its investment. It probably should set a _____ pricing objective.
A. profit maximization.
B. target return.
C. sales-oriented.
D. status-quo.
E. None of the above.

17-84.
E
Comp.
Hard
p. 488

Seeking a profit maximization pricing objective:
A. will help a firm to earn "all the traffic will bear."
B. requires some knowledge of the firm's demand curve to be implemented effectively.
C. with no competitors and an inelastic demand curve is likely to lead to "high" prices in the short run.
D. may lead to a low penetration price.
E. All of the above are true.

17-**85.**
C
Comp.
Med.
p. 488

Profit maximization pricing objectives:
A. almost always lead to high prices.
B. are generally not in the public interest.
C. seek to get as much profit as possible.
D. may be stated as a desire to achieve rapid sales growth.
E. All of the above.

17-**86.**
B
Def.
Easy
p. 488

An "all the traffic will bear" pricing objective is a _____ objective.
A. target return
B. profit maximization
C. growth in market share
D. meeting competition
E. nonprice competition

17-**87.**
A
Def.
Easy
p. 488-89

Which of the following is a SALES-ORIENTED pricing objective?
A. Growth in market share
B. Target return
C. Nonprice competition
D. Satisfactory profits
E. Meeting competition

17-**88.**
B
App.
Easy
p. 488-89

Heritage Brick's marketing manager is setting her pricing policies to "increase market share to 8%." Her pricing objective seems to be:
A. status-quo oriented.
B. sales oriented.
C. profit oriented.
D. target return oriented.
E. None of the above.

17-**89.**
D
App.
Med.
p. 488-89

Australian Outback Products Co. has introduced a new product and set the price to help achieve "the 1% share we need to be in the game." This is an example of a:
A. status-quo objective.
B. profit-oriented objective.
C. target return objective.
D. sales-oriented objective.
E. profit maximization objective.

17-**90.**
E
Comp.
Hard
p. 489

Sales-oriented objectives stated in market share terms:
A. make some sense when a market is growing rapidly.
B. help focus attention on the competition.
C. are subject to the same limitations of other sales-oriented objectives.
D. are common in consumer packaged products firms.
E. All of the above are true.

17-**91.**
D
Comp.
Med.
p. 488-89

Sales-oriented pricing objectives:
A. may include market share targets as well as dollar or unit sales targets.
B. might be achieved and still result in losses.
C. are especially risky during times when a firm's costs are rising rapidly.
D. All of the above are true.
E. None of the above is true.

17-**92.**
B
Comp.
Med.
p. 489

The problem with sales-oriented pricing objectives is that:
A. many managers are evaluated by their level of sales.
B. larger sales don't necessarily lead to higher profits.
C. the number of units sold does not consider possible growth in the market.
D. sales growth usually leads to declining profits.
E. All of the above.

17-**93.**
B
App.
Easy
p. 489

A firm which is very concerned about increases in market share should adopt a
_____ pricing objective.
A. profit-oriented
B. sales-oriented
C. nonprice competition
D. status quo
E. target return

17-**94.**
B
App.
Med.
p. 489

Which of the following statements would be most likely to be made by a manager with a status-quo pricing objective?
A. "A price of $10.00 will penetrate the market."
B. "A price of $10.00 will not start a price war with our competitors."
C. "A price of $10.00 should maximize profits."
D. "A price of $10.00 will provide a 30% return on investment."
E. "A price of $10.00 should result in a 9% increase in sales."

17-**95.**
E
Def.
Easy
p. 489

Which of the following is a STATUS-QUO pricing objective?
A. Growth in sales
B. Maximize profits
C. Growth in market share
D. Satisfactory profits
E. Meeting competition

17-**96.**
A
App.
Med.
p. 490

Faced with many "me-too" competitors, Sonic Burgers, Inc. has set its price level to "meet competition"--while emphasizing nonprice competition. Sonic Burgers' pricing objective seems to be a _____ objective.
A. status quo
B. sales-oriented.
C. profit-oriented
D. satisfactory profits
E. maintaining market share

17-**97.**
E
Int.
Hard
p. 490

Regarding pricing objectives, a good marketing manager knows that:
A. sales-oriented objectives usually lead to high profits.
B. target return objectives usually lead to a large profit.
C. status quo pricing objectives can be part of an extremely aggressive marketing strategy.
D. profit maximization objectives don't always lead to high prices.
E. Both C and D.

17-**98.**
D
Def.
Med.
p. 490

Prices are "administered" when:
- A. they fall below "suggested list price."
- B. prices can change every time a customer asks for a price.
- C. government regulators set prices.
- D. firms consciously set their own prices.
- E. they are set by bargaining between buyers and sellers.

17-**99.**
D
Def.
Easy
p. 490

When individual firms set their own prices--sometimes holding them steady for long periods of time--rather than letting daily market forces determine prices, such prices are called:
- A. flexible prices.
- B. parallel prices.
- C. equilibrium prices.
- D. administered prices.
- E. fixed prices.

17-**100.**
A
Def.
Med.
p. 491

A one-price policy means:
- A. offering the same price to all customers who purchase products under essentially the same conditions and in the same quantities.
- B. never using temporary sales or rebates.
- C. selling to different customers at different prices.
- D. setting a price at the "right" level from the start and never changing it.
- E. None of the above.

17-**101.**
B
Def.
Easy
p. 491

Offering the same price to all customers who purchase products under essentially the same conditions and in the same quantities is a _____ policy.
- A. penetration pricing
- B. one-price
- C. value pricing
- D. flexible-price
- E. skimming pricing

17-**102.**
D
App.
Med.
p. 492

The marketing manager for Aerial Photography, Inc. says his sales reps have gotten in the habit of setting prices which do not produce a profit. Aerial Photography apparently is using:
- A. penetration pricing.
- B. introductory price dealing.
- C. administered pricing.
- D. flexible pricing.
- E. profit minimization pricing.

17-**103.**
A
App.
Easy
p. 491-92

A business products producer which has given its salespeople the right to adjust prices when necessary to get new business is using a _____ policy.
- A. flexible-price
- B. target-return pricing
- C. penetration pricing
- D. one-price
- E. skimming pricing

17-**104.**
E
Comp.
Med.
p. 491-92

Nationwide Equipment Co. produces industrial equipment that it sells through its national sales force. Its sales reps often must negotiate with customers to match the low prices of foreign competitors. Apparently, the firm has
A. an "F.O.B.-Seller's Factory" price policy.
B. been violating the Robinson-Patman act.
C. a skimming price policy.
D. a status quo pricing objective.
E. a flexible-price policy.

17-**105.**
E
App.
Med.
p. 492

A flexible-price policy is MOST LIKELY to be set by a retailer selling:
A. milk.
B. women's shoes.
C. golf balls.
D. T-shirts.
E. cars.

17-**106.**
A
App.
Med.
p. 493

Which pricing policy would probably be best for a profit-oriented producer introducing a really new product with a very inelastic demand curve?
A. Skimming pricing
B. Meeting competition pricing
C. Below-the-market pricing
D. Penetration pricing
E. Introductory price dealing

17-**107.**
C
Def.
Easy
p. 493

Trying to get the "cream" of a market (i.e., the top of a demand curve) at a high price before aiming at the more price-sensitive customers is consistent with a(an):
A. flexible-price policy.
B. sales-oriented pricing policy.
C. skimming pricing policy.
D. introductory price dealing policy.
E. penetration pricing policy.

17-**108.**
D
Comp.
Med.
p. 494

A "skimming pricing policy":
A. should be used if a firm expects strong competition very soon.
B. is most useful when demand is very elastic.
C. is typically used during the sales decline stage of the product life cycle.
D. usually involves a slow reduction in price over time.
E. means temporary price cuts to speed new products into a market.

17-**109.**
E
App.
Med.
p. 494

If a producer's marketing manager doesn't know the shape of the demand curve for a new product, the initial price level policy should probably be a _____ policy.
A. flexible-pricing
B. target-return pricing
C. introductory pricing
D. penetration price
E. skimming price

17-110.
D
Def.
Easy
p. 494

Trying to sell a firm's new product to a large market at one low price is known as:
- A. a skimming pricing policy.
- B. introductory price dealing.
- C. nonprice competition.
- D. a penetration pricing policy.
- E. a flexible-pricing policy.

17-111.
E
Comp.
Med.
p. 494

A "penetration pricing policy":
- A. is the same as a "meeting competition" price-level policy.
- B. is wise when demand is fairly inelastic--offering an "elite" market.
- C. involves temporary price cuts to speed new products into market.
- D. involves a series of step-by-step price reductions along an inelastic demand curve.
- E. may be wise if a firm expects strong competition very soon after its product introduction.

17-112.
D
App.
Med.
p. 494

Which pricing policy is probably "best" for a profit-oriented, low-cost producer who is introducing a new product into a market with elastic demand and is expecting strong competition very soon after product introduction?
- A. Skimming pricing
- B. Introductory price dealing
- C. Meeting competition pricing
- D. Penetration pricing
- E. Status-quo pricing

17-113.
D
Comp.
Easy
p. 495

Introductory price dealing:
- A. would not be used if other competitors already had competing products on the market at a price consumers found acceptable.
- B. is often viewed by competitors as a "stay out" price.
- C. usually sets off price wars.
- D. is different from penetration pricing.
- E. can apply only to final consumers, not channel members.

17-114.
D
App.
Med.
p. 495

Unilever is introducing a new brand of car window cleaner in market maturity. To speed its entry into the market--without encouraging price competition--Unilever should use:
- A. a flexible-price policy.
- B. a one-price policy.
- C. a penetration pricing policy.
- D. introductory price dealing.
- E. a skimming pricing policy.

17-115.
B
Def.
Easy
p. 495

Using temporary price cuts to speed a producer's new product into a market is known as:
- A. a skimming pricing policy.
- B. introductory price dealing.
- C. a flexible-price policy.
- D. a penetration pricing policy.
- E. a meeting competition pricing policy.

17-**116.**
E
Comp.
Med.
p. 493-95

When setting a price level policy, a good marketing manager knows that:
A. introductory price dealing usually does not increase sales.
B. a penetration price makes the most sense when there is a large "elite" market.
C. a "skimming" price may lead to low profits if demand is very elastic.
D. it's easy to raise prices if the initial price is too low.
E. none of the above is true.

17-**117.**
A
Def.
Easy
p. 497

Final customers or users are normally asked to pay _____ prices for products they buy.
A. basic list
B. phony list
C. discounted
D. wholesale list
E. unchanging list

17-**118.**
E
Def.
Easy
p. 497

_____ are reductions from list price that are given by a seller to a buyer who either gives up some marketing function or provides the function himself.
A. PMs
B. Phony prices
C. Spiffs
D. Markups
E. Discounts

17-**119.**
E
Comp.
Easy
p. 497

Quantity discounts are offered by sellers to:
A. reduce shipping or selling costs.
B. encourage customers to purchase larger quantities.
C. shift some of the storing function to buyers.
D. encourage buyers to make additional purchases.
E. All of the above.

17-**120.**
D
Comp.
Med.
p. 498

Offering a CUMULATIVE quantity discount seeks to:
A. reduce the seller's shipping costs.
B. eliminate some marketing function.
C. shift some of the storing function to the buyer.
D. encourage the buyer to make additional purchases.
E. All of the above.

17-**121.**
E
Comp.
Med.
p. 498

If a producer wants to stabilize demand over time by encouraging repeat business, it should probably use
A. uniform delivered pricing.
B. phony list prices.
C. a seasonal discount.
D. a cash discount.
E. a cumulative quantity discount.

17-**122.**
A
App.
Med.
p. 498

Firestone, Inc. offers its customers a 10 percent discount if they buy at least $200,000 worth of products during a year. The products may be bought in one order--or spread out over several orders. Firestone, Inc. is offering a:
   A. cumulative quantity discount.
   B. brokerage allowance.
   C. seasonal discount.
   D. noncumulative quantity discount.
   E. cash discount.

17-**123.**
A
App.
Med.
p. 498

Ceramics Distributing Co. wants to keep its inventory low. Which of the following would be LEAST likely to encourage customers to take over more responsibility for the storage function?
   A. offering a cumulative quantity discount
   B. offering a stocking allowance
   C. offering a noncumulative quantity discount
   D. offering a seasonal discount

17-**124.**
C
App.
Med.
p. 498

Ceramics Distributing Co. wants to keep its inventory low. Which of the following would be MOST likely to encourage customers to take over more responsibility for the storage function?
   A. setting a skimming price
   B. specifying invoice terms of 2/10, net 30
   C. offering a noncumulative quantity discount
   D. using zone pricing
   E. offering a cash discount

17-**125.**
E
Comp.
Med.
p. 498

Offering a NONCUMULATIVE quantity discount seeks to:
   A. reduce the seller's shipping costs.
   B. encourage bigger orders.
   C. discourage small orders.
   D. shift some of the storing function to the buyer.
   E. All of the above.

17-**126.**
E
App.
Easy
p. 498

Calumet Pottery Supply allows a 10 percent reduction off its list price of Jepson clay whenever a middleman orders more than 100 cases in one shipment. This is a:
   A. cash discount.
   B. seasonal discount.
   C. cumulative quantity discount.
   D. PM.
   E. noncumulative quantity discount.

17-**127.**
B
Def.
Easy
p. 498

A discount that is offered to encourage buyers to stock earlier than present demand requires is:
   A. a cash discount.
   B. a seasonal discount.
   C. a quantity discount.
   D. "push money."
   E. a trade discount.

17-**128.**
D
Math.
Med.
p. 499

The following terms appeared on an invoice dated May 20 which was sent by a manufacturer to a retail store: 2/10, net 30. The amount of the invoice was $2,000. Assuming the retailer paid the invoice on June 1 (10 days after the products were delivered), how much should he have paid?
 A. $1,900
 B. $1,800
 C. $2,000
 D. $1,960
 E. $2,040

17-**129.**
E
Math.
Hard
p. 499

The cash discount term "2/10, net 30" means that:
 A. the invoice is dated February 10 and must be paid by February 30.
 B. the buyer will, in effect, be borrowing at a 36 percent annual interest rate if he takes 30 days to pay the invoice.
 C. the buyer must make a 2 percent down payment--with the balance due in 10 to 30 days.
 D. a 2 percent discount off the face value of the invoice is permitted if the bill is paid within 10 days.
 E. Both B and D are true.

17-**130.**
D
Math.
Med.
p. 499

A firm has just received an invoice for $1,000 with the following terms: 3/10, net 30. In this case, the firm:
 A. should not worry about earning the cash discount because the amount is small.
 B. can take a 10 percent discount if it pays within 3 days, and otherwise the full amount is due in 30 days.
 C. can take a 3 percent discount if it pays the invoice on the 30th day.
 D. in effect, will be borrowing at an annual rate of 54 percent if it pays the invoice in 30 days.
 E. should pay $900 if it pays within 10 days.

17-**131.**
C
Math.
Hard
p. 499

Cash discount terms of 2/10, net 60 on an invoice would--in effect-- amount to borrowing at an annual interest rate of about _____ percent if the buyer did not pay the invoice for 60 days.
 A. 22
 B. 72
 C. 14
 D. 18
 E. 36

17-**132.**
E
Math.
Hard
p. 499

Cash discount terms of 2/10, net 30 on an invoice would--in effect-- amount to borrowing at an annual interest rate of about _____ percent if the buyer did not pay the invoice for 30 days.
 A. 10
 B. 30
 C. 18
 D. 12
 E. 36

17-**133.**
B
Math
Med.
p. 499

When a buyer receives an invoice for $100 with terms of "2/15 net 30" he can expect to pay:
   A. $100 if he pays anytime in the first 30 days.
   B. less than $100 if he pays during the first 15 days.
   C. $100 if he pays anytime during the first fifteen days.
   D. more than $100 if he pays from day fifteen through day thirty.
   E. the full $100 if he waits more than 30 days to pay.

17-**134.**
D
App.
Med.
p. 499

A wholesaler has been offering his customers payment terms of 3/10, net 60. He wants to tighten his terms because interest rates have gone up. He could change his terms to:
   A. 3/10, net 90.
   B. 3/20, net 60.
   C. 4/10, net 60.
   D. 3/10, net 30.
   E. None of the above would be in the intended direction.

17-**135.**
B
Def.
Med.
p. 499

A marketing manager might offer a cash discount to channel members to:
   A. increase sales during a slow period.
   B. encourage buyers to pay their bills quickly.
   C. reduce shipping or selling costs.
   D. encourage them to buy in larger quantities.
   E. All of the above.

17-**136.**
D
App.
Med.
p. 500

Sierra Leather Furniture gives its wholesalers discounts of 30 percent and 10 percent--expecting the wholesalers to pass the 30 percent discount on to their retail customers. These discounts off the manufacturer's suggested retail prices--to cover the costs of the jobs the middlemen will do--are _____ discounts.
   A. seasonal
   B. illegal
   C. cash
   D. trade (functional)
   E. quantity

17-**137.**
E
Def.
Easy
p. 500

Producers offer trade (functional) discounts to:
   A. encourage customers to buy out-of-season merchandise.
   B. encourage customers to pay their bills quickly.
   C. prevent retailers from becoming wholesalers.
   D. encourage quantity purchases by customers.
   E. cover the cost of work wholesalers or retailers are expected to do.

17-**138.**
D
Comp.
Med.
p. 500

Trade (functional) discounts
   A. are illegal unless they are offered to meet a competitor's price.
   B. are not offered by sellers who use administered prices.
   C. are a type of cash discount.
   D. reflect the fact that marketing activities can often be shifted and shared in the channel in different ways.
   E. are typically offered to consumers but not to middlemen.

17-**139.**
A
Comp.
Med.
p. 500-501

Everyday low pricing of consumer convenience products:
  A. tends to reduce fluctuations in prices customers actually pay.
  B. has been used by many retailers even though no producers have adopted this approach.
  C. makes it easy to quickly compete on price--without changing the basic strategy--when a competitor offers a particularly large discount for a short period of time.
  D. relies on frequent discounts and allowances from the producer.
  E. confuses customers and increases selling costs.

17-**140.**
D
App.
Easy
p. 501

A producer of plastic water bottles that can be attached to bikes gives retailers a 3 percent price reduction to advertise its products locally. This is an example of:
  A. value pricing.
  B. push money.
  C. everyday low pricing.
  D. an advertising allowance.
  E. a cash discount.

17-**141.**
D
App.
Easy
p. 501

A reduction from list price given to middlemen to get shelf space for a product is a:
  A. shelf allocation.
  B. brokerage allowance.
  C. trade allowance.
  D. slotting allowance.
  E. Push money allowance.

17-**142.**
D
App.
Easy
p. 501

A reduction from list price given to middlemen to get shelf space for a product is a:
  A. shelf allocation.
  B. brokerage allowance.
  C. trade allowance.
  D. stocking allowance.
  E. Push money allowance.

17-**143.**
C
Comp.
Med.
p. 501

A retailer might expect a stocking allowance:
  A. for paying the supplier's invoice before the product is delivered.
  B. to pass along to retail salesclerks who aggressively sell the product.
  C. to offset the handling costs for a new product.
  D. if the manufacturer can't fill an order by the promised delivery date.
  E. None of the above--stocking allowances only apply to wholesalers.

17-**144.**
A
App.
Med.
p. 501

"Push money" is most likely to be offered to:
  A. cosmetics salespeople at a department store.
  B. salesclerks at a grocery store.
  C. component materials sales reps.
  D. industrial supplies sales reps.
  E. Each of the above is equally likely to receive "push money."

17-**145.**
D
Def.
Easy
p. 501

Some manufacturers give _____ to retailers to pass on to the retailers' salesclerks to encourage aggressive selling of specific items or lines.
A. advertising allowances
B. cash discounts
C. slotting allowances
D. "push money"
E. trade discounts

17-**146.**
E
Comp.
Hard
p. 501

Careful handling of "trade-ins"--to avoid reducing the list price--is especially important for sellers of:
A. expense items.
B. raw materials.
C. emergency products.
D. component materials.
E. expensive accessory products.

17-**147.**
A
Int.
Med.
p. 503

Which of the following geographic pricing policies would probably handicap a producer wanting to compete with other producers who are closer to a potential buyer?
A. F.O.B. mill
B. F.O.B. delivered
C. Zone pricing
D. Freight absorption
E. All of the above.

17-**148.**
D
Comp.
Hard
p. 503

If a producer wants title to pass to a buyer immediately--but still wants to pay the freight bill--the invoice should read:
A. F.O.B. buyer's factory.
B. F.O.B. shipping point.
C. F.O.B. delivered.
D. F.O.B. seller's factory--freight prepaid.
E. F.O.B. mill.

17-**149.**
B
App.
Med.
p. 503

A seller's invoice reads: "Seller pays the cost of loading said merchandise onto a common carrier. At the point of loading, title to such products passes to the buyer, who assumes responsibility for damage in transit, except as covered by the transportation agency." This shipment has been shipped:
A. F.O.B. delivered.
B. F.O.B. shipping point.
C. F.O.B. mill, freight absorbed.
D. F.O.B. buyer's factory.
E. F.O.B. seller's factory--freight prepaid.

17-**150.**
E
Comp.
Easy
p. 503

"Zone pricing":
A. allows a uniform delivered price to be charged to all buyers in each zone.
B. simplifies the calculation of transportation charges.
C. means making an average freight charge to all buyers within some geographic area.
D. may make it possible to compete with sellers located closer to the buyer.
E. All of the above.

17-**151.**
A
App.
Med.
p. 503

A producer in Philadelphia uses "zone pricing." It's selling widgets for $150/ton in the Eastern Zone--which includes Richmond and Baltimore. The actual freight cost from its plant to Baltimore is $70/ton and from its plant to Richmond is $80/ton. In this situation:
  A. one ton of widgets costs a Baltimore buyer the same as an Richmond buyer.
  B. both buyers would pay $225 for one ton of widgets.
  C. one ton of widgets delivered to Richmond would cost the buyer $230.
  D. one ton of widgets delivered to Baltimore would cost the buyer $220.
  E. Both C and D.

17-**152.**
C
Comp.
Med.
p. 503

Uniform delivered pricing:
  A. usually results in higher delivered prices for everyone.
  B. results in all buyers paying less than the actual transportation costs.
  C. is most often used when transportation costs are relatively low.
  D. is just an extension of F.O.B. pricing.
  E. All of the above.

17-**153.**
D
App.
Med.
p. 503

A producer of electrical parts in Kansas City wants to expand into the West Coast market--where price competition is tough. It probably should use:
  A. F.O.B. mill pricing.
  B. uniform delivered pricing.
  C. zone pricing.
  D. freight absorption pricing.
  E. either A or B.

17-**154.**
D
App.
Hard
p. 503

Cherokee Cable Corporation, sells heavy wire cable to large construction companies around the country. Customers pay shipping from a central warehouse in Dallas. Recently, a new competitor in Atlanta has been taking away some of Cherokee Cable's Southern customers. If Cherokee Cable wants to compete in those distant markets, but not increase the cost of its product to other customers, it would probably switch to
  A. zone pricing.
  B. specifying "F.O.B. Dallas" in its contracts.
  C. uniform delivered pricing.
  D. freight absorption pricing.
  E. None of the above would help Cherokee Cable Corporation with its problem.

17-**155.**
A
Comp.
Med.
p. 503

Freight absorption pricing:
  A. amounts to cutting list price to appeal to new geographic markets.
  B. forces all buyers to pay higher shipping costs.
  C. tends to restrict firms from competing in distant markets.
  D. tends to decrease competition.
  E. Both B and C.

17-**156.**
C
Int.
Med.
p. 503

Regarding geographic pricing policies:
  A. uniform delivered pricing tends to decrease the size of a firm's market.
  B. F.O.B. pricing tends to increase the size of a firm's market.
  C. freight absorption pricing tends to increase the size of a firm's market.
  D. zone pricing encourages large orders.
  E. All of the above.

17-**157.**
D
Comp.
Med.
p. 504-505

Which of the following statements concerning "value pricing" is FALSE?
A. Value pricing tries to build customer loyalty.
B. Companies using value pricing guarantee what they offer.
C. Value pricing involves setting a fair price level for a marketing mix that meets customers' needs.
D. Value pricing means using "budget" or "cheap" prices.
E. The focus of value pricing is on the customer's requirements--and the whole strategy.

17-**158.**
B
Comp.
Med.
p. 505

A producer's price level decision is made by the market in:
A. a monopoly.
B. pure competition.
C. monopolistic competition.
D. All of the above.
E. None of the above.

17-**159.**
D
Comp.
Hard
p. 506

Regarding price-level policies:
A. meeting competition is the only sensible policy in monopolistic competition.
B. in an oligopoly situation, pricing "above the market" usually leads to an increase in profit.
C. a firm in pure competition may increase profit by pricing "below the market."
D. charging a lower price than seeming competitors may not mean that a firm is selling "below the market."
E. All of the above.

17-**160.**
A
Comp.
Med.
p. 507

In an oligopoly situation, a wise marketing manager will probably set the firm's price level:
A. at the competitive level.
B. on a negotiated basis--that is, customer by customer.
C. above competitors' prices.
D. at least 10 percent below the price leader's price.
E. below competitors' prices.

17-**161.**
D
Comp.
Hard
p. 507

Some critics charge that firms in oligopoly situations practice "conscious parallel action." These critics apparently think the firms:
A. seek too high a target return objective.
B. give quantity discounts which are "too large."
C. raise prices to match increases in other industries.
D. are "conspiring" to set prices.
E. administer prices.

17-**162.**
E
Def.
Easy
p. 507

"Unfair trade practice acts":
A. require different types of retailers to charge different retail prices.
B. make price fixing illegal.
C. eliminate price competition on manufacturers' brands.
D. prohibit middlemen from taking excessive markups.
E. put a lower limit on prices, especially at the wholesale and retail levels.

17-**163.**
E
Comp.
Med.
p. 508

"Unfair trade practice acts":
    A. prohibit very high markups at the retail level.
    B. allow manufacturers to set retail prices for branded products.
    C. prohibit price fixing among retailers.
    D. allow middlemen to sell below cost.
    E. protect certain limited-line retailers from "ruinous" price competition.

17-**164.**
C
Comp.
Med.
p. 508

Antidumping laws:
    A. protect consumers from the high prices charged by monopolistic foreign producers.
    B. set the maximum price a foreign producer can charge.
    C. are used in an effort to control the minimum price of imported products.
    D. make it illegal for a foreign producer to sell a product at a price level lower than domestic producers.
    E. force foreign producers to sell below cost if they want to compete with a nation's domestic producers.

17-**165.**
C
Def.
Easy
p. 508

Some customers encourage the use of _____ by paying more attention to supposed price discounts than to the actual prices (and values).
    A. unchanging list prices
    B. basic list prices
    C. phony list prices
    D. fair trade prices

17-**166.**
A
App.
Med.
p. 509

Recently, some executives for highway construction companies agreed to stop competing with each other on price and to meet every three months to decide their price for the next quarter. In this situation:
    A. the Sherman Act has been violated.
    B. the Robinson-Patman Act has been violated by price discrimination.
    C. the executives are exercising their right to free trade.
    D. the unfair trade practice acts have been violated.
    E. as long as prices don't increase--the executives have done nothing wrong.

17-**167.**
E
Def.
Easy
p. 509

"Price fixing" means:
    A. changing a price that was set at the wrong level by the financial manager.
    B. pricing a product that will be sold in a foreign market at a level below the cost of production.
    C. selling products of like grade and quality to different buyers at different prices.
    D. a firm consciously setting its prices.
    E. competitors getting together to raise, lower, or stabilize prices.

17-**168.**
B
Def.
Med.
p. 509

Which of the following laws specifically makes illegal any price discrimination which injures competition?
    A. Magnuson-Moss Act
    B. Robinson-Patman Act
    C. Wheeler-Lea Act
    D. FTC Act
    E. Sherman Act

17-**169.**
A
Def.
Med.
p. 509

Which of the following laws focuses specifically on price discrimination?
A. Robinson-Patman Act
B. Magnuson-Moss Act
C. Sherman Act
D. Wheeler-Lea Act
E. Federal Trade Commission Act

17-**170.**
D
Comp.
Med.
p. 509

A large producer who offers no discounts and the same prices to all customers in the U.S.:
A. does not have pricing objectives.
B. ignores the benefits of administered pricing.
C. probably ignores nonprice competition too.
D. may be "playing it safe" because of concern about the Robinson-Patman Act.
E. is probably violating the antidumping laws.

17-**171.**
E
Def.
Easy
p. 509

The Robinson-Patman Act says that to be legal, price differences must be based on:
A. a need to meet competition
B. a reasonable profit margin as determined by the FTC
C. freight costs
D. cost differences
E. Both A and D.

17-**172.**
D
Comp.
Hard
p. 509

The court decisions in the Borden case clearly show that:
A. products of "like grade and quality" must be offered to all buyers at the same price--even if sold under different labels.
B. manufacturers who supply retailers with dealer brands can not force the retailer to charge consumers the manufacturer's suggested list price.
C. price fixing is always illegal.
D. a manufacturer can charge different prices for different brands of physically identical products as long as the price differentials do not exceed the recognized consumer appeal of the higher-priced brands.
E. manufacturers cannot charge different prices for dealer brands and manufacturer brands.

17-**173.**
D
Comp.
Med.
p. 509

Price discrimination:
A. by firms selling to final consumers is illegal, but it is usually legal in selling to middlemen.
B. is not covered by Federal laws, but in some states it is illegal.
C. is always illegal.
D. may be legal if the firm can prove that different prices were set based on different costs.
E. None of the above is true.

17-**174.**
E
Int.
Easy
p. 509

A manufacturer could try to defend itself against charges of price discrimination under the Robinson-Patman Act by claiming that:
A. the products were not of "like grade and quality."
B. any price differences were to "meet competition in good faith."
C. the price differences did not injure competition.
D. the price differences were justified on the basis of cost differences.
E. All of the above are possible defenses against price discrimination charges.

17-175.
A
App.
Hard
p. 509

Jackson Motors, Inc. normally sells its electric motors to all buyers for $100. However, a competitor offered to sell similar motors to one of Jackson Motors' biggest customers for only $80 and Jackson Motors offered that customer--but not its other customers--a $80 selling price. According to the Robinson-Patman Act:

  A. Jackson Motors has not violated the law--it is just meeting competition.
  B. Jackson Motors is breaking the law--unless it offers to sell motors to all of its customers for $80.
  C. Jackson Motors cannot lower its $100 selling price.
  D. Jackson Motors cannot use the "meeting competition in good faith" defense unless it beats its competitor's $80 selling price.
  E. Jackson Motors AND its competitor are both guilty of price fixing.

17-176.
B
Comp.
Med.
p. 509

Advertising allowances offered by producers can be ILLEGAL unless they are made available:

  A. for products of "like grade and quality."
  B. to all customers on proportionately equal terms.
  C. to all buyers in equal dollar amounts.
  D. on all products sold by the producer.
  E. within an FTC approved agreement.

Chapter 18

Price Setting in the Business World

True-False Questions:

18-1.
True
p. 515

A markup is the dollar amount added to the cost of products to get the selling price.

18-2.
False
p. 515

According to the text, markup (percent) means percentage of cost unless otherwise stated.

18-3.
True
p. 515

If a retailer adds a 25-cent markup to a product which costs the retailer $1.00, then according to the text the retailer's markup is 20 percent.

18-4.
False
p. 515

If a retailer adds a 25-cent markup to a product which costs the retailer $1.00, then according to the text the retailer's markup is 25 percent.

18-5.
False
p. 515

Most retailers and wholesalers set prices by using a different markup percent for each different product carried.

18-6.
True
p. 516

A "markup chain" can be used to calculate the price structure in a whole channel.

18-7.
True
p. 516-17

A certain item has a production cost of $24. The manufacturer takes a 25 percent markup, the wholesaler takes a 20 percent markup, and the retailer takes a 50 percent markup. Therefore, the item has a retail selling price of $80.

18-8.
False
p. 517

Retailers who earn high profits generally use higher markups than retailers who have low profits.

18-9.
True
p. 517

Items with lower markups may be more profitable--if the stockturn is higher.

18-10.
True
p. 517

Firms with high markups and low turnover rates may earn lower profits than firms with low markups and high turnover rates.

18-11.
False
p. 517

The stockturn rate is the number of times the average inventory must turnover to make a profit in a given year.

18-12.
False
p. 518

Average-cost pricing consists of adding a 20 percent markup to the average cost of an item.

18-13.
False
p. 519

Average-cost pricing guarantees that the firm will earn enough to at least cover its costs.

18-14.
True
p. 519

A major problem with average-cost pricing is that it does not allow for cost variations at different levels of output.

18-15.
True
p. 520

Total fixed costs do not change when output increases.

18-16.
True
p. 520

At zero output, total variable cost is zero.

18-17.
True
p. 520

A firm's total cost increases only when its variable cost increases.

18-18.
True
p. 521-22

If a firm's average variable cost is constant per unit, then the firm's average cost decreases continually as output increases because average fixed cost decreases continually.

18-19.
False
p. 521-22

A firm's average fixed cost increases as its output increases.

18-20.
True
p. 521-22

Average fixed costs are lower when a large quantity is produced.

18-21.
True
p. 521-22

As output increases, a firm's average fixed cost probably will go down.

18-22.
False
p. 521-22

Even if a firm's average variable cost remains constant per unit, its average cost will increase as output increases.

18-23.
False
p. 522

If a manager sells more than was expected when average-cost pricing was used to set a price, the firm will lose money.

18-24.
False
p. 522

Average-cost pricing works well if the firm actually sells the quantity which was used in setting the price, but losses may result if actual sales are much higher than were expected--due to higher total variable costs.

18-25.
True
p. 522

When setting prices, the marketing manager should consider the firm's demand curve, or else the price may not even cover the firm's total cost.

18-26.
True
p. 522

Average-cost pricing works best in situations where demand conditions do not change a lot.

18-27.
True
p. 523

Experience curve pricing is a variation of average-cost pricing--but based on what average costs are expected to be in the future.

18-28.
True
p. 524

Target return pricing is a variation of average-cost pricing--and has the same basic weakness as other average-cost methods.

18-29.
True
p. 524

In target return pricing, the desired target return is added to total cost; otherwise, it's the same as average-cost pricing.

18-30.
False
p. 527

Break-even analysis is particularly accurate because it recognizes that the demand curve is downward sloping.

18-31.
False
p. 528

The marginal revenue curve and the demand curve are the same thing.

18-32.
True
p. 529-30

Even if a manager's estimate of a demand curve is not exact, there is usually a profitable range around the price that would maximize profit.

18-33.
True
p. 531

In oligopolies, a price leader usually emerges and sets a price for all to follow.

18-34.
False
p. 531

Price leaders usually emerge in pure competition--and they set a price for all to follow.

18-35.
True
p. 533

Value in use pricing considers what a customer will save by buying a product.

18-36.
False
p. 534

The price most consumers expect to pay for a product is called the leader price.

18-**37.**
True
p. 535

Leader pricing is typically used with well-known, widely used items which are not stocked heavily by consumers.

18-**38.**
False
p. 535

It makes sense for a manager to use leader pricing on a product only if consumers are unlikely to be aware of the normal price.

18-**39.**
True
p. 535

Leader pricing is normally used with products for which consumers do have a specific reference price.

18-**40.**
False
p. 535

The Federal Trade Commission encourages bait pricing because it reduces the prices that consumers pay for products.

18-**41.**
False
p. 536

"Psychological pricing" involves setting prices which end in certain numbers, while "odd-even pricing" is setting prices which have special appeal to target customers.

18-**42.**
False
p. 536

The major disadvantage of price lining is that it is complicated for both clerks and customers.

18-**43.**
True
p. 536

Price lining tends to result in faster turnover, fewer markdowns, quicker sales, and simplified buying.

18-**44.**
True
p. 537

"Demand-backward pricing" involves a producer estimating an acceptable final consumer price and working backward to determine what the producer can charge in the channel.

18-**45.**
True
p. 537

Demand estimates are required for demand-backward pricing to be successful.

18-**46.**
True
p. 537

Prestige pricing is most common for luxury products such as furs, jewelry, and perfume.

18-**47.**
False
p. 537

Prestige pricing involves setting a rather high price because the product has a normal down-sloping demand curve.

18-**48.**
True
p. 538

"Full-line pricing" is setting prices for a whole line of products.

18-**49.**
False
p. 538

With complementary product pricing, different price levels are set on different products because the products are targeted at different market segments.

18-50.
True
p. 539

Product-bundle pricing may encourage customers to spend more and buy products that they would not buy otherwise.

18-51.
True
p. 539

Bid pricing is offering a specific price for each possible job, rather than setting a price that applies to all potential customers.

18-52.
False
p. 540

With bid pricing, it is best for the bidder to use the same overhead and profit rates on all jobs since that will make it easy to estimate costs and eventually will increase profits.

Multiple Choice Questions

18-53.
C
Def.
Easy
p. 514

Most firms in the business world set their prices using:
A. federal price guidelines.
B. demand-oriented price setting.
C. cost-oriented price setting.
D. supply and demand analysis.
E. marginal analysis.

18-54.
B
Def.
Med.
p. 515

The text says "markups":
A. should always be stated as a percentage of cost.
B. are a percentage of selling price--unless otherwise stated.
C. are never stated as a percentage of cost.
D. should never be stated in dollar amounts.
E. All of the above except B.

18-55.
B
Def.
Easy
p. 515

The text says "markup" means percent of:
A. "mark-on."
B. selling price--unless otherwise stated.
C. fixed cost.
D. delivered cost--unless otherwise stated.
E. cost of sales.

18-56.
A
Math.
Med.
p. 515

A retailer pays a wholesaler $24.00 for an item and then sells it with a 25 percent markup. The retailer's selling price is:
A. $32.00.
B. $56.00.
C. $48.00.
D. $30.00.
E. None of the above.

18-57.
E
Math.
Med.
p. 515

An item costs a retailer $140. If a 30 percent markup is desired, what should the retail selling price be?
A. $191.00
B. $242.00
C. $182.00
D. $140.30
E. $200.00

18-58.
B
App.
Med.
p. 515

The Horizons Cycle Shop bought 3 motorcycles for $2,100, and sold each one for $1,000. The markup percent was:
A. 33 1/3.
B. 30.
C. 142.
D. 50.
E. There is not enough information to tell.

18-59.
C
App.
Hard
p. 515

Michael Soles--owner of Soles Shoe Store--recently discovered that shoe stores in his trading area have an average markup of 40 percent. Upon investigation, Michael found that his average markup is $15 on shoes that he sells for $45. This suggests that:
A. Michael has higher-than-average costs.
B. Michael is pricing his products higher than his competitors.
C. Michael is taking a smaller average markup than his competitors.
D. Michael has a relatively high stockturn rate.
E. Michael's markups in dollar amounts are about the same as his competitors.

18-60.
C
Comp.
Easy
p. 516

Different firms in the same line of business are likely to use the same markup percent:
A. because they all want to have the same selling price.
B. because this is a government requirement.
C. because they are likely to have similar operating expenses.
D. because this is what is acceptable to manufacturers.
E. only if they are in pure competition.

18-61.
D
Comp.
Med.
p. 516

The typical markup (percent) is the:
A. cost of an item divided by its selling price--times 100.
B. selling price minus the cost of the item, divided by the cost of the item--times 100.
C. selling price of an item, divided by its cost--times 100.
D. selling price minus the cost of the item, divided by the selling price--times 100.
E. selling price minus the cost of the item, divided by the average fixed cost--times 100.

18-62.
D
Comp.
Med.
p. 516

A markup chain:
A. only applies to consumer products, not to business products.
B. implies that a retailer must always apply a smaller markup than a wholesaler.
C. causes lower prices in longer channel systems.
D. determines the price structure in a channel of distribution.
E. None of the above is true.

18-63.
B
Math.
Hard
p. 517

Blue Ridge Weavers wants to set its selling price on an item so that the retail list price will be $50--taking into account the usual markups of 10 percent at wholesale and 30 percent at retail. At what price should Blue Ridge Weavers sell the item?
A. $32.50
B. $31.50
C. $35.00
D. $34.00
E. $38.00

18-**64.**
C
Math.
Hard
p. 517

High Meadow Mfg. Co. sold its product through wholesalers and retailers--allowing the wholesalers a markup of 25 percent and retailers a markup of 40 percent. If the retail selling price is $100 and the manufacturer's cost is $30, what markup in dollars did High Meadow receive on the sale of this product?
   A. $5.00
   B. $13.50
   C. $15.00
   D. $10.00
   E. $20.00

18-**65.**
B
Math.
Hard
p. 517

TopKnotch Mfg. Co. has a production cost of $280. It sells its product to a wholesaler for $400. The wholesaler then sells the item to retailers for $500 and the retailers sell the item for $1,000. Which of the following is true about this "markup chain?"
   A. The wholesaler's markup is 25 percent.
   B. The manufacturer is taking a markup of 30 percent.
   C. The retailers' markup is 100 percent.
   D. All of the above are true.
   E. None of the above is true.

18-**66.**
B
App.
Hard
p. 517

Wilson sells a basketball to a wholesaler for $16, and the wholesaler applies a 20 percent markup. A retailer then applies a 33.3 percent markup. The final selling price is:
   A. $24.53.
   B. $30.00.
   C. $25.59.
   D. $28.00.
   E. Cannot be determined from the information given.

18-**67.**
A
App.
Hard
p. 517

A producer makes an item for $32 and sells it with a 50 percent markup to a wholesaler. The wholesaler then applies a 20 percent markup. A retailer then uses a 60 percent markup. The final retail selling price is:
   A. $200.00.
   B. $73.60.
   C. $64.00.
   D. $80.00.
   E. Cannot be determined without stockturn information.

18-**68.**
E
Int.
Med.
p. 517

Regarding markups and turnover:
   A. supermarket operators have found that high-margin products are generally more profitable that low-margin products.
   B. higher markups do not always lead to higher profits.
   C. low stockturn rates increase costs by tying up working capital in inventory.
   D. to earn higher profits, all firms should lower their markups and seek faster turnover.
   E. Both B and C.

18-**69.**
A
Comp.
Med.
p. 517

Which of the following is a TRUE statement about markups?
A. A firm can lose money even when using a high markup.
B. Markup percents are computed as a percent of the cost of the product.
C. It's easier for a producer to administer the prices consumers pay for products if the markup used varies from one middleman to the next.
D. The lower the markup, the lower the profit.
E. None of the above is true.

18-**70.**
E
App.
Easy
p. 517

A middleman seeking high profits should:
A. use the lowest markup that will still cover selling expenses.
B. use experience curve pricing.
C. use high markups.
D. choose the markup which maximizes turnover.
E. try to find the markup level related to the most profitable price.

18-**71.**
C
Def.
Med.
p. 517

"Stockturn rate" means:
A. the number of days required to sell a given output of products.
B. the amount of time needed to sell every item in a retailer's inventory.
C. the number of times the average inventory is sold in a year.
D. the rate at which products enter and leave a middleman's establishment.
E. All of the above.

18-**72.**
A
Def.
Easy
p. 517

The number of times a middleman's average inventory is sold in a year is called the:
A. stockturn rate.
B. asset factor.
C. inventory ratio.
D. markup ratio.
E. ROI (return on inventory).

18-**73.**
D
Int.
Hard
p. 517

Regarding markups and turnover:
A. high markups usually lead to high profits.
B. speeding turnover usually decreases profits.
C. items sold at low markups (e.g., 20 percent) cannot be profitable.
D. depending on the industry--a stockturn rate of 1 or 2 may be quite profitable.
E. All of the above.

18-**74.**
E
Math.
Med.
p. 517

If a retailer's annual stockturn rate shifted to 20 from 5, then selling products costing $100,000 would require _____ rather than $20,000 in working capital to carry the needed inventory.
A. $10,000
B. $80,000
C. $8,000
D. $500
E. $5,000

18-**75.**
C
Comp.
Med.
p. 517

A high stockturn rate:
A. is only possible with a low markup percent.
B. is likely to result in low profits.
C. reduces the inventory investment and can improve profits.
D. increases the space needed for inventory.
E. None of the above is true.

18-**76.**
D
App.
Easy
p. 518

Retailers of which of the following products would probably have the highest stockturn rate?

A. furniture
B. women's clothing
C. hardware
D. fresh seafood
E. bowling balls

18-**77.**
E
App.
Med.
p. 518

Best Buy sets its prices below other electronics stores in its service area and generally attracts more customers than the others. Best Buy apparently hopes to earn a profit by

A. achieving status quo pricing objectives.
B. setting prices based on "value in use."
C. relying on a high margin percent.
D. being the price leader in an oligopoly market.
E. achieving a high stockturn rate.

18-**78.**
D
Def.
Easy
p. 518

Setting prices by adding a "reasonable" markup to a firm's average cost is called:

A. break-even pricing.
B. add-on pricing.
C. target-return pricing.
D. average-cost pricing.
E. marginal analysis.

18-**79.**
B
Comp.
Hard
p. 519

Average cost pricing

A. always results in a profit that is less than what was expected.
B. will work out as expected when the firm's actual average fixed cost per unit is what was estimated when prices were set.
C. sets the price at the point where average fixed cost is equal to average variable cost.
D. ignores variable costs.
E. is the only way to insure that the firm will set a profitable price.

18-**80.**
B
Comp.
Med.
p. 520

Total fixed cost:

A. is the sum of all expenses which are closely related to output.
B. is the sum of those costs which do not change in total no matter how much is produced.
C. may vary in the short run--but is more or less fixed in the long run.
D. is the sum of all costs of manufacturing and distributing a product.
E. would be zero if the quantity produced were zero.

18-**81.**
A
Def.
Med.
p. 520

The sum of those costs that do not change in total--no matter how much is produced--is called:

A. total fixed cost.
B. total cost.
C. total variable cost.
D. total direct cost.
E. both A and C.

18-82. Which of the following would NOT be included in a producer's total fixed cost?
E
A. Rent
App.
B. Property taxes
Med.
C. Insurance
p. 520
D. Depreciation
E. Component parts

18-83. The sum of those changing expenses which are closely related to output is called:
D
A. total fixed cost.
Def.
B. total cost.
Med.
C. total overhead cost.
p. 520
D. total variable cost.
E. Both C and D.

18-84. Total variable cost:
E
A. is zero when the quantity produced is zero.
Comp.
B. is the sum of those changing expenses that are closely related to output.
Med.
C. may decrease as the quantity produced is increased.
p. 520
D. All of the above are true.
E. Both A and B are true.

18-85. A sales rep is paid a commission on each product sold. The commission is:
B
A. part of the total fixed cost.
App.
B. part of the total variable cost.
Easy
C. not included in figuring average cost.
p. 520
D. part of the total cost, but not specifically a fixed cost or a variable cost.
E. None of the above is true.

18-86. Which of the following would NOT be included in a firm's total variable cost?
C
A. Outgoing freight
App.
B. Packaging materials
Easy
C. Depreciation on buildings
p. 520
D. Expenses for parts
E. Sales commissions

18-87. Total cost:
A
A. increases directly with increases in total variable cost.
Comp.
B. is zero at zero output.
Med.
C. is fixed in total no matter how much is produced.
p. 520
D. increases directly with increases in total fixed cost.
E. All of the above are true except A.

18-88. Average cost is obtained by dividing:
C
A. total fixed cost by the related quantity.
Def.
B. marginal cost by marginal revenue.
Easy
C. total cost by the related quantity.
p. 520
D. average fixed cost and average variable cost by the quantity produced.
E. total variable cost by the related quantity.

18-**89.**
D
App.
Easy
p. 520

A college "marketing club" printed 1,000 "We're Number 1" bumper stickers for sale at $3.00 each as a fund-raiser. Its fixed costs were $500, and the variable cost for each sticker was $.50. The club's average cost was:
  A. $2.00.
  B. $2.50.
  C. $ .50.
  D. $1.00.
  E. There is not enough information to tell.

18-**90.**
C
Comp.
Med.
p. 521

Average fixed costs:
  A. increase as the quantity produced increases.
  B. decline for a while as output increases and then begin to rise again.
  C. decrease steadily as output increases.
  D. are less than average variable costs at all output levels.
  E. Both C and D.

18-**91.**
E
Comp.
Hard
p. 521

When a firm's average variable cost is constant--no matter how much is produced--then the firm's:
  A. average cost will increase as the quantity produced increases.
  B. fixed cost must be zero.
  C. average cost will also be constant.
  D. average fixed cost will also be constant.
  E. average cost will decrease as the quantity produced increases.

18-**92.**
B
Comp.
Med.
p. 522

The big problem with average-cost pricing is that:
  A. fixed costs are hard to estimate.
  B. it ignores the firm's demand curve.
  C. it doesn't consider the effect of variable costs.
  D. there is no way to include a desired profit per unit.
  E. None of the above is true.

18-**93.**
B
Comp.
Hard
p. 522

"Average-cost pricing":
  A. will result in losses if actual sales are much higher than expected.
  B. might cause a firm to charge too high or too low a price--and reduce its profits.
  C. usually assumes the firm will sell a larger quantity than the year before.
  D. cannot be profitable--because it ignores demand.
  E. All of the above.

18-**94.**
E
Comp.
Med.
p. 522

The major weakness of "average-cost pricing" is that:
  A. it ignores likely customer demand at different prices.
  B. it usually leads to losses instead of profits.
  C. average fixed cost changes at different levels of output.
  D. it is too hard for most managers to use.
  E. Both A and C.

18-95.
D
Comp.
Hard
p. 522

Average cost pricing
A. will result in disappointing profits when the firm sells more than it expected to sell.
B. will never lead to a higher than expected profit.
C. takes the demand curve into account when calculating a price.
D. is most likely to result in the expected level of profit when demand is inelastic within the range of possible prices.
E. All of the above are true.

18-96.
D
Def.
Easy
p. 523

Average-cost pricing which uses an estimate of FUTURE average costs is called _____ pricing.
A. demand-backward
B. break-even
C. target return
D. experience curve
E. variable cost

18-97.
D
Comp.
Hard
p. 523

Experience curve pricing:
A. assumes that future costs will be about the same as past costs.
B. is less risky than average cost pricing--since it is based on past experience rather than forecasts of the future.
C. leads to prices that are "too high" if costs stay the same.
D. assumes that average costs will be lower in the future.
E. is most heavily used in the maturity stage of the product life cycle.

18-98.
D
Comp.
Med.
p. 523

Experience curve pricing:
A. usually leads to high prices.
B. assumes that average costs will neither increase nor decrease in the future.
C. works better than average-cost pricing because it is based on demand estimates.
D. usually assumes that average costs will be lower in the future.
E. Both B and C are true.

18-99.
A
Comp.
Hard
p. 523

Experience curve pricing
A. is based on predictions about future cost levels.
B. sets the price at the level where marginal cost is equal to marginal revenue.
C. avoids the major pitfall of average cost pricing.
D. is used when a firm wants to make high profits immediately.
E. All of the above are true.

18-100.
E
Comp.
Med.
p. 522-24

Which of the following pricing approaches specifically considers the concept of elasticity of demand?
A. experience curve pricing.
B. average-cost pricing.
C. markup pricing.
D. target return pricing.
E. None of the above.

18-**101.**
C
Def.
Easy
p. 524

"Target return pricing":
   A. is a type of demand-oriented pricing.
   B. is very different from average-cost pricing.
   C. seeks to earn a percentage return on investment or a specific total dollar return.
   D. guarantees that the target objective will be hit because the target return is included in the total cost.
   E. All of the above.

18-**102.**
E
Math.
Hard
p. 524

Vanguard Corp. uses target return pricing and is hoping to earn a 20 percent return on its investment of $1 million during the coming year. Vanguard sold 30,000 units last year and hopes the same quantity will be sold this year. If Vanguard has fixed costs of $250,000 and variable costs of $10 per unit, what price should the firm set to achieve its target return?
   A. $58.30
   B. $60.00
   C. $20.00
   D. $30.00
   E. $25.00

18-**103.**
A
Math.
Hard
p. 524

Komatsu Mfg. Co. uses target return pricing and expects to sell 40,000 units of its product in the coming year. Its fixed costs will be $500,000 and its variable costs will be about $20 per unit. If Komatsu seeks to earn a 20 percent return on its investment of $500,000, what price should it charge?
   A. $35.00
   B. $32.50
   C. $21.00
   D. $22.50
   E. $20.00

18-**104.**
A
Comp.
Med.
p. 524

When a firm uses "long-run target return" pricing:
   A. it assumes that in some years the target return won't be earned.
   B. prices tend to go up and down a lot.
   C. it assumes that its plant will always produce at or close to full capacity.
   D. much attention is paid to current demand when setting current prices.
   E. All of the above.

18-**105.**
D
Def.
Easy
p. 525

A firm's "break-even point" is that point where:
   A. maximum profit is earned.
   B. total variable cost just equals total revenue.
   C. the target return on investment is earned.
   D. total cost just equals total revenue.
   E. Both C and D are true.

18-**106.**
E
Comp.
Med.
p. 527

Break-even analysis usually:
   A. makes it appear that any quantity can be sold at the assumed price.
   B. suggests that profits will grow rapidly as sales volume increases beyond the break-even point.
   C. is quite accurate in maximizing profit.
   D. assumes a U-shaped average variable cost curve.
   E. Both A and B.

18-**107.**
E
Comp.
Med.
p. 525-27

Break-even charts usually assume that:
A. total cost and total revenue curves are straight lines.
B. average variable cost is constant per unit.
C. the break-even point is reached when total cost just equals total revenue.
D. any quantity can be sold at the assumed price.
E. All of the above.

18-**108.**
D
Comp.
Hard
p. 526

A typical break-even analysis assumes that:
A. the fixed-cost contribution per unit increases as units sold increases.
B. average fixed cost per unit is the same regardless of quantity sold.
C. demand curves are downward sloping.
D. average variable cost is the same regardless of quantity sold.
E. None of the above is true.

18-**109.**
D
App.
Med.
p. 525

Spruce Pine Mfg. Co. has total fixed costs of $300,000 a year. The owner estimates that average variable costs for its product will be about $30 next year. The selling price to wholesalers will be $50. The break-even point is:
A. 6,000 units.
B. 10,000 units.
C. 12,000 units.
D. 15,000 units.
E. None of the above is correct.

18-**110.**
A
Math.
Med.
p. 525

You are considering opening a fast-food store. Your fixed costs for the required land, building, parking lot paving, kitchen equipment, and neon sign will be $1,000,000. The variable cost will be $1.89 for servings which will sell for $2.89. How many servings must you sell to break even?
A. 1,000,000
B. 1,200,000
C. 2,890,000
D. 189,000
E. Cannot be determined from the data given.

18-**111.**
A
Math.
Hard
p. 526

Given the following data, compute the BEP in DOLLARS:
Selling price = $2.00
Variable cost = $1.00
Fixed cost = $150,000
A. $300,000
B. $400,000
C. $100,000
D. $200,000
E. $50,000

18-**112.**
B
Math.
Med.
p. 525

Given the following data, determine the break-even point in units:
Total fixed cost = $120,000
Variable cost per unit = $0.60
Selling price per unit = $1.10
  A. 100,000
  B. 240,000
  C. 200,000
  D. 218,182
  E.   50,000

18-**113.**
B
Math.
Med.
p. 525

Given the following data, compute the BEP in units:
Selling price = $2.00
Variable cost = $0.75
Fixed cost = $250,000
  A. 333,334
  B. 200,000
  C. 125,000
  D. 400,000
  E. Cannot be determined with this information.

18-**114.**
A
Comp.
Med.
p. 525

In a typical break-even analysis, a firm's fixed-cost contribution per unit:
  A. is the assumed selling price per unit minus the variable cost per unit.
  B. is the assumed selling price per unit minus the average fixed cost.
  C. usually decreases as the quantity produced increases.
  D. is total fixed cost divided by the quantity produced.
  E. usually increases as the quantity produced increases.

18-**115.**
B
Math.
Easy
p. 525

If a firm's total fixed cost is $400,000 and its fixed cost contribution per unit is $10, its break-even in units is:
  A. 30,000.
  B. 40,000
  C. 10,000.
  D. 20,000.
  E. Cannot be determined with this information.

18-**116.**
A
Comp.
Med.
p. 527

Break-even analysis can show:
  A. which prices will not be profitable.
  B. the most profitable price for a firm's product.
  C. how the firm's variable cost per unit will drop as output rises.
  D. the firm's most profitable output level.
  E. when a firm should cut its price to increase sales.

18-**117.**
D
Comp.
Hard
p. 525-27

Break-even analysis
  A. can be adapted to evaluate the quantity that needs to be sold to earn a target profit--by adding the target profit to fixed costs.
  B. may result in a "break-even" quantity that it would be impossible to sell at the assumed price.
  C. focuses on the contribution of each unit sold to the reduction of fixed costs.
  D. All of the above are true.
  E. None of the above is true.

18-**118.**
A
Comp.
Hard
p. 527

Break-even analysis
A. assumes that the demand curve is perfectly horizontal at the selling price.
B. reveals the price that will earn the highest profit.
C. cannot be used for comparing several different alternatives (for example, assuming different prices).
D. all of the above.
E. none of the above.

18-**119.**
C
Comp.
Med.
p. 527

Break-even analysis can be useful for:
A. estimating future sales.
B. setting the most profitable price.
C. comparing pricing alternatives.
D. relating assumed prices to demand estimates.
E. All of the above.

18-**120.**
D
Comp.
Med.
p. 527

A typical break-even analysis assumes that:
A. the total revenue curve is a straight line.
B. the demand curve faced by the firm is horizontal.
C. the average variable cost is the same at different levels of output.
D. All of the above.
E. None of the above.

18-**121.**
B
Comp.
Hard
p. 527

Regarding break-even analysis, a good marketing manager knows that:
A. a high fixed-cost contribution per unit will lead to high profits.
B. assuming a straight-line total revenue curve incorrectly suggests that any quantity can be sold at the assumed price.
C. break-even analysis is useless for comparing pricing alternatives.
D. the usual straight-line total cost curve applies only when economies of scale exist.
E. All of the above are true.

18-**122.**
C
Comp.
Med.
p. 527

Marginal analysis
A. assumes that the firm's total revenue curve is a straight line.
B. bases the analysis on the cost of the first few units sold.
C. explicitly considers demand when calculating price.
D. All of the above are correct.
E. None of the above is correct.

18-**123.**
E
Comp.
Easy
p. 527-28

Marginal analysis:
A. can be very useful if a firm's pricing objective is profit maximization.
B. focuses on the last unit which will be sold.
C. can be used to find the most profitable price and quantity.
D. can help find where marginal revenue and marginal cost are equal.
E. All of the above.

18-**124.**
B
Comp.
Hard
p. 527

A firm in monopolistic competition with a down-sloping demand curve:
- A. does not have to worry about price competition due to the nature of its demand curve.
- B. can use marginal analysis to help it maximize profits.
- C. will have to charge the "market price" which is set by the intersection of industry supply and demand.
- D. could use marginal analysis to compare alternatives--but this would not help in pricing because this method focuses on selling one more unit and therefore ignores total profitability.
- E. All of the above are true.

18-**125.**
C
Comp.
Hard
p. 528

A firm in monopolistic competition has "marginal revenue" which:
- A. is always greater than its marginal cost.
- B. is always shown above its related down-sloping demand curve when plotted on a graph.
- C. is the change in total revenue which results from the sale of one more unit of a product.
- D. is always positive (i.e., greater than zero).
- E. All of the above.

18-**126.**
B
App.
Hard
p. 528

If a demand curve were elastic within a price range, then:
- A. marginal revenue would be negative within this price range.
- B. lowering the price within this range would increase total revenue.
- C. the marginal revenue curve would be above the demand curve in this range.
- D. in this range, raising price would increase total revenue.
- E. All of the above.

18-**127.**
D
App.
Med.
p. 528

A marketing manager has just estimated that her firm's marginal revenue will become negative if a proposed price cut is made. This means that:
- A. demand must be very elastic.
- B. marginal cost must be negative already.
- C. the firm is in pure competition.
- D. more units may be sold--but total revenue will be less than it would be at the higher price.
- E. None of the above--a firm's marginal revenue can't be negative.

18-**128.**
A
Int.
Hard
p. 528-29

A typical break-even analysis assumes that:
- A. the marginal revenue from an additional unit sold is constant.
- B. the fixed-cost contribution per unit decreases as units sold increases.
- C. marginal cost from an additional unit sold is dropping.
- D. All of the above.
- E. None of the above.

18-**129.**
C
Comp.
Med.
p. 529

"Marginal cost" is:
- A. always less than average variable cost.
- B. more affected by fixed costs than by variable costs.
- C. the change in total cost that results from producing one more unit.
- D. All of the above.
- E. None of the above.

18-**130.** The change in a company's total cost from producing one more unit is called:
B
Def.   A. average total cost.
Easy   B. marginal cost.
p. 529   C. average fixed cost.
             D. variable cost.
             E. average variable cost.

18-**131.** Regarding a producer's cost structure:
E
Comp.   A. marginal cost begins to rise at a lower level of output than average cost.
Hard   B. total fixed costs increase continuously as more units are produced.
p. 529   C. average cost is the extra cost of producing one more unit.
             D. average costs usually drop for awhile and then start to rise when the economies of scale "run out."
             E. Both A and D are true.

18-**132.** To maximize its profit, a producer should set a price (and produce that related output) where:
A
Def.   A. marginal cost is just less than or equal to marginal revenue.
Med.   B. marginal cost is at its minimum.
p. 529   C. price is as high as possible.
             D. total revenue equals total cost.
             E. marginal revenue is zero.

18-**133.** The "rule for maximizing profit" is that a producer should set a price such that:
E
             A. the difference between marginal revenue and marginal cost is the greatest.
Def.   B. marginal revenue is at a maximum.
Med.   C. average cost is at a minimum.
p. 529   D. marginal profit is maximized.
             E. marginal cost is just less than or equal to marginal revenue.

18-**134.** A good marketing manager for a producer knows that the most profitable price and level of output:
A
Comp.   A. is where the positive difference between the total revenue and total cost curves is the greatest.
Hard   B. is where the difference between marginal revenue and marginal cost is the greatest.
p. 529   C. is where total revenue equals total cost.
             D. is where marginal revenue is maximized.
             E. Both A and C are true.

18-**135.** If a producer selects an output level and price where marginal revenue is equal to marginal cost:
D
Comp.   A. marginal profit will be at its maximum.
Hard   B. total revenue will be at a maximum.
p. 529   C. profits will continue to grow beyond this break-even point.
             D. profit will be maximized.
             E. any increase in price will cause marginal revenue to go negative.

18-**136**.
B
Comp.
Med.
p. 529

Compared with the typical break-even analysis, marginal analysis recognizes that:
A. marginal revenue is always the same as quantity produced increases.
B. there usually are two break-even points.
C. variable costs per unit are always the same as output increases.
D. All of the above are true.
E. None of the above is true.

18-**137**.
B
Comp.
Med.
p. 530

If a profit-oriented marketing manager doesn't know the exact shape of the firm's demand curve, marginal analysis:
A. is useless.
B. may be useful anyway--because a profitable region usually surrounds the best price.
C. will suggest the same price as break-even analysis.
D. suggests that the only sensible approach is to follow the price leader.
E. None of the above is true.

18-**138**.
A
Comp.
Med.
p. 529

Marginal analysis
A. reveals the range of prices that should be profitable.
B. can be used to set prices, but it does not give you any idea what quantity might be sold at that price.
C. is not applicable to oligopoly situations.
D. All of the above are true.
E. None of the above is true.

18-**139**.
E
Comp.
Hard
p. 529

Using traditional demand and supply analysis, a producer finds that it has two break-even points--rather than just one. This means that:
A. something is wrong--there never is more than one break-even point.
B. seeking a maximum profit point is hopeless.
C. the producer's demand curve must be horizontal.
D. the producer doesn't have any economies of scale.
E. there is a profitable operating range around the price that maximizes profit.

18-**140**.
B
Comp.
Med.
p. 530

A profit-oriented producer probably should stop operations temporarily--or go out of business--when:
A. marginal costs start to increase.
B. marginal or variable costs cannot be covered.
C. the producer doesn't cover all its fixed costs in the short run.
D. marginal revenue starts to decrease.
E. total revenue falls below total costs.

18-**141**.
C
App.
Hard
p. 530

A profit-oriented marketing manager in pure competition should produce that quantity which is indicated by the intersection of his flat demand curve and his:
A. average variable cost curve.
B. total cost curve.
C. marginal cost curve.
D. average cost curve.
E. None of the above.

18-**142.**
D
App.
Easy
p. 530

A profit-maximizing oligopolist should set a price by using:
A. target return pricing.
B. average-cost pricing.
C. leader pricing.
D. marginal analysis.
E. cost-oriented pricing.

18-**143.**
A
Comp.
Med.
p. 530

A profit-maximizing oligopolist knows that his marginal cost curve usually intersects a:
A. marginal revenue curve that drops vertically at some price.
B. horizontal marginal revenue curve.
C. smoothly down-sloping marginal revenue curve.
D. negative marginal revenue curve.
E. S-shaped marginal revenue curve.

18-**144.**
D
Comp.
Easy
p. 531

A "price leader" in an oligopoly should know that:
A. all firms in this product-market probably will have the same costs.
B. "conscious parallel action" is illegal.
C. competitors are sure to raise their prices if he raises his price.
D. "followers" may try secret price cutting (to expand sales) if they are not able to make a reasonable profit.
E. All of the above.

18-**145.**
B
Comp.
Med.
p. 531

In oligopoly situations,
A. one firm usually acts as the price leader--and orders the other firms to set the same price.
B. "conscious parallel action" in price setting is criticized, but it is legal as long as there is no conspiracy.
C. each firm usually charges a different price.
D. it is legal for competitors to get together and agree what each firm will charge.
E. None of the above is correct.

18-**146.**
D
Comp.
Med.
p. 535

Which of the following statements concerning "reference prices" is FALSE?
A. A reference price is the price consumers expects to pay for an item.
B. Marketing research can be used to identify groups with different reference prices.
C. Different customers may have different reference prices for the same type of purchase.
D. Leader pricing is normally used with products for which consumers do not have a specific reference price.
E. None of the above is false.

18-**147.**
B
App.
Easy
p. 535

A retailer of men's suits who is advertising a popular brand of dress shirts at a reduced price to attract customers is using:
A. price lining.
B. leader pricing.
C. odd-even pricing.
D. bait pricing.
E. prestige pricing.

18-**148.**
A
App.
Easy
p. 535

A CVS drugstore that is trying to attract customers by advertising a special bargain price on a popular brand of cold remedy during the cold season is using:
A. leader pricing.
B. bait pricing.
C. prestige pricing.
D. odd-even pricing.
E. price lining.

18-**149.**
E
App.
Med.
p. 535

Eckerd Drugs advertises that its Tylenol prices are "the lowest in town" in order to stimulate sales of other products along with Tylenol. This is an example of:
A. skimming.
B. value in use pricing.
C. bait pricing.
D. price lining.
E. leader pricing.

18-**150.**
C
Comp.
Med.
p. 535

Leader pricing:
A. seeks a big profit on the leader items.
B. is usually used for a retailer's major product line--to give it a competitive advantage.
C. is different from bait pricing in that the marketing manager really expects to sell leader priced items.
D. assumes that some part of the demand curve is upward sloping to the right.
E. is banned in interstate commerce.

18-**151.**
A
App.
Easy
p. 535

A computer store regularly advertises a very low price for a well-known brand of disks. When the customers come in, however, the salespeople point out the disadvantages of this particular brand and try to persuade them to buy other disks at much higher prices. This retailer is using:
A. bait pricing.
B. odd-even pricing.
C. psychological pricing.
D. leader pricing.
E. price lining.

18-**152.**
E
Def.
Easy
p. 535

A retailer who advertises a low price on an item--with no intent to sell that item--but only to attract customers to try to sell more expensive products is using:
A. full-line pricing.
B. leader pricing.
C. odd-even pricing.
D. psychological pricing.
E. bait pricing.

18-**153.**
E
App.
Easy
p. 535

A tire retailer is advertising a very low price on a popular size tire. When a customer comes into the store, the clerk says the low-priced item is sold out, and tries to convince the customer to buy the top-of-the-line model--claiming the low priced model is not a very good buy even at the low price. This is an example of:
A. leader pricing.
B. full-line pricing.
C. value in use pricing.
D. price lining.
E. bait pricing.

18-**154.**
C
Int.
Hard
p. 536

Regarding pricing:
A. the use of prestige and psychological pricing shows that most retailers do not consider demand when setting prices.
B. bait pricing tries to attract customers on the high end of a demand curve.
C. the FTC considers bait pricing a deceptive act and has banned its use in interstate commerce.
D. leader-priced items are priced very low to get customers into the store--not to sell these items.
E. All of the above are true.

18-**155.**
D
App.
Med.
p. 536

Danielle Paxton believes that customers in her dress shop find certain prices very appealing. Between these price levels, all prices are seen as roughly the same--and price cuts in these ranges generally do not increase the quantity sold (i.e., the demand curve tends to drop vertically within these price ranges). Therefore, Danielle prices her items as close as possible to the top of each such price range. This is:
A. bait pricing.
B. prestige pricing.
C. leader pricing.
D. psychological pricing.
E. odd-even pricing.

18-**156.**
E
App.
Easy
p. 536

Some retailers feel that their potential customers find certain prices appealing, but between these prices the customers see prices as roughly the same--and thus price cuts within these ranges will not increase the quantity sold (i.e., the demand curve is vertical within these "same price" ranges). These retailers probably use _____ if they want to maximize profit.
A. average-cost pricing
B. bait pricing
C. leader pricing
D. prestige pricing
E. psychological pricing

18-**157.**
A
Def.
Med.
p. 536

Some retailers use certain prices more often than other prices. They seem to assume that their customers will buy less for a while as prices are lowered--and then more when some "magic" price is approached. This is:
A. odd-even pricing.
B. demand-backward pricing.
C. leader pricing.
D. prestige pricing.
E. psychological pricing.

18-**158.**
D
App.
Hard
p. 536

Which of the following prices is most likely to be seen if a firm is using odd-even pricing?
A. $9.00
B. $2.03
C. $6.60
D. $99.95
E. $100.00

18-**159.**
C
App.
Med.
p. 536

Alex's Knot Shop prices its ties at $5 intervals from $10 to $25 because most customers find these prices appealing and easier to compare. This is:
A. prestige pricing.
B. penetration pricing.
C. price lining.
D. odd-even pricing.
E. value in use pricing.

18-**160.**
B
Def.
Easy
p. 536

Setting a few price levels for a product line and then marking all items at these price levels is:
A. leader pricing.
B. price lining.
C. product-bundle pricing.
D. penetration pricing.
E. odd-even pricing.

18-**161.**
B
Comp.
Med.
p. 536

Price lining:
A. is quite similar to prestige pricing.
B. can simplify both buying and selling.
C. tends to reduce turnover rates.
D. results in larger inventories.
E. All of the above.

18-**162.**
A
Def.
Easy
p. 537

"Demand-backward" pricing:
A. starts with an acceptable final consumer price and works backward to what producers can charge.
B. ignores demand estimates.
C. is only sensible when the channel captain is a large retailer.
D. is an average-cost pricing approach.
E. All of the above.

18-**163.**
A
App.
Med.
p. 537

Good Health Co. has set a suggested retail list price of $40 on its new vitamin tablets on the assumption that its target market will find the product attractive at this price. From this suggested retail list price, Good Health has subtracted its usual chain of markups for wholesalers and retailers to obtain its own selling price of $17. This is:
A. demand-backward pricing.
B. full-line pricing.
C. average-cost pricing.
D. odd-even pricing.
E. prestige pricing.

18-**164.**
E
Def.
Easy
p. 537

Setting relatively high prices to suggest high-quality or high-status is:
A. odd-even pricing.
B. price lining.
C. leader pricing.
D. psychological pricing.
E. prestige pricing.

18-**165.**
D
Comp.
Med.
p. 537

The idea that people will pay extra for "quality" and status is the idea behind
A. price lining.
B. average cost approaches to pricing.
C. penetration skimming.
D. prestige pricing.
E. psychological pricing.

18-**166.**
B
Comp.
Med.
p. 537

Which of the following pricing approaches should be used by a profit-oriented retailer if its demand curve is down-sloping to the right for awhile--but then actually bends back to the left at lower prices?
A. Psychological pricing
B. Prestige pricing
C. Average-cost pricing
D. Bait pricing
E. Penetration pricing

18-**167.**
E
Comp.
Med.
p. 538

Regarding "full-line pricing," which of the following statements is TRUE?
A. A good marketing manager usually tries to price products in a line so that the prices will seem logically related and make sense to target customers.
B. The marketing manager should try to cover all costs on the whole product line.
C. Most customers seem to feel that prices in a product line should be somewhat related to cost.
D. Not all companies that make a line of products must use full-line pricing.
E. All of the above are true.

18-**168.**
A
App.
Med.
p. 538-39

When Nintendo sets a relatively low price on its game units to stimulate more demand for its game cartridges, it is using
A. complementary product pricing.
B. product-bundle pricing.
C. price lining.
D. bait pricing.
E. cost plus pricing.

18-**169.**
C
App.
Med.
p. 539

When Eckerd Drugstores advertises one price for the cost of a roll of film and the cost of processing it, they are using
A. complementary product pricing.
B. flexible pricing.
C. product-bundle pricing.
D. a one-price policy.
E. bait pricing.

18-**170.**
E
Def.
Easy
p. 539

If a service firm sets a specific price for each possible job--rather than setting a price which applies for all potential customers--it is most likely using:

A. product-bundle pricing.
B. a one-price policy.
C. price lining.
D. average-cost pricing.
E. bid pricing.

18-**171.**
D
Comp.
Hard
p. 539

Regarding bid pricing:

A. the same overhead changes and profit rates should apply to all bids--to avoid legal problems.
B. most firms should try to bid for as many jobs as possible--to spread risk.
C. all business buyers are legally required to accept the lowest bid--if they ask for bids.
D. the big problem for sellers is assembling all the costs--including the variable and fixed costs--that apply to a particular job.
E. All of the above are true.

18-**172.**
B
Comp.
Med.
p. 540-41

Which of the following statements concerning "negotiated price" is FALSE?

A. The negotiated price is set by bargaining between the buyer and the seller.
B. Negotiated pricing is not a demand-oriented approach.
C. Bargaining may involve the whole marketing mix, not just the price level.
D. Sellers must know their costs to negotiate effectively.
E. None of the above is false.

Chapter 19

Implementing and Controlling Marketing Plans: Evolution and Revolution

True-False Questions:

19-1.
True
p. 547,559

Traditional accounting reports are usually too general to be much help to the marketing manager in controlling marketing plans.

19-2.
True
p. 549

Electronic communication and e-commerce has speeded up the information needed for better control.

19-3.
True
p. 549

The development of inexpensive computer systems has helped small and large companies control their marketing strategies.

19-4.
False
p. 551

The ideal of doing things better, faster, and at lower cost is easy to implement once it is accepted.

19-5.
False
p. 551

Implementing a strategy is straightforward; there are usually only a limited number of ways things can go wrong.

19-6.
False
p. 552

The total quality management approach recognizes that defects are an inevitable part of mass production, and that the cost of replacing defective goods is just a cost of doing business.

19-7.
True
p. 553

The Japanese success showed that one of the biggest costs of poor quality is lost customers.

19-8.
False
p. 553

The cost of replacing defective parts is the biggest cost of poor quality.

19-9.
False
p. 553

Total quality management applies when the firm's product is a physical good, but not if it is a service.

19-**10.**
False
p. 556

The two keys to improving how people implement quality service are: (1) training and (2) more inspectors.

19-**11.**
True
p. 556

Empowerment means giving employees the authority to correct a problem on their own.

19-**12.**
True
p. 556

A marketing manager must use effective communication to manage customer expectations--or customers will be dissatisfied because they expect more than the firm can offer.

19-**13.**
False
p. 557

In a service operation, customer satisfaction usually increases when routine services and services that require special attention are grouped together--so all customers are treated equally.

19-**14.**
True
p. 557

Services that require special attention can often be made "routine" with training.

19-**15.**
True
p. 558

A company may decide to benchmark its sales reps against the sales reps of a competitor or against the sales reps of a firm in a completely different industry.

19-**16.**
True
p. 558

A company picking a basis of comparison for evaluating how well its sales reps are performing is an example of benchmarking.

19-**17.**
True
p. 558-59

The money spent to improve quality should not only satisfy customers but also justify the cost through improved profit.

19-**18.**
False
p. 559

A manager shouldn't worry about making a financial return from money spent on a quality program as long as customers recognize that the quality is high.

19-**19.**
True
p. 559

According to the "80/20 rule," it is common to find that about 80 percent of a firm's business comes from only about 20 percent of its customers.

19-**20.**
False
p. 560

The best way to do a sales analysis is to first break down sales by customer type, and then geographic region.

19-**21.**
False
p. 560-61

Because too much sales data can drown a manager, it's best to start by asking only for breakdowns that involve customer type.

19-**22.**
True
p. 561

Advances in computer software have accelerated the move to cost analysis and performance analysis.

19-23.
True
p. 561

Statistical packages that produce graphs can make it easier to see patterns that are hidden in a table of numbers.

19-24.
True
p. 561

Performance analysis looks for exceptions or variations from planned performance.

19-25.
False
p. 561

As with sales analysis, performance analysis is limited to sales data.

19-26.
True
p. 563

Marketing managers use performance indexes to compare what did happen with what ought to have happened.

19-27.
True
p. 563

The main advantage of performance indexes is that they make it easier to compare numbers in a performance analysis.

19-28.
False
p. 566

The "iceberg principle" says that looking at detailed breakdowns of data is not very useful, since most relevant information is revealed in good summaries.

19-29.
False
p. 567

Cost analysis and performance analysis are the same thing.

19-30.
False
p. 568

Experience shows that it doesn't make sense for marketing managers to allocate costs to specific market segments or products.

19-31.
True
p. 568

In general, the more products a company has the more difficult it will be to allocate costs.

19-32.
True
p. 568

With the full-cost approach to marketing cost analysis, all costs are allocated to products, customers, or other categories.

19-33.
False
p. 568

With the contribution-margin approach to marketing cost analysis, all costs are allocated to products, customers, or other categories.

19-34.
True
p. 568

The contribution-margin approach to marketing cost analysis focuses attention on variable costs rather than total costs.

19-35.
False
p. 569

The contribution-margin and the full-cost approaches to marketing cost analysis are different, but they should lead to the same action implications.

19-**36.**
True
p. 570

The full-cost approach to marketing cost analysis is likely to lead to arguments among product managers about how costs are to be allocated.

19-**37.**
False
p. 570

When it comes to marketing cost analysis, a sales rep is likely to favor the full-cost approach over the contribution-margin approach.

19-**38.**
False
p. 572

A marketing audit is a systematic procedure for allocating the full costs of marketing to the appropriate functional accounts.

19-**39.**
True
p. 572

A marketing audit is a systematic, critical, and unbiased review and appraisal of the basic objectives and policies of the marketing function.

19-**40.**
False
p. 572

Marketing audits consider future marketing plans, so they are not concerned with a company's current marketing strategies.

19-**41.**
False
p. 572

In a marketing audit, the auditor evaluates the plans being implemented, but not the quality of the effort.

19-**42.**
True
p. 573

A marketing audit evaluates the whole marketing program as well as individual plans.

Multiple Choice Questions

19-**43.**
D
Def.
Easy
p. 546

Control helps marketing managers learn how:
- A. to plan for the future.
- B. implementation is working.
- C. ongoing plans are working.
- D. All of the above.
- E. None of the above.

19-**44.**
B
Comp.
Med.
p. 547-49

With respect to marketing control,
- A. all cost records should be kept in the marketing department.
- B. faster feedback can often be the basis for a competitive advantage.
- C. many advances have been made, but there is still no effective way for a manager to be sure that a product is actually selling to the intended target market rather than some other group.
- D. All of the above are true.
- E. None of the above are true.

19-45.
C
Comp.
Med.
p. 548-49

To improve the effectiveness of the marketing control process, the marketing manager should:

A. realize that most errors are made because managers react to detailed information too quickly--instead of waiting to see what patterns show up in summary reports.
B. be the supervisor for the data-processing manager.
C. have all relevant data collected in an accessible and speedy manner.
D. be certain that all cost records are kept in a central location controlled by the marketing department.
E. All of the above.

19-46.
E
App.
Easy
p. 553

A marketing manager might use the total quality management approach to:

A. reduce defects in goods produced in factories.
B. train better salespeople.
C. improve customer service.
D. make delivery schedules more reliable.
E. all of the above.

19-47.
D
Def.
Easy
p. 555

After a problem has been identified, a fishbone diagram helps managers solve the problem by:

A. identifying how customer satisfaction can be improved.
B. creating a visual aid of why things go wrong.
C. organizing cause-and-effect relationships.
D. all of the above.
E. none of the above.

19-48.
E
Comp.
Med.
p. 556

Building quality into services:

A. is made easier by grouping services that require special attention with those that are routine.
B. can be accomplished by lowering customer expectations.
C. is not necessary unless the service is guaranteed.
D. can be easily accomplished with surprise quality inspections.
E. can be improved by giving employees the authority to correct a problem on their own.

19-49.
E
Def.
Med.
p. 558

It might be sensible for a company to benchmark each of its sales reps against:

A. another firm's sales reps who earn high customer satisfaction scores.
B. its other sales reps.
C. a competitor's sales reps.
D. sales reps of a firm in a different industry.
E. any of the above.

19-50.
D
Int.
Med.
p. 559

Regarding controlling marketing programs:

A. "sales analysis" and "performance analysis" mean the same thing.
B. traditional accounting reports are very useful for controlling marketing programs.
C. sales analysis is so revealing that there is no such thing as having TOO MUCH data.
D. the control process helps marketing managers learn how ongoing plans are working.
E. All of the above are true.

19-**51.**
C
Comp.
Easy
p. 559

The 80/20 rule suggests that
A. 20 percent of marketing effort is wasted.
B. 80 percent of marketing effort is well implemented, but the remaining 20 percent is out of control.
C. 80 percent of the business comes from 20 percent of the customers.
D. it will take 80 percent more effort to get 20 percent more business.
E. None of the above is true.

19-**52.**
D
Comp.
Easy
p. 559

The "80/20 rule" says that:
A. only 20 out of every 100 firms use formal accounting controls.
B. a firm should hire 20 sales reps for every 80 customers.
C. marketing accounts for 80 percent of a typical consumer's dollar.
D. even though a firm is showing a profit, 80 percent of its business might be coming from only 20 percent of its customers.
E. usually about 20 percent of a firm's customers are unprofitable.

19-**53.**
B
App.
Med.
p. 559

Which of the following statements illustrates the 80/20 rule?
A. "80 percent of our target market doesn't respond to our marketing mix, and we only have a 20 percent market share."
B. "Of the hundred retailers who carry our products, the top twenty account for nearly 80 percent of our total business."
C. "20 percent of our marketing effort is wasted, but we don't know which 20 percent."
D. "We don't know whether our profits are 20 percent higher than we deserve, or only 80 percent of what might be easily obtained."
E. None of the above.

19-**54.**
A
Comp.
Med.
p. 560

When involved in the control process, the marketing manager should view company profit
A. as a gross index of performance that should be further broken down into smaller components.
B. as a guide to future operations.
C. as the test of whether or not the marketing mix is successful.
D. All of the above are true.
E. None of the above is true.

19-**55.**
E
Comp.
Med.
p. 560

Detailed sales analysis is:
A. not worth the cost unless the firm is very unprofitable.
B. based on the information available on traditional accounting reports.
C. important for producers, but usually not that valuable for retailers.
D. most useful when it analyzes costs from different possible target markets.
E. None of the above is true.

19-**56.**
B
Comp.
Med.
p. 560

Marketing sales analysis:
A. keeps track of whether a firm's sales are increasing or decreasing.
B. requires a detailed breakdown of a company's sales records.
C. is very hard to do--because computers must be involved.
D. looks for exceptions or variations from planned performance.
E. tries to avoid the 80/20 rule.

19-**57.**
E
Def.
Med.
p. 560

Sales analysis is a:
A. well-accepted trend analysis method.
B. necessity for making all important marketing decisions.
C. way of assuring that future sales will be profitable.
D. detailed report of likely profitability.
E. detailed breakdown of a company's sales records.

19-**58.**
D
Comp.
Easy
p. 560

Sales analysis:
A. requires more information than is available from traditional accounting reports.
B. can be done in different ways--there is no single "best way."
C. often studies how sales patterns change over time.
D. All of the above are true.
E. None of the above is true.

19-**59.**
D
Comp.
Med.
p. 560-61

Sales analysis:
A. typically involves reorganizing existing information rather than gathering new information.
B. may involve analyzing many different breakdowns of overall sales.
C. is usually a good first step when setting up a control system.
D. All of the above are true.
E. None of the above is true.

19-**60.**
E
App.
Easy
p. 560-61

The best way to break down and analyze sales data is:
A. by order size.
B. by geographic region.
C. by customer type.
D. by product, package, size, grade or color.
E. any of the above, depending on the situation.

19-**61.**
E
App.
Easy
p. 560-61

The most useful breakdown of data in a sales analysis is by:
A. size of order.
B. product, package size, grade, or color.
C. customer type.
D. geographic region.
E. any or all of the above--depending on the situation.

19-**62.**
A
Comp.
Med.
p. 561

The major difference between a sales analysis and a performance analysis is that:
A. performance analysis looks at variations from planned performance, while sales analysis shows what happened.
B. sales analysis looks at individual transactions, while performance analysis groups them into categories.
C. sales analysis is a control procedure, while performance analysis is part of implementation.
D. sales analysis is concerned with expected sales, while performance analysis is concerned with past sales.
E. sales analysis is used to find profitable sales patterns, while performance analysis seeks unprofitable patterns.

19-63.
B
Comp.
Med.
p. 561

Compared with sales analysis, PERFORMANCE ANALYSIS:
A. shows which customers should be dropped.
B. looks for exceptions or variations from planned performance.
C. does not do as much comparing against standards.
D. shows how to improve performance.
E. All of the above.

19-64.
E
Def.
Easy
p. 561

A marketing "performance analysis" is most likely to compare:
A. an individual sales rep's performance to total company sales.
B. a firm's sales with its competitors' sales.
C. sales by product to sales by territory.
D. advertising cost to sales.
E. planned sales with actual sales.

19-65.
B
Comp.
Med.
p. 561

The main purpose of a performance analysis is to:
A. see whether or not the 80/20 rule applies in a particular situation.
B. uncover variations in performance that may be hidden in summary information.
C. determine who should recieve a performance bonus when profit is greater than expected.
D. determine if the marketing budget is large enough to achieve the expected sales performance.
E. provide a detailed breakdown of a company's sales records.

19-66.
E
App.
Hard
p. 561

Which of the following statements might result from a performance analysis?
A. Our California salesman sold more aluminum tubing than any of our other reps.
B. Sophia Sanchez calls on two of our three biggest customers.
C. Joshua Voigt sold less tubing to wholesalers than to manufacturers.
D. Walker Brown sold more aluminum tubing than steel tubing.
E. Pele Ruiz's sales are over his quota.

19-67.
E
App.
Med.
p. 561

Joe Canon is a sales manager for IBM. He has asked his assistant to prepare an analysis that shows what percent over or under quota each sales rep was during the last year. This is an example of
A. using natural accounts.
B. the contribution-margin approach.
C. sales analysis.
D. target market analysis.
E. performance analysis.

19-68.
D
Comp.
Med.
p. 563

Performance analysis:
A. is based on qualitative factors, as contrasted with sales and cost analysis which are based on quantitative data.
B. is most useful in situations where the iceberg principal is not likely to be a concern.
C. indicates why problems have occurred and how to solve them.
D. may be based on several different performance indexes.
E. All of the above are true.

19-69.
B
Comp.
Hard
p. 563

A good reason for using performance indexes is to:
  A. convert sales data to profit data.
  B. make it easier to compare situations.
  C. find territories where actual sales are very high or low.
  D. direct management attention to territories where the market potential is greatest.
  E. None of the above is true.

19-70.
B
Def.
Easy
p. 563

Performance indexes:
  A. are based on the "iceberg principle."
  B. show the relation of one value to another.
  C. are used mainly to eliminate lazy salespeople.
  D. provide a qualitative measure of what "ought to happen."
  E. are calculated from the Consumer Price Index.

19-71.
C
App.
Med.
p. 563

If Salesperson A has a performance index of 80 and Salesperson B has a performance index of 120:
  A. Salesperson A's performance should be used as a model to improve everyone's performance.
  B. Salesperson B's performance should be improved to bring it up to "average."
  C. Salesperson A may be having some problems.
  D. Salesperson B should be fired.
  E. the two average out to 100--and "all is well."

19-72.
D
App.
Hard
p. 563

Information about five sales reps and their territories is presented below. Which would have the highest performance index?

REP'S NAME	TERRITORY POTENTIAL AS A PERCENT OF TOTAL	ACTUAL SALES
A. Aayak	30%	$290,000
B. Bellio	30%	$210,000
C. Cadams	10%	$120,000
D. Dooty	10%	$150,000
E. Eayma	20%	$230,000

19-73.
B
App.
Med.
p. 563

Avon, Inc., has analyzed the market potential in its territories and set sales quotas for its salespeople. It is now in a good position to develop _____ indexes at the end of the year.
  A. MIS
  B. performance
  C. PERT
  D. sales
  E. contribution

19-74.
D
Def.
Easy
p. 566

The "iceberg principle":
  A. explains why some firm's sales are "cooler" that others.
  B. explains why some customers are more profitable than others.
  C. suggests that sales will vary from one territory to another.
  D. suggests that much good information may be hidden in summary data.
  E. says that sales reps should never make "cold calls" on customers.

19-75.
C
Comp.
Med.
p. 566

The iceberg principle suggests that:
  A. most competitors' strategies are not obvious on the surface.
  B. small customers usually have the most hidden profit potential.
  C. conclusions based on summary information are often misleading.
  D. no matter what control procedure is used, most major problems are impossible to detect until it is too late.
  E. None of the above is true.

19-76.
E
App.
Med.
p. 566

Which of the following statements best explains the "iceberg principle"?
  A. Several salespeople in a sales force usually meet their quotas while many others don't.
  B. Many salespeople don't make their quotas because they only try to sell to large customers.
  C. Most consumer decisions are at the 90 percent pre-conscious level.
  D. Ten percent of a firm's customers usually account for 90 percent of its sales.
  E. Good performance in some areas may hide poor performance in other areas if only averages are evaluated.

19-77.
D
App.
Hard
p. 566

Which of the following statements by a sales manager best reflects an understanding of the iceberg principle?
  A. "Detailed cost analysis gets you focused on small parts of the problem, whereas general summaries make it easier to see the really big problems."
  B. "Most costs that look like they're fixed are actually changing all of the time."
  C. "Don't tell me that you're certain we're going to increase sales. They were certain that an iceberg couldn't sink the Titanic!"
  D. "Let's not dwell on sales data summaries--let's get below the surface and study the details.
  E. "Cost problems always show up first--but controlling expenses doesn't mean that you won't run into revenue problems."

19-78.
A
Def.
Easy
p. 566

Averages are useful for summarizing data--but only analyzing "averages" may be misleading according to:
  A. the "iceberg principle."
  B. AIDA.
  C. hypothesis--testing theory.
  D. the "law of central tendency."
  E. the "50/50" rule.

19-79.
E
App.
Med.
p. 566

A sales manager has just discovered that one of his sales reps has sales about 20 percent below his quota. The sales manager should conclude:
  A. that the sales rep's quota was set too high.
  B. that the sales rep lacks the desire to succeed.
  C. that "all is well" because other salespeople had sales that were at least 20 percent over their quotas.
  D. that the salesperson's performance index is 4 (i.e., 80:20).
  E. nothing thus far--because of the "iceberg principle."

19-**80.**
A
Comp.
Med.
p. 566

General summaries of overall marketing cost data
  A. may hide problems rather than highlighting them.
  B. are usually the key to identifying how to improve the marketing plan.
  C. should not be too detailed--since detailed analysis requires allocating costs that are actually fixed.
  D. are usually enough to reveal areas where changes are needed.
  E. All of the above are true.

19-**81.**
B
App.
Med.
p. 566

Marketing cost analysis shows that one of Buildco, Inc.'s customers is unprofitable, so Buildco should:
  A. refuse to sell to that customer.
  B. try to determine why this customer is unprofitable.
  C. drop the customer and shift all fixed costs to the other customers.
  D. assign a new salesperson to that account.
  E. immediately develop a plan to sell more to that customer.

19-**82.**
A
Comp.
Med.
p. 567

Using cost analysis to analyze the money being spent by a firm is analogous to using _____ to analyze the money coming into the firm.
  A. sales analysis
  B. traditional accounting reports
  C. performance analysis
  D. the iceberg principle
  E. TQM methods

19-**83.**
A
App.
Hard
p. 568

Lori Winters, a regional sales manager, is interested in the profitability of the different sales reps in her region. She has used a variety of different approaches for allocating fixed sales expenses to the different sales reps, but she reaches very different conclusions depending on which allocation approach is used. In this case, it would be wise for Ms. Winters to supplement her other analyses with an analysis based on
  A. the contribution-margin approach.
  B. the full cost approach.
  C. the marketing audit approach.
  D. none of the above.
  E. all of the above.

19-**84.**
B
Def.
Easy
p. 568

The text's "full-cost approach" to marketing cost analysis:
  A. looks only at each customer or product's "contribution margin."
  B. allocates all costs to products, customers, or other categories.
  C. looks only at those costs which are directly related to particular alternatives.
  D. is misleading and should be avoided.
  E. All of the above.

19-**85.**
A
Comp.
Med.
p. 568

The "contribution-margin approach" to marketing cost analysis:
  A. considers only those costs which are directly related to particular alternatives.
  B. is especially useful for estimating the long-run profit of a proposed strategy.
  C. allocates variable costs which are hard to measure to overhead.
  D. is especially useful for determining if there should be more controls on fixed costs.
  E. All of the above.

19-**86.**
C
Def.
Med.
p. 568

The "contribution margin approach" to marketing cost analysis:
- A. allocates all costs to products or customers.
- B. should always be used instead of the full-cost approach--so that fixed costs are fully considered.
- C. focuses management's attention on variable costs rather than total costs.
- D. assumes that all costs must be allocated.
- E. None of the above.

19-**87.**
B
Comp.
Hard
p. 568

Regarding marketing cost analysis,
- A. the full-cost approach usually should be used as there are almost always some fixed costs to be allocated.
- B. the contribution-margin approach focuses attention on variable costs.
- C. fixed costs should be allocated according to the contribution-margin approach.
- D. the action implications will be the same whether the full-cost or contribution-margin approach is used.
- E. the contribution-margin approach provides the most complete allocation of total expenses.

19-**88.**
B
Comp.
Med.
p. 568

The main difference between the full-cost approach and the contribution-margin approach to marketing cost analysis is:
- A. The contribution-margin approach uses both mechanical and logical reasoning to allocate marketing costs.
- B. The full-cost approach allocates all costs--even fixed costs--to products, customers, or other categories.
- C. The contribution-margin approach allocates all costs to show how profitable various customers are.
- D. The full-cost approach focuses on variable costs rather than total costs.

19-**89.**
D
Comp.
Med.
p. 568

With the "contribution-margin approach" to marketing cost analysis,
- A. all costs are allocated to products, customers, or other categories.
- B. fixed costs are allocated based on the profit contribution to the firm.
- C. variable costs are treated as common costs.
- D. common costs which are hard to allocate are ignored.
- E. None of the above is true.

19-**90.**
D
Comp.
Hard
p. 569

Regarding the "contribution-margin approach" to marketing cost analysis, which of the following statements is TRUE?
- A. The total net profit obtained with this approach is different from that obtained using the "full-cost approach."
- B. It is concerned with the amount contributed by a product or customer toward covering variable costs--after fixed costs have been covered.
- C. This approach stresses the need for evaluating fixed costs.
- D. This approach may suggest a different action than the "full-cost approach."
- E. All of the above are true.

19-**91.**
A
App.
Hard
p. 570

When the "full-cost approach" to marketing cost analysis is used, allocating fixed costs on the basis of sales:
A. may make low-volume customers appear more profitable than they are.
B. increases each customer's contribution margin.
C. decreases the profitability of the whole business.
D. makes large-volume customers appear more profitable that they are.
E. increases the profitability of the whole business.

19-**92.**
E
Comp.
Hard
p. 570

Which of the following would be the BEST reason to use the "full-cost approach" when comparing the performance of several product managers?
A. Unlike the "contribution-margin approach," it charges managers only for the expenses which are directly related to their operations.
B. This approach is required by Federal tax laws.
C. It charges each product manager only for those expenses which he controls.
D. It allows management to consider only the variable costs related to different products.
E. It makes each manager bear a share of the overhead expenses which were made for everyone's benefit.

19-**93.**
A
App.
Hard
p. 569-70

A company produces three product lines and a different marketing manager is responsible for each line. Most marketing expenses are specific to each line, but a common sales force sells all three lines. Sales reps are paid by commission, with a different commission for each product line. In this case, in a marketing cost analysis,
A. the contribution-margin approach would probably divide personal selling expense based on commission expense for each product line.
B. a full-cost approach would ignore commission expense since it is not a fixed cost.
C. sales commissions are a variable expense and would not be considered in the contribution-margin approach.
D. the full-cost approach would be easier to do if all sales reps were paid a straight salary.
E. None of the above is true.

19-**94.**
A
Comp.
Hard
p. 568-70

When deciding how to evaluate costs, a marketing manager should realize that
A. the best method for dealing with fixed costs depends on the objectives of the analysis.
B. according to the iceberg principle too much detail in cost analysis obscures the big problems by calling attention to the superficial problems.
C. the full cost approach is misleading and should not be used.
D. the contribution-margin approach ignores necessary fixed costs and should not be used.
E. None of the above.

19-**95.**
B
Def.
Easy
p. 572

A systematic, critical, and unbiased review and appraisal of the basic objectives and policies of the marketing function--and of the organization, methods, procedures, and people employed to implement the policies--is called a:
A. MIS report.
B. marketing audit.
C. management review.
D. marketing information system.
E. marketing analysis survey.

19-**96.**
D
Comp.
Easy
p. 572

A marketing audit should help determine if:
A. current marketing strategies are good ones.
B. the company's marketing objectives are reasonable.
C. implementation of a marketing program was effective.
D. All of the above.
E. None of the above.

19-**97.**
E
Def.
Easy
p. 572

A marketing audit is:
A. an evaluation of day-to-day marketing operations.
B. an analysis of the profitability of all profit centers.
C. a review of a marketing program during a crisis.
D. a detailed look by a CPA at how the company's marketing costs are allocated.
E. a systematic, critical, and unbiased review and appraisal of the objectives and policies of the marketing function.

19-**98.**
D
Comp.
Med.
p. 573

A "marketing audit" should:
A. be done by someone inside the finance department.
B. be conducted whenever a crisis arises.
C. be conducted by the person most familiar with each of the firm's marketing plans.
D. evaluate a company's whole marketing program on a regular basis.
E. All of the above.

Chapter 20

Managing Marketing's Link with Other Functional Areas

True-False Questions:

20-1.
False
p. 578-79

A marketing strategy that is focused on a real breakthrough opportunity will usually be successful even if there are obstacles in getting help from other functional areas in the firm.

20-2.
True
p. 579

Turning a strategy into a profitable business usually requires money, people, and other resources, such as production capacity, as well as a marketing plan.

20-3.
True
p. 580

Coordinating the linkages between different functional areas is likely to be easier when a new strategy involves only a minor modification to a plan that the firm is already implementing.

20-4.
True
p. 580

Coordinating the linkages between different functional areas is likely to be more difficult and critical when a strategy involves development of a totally new product idea rather than a minor change to an existing plan.

20-5.
False
p. 580

Coordinating the linkages between marketing and other functional areas is likely to be easier when a strategy involves developing a totally new product idea rather than just modifying an existing plan and established ways of doing things.

20-6.
False
p. 580

Capital is the financial term for the amount of cash that a firm has in a bank checking account or other readily available form.

20-7.
True
p. 580

Capital is the financial term for the amount of money invested in a firm.

20-8.
False
p. 580

Capital is the money needed to pay the personnel expenses required during the period of a marketing plan.

20-9.
False
p. 580

A marketing manager usually has responsibility for finding and allocating a firm's capital.

20-10.
True
p. 580

Finding and allocating capital is usually the responsibility handled by a firm's chief financial officer.

20-11.
False
p. 580

When evaluating possible strategies, a marketing manager shouldn't have to worry about screening based on financial criteria because the finance area's main job is to get the capital needed to implement the firm's marketing plan.

20-12.
True
p. 580

A marketing plan is more likely to be funded if the marketing manager has included financial measures as quantitative criteria when screening possible opportunities.

20-13.
False
p. 581

"Working capital" is the money needed to pay for investments in facilities, equipment and other "fixed assets" needed to do the firm's basic work.

20-14.
True
p. 581

"Working capital" is the money needed to pay for short term expenses--such as employee salaries, advertising, and marketing research--as they occur.

20-15.
True
p. 581

It would probably be a bad idea to go to work as a salaried salesperson selling installations for a firm that didn't have any working capital.

20-16.
False
p. 581

A firm's working capital may come from either internal sources--such as company bonds--or external sources--such as money paid by customers.

20-17.
True
p. 581

A firm's working capital may come from either internal sources--such as sales revenue and profits--or external sources--such as money from sales of stocks or bonds.

20-18.
False
p. 581

Capital comes from external sources and working capital comes from internal sources.

20-19.
False
p. 581

Internal sources for capital include loans, stocks, and bonds.

20-20.
True
p. 581

A strategy that's expected to "pay it's own way" must be based on a plan that generates the working capital needed to implement the plan.

20-21.
False
p. 581

With externally generated funding a firm's marketing program may be expected to "pay its own way."

20-22.
False
p. 581

It's not sensible for a firm to implement a marketing plan if the plan doesn't generate at least enough initial revenue to cover working capital needs.

20-**23.**
True
p. 581

Selling stock is a common way to raise money for capital and involves selling shares in the ownership of the company.

20-**24.**
True
p. 581

The value of a firm's stock is more likely to increase when its profits are growing.

20-**25.**
False
p. 582

Compared to most U.S. firms, Japanese firms have a reputation for expecting a marketing plan to be profitable in a much shorter period of time.

20-**26.**
True
p. 582

There's more risk for financial investors when the potential profits from a marketing plan are off in the future rather than immediate.

20-**27.**
False
p. 583

A bank (or other institution) that provides debt financing to fund a marketing plan is usually more willing to take risks than are investors who buy stock.

20-**28.**
True
p. 583

Before profits accumulate, a firm's selling price must cover all of the costs of doing business, including the interest charge on borrowed money.

20-**29.**
True
p. 583

Some banks work aggressively to attract business customers who want loans, but most commercial lenders like to avoid risk and making loans that are not secured with assets.

20-**30.**
True
p. 583

A company with a successful marketing strategy has its own internal source of funds--profits.

20-**31.**
False
p. 583

A company with a successful marketing strategy has its own external source of funds--profits.

20-**32.**
True
p. 583

A company with a profitable strategy has its own internal source of funds.

20-**33.**
True
p. 583

Paying for growth by reinvesting cash generated from operations is usually less expensive than borrowing money because no interest expense is involved.

20-**34.**
True
p. 584

A cash flow statement is a financial report that forecasts how much cash will be available after paying expenses.

20-**35.**
False
p. 584

Forecasting the amount of cash that will be available after paying expenses is straight forward because it's always equal to the firm's "bottom line"--the net profit figure shown on the operating statement.

20-**36.**
True
p. 584

When finances are tight, it's sensible to look for strategy alternatives that get a better return on money that is already invested.

20-**37.**
True
p. 584

When a marketing strategy increases revenue and profit contribution without increasing fixed costs and capital invested, the firm's profit and return on investment also increase.

20-**38.**
True
p. 584-85

Indirect distribution usually requires less investment capital than direct approaches.

20-**39.**
True
p. 585

Capital requirements are likely to be less when intermediaries take on much of the responsibility for promotion in the channel.

20-**40.**
True
p. 585

Promotion blends that focus on stimulating consumer pull usually require a big front-end investment in advertising and consumer promotions.

20-**41.**
True
p. 585

Production capacity is the ability to produce a certain quantity and quality of specific goods or services.

20-**42.**
False
p. 585

Concerns about production capacity apply to physical goods but they are not relevant when the product is a service.

20-**43.**
True
p. 585

While excess capacity can be costly, it can be a part of a sensible plan for preventing lost sales if demand suddenly picks up.

20-**44.**
True
p. 586

If demand is irregular, a firm's production flexibility is likely to influence the severity of stock-out problems in the channel of distribution.

20-**45.**
False
p. 586

Problems of matching supply and demand are likely to be greatest when a marketing plan calls for a regional roll out rather than a national roll out.

20-**46.**
True
p. 586

Problems of matching supply and demand are likely to be greatest when a marketing plan calls for quick expansion into many different types of channels.

20-**47.**
True
p. 586

Problems of matching supply and demand for a new product are likely to be greatest when a marketing plan calls for quick expansion into many different types of channels at the same time.

20-**48.**
True
p. 586

Production capacity is more easily matched to the distribution of a new product if that distribution is staged.

20-**49.**
True
p. 586

A virtual corporation may not make anything at all.

20-**50.**
True
p. 586

A virtual corporation is likely to look for a capable supplier to produce a product that meets the specs laid out in the firm's marketing plan.

20-**51.**
False
p. 587

A virtual corporation is one that achieves great flexibility in production by using computer-controlled manufacturing equipment.

20-**52.**
True
p. 587

A virtual corporation is one where the firm is primarily a coordinator--with a good marketing concept.

20-**53.**
False
p. 587

When a firm is a virtual corporation, it acts primarily as a producer--and leaves it to another firm to coordinate functions such as marketing, finance, and human resources.

20-**54.**
True
p. 587

While out-sourcing production may increase a firm's flexibility in some ways, it may also make production costs higher and quality control more difficult.

20-**55.**
True
p. 587

A virtual corporation may enjoy flexibility in operations, but often at higher cost or with less control of quality and schedules.

20-**56.**
True
p. 587

Production flexibility allows a firm to provide business customers with the just-in-time delivery service or rapid response replenishment of inventories that they expect.

20-**57.**
True
p. 587

Production flexibility allows a firm to make better use of EDI or some other type of computerized reorder system--because the firm can respond to customer needs more quickly.

20-**58.**
True
p. 588

Mass customization serves individual needs.

20-**59.**
False
p. 588

The mass-customization approach is not useful if a firm wants to focus on a particular market segment.

20-**60.**
True
p. 588

Mass customization applies the principles of mass production to the challenge of meeting the unique needs of individual customers.

20-**61.**
True
p. 588

With the mass-customization approach, a firm tries to find a low-cost way to give individual customers more or better choices.

20-62.
True
p. 588

A firm that relies on mass customization tries to get a competitive advantage by finding a low-cost way to give each customer in its target market more or better choices.

20-63.
False
p. 588

Mass customization is based on the idea that all of the people in a particular market have the same needs.

20-64.
True
p. 589

Cost advantages that are gained from economies of scale in production may later be lost to inventory carrying costs.

20-65.
True
p. 589

It makes sense for a firm to produce where it can produce most economically--if the cost of transporting and storing products to match demand doesn't offset the production savings.

20-66.
True
p. 590

Task transfer is using telecommunications to move service operations to places where there are pools of skilled workers.

20-67.
True
p. 591

Marketing managers should strive to cut production costs that don't add value for customers.

20-68.
True
p. 591

It's often hard for a marketing manager to be familiar with all of the costs associated with a product (or customer) without help from the firm's accountants.

20-69.
True
p. 591

Accounting statements that are prepared for tax purposes and for outside investors often aren't helpful for managers who need to make decisions about marketing strategy.

20-70.
True
p. 591

Marketing cost analysis usually requires a new way of classifying accounting data based on functional accounts rather than the natural accounts typically used for financial analysis.

20-71.
False
p. 591

Marketing cost analysis usually requires a new way of classifying accounting data based on natural accounts rather than the functional accounts that are typically used for financial analysis.

20-72.
True
p. 591

Marketing cost analysis usually requires a new way of classifying accounting data.

20-73.
False
p. 591

Natural accounts show the purpose for which expenditures are made.

20-74.
True
p. 591

Functional accounts show the purpose for which expenditures are made.

20-**75.**
True
p. 591

The titles of functional cost accounts show the purpose for which expenditures are made.

20-**76.**
False
p. 591

Examples of functional accounts include taxes, supplies, and wages.

20-**77.**
True
p. 592

The first step in marketing cost analysis is to reclassify all the dollar cost entries in the natural accounts into functional cost accounts.

20-**78.**
False
p. 592

The first step in marketing cost analysis is to reclassify all of the costs in functional accounts into natural accounts.

20-**79.**
True
p. 592

For marketing cost analysis, it's often useful to reallocate costs in various natural accounts to specific products or customers.

20-**80.**
True
p. 592-96

Advertising costs can often be allocated to specific products, just as the cost of labor in the factory can be allocated to specific products.

20-**81.**
True
p. 597

Human resource issues include recruiting and hiring new employees, deciding how people will be compensated, and what to do when a job is not being performed well or is no longer necessary.

20-**82.**
True
p. 597

Many of the people affected by a new strategy may not be under the control of the marketing manager.

20-**83.**
True
p. 598

It is the marketing manager's job to communicate with others in the organization and explain the new strategy, what needs to happen, and why.

20-**84.**
False
p. 598

It is the chief executive's job to communicate with others in the organization and explain the new marketing strategy, what needs to happen, and why.

20-**85.**
True
p. 598

The marketing manager needs to work with the human resources manager--or with other managers--who will participate in preparing the firm's personnel for changes required by a new marketing strategy.

20-**86.**
True
p. 598

Rapid growth strains human resources because it's a challenge getting enough qualified people to do what needs to be done.

20-**87.**
True
p. 598

Training is especially important during rapid growth of a company because it takes time to hire people and get them up to speed.

20-88.
True
p. 599

In planning a new strategy or reorganization, it's important to keep in mind that people can effectively absorb only so much change in a limited period.

20-89.
True
p. 599

Marketing managers should plan time for strategy changes and not put undue pressure on the people in their organization to perform heroic efforts.

20-90.
True
p. 599

The human resources challenges of dealing with rapidly expanding marketing efforts are generally less traumatic than the challenges involved with decisions to drop products, channels of distribution, or even certain types of customers.

20-91.
True
p. 599

A new marketing strategy often upsets established ways of doing things in the organization.

20-92.
True
p. 600

A marketing plan for a new strategy needs to take into consideration the time--and effort--that will be required to get people up to speed on the new jobs they will be expected to do.

20-93.
True
p. 600

It is the responsibility of the chief executive--not the marketing manager-- to make the strategic planning decisions that concern how a firm is going to use its overall resources--from marketing, production, finance and other areas.

20-94.
False
p. 600

It is the responsibility of the marketing manager to make the strategic planning decisions that concern how a firm is going to use its overall resources--from marketing, production, finance and other areas.

20-95.
True
p. 600

Marketing strategies and plans that the marketing manager recommends are more likely to be accepted--and then successfully implemented--if the links between marketing and other functional areas have been carefully considered from the outset.

Multiple Choice Questions

20-96.
E
App.
Easy
p. 581

Working capital may be used to pay for:
    A. advertising
    B. what a firm owes suppliers
    C. employee salaries
    D. marketing research
    E. all of the above

20-97.
E
App.
Easy
p. 581

Working capital may be used to pay for:
    A. advertising
    B. storing
    C. employee salaries
    D. what a firm owes suppliers
    E. all of the above

20-**98.**
E
App.
Easy
p. 581

Working capital may be used to pay for:
A. what a firm owes suppliers
B. what it costs to store inventory
C. employee salaries
D. marketing research
E. all of the above

20-**99.**
E
App.
Easy
p. 581

Working capital may be used to pay for:
A. what it costs to store inventory
B. marketing research
C. advertising
D. what a firm owes suppliers
E. all of the above

20-**100.**
E
App.
Easy
p. 581

Which of the following would NOT be paid for using working capital?
A. advertising expense
B. what it costs to store inventory
C. what a firm owes suppliers
D. employee salaries
E. the cost of new facilities

20-**101.**
E
App.
Easy
p. 581

Which of the following would NOT be paid for using working capital?
A. employee salaries
B. what it costs to store inventory
C. what a firm owes suppliers
D. marketing research costs
E. the cost of new production equipment

20-**102.**
A
App.
Easy
p. 581

Which of the following typically would NOT be paid for using working capital?
A. purchase of new facilities
B. what it costs to store inventory
C. what a firm owes suppliers
D. employee salaries
E. marketing research costs

20-**103.**
D
App.
Easy
p. 581

Which of the following would NOT be paid for using working capital?
A. employee salaries
B. what it costs to store inventory
C. what a firm owes suppliers
D. purchase of new facilities
E. advertising expense

20-**104.**
E
Def.
Easy
p. 581

Capital sources include:
A. bonds
B. profits
C. loans
D. stocks
E. all of the above

20-**105.**
E
Def.
Easy
p. 581

Working capital might come from:
- A. sale of bonds
- B. a previous period's profits
- C. loans
- D. sale of stocks
- E. any of the above

20-**106.**
E
Int.
Easy
p. 581

Which of the following is NOT a way to stimulate profit growth?
- A. get the marketing job done at lower cost
- B. do a better job of holding onto customers
- C. pursue new market opportunities
- D. be more efficient with current activities
- E. all of the above are ways to keep profits growing

20-**107.**
E
Int.
Med.
p. 581-83

If a marketing plan requires that the firm obtain additional capital, a manager should remember that:
- A. Interest expense on a loan may impact prices and profits.
- B. A company with a successful marketing strategy has its own internal source of funds--profits.
- C. Institutions that loan money are usually even less willing to take a risk than are investors who buy stock.
- D. The firm may be able to sell stock to its own employees.
- E. All of the above are true.

20-**108.**
C
Int.
Med.
p. 583

Which of the following statements is FALSE in regard to borrowing money?
- A. Interest expense on a loan may impact prices and profits.
- B. A company with a successful marketing strategy has its own internal source of fund--profits.
- C. Institutions that loan money are usually more willing to take a risk than are investors who buy stock.
- D. The firm may be able to sell stock to its own employees.
- E. None of the above is false.

20-**109.**
D
Int.
Med.
p. 585

Indirect distribution typically requires less capital than direct distribution because:
- A. agent middlemen may take on much of the selling effort and not expect any compensation until the revenue is in on what they've sold.
- B. intermediaries may provide the capital required for logistics facilities.
- C. merchant wholesalers and retailers usually pay for products when they purchase them and then take over the costs of carrying inventory.
- D. all of the above.
- E. none of the above--indirect distribution usually requires more capital.

20-**110.**
D
Int.
Med.
p. 585

Which of the following statements concerning push versus pull is correct?
A. Pushing a product (through a channel) means getting customers to ask middlemen for the product.
B. It is less risky for a firm with limited working capital to rely on pull rather than push.
C. Pulling a product (through a channel) means targeting middlemen with normal promotion efforts such as personal selling, advertising, and sales promotion.
D. Promotion blends that focus on stimulating consumer pull usually require more working capital for advertising than do those that rely on push.
E. None of the above is correct.

20-**111.**
E
App.
Med.
p. 585-86

If a firm has excess production capacity, it
A. can serve as a safety net if demand suddenly picks up.
B. may be a sign that there's too much competition.
C. may make sense for the marketing manager to try to find new markets for current products.
D. can be costly.
E. all of the above.

20-**112.**
E
Int.
Easy
p. 585-86

Which of the following aspects of production capacity should be considered in marketing planning?
A. A firm can produce only limited quantities of its current product without a major investment in new facilities.
B. Other firms are available to handle production on a contract or supplier basis.
C. A firm's production capacity allows it to produce some products quickly but not others.
D. A firm has more production capacity than it can use.
E. All of the above.

20-**113.**
D
Comp.
Med.
p. 586

The challenges of matching supply and demand are likely to be greater when a marketing plan calls for:
A. an international roll out instead of a regional roll out.
B. quick expansion into many different types of channels.
C. simultaneously expanding into many different market areas rather than expanding into one market after another.
D. Any of the above would increase the challenge of matching supply and demand.
E. none of the above.

20-**114.**
B
Comp.
Med.
p. 586

The problems of matching supply and demand are likely to be less severe when a marketing plan calls for:
A. rapid penetration into many different types of channels.
B. the staged distribution of a new product.
C. quick expansion into many different market areas at once.
D. a national roll out instead of a regional roll out.

20-**115.**
E
Def.
Easy
p. 586-87

Virtual corporations
A. may not make anything at all
B. look for capable suppliers to produce the actual products
C. act primarily as coordinators
D. try to come up with good marketing plans
E. all of the above

20-**116.**
E
Def.
Easy
p. 586-87

A virtual corporation
A. does all of its production "in house"
B. looks for capable suppliers who can meet the specs it lays out
C. acts primarily as a producer
D. needs to have a good marketing plan
E. B and D only

20-**117.**
E
Def.
Easy
p. 586-87

A virtual corporation
A. acts primarily as a coordinator
B. has no need for suppliers because it produces everything it needs or sells.
C. does none of its production "in house"
D. all of the above
E. A and C only

20-**118.**
A
Def.
Easy
p. 588

With the mass customization approach, a firm
A. tailors the principles of mass production to meet the unique needs of individual customers in its target market
B. tries to justify high prices by customizing its offering for everyone in a mass market
C. gives up segmenting to go after the mass market
D. all of the above
E. none of the above

20-**119.**
A
Int.
Med.
p. 588

Which of the following statements about mass customization is true?
A. Levi's Personal Pair personalized jeans program for women is a good example of mass customization.
B. Mass customization avoids the need for working capital.
C. Mass customization requires a firm to give up segmentation thinking to pursue larger, more heterogeneous markets.
D. The mass-customization approach applies only to services, and they often must be custom produced anyway.

20-**120.**
D
Int.
Med.
p. 588

Which of the following statements about mass customization is true?
A. Mass customization means that a firm is targeting the mass market but that it tries to customize the design of a product so it is different from what a competitor offers.
B. Mass customization requires a firm to give up segmentation thinking to pursue larger, more heterogeneous markets.
C. The mass-customization approach applies only to services, and they often must be custom produced anyway.
D. Levi's Personal Pair personalized jeans program for women is a good example of mass customization.
E. None of the above is true.

20-**121.**
B
Comp.
Med.
p. 591-92

Marketing cost analysts start with the assumption that:
A. "natural accounts" are more useful than "functional accounts."
B. marketing expenditures are made for a specific purpose--and so it makes sense to allocate costs to different market segments, customers, or products.
C. all marketing expenditures should be treated as overhead expenses.
D. overall profit is what counts--so it isn't critical if some market segments, products, or customers are unprofitable.
E. All of the above.

20-**122.**
D
Comp.
Med.
p. 592

A major purpose of marketing cost analysis is to:
A. offset the limitations of performance analysis.
B. determine which costs are fixed and which are variable.
C. divide costs into natural accounts.
D. show the marketing manager where costs occur in relation to serving particular customers.
E. avoid the pitfalls of the contribution-margin approach to allocating costs.

20-**123.**
C
App.
Med.
p. 592

A firm is doing a marketing cost analysis involving two products, three target markets, and $6 million in advertising costs. The firm should:
A. allocate $2 million of the advertising costs to each target market.
B. allocate these costs to general overhead.
C. determine the purpose of the advertising and allocate costs to products and target markets accordingly.
D. allocate these costs to each product and target market on the basis of their percentage of total sales.
E. allocate $3 million of the advertising costs to each product.

20-**124.**
B
Int.
Med.
p. 591

Regarding marketing cost analysis:
A. there is only one right way to allocate functional costs.
B. traditional accounting analysis doesn't analyze the purpose of marketing costs.
C. marketing costs usually should be allocated to general overhead.
D. functional accounts and natural accounts usually have the same names.
E. All of the above are true.

20-**125.**
B
Comp.
Easy
p. 591

"Natural accounts" are:
A. usually allocated to functional accounts by the MIS method.
B. accounts to which various costs are charged in the normal accounting cycle.
C. misleading for calculating a firm's total profitability.
D. usually named to show the purpose for which expenditures are made.
E. All of the above.

20-**126.**
E
Def.
Easy
p. 591

Accounts such as rent, salaries, taxes and auto expenses are called _____ accounts.
A. functional
B. general business
C. cost analysis
D. distribution
E. natural

20-**127.**
B
Def.
Med.
p. 591

As compared to natural accounts, FUNCTIONAL ACCOUNTS:
A. are the accounts to which various costs are charged in the normal accounting cycle.
B. show the purpose for which expenditures are made.
C. include items such as storing, salaries, and taxes.
D. All of the above.
E. Both A and C above.

20-**128.**
D
App.
Med.
p. 592

Which of the following is NOT a FUNCTIONAL cost account?
A. Packaging
B. Selling
C. Order entry
D. Rent
E. Billing

20-**129.**
B
App.
Med.
p. 592

Which of the following is an example of a FUNCTIONAL cost account?
A. Auto repairs
B. Advertising
C. Taxes
D. Social Security
E. Any of the above--because functional accounts include any costs which are used in the normal preparation of a company's operating statement.

20-**130.**
D
Comp.
Med.
p. 591

Classifying marketing costs in terms of their purpose--why the money was spent--requires the use of
A. iceberg accounts.
B. marketing audit accounts.
C. expense accounts.
D. functional accounts.
E. natural accounts.

20-**131.**
C
Int.
Med.
p. 592

Regarding marketing cost analysis, which of the following statements is TRUE?
A. Natural accounts are set up to indicate the purpose for which the expenditures were made.
B. The contribution-margin approach focuses attention on all costs equally.
C. The first step is to reclassify all costs in the natural accounts into functional accounts.
D. The total of costs in the natural accounts will often differ from the total of those in the functional accounts.
E. All of the above are true.

20-**132.**
D
App.
Med.
p. 592

A marketing manager who wants to calculate the cost of marketing several products to several target markets will probably have to:
A. read all requisitions very carefully.
B. allocate advertising expense to general overhead.
C. reorganize some of the company`s functional cost accounts to natural accounts.
D. reclassify all natural accounts into functional accounts.
E. None of the above--it is impossible to link the costs of marketing to target markets.

20-**133.**
C
Comp.
Hard
p. 592

A major difference between functional accounts and natural accounts is that functional accounts

A. are based on the contribution-margin approach and natural accounts are based on the full cost approach.

B. always total to a lower overall expense than the total of the natural accounts.

C. might be used to compare the costs of serving different customers--but natural accounts are not suited to that purpose.

D. are the basis for most accounting systems, but natural accounts are more useful for marketing managers.

E. do not consider fixed costs, but natural accounts do.

20-**134.**
E
Def.
Easy
p. 597

Human resource issues include:

A. retraining employees for other jobs within the company.

B. deciding what to do when a job is not being performed well.

C. recruiting and hiring new employees.

D. deciding how people will be compensated.

E. all of the above.

20-**135.**
A
Int.
Med.
p. 597

Which of the following statements concerning human resources is NOT true?

A. Most of the people affected by a new strategy are under the control of a marketing manager.

B. Communication is very important because you can't expect people to pull together in an organization-wide effort if they don't know what's going on.

C. People are one of a company's most important resources.

D. It is the marketing manager's job to communicate with others in the organization and explain the new strategy, what needs to happen, and why.

E. All of the above are true.

Chapter 21

Developing Innovative Marketing Plans

True-False Questions:

21-1.
True
p. 607

A marketing plan usually spells out the time schedule for a marketing strategy as well as the time-related details.

21-2.
False
p. 609

A S.W.O.T. analysis identifies the "special weapons or tactics" used by the competitor in a product market that has the most profitable marketing mix.

21-3.
False
p. 609

S.W.O.T. analysis is based on the idea that one of the best ways to develop a strategy is to identify and copy the marketing "strategies, weapons, outlook and tactics" of the firm's most effective competitor.

21-4.
True
p. 609

A good S.W.O.T. analysis helps a manager focus on a strategy that takes advantages of the firm's opportunities and strengths while avoiding its weaknesses and threats to its success.

21-5.
True
p. 609

The letters in "S.W.O.T. analysis" are an abbreviation for the first letters of the words "strengths, weaknesses, opportunities and threats"

21-6.
False
p. 609

The letters in "S.W.O.T. analysis" are an abbreviation for the first letters of the words "special weapons or tactics."

21-7.
False
p. 613

A good marketing strategy will work well throughout the different stages of the product life cycle.

21-8.
False
p. 613

As the product life cycle moves on, the marketing manager should expect to see the market move closer to monopoly.

21-9.
True
p. 614

Market potential refers to what a whole market segment might buy.

21-10.
False
p. 614

A sales forecast is an estimate of what a whole market segment will buy.

21-11.
True
p. 614

A sales forecast is an estimate of how much an industry or firm hopes to sell to a market segment.

21-12.
True
p. 614

Market potential refers to how much a whole market segment will buy while sales forecast refers to how much one firm hopes to sell to that market segment.

21-13.
False
p. 614

When comparing the figures for market potential and sales forecast for the same market segment, the sales forecast figure should always be larger.

21-14.
True
p. 614

When forecasting sales, a common approach is to develop a national income forecast, then an industry sales forecast, and finally specific company and product forecasts.

21-15.
True
p. 615

A weakness of the trend-extension method of sales forecasting is that it assumes past conditions will continue unchanged in the future.

21-16.
True
p. 616

The basic formula used in the factor method of sales forecasting is: some variable, such as past sales, times some related factor equals the sales forecast.

21-17.
False
p. 616

Sales and Marketing Management's "Buying Power Index" is not very useful for sales forecasting because it only considers the population in markets.

21-18.
True
p. 616

Sales forecasts based on Sales and Marketing Management's "Buying Power Index" assume that sales are related to a market's population, income, and retail sales.

21-19.
False
p. 616

The factor method is widely used by producers of consumer products, but it isn't relevant for producers of business products.

21-20.
True
p. 616

An auto manufacturer that bases its sales forecast on increases in population and income is using the "factor method."

21-21.
True
p. 619

The "jury of executive opinion" method of sales forecasting combines the opinions of experienced executives in a firm.

21-22.
False
p. 620

The main disadvantage of the "jury of executive opinion" method of sales forecasting is that it is very slow.

21-23.
True
p. 620

The likely reaction of customers to possible changes in a marketing mix can sometimes be estimated using market tests and surveys of final buyers.

21-**24.**
True
p. 621

Inexpensive computer programs and spreadsheet analysis can make it easier for marketing managers to plan and implement marketing programs.

21-**25.**
True
p. 623

If a marketing manager doesn't schedule implementation carefully, the whole strategy may miss the target.

21-**26.**
True
p. 626

PERT and similar approaches help a marketing manager see which marketing activities have to be done and in what order.

21-**27.**
True
p. 627

A marketing program blends all of a firm's marketing plans into one big plan.

21-**28.**
True
p. 628

Exporting is sometimes just a way for a firm to get rid of surplus products.

21-**29.**
True
p. 628

Exporting is often the first step into international marketing.

21-**30.**
False
p. 628

Exporting usually involves very little government "red tape."

21-**31.**
True
p. 628

Of the six basic kinds of involvement in international marketing, exporting is the least permanent.

21-**32.**
True
p. 628

Exporting has an advantage compared to other types of international involvement, because it is usually easier to drop or change arrangements as the firm's needs change.

21-**33.**
True
p. 629

In a licensing agreement, the licensee takes most of the risk because it must invest some capital to use the right granted by the licensor.

21-**34.**
True
p. 629

Contract manufacturing involves turning production over to a foreign "partner," while retaining control of the marketing process.

21-**35.**
True
p. 629

A firm that has a lot of "marketing know-how," but expects production problems in a foreign market, might be wise to use contract manufacturing.

21-**36.**
True
p. 629

Management contracting is a relatively low risk way of entering foreign markets, since no commitment is made to fixed facilities.

21-**37.**
True
p. 629-30

Joint venturing gives a firm less control than if it created a wholly-owned subsidiary.

21-**38.**
False
p. 630

A multinational corporation is a firm which exports at least one of its products to one or more foreign markets around the world.

21-**39.**
True
p. 630

A multinational corporation may be "based" in one country, but it makes business decisions based on the best choices available anywhere in the world.

21-**40.**
False
p. 631

The organizational setup for a multinational corporation should be centralized and provide a great deal of structure and control over local managers--to be certain they meet the plans top management assigns to them.

Multiple Choice Questions

21-**41.**
D
Def.
Easy
p. 607

Good marketing managers plan:
A. marketing programs.
B. marketing strategies.
C. marketing plans.
D. All of the above.
E. None of the above.

21-**42.**
D
Comp.
Med.
p. 607

A marketing plan:
A. is a combination of several marketing strategies.
B. must cover a one-year period.
C. consists of a target market and an appropriate marketing mix.
D. includes the time-related details for implementing a marketing strategy.
E. All of the above.

21-**43.**
E
Def.
Easy
p. 607

A marketing plan should be developed for a:
A. five-year period.
B. year.
C. quarter.
D. month
E. Any of the above--depending on the situation.

21-**44.**
E
Comp.
Med.
p. 607

A marketing PROGRAM will:
A. explain what marketing mix the firm will use for each of its target markets.
B. include time-related details for each strategy.
C. plan day-to-day operations for each department.
D. All of the above are true.
E. A and B are true.

21-**45.**
E
Def.
Med.
p. 609

A S.W.O.T. analysis
A. seeks to reduce the risk of competitive surprises by scanning the market for "signals, warnings, omens, and tips."
B. focuses on what a firm plans to do to "Satisfy Wishes Of a Target" customer.
C. summarizes a firm's "strategy, wishes (of its customers), outlook and tactics."
D. helps defend against potential competitors by developing a set of competitive "safeguards, weapons, offensives, and tactics."
E. identifies a firm's "strengths, weaknesses, opportunities and threats."

21-**46.**
A
Comp.
Med.
p. 609

A S.W.O.T. analysis
A. seeks to improve strategy planning by "Scanning for Warnings, Omens, and Tips" about competitors' plans.
B. None of the above is a good answer.
C. is not necessary if competitors have already entered the market.
D. defends against potential competitive threats by planning specific "safeguards, weapons, or tactics."
E. should help a manager develop a strategy that leads to a competitive advantage.

21-**47.**
E
Comp.
Med.
p. 609

A S.W.O.T. analysis can help a marketing manager:
A. develop a competitive advantage.
B. define what business and markets the firm wants to compete in.
C. narrow down to a specific target market and marketing mix from the many alternatives available.
D. see the pros and cons of different possible strategies.
E. all of the above.

21-**48.**
A
Comp.
Med.
p. 609

Ideally, the ingredients of a good marketing mix should:
A. flow logically from all the relevant dimensions of a target market.
B. match the ingredients typically used by key competitors.
C. be determined by which ingredients cost the least.
D. not include much advertising because it's expensive.
E. All of the above are true.

21-**49.**
E
Comp.
Easy
p. 609-10

Marketing strategy planning is difficult for marketing managers because:
A. they rarely know enough about the needs and attitudes of their target markets.
B. other dimensions of the marketing environment may force changes in possible marketing mixes.
C. proposed plans for each of the "four Ps" have to be blended together.
D. competitors are usually trying to satisfy the same or similar needs.
E. All of the above are true.

21-**50.**
A
Comp.
Med.
p. 609

Regarding marketing strategy planning:
A. marketing managers seldom know as much as they would like to about the needs and attitudes of their target markets.
B. marketing managers implement marketing STRATEGIES--NOT marketing plans.
C. the marketing environment may force marketing managers to change target markets--but their marketing mixes usually are not affected.
D. it is easier in large firms because marketing managers can count on specialists to plan each of the "four Ps."
E. All of the above are true.

21-**51.**
C
Comp.
Med.
p. 610

When attempting to design a marketing mix for a new product, a marketing manager might start evaluating what a "typical" marketing mix for the product might look like by
A. estimating the cost of producing the product.
B. developing a leading series.
C. deciding what product class best fits the product.
D. using the buying power index.
E. determining the qualifying dimensions of the product's target market.

21-**52.**
C
Comp.
Med.
p. 610

Regarding product classes and marketing mix planning, a good marketing manager knows that:
A. the more "typical" the marketing mix, the more profitable it will be.
B. a marketing mix usually will fail if it varies much from the "typical" mix for that type of product.
C. the "typical" mix for a product's typical product class may not satisfy a market segment that sees the product in another product class.
D. All of the above are true.
E. None of the above is true.

21-**53.**
D
Comp.
Med.
p. 613

When developing a marketing plan for a new product that is about to enter the market introduction stage of its product life cycle, a marketing manager should:
A. plan to change the marketing strategy every six months.
B. choose the best possible marketing strategy and stay with it throughout its product life cycle.
C. plan to sell the product until its whole life cycle is over.
D. plan to change the marketing strategy as the product moves through its life cycle.
E. change the marketing strategy only when the marketing environment changes.

21-**54.**
B
App.
Hard
p. 613

Marie Callender has developed a new brand of frozen dinners to compete with the well-established brands. It probably should use a marketing mix of:
A. exclusive distribution, skimming pricing, and persuasive advertising.
B. intensive distribution, introductory price dealing, selective demand advertising, and a combined "push" and "pull" policy.
C. intensive distribution, price cutting, reminder advertising, and a "pull" policy.
D. selective distribution, penetration pricing, pioneering advertising, and a "push" policy.
E. selective distribution, skimming pricing, selective demand advertising, and a "push" policy.

21-**55.**
C
App.
Med.
p. 613

Pioneer has developed a really new consumer electronics item--a heterogeneous shopping product with unique patented features. It probably should use a marketing mix of:
A. exclusive distribution, price cutting, reminder advertising, and a "push" policy.
B. exclusive distribution, penetration pricing, informative and persuasive advertising, and a "pull" policy.
C. selective distribution, skimming pricing, pioneering advertising, and a "push" policy.
D. selective distribution, penetration pricing, persuasive advertising, and a "pull" policy.
E. intensive distribution, persuasive advertising, price dealing, and a "push" policy.

21-**56.**
D
Comp.
Easy
p. 613

As a product moves through its product life cycle stages:
A. price cutting tends to decrease.
B. competition tends to move toward monopoly.
C. distribution moves from intensive to selective.
D. promotion tends to become less informative and more persuasive.
E. All of the above.

21-**57.**
D
Comp.
Med.
p. 613

As a product moves through its product life cycle stages:
A. consumers are offered less product variety.
B. distribution tends to become more and more exclusive.
C. competition forces firms to skim instead of just meeting competition.
D. the promotion emphasis is on building selective demand.

21-**58.**
E
Comp.
Easy
p. 613

As a product moves from the early to the later stages of the product life cycle:
A. distribution moves toward being more intensive.
B. firms either cut prices or just meet competition.
C. promotion becomes frantically competitive.
D. products tend to become more similar.
E. All of the above.

21-**59.**
A
Def.
Easy
p. 614

"Market potential" is:
A. what a whole market segment might buy.
B. how much a firm hopes to sell to a market segment.
C. how much an industry hopes to sell to a market segment.
D. an estimate of the national income for the coming year.
E. All of the above.

21-**60.**
C
App.
Easy
p. 614

A marketing researcher estimates that during the next year a market's total purchases of a new product will be $250,000. One firm expects to sell $110,000 worth. It knows that its profits will be about 10 percent of its sales. This firm's sales forecast is:
A. $90,000
B. $250,000
C. $110,000
D. $11,000
E. There is not enough information to tell.

21-**61.**
B
App.
Med.
p. 614

A marketing manager knows that the current market potential for his company's product is close to $1,000,000. He knows that the market is growing at about 20 percent a year, and that his firm usually wins about 25 percent of the total sales. A market analyst forecasts that the company should have $800,000 in sales next year.
A. The sales manager should worry that his competitors seem to be getting stronger.
B. The marketing manager should not make any plans based on the forecast, since he knows it must be way off.
C. The marketing manager should plan on selling less dollar volume next year.
D. The marketing manager should be disappointed that his sales are not projected to grow at a rate as fast as the market.

21-**62.**
C
App.
Med.
p. 614

A retailer has estimated that her store has a market potential of about $3 million for the coming year. From this information, we know that:

    A. the owner has not yet planned her marketing strategy for the coming year.
    B. the store will sell about $3 million of goods and services during the coming year.
    C. the store's sales forecast is probably LESS that $3 million.
    D. if the store maintains its present 20 percent market share, its competitors' sales should total about $15 million.
    E. Both B and C are true.

21-**63.**
B
App.
Med.
p. 614

A marketing researcher estimates that all the users and potential users of a special industrial tool might buy about $600,000 worth next year. The marketing manager for one firm that sells the tools knows that her company sold $80,000 worth of tools last year and that her profits will be about 10 percent of sales. The market potential in this case is probably about:

    A. $16,000
    B. $600,000
    C. $80,000
    D. $8,000

21-**64.**
D
Comp.
Med.
p. 614

A national income forecast:

    A. eliminates the need for making industry sales forecasts.
    B. usually shows very little about an individual firm's sales prospects.
    C. usually must be developed by a marketing manager.
    D. is a good starting point for forecasting industry and company sales.
    E. All of the above.

21-**65.**
B
Comp.
Hard
p. 614

Developing a sales forecast for a broad industry:

    A. is easier when a firm segments its product-markets very carefully.
    B. is often very similar to developing a national income forecast.
    C. is usually done by a marketing manager.
    D. is relatively easy because computers can eliminate the "guess" work.
    E. All of the above are true.

21-**66.**
A
App.
Med.
p. 614

If you want to forecast the sales of one of your major products, your first step probably should be to:

    A. develop or obtain a national income forecast.
    B. carefully estimate your costs at various sales levels.
    C. develop company and product forecasts.
    D. develop an industry sales forecast.

21-**67.**
B
Def.
Easy
p. 615

The sales forecasting approach which extends past sales into the future is called:

    A. future analysis.
    B. trend extension.
    C. input-output analysis.
    D. market potential analysis.
    E. market extension.

21-**68.**
E
App.
Hard
p. 615

For which of the following products would trend extension probably be MOST suitable for sales forecasting?
A. Cars
B. Equipment used to produce microcomputers
C. Snow skis
D. Industrial pollution control equipment
E. Margarine

21-**69.**
D
Int.
Med.
p. 615

Regarding sales forecasting:
A. marketing managers usually develop their own national income and industry forecasts.
B. trend extension cannot be used when past sales have varied.
C. the final step should be to develop an industry sales forecast.
D. trend extension assumes that past conditions will continue unchanged into the future.
E. only one forecasting method should be used because different techniques give different forecasts.

21-**70.**
C
Comp.
Hard
p. 615

Relying on trend extension approaches for forecasting sales is a lot like going down a river in a canoe and steering the canoe
A. with help from radar equipment that detects obstacles before you get close to them.
B. only when you encounter a waterfall.
C. by looking backwards up the river.
D. based on a detailed map of the river someone else has drawn.
E. based on directions from others in the canoe who are looking ahead for rapids.

21-**71.**
D
Def.
Easy
p. 616

The factor method of sales forecasting tries to find a relation between the company's sales and:
A. industry sales.
B. how much working capital it needs.
C. national income.
D. some other factor (or factors).
E. the company's marketing mix.

21-**72.**
D
Comp.
Hard
p. 616

SALES & MARKETING MANAGEMENT'S "Buying Power Index" (BPI) reflects each geographic market's share of total U.S.:
A. population.
B. income.
C. retail sales.
D. All of the above.
E. Only A and C above.

21-**73.**
A
App.
Med.
p. 616

A marketing manager who uses SALES AND MARKETING MANAGEMENT'S "Buying Power Index" (BPI) to forecast sales is using the:
A. factor method (using several factors).
B. NAICS code method.
C. factor method (using one factor).
D. trend management method.
E. substitute method.

21-**74.**
D
Math.
Hard
p. 616

Tammy Patterson is the sales rep for an area with a "Buying Power Index" (BPI) of 0.45. If her firm's national sales forecast is $30,000,000, calculate a "reasonable" sales forecast for Tammy's area.

A. $900,000
B. $90,000
C. $666,666
D. $135,000
E. $1,350,000

21-**75.**
B
Def.
Easy
p. 619

A listing of the percent change in a firm's product-market sales for the last ten years is a:

A. BPI model.
B. time series.
C. factor file.
D. sales forecast.
E. Pareto chart.

21-**76.**
D
Def.
Med.
p. 619

A "leading series"

A. is a series of leaders.
B. simplifies trend extension when historical data is not available.
C. is usually qualitative, while a time series is quantitative.
D. is a time series which changes in the same direction but ahead of the series to be forecasted.
E. shows the sales of leading firms in major industries.

21-**77.**
A
Def.
Easy
p. 619

The hope of all sales forecasters is to find:

A. an accurate leading series.
B. a U-shaped sales curve.
C. a low buying power index.
D. a flat time series.
E. All of the above.

21-**78.**
E
App.
Hard
p. 619

A tractor dealer in Nebraska has noted that sales of new tractors go up or down about a month after the prime rate of interest for loans goes up or down. It appears that

A. this situation is not well suited to a forecast based on trend extension.
B. the manager should include the interest rate if he is trying to develop indices to use in forecasting.
C. interest rates are a leading series for new tractor sales.
D. he might be able to use time series techniques to develop a forecast.
E. All of the above are correct.

21-**79.**
C
Comp.
Med.
p. 620

The "jury-of-executive-opinion" sales forecasting approach has an advantage in that:

A. executives usually know about outside market forces.
B. no other quantitative estimates are necessary.
C. a forecast can be obtained quickly and easily.
D. past trends are usually ignored.
E. trend extension is minimized.

21-**80.**
E
Def.
Easy
p. 619

The "jury-of-executive-opinion" approach to sales forecasting combines the opinions of experienced executives from:
A. sales.
B. purchasing.
C. marketing.
D. finance.
E. Any or all of the above.

21-**81.**
B
Comp.
Med.
p. 620

The "jury-of-executive-opinion" approach to sales forecasting
A. is less accurate than trend extension.
B. can be done quickly.
C. is effective even if the individual executives aren't very well informed.
D. B and C are true.
E. All of the above are true.

21-**82.**
E
App.
Hard
p. 619-20

AgriGrow, Inc. is an agricultural research firm that develops and markets seeds for fast-growth crops. This product-market is in the growth stage of the product life cycle--and sales depend not only on the right marketing mix but also on a variety of other concerns such as competitors' new products, the weather, and ever-changing Federal farm subsidy programs. The AgriGrow marketing manager wants to develop a sales forecast, and in this situation
A. trend extension approaches are likely to yield the most accurate forecast.
B. NAICS codes can be used as factors.
C. the Survey of Buying Power (and the buying power index) should work well.
D. the best bet is to search for a leading series.
E. a jury of executive opinion is probably the best bet.

21-**83.**
E
App.
Hard
p. 620

Which of the following sales forecasting methods would be most appropriate when middlemen's reactions and competitors' activities are very important to sales?
A. The factor method
B. Jury of executive opinion
C. Use of a carefully selected "leading series"
D. Trend extension of past sales
E. Sales force estimates

21-**84.**
E
Comp.
Easy
p. 619-20

Sales forecasting using the jury of executive opinion, sales force estimates, and/or market tests may be especially useful when:
A. the company's marketing mix has changed a lot.
B. the company is introducing new products.
C. conditions are changing in the marketplace.
D. the company is in unstable, fluctuating markets.
E. All of the above.

21-**85.**
B
App.
Med.
p. 620

To OBJECTIVELY estimate how sales to present customers may change because of possible marketing mix changes, a marketing manager should use:
A. a jury of executive opinion.
B. a market test.
C. trend extension.
D. a sales force estimate.

21-**86.**
A
Comp.
Med.
p. 620-21

According to the text, the best approach for estimating the cost of various parts of a marketing plan is to:
- A. use the "task method."
- B. do a spreadsheet analysis to determine what combination of individual expenses sums to the desired overall budget.
- C. start with an estimate of the overall budget and then allocate a share (percent) of the total to each marketing activity.
- D. ask firms that are not competitors what similar marketing activities cost them.
- E. None of the above.

21-**87.**
D
Comp.
Med.
p. 626

A PERT chart is most likely to be useful for
- A. setting the marketing budget.
- B. mapping the firm's competitive position.
- C. forecasting sales.
- D. scheduling the implementation of the marketing plan.
- E. quality control in service operations.

21-**88.**
B
Comp.
Med.
p. 626

Which of the following is the best example of the type of information a marketing manager will need to use PERT in planning a new product introduction?
- A. The cost of new sales reps.
- B. How long it will take to hire 3 new sales reps.
- C. The type of sales presentation to use.
- D. The importance of personal selling for the relevant product class.
- E. None of the above is a good example.

21-**89.**
D
Comp.
Easy
p. 626

The critical path method (CPM) will be most useful to a marketing manager:
- A. for projecting when the product life cycle will go from stage to stage.
- B. for estimating the total cost of defective parts.
- C. in estimating how much competitors budget for critical marketing activities.
- D. in seeing that the critical activities of a marketing plan are completed on time.
- E. in selecting the best channel of distribution.

21-**90.**
A
Comp.
Med.
p. 626

Flowcharting approaches--such as CPM and PERT:
- A. require that all the tasks which must be done to reach a firm's objectives be identified "up front."
- B. show the actual starting and ending dates for all necessary activities.
- C. do not indicate how long a project will take to complete.
- D. require that all marketing activities must be done in sequence.
- E. All of the above.

21-**91.**
A
Def.
Easy
p. 627

"Marketing program" means:
- A. a "big" plan for implementing several marketing plans at the same time.
- B. a one-year marketing plan.
- C. a promotion plan.
- D. a detailed explanation of how to implement a marketing strategy.
- E. all the details of a marketing mix.

21-**92.**
E
Comp.
Easy
p. 621-27

A profit-oriented marketing manager seeking the "best" marketing program
  A. should find spreadsheet analysis helpful if many alternatives have to be evaluated.
  B. may use a "trial-and-error" approach with possible plans.
  C. must match potential revenues and profits with available resources.
  D. must rely on his own judgment--aided by some calculations.
  E. All of the above.

21-**93.**
E
Def.
Easy
p. 628

Selling products manufactured in the United States to foreign customers--often without any product changes--is called:
  A. joint ventures.
  B. licensing.
  C. importing.
  D. contract manufacturing.
  E. exporting.

21-**94.**
B
Comp.
Med.
p. 628

Which of the following is typically the lowest risk approach for moving into international markets:
  A. contract manufacturing
  B. exporting
  C. joint venturing
  D. wholly owned subsidiaries
  E. management contracting

21-**95.**
B
App.
Med.
p. 629

A producer that enters into a licensing agreement with a foreign company to better reach foreign customers is MOST likely to sell the rights to use its:
  A. production facilities.
  B. brand name.
  C. channels of distribution.
  D. sales force.
  E. Any of the above are equally likely.

21-**96.**
D
Comp.
Med.
p. 629

Licensing, in international marketing,
  A. refers to foreign middlemen agreeing to sell products produced in this country.
  B. requires a producer to pay a licensing fee to the country where it wants to sell its products.
  C. increases the risk that a company's production facilities will be taken over by the foreign country.
  D. means a company selling the right to use a process, trademark, patent, or other right for a fee or royalty.
  E. None of the above is true.

21-**97.**
B
Int.
Med.
p. 629

Which of the following is the easiest way for a firm to enter foreign markets?
  A. joint ventures
  B. licensing
  C. multinational bargaining
  D. contract manufacturing
  E. wholly-owned subsidiaries

21-**98.**
A
Def.
Easy
p. 629

_____ (as a way to enter foreign markets) means selling the right to use some process, trademark, patent, or other right for a fee.
A. licensing
B. contract manufacturing
C. subsidiaring
D. joint venturing
E. exporting

21-**99.**
A
App.
Med.
p. 629

If Wilkinson were to sell Norelco the exclusive rights to produce and sell its brand of shavers in Japan for a 5 percent royalty on all sales, it would be using:
A. licensing.
B. joint venturing.
C. management contracting.
D. exporting.
E. contract manufacturing.

21-**100.**
D
Comp.
Med.
p. 629

A firm can take advantage of lower cost local labor in a foreign market and still control foreign distribution and sales by using
A. licensing.
B. exporting.
C. joint venturing.
D. contract manufacturing.
E. wholly owned subsidiaries.

21-**101.**
D
Def.
Med.
p. 629

When a producer enters a foreign market by turning over production to a foreign firm--while doing marketing itself--it is using:
A. exporting.
B. joint venturing.
C. management contracting.
D. contract manufacturing.
E. licensing.

21-**102.**
E
App.
Med.
p. 629

To avoid foreign labor problems, Niagara, Inc. has foreign firms manufacture its patented products while Niagara retains full control of marketing in those foreign countries. Niagara is involved in:
A. management contracting.
B. joint venturing.
C. licensing.
D. exporting.
E. contract manufacturing.

21-**103.**
B
Comp.
Med.
p. 629

If a producer agrees to enter into a management contracting arrangement with a zinc mining operation in Chile,
A. the company should be prepared to invest large amounts in mining facilities.
B. the company should be prepared to send people to Chile.
C. success will depend on how well the Chilean managers know what needs to be done.
D. the company must assume no political problems will arise, otherwise the risk is very high.
E. None of the above is true.

21-**104.**
A
App.
Med.
p. 629

Worldwide Drilling, Inc. of Fort Worth, Texas, operates an oil well in Russia for its owners. Worldwide is involved in:
A. management contracting.
B. exporting.
C. contract manufacturing.
D. a joint venture.
E. licensing.

21-**105.**
E
Def.
Easy
p. 629

If a firm's involvement in international marketing is limited to managing others' production facilities, it is using:
A. exporting.
B. licensing.
C. contract manufacturing.
D. joint venturing.
E. management contracting.

21-**106.**
E
App.
Med.
p. 629-30

Oceanside Tools, Inc. of Newport, Rhode Island has agreed to work with a Thai company to produce and sell chemicals in Thailand. The U.S. firm will provide technical and marketing know-how, while its Thai partner will provide knowledge of Thai markets and political connections. The partners will share the costs and profits 50/50. This type of international involvement is called:
A. contract manufacturing.
B. management contracting.
C. licensing.
D. multinational marketing.
E. joint venturing.

21-**107.**
D
App.
Med.
p. 630

Midwest Tools, Inc. of Indianapolis, Indiana owns a plant in Poland for manufacturing and selling machine tools in Europe. This type of international involvement is called:
A. contract manufacturing.
B. licensing.
C. a joint venture.
D. a wholly-owned subsidiary.
E. management contracting.

21-**108.**
D
Comp.
Med.
p. 630

A multinational corporation:
A. sells patents to foreign firms.
B. earns over 50 percent of its profits in international markets.
C. is any corporation involved in international markets.
D. has investments in several countries and makes its major decisions on a global basis.
E. All of the above.

21-**109.**
B
Def.
Easy
p. 630

Companies which have a direct investment in several countries and run their businesses depending on the choices available anywhere in the world are:
A. contract manufacturers.
B. multinational corporations.
C. exporters.
D. licensers.
E. management contractors.

21-110.
C
Comp.
Hard
p. 631

What do firms like Eastman Kodak, Shell, Honda, Gillette, IBM, and Goodyear have in common?
   A. They are all American companies.
   B. They all earn more than 80 percent of their sales and profits in foreign markets.
   C. They are all multinational corporations.
   D. They all can use the SALES AND MARKETING MANAGEMENT'S BPI to estimate sales potential in foreign markets.
   E. All of the above.

21-111.
A
Comp.
Med.
p. 631

Multinational corporations:
   A. see world market opportunities.
   B. locate their major production and distribution facilities in their "home" countries.
   C. are companies that do a lot of importing and exporting.
   D. All of the above are true.
   E. None of the above is true.

21-112.
C
App.
Med.
p. 631

Which of the following BEST illustrates a multinational corporation?
   A. Faced with decreasing sales in its domestic market, CrocDun, Ltd. of Australia is trying to sell its swollen inventory of hunting knives at "special prices" in the United States.
   B. A large U.S. chain is importing products from China.
   C. To be more competitive in the European market, U.S. firms are buying or setting up factories in Germany and France.
   D. Chrysler has licensed a Japanese firm to produce and sell cars in Africa.
   E. All of the above.

21-113.
A
App.
Med.
p. 631

Which of the following BEST illustrates a MULTINATIONAL CORPORATION?
   A. P&G recently opened new production facilities in Mexico to meet needs in Latin America.
   B. Chick-Filet, a fast-food franchise operation out of Atlanta, Georgia has licensed a firm in Jamaica to operate five Chick-Filet restaurants.
   C. Peachtree, Inc. exported $500,000 of peaches from South Carolina to Canada.
   D. Java, Inc. recently purchased a carload of coffee beans from Colombia.
   E. All of the above are good examples.

21-114.
D
Comp.
Med.
p. 631

A multinational company differs from a major exporter in that:
   A. the exporter is concerned with foreign policy primarily as it affects his sales.
   B. the multinational does not make decisions based on his home country's perspective.
   C. the multinational considers every aspect of the business from a global perspective.
   D. All of the above are differences.
   E. None of the above is true.

Chapter 22

Ethical Marketing in a Consumer-Oriented World: Appraisal and Challenges

True-False Questions:

22-1.
True
p. 637

When evaluating marketing, it is best to evaluate micro-marketing and macro-marketing separately.

22-2.
True
p. 637

In the United States, the aim of the economic system has been to satisfy consumers' needs as they--the consumers--see them.

22-3.
True
p. 637-38

At the macro level, consumer satisfaction is difficult to measure because there is no practical way to measure economic utility.

22-4.
False
p. 638-39

At the macro level, consumer satisfaction can easily and objectively be measured using the practical methods already available to measure time, possession, form and place utilities.

22-5.
False
p. 639

Consumer satisfaction at the micro level cannot be measured because firms cannot determine how well their products satisfy customers.

22-6.
False
p. 640

According to the text, micro-marketing does NOT cost too much in the United States--but macro-marketing often DOES cost too much.

22-7.
True
p. 640

Micro-marketing often does cost too much because many firms improperly blend the four Ps and misunderstand both their customers and the marketing environment that affects their operation.

22-8.
True
p. 640

Using total quality management to implement marketing plans is one way to improve a marketing mix.

22-9.
True
p. 640

Making sure that the customer benefits of a marketing mix exceed the customer's costs of obtaining those benefits is one way to gain a competitive advantage.

22-**10.**
False
p. 640

Aggressive spending on promotion can usually make up for other types of mistakes.

22-**11.**
False
p. 642

Monopolistic competition is the result of control of markets by business, not consumer demands.

22-**12.**
True
p. 642

Monopolistic competition is caused by customer preferences, not business manipulation of markets.

22-**13.**
False
p. 643

Monopolistic competition may result in high costs--and therefore it does not do a good job of serving consumers the way they want to be served.

22-**14.**
True
p. 643

Micro-marketing efforts help the economy grow by stimulating innovation.

22-**15.**
True
p. 643

Advertising is probably the most criticized of all micro-marketing activities.

22-**16.**
False
p. 643

According to the text, the proper function of marketing is to persuade consumers to buy what firms want to sell.

22-**17.**
False
p. 643

A marketing manager who is willing to spend enough on persuasive promotion can usually get consumers to buy anything the company chooses to produce.

22-**18.**
True
p. 643

People have always been materialistic, even in the most primitive societies.

22-**19.**
False
p. 644-45

The text argues that the plight of the homeless is a result of the forces of market competition in our market-directed economies.

22-**20.**
False
p. 645-47

A good business manager should adhere to the idea "if it ain't broke, don't fix it."

22-**21.**
True
p. 647

The text argues that international competition will actually improve macro-marketing systems worldwide.

22-**22.**
False
p. 650

The legal environment sets the maximum standards of ethical behavior in a society.

22-23.
True
p. 650

The legal environment sets the minimum standards of ethical behavior in a society.

22-24.
True
p. 650-51

Consumers--as well as business firms--should behave in a more socially responsible manner to improve the performance of our macro-marketing system.

22-25.
True
p. 652

In the future, consumers' needs will probably become more subtle.

Multiple Choice Questions

22-26.
A
Def.
Easy
p. 637

Given the nature of marketing--and the kinds of criticism it typically gets--marketing should be evaluated:
A. at both the micro and the macro level.
B. mainly at the macro level.
C. mainly at the micro level.
D. None of the above.

22-27.
C
Comp.
Hard
p. 637

When evaluating the effectiveness of the macro-marketing systems of different countries,
A. the evaluation should be limited to basic economic objectives which are common across countries.
B. the best approach is to see if firms are making a profit.
C. it doesn't make sense to try to compare the effectiveness of systems for different nations that have different objectives.
D. the evaluation should be based on how well each system satisfies consumers' needs as they--the consumers--see them.
E. All of the above are true.

22-28.
D
Comp.
Med.
p. 637

The basic objective of the U.S. market-directed economic system is to:
A. ensure the survival of business firms.
B. find a reasonable balance between consumer satisfaction and business profits.
C. reduce the cost of marketing activities.
D. satisfy consumer needs as the consumers themselves see them.
E. satisfy consumer needs as seen by marketing managers.

22-29.
B
Def.
Med.
p. 637

The basic objective of the U.S. market-directed economic system is to:
A. minimize inflation.
B. satisfy consumer needs as they--the consumers--see them.
C. provide each person with an equal share of the economic output.
D. achieve an annual growth rate of at least 10 percent.
E. make the most efficient use of the country's resources.

22-30.
E
Comp.
Med.
p. 637-38

Given the U.S. economy's basic objective, the best measure of the effectiveness of the U.S. macro-marketing system is:
A. GNP growth.
B. the equality of income distribution.
C. how efficiently resources are used.
D. how many new products are introduced.
E. the level of consumer satisfaction.

22-31.
A
Comp.
Med.
p. 637-38

Given the American economy's basic objective of meeting consumers' needs as THEY--the consumers--see them, it is sensible to evaluate our MACRO-marketing system in terms of:
A. the level of consumer satisfaction.
B. how efficiently our resources are used.
C. the value of the inputs to the system.
D. our standard of living--as measured by GNP.
E. total business profits.

22-32.
B
Comp.
Med.
p. 638-39

Measuring macro consumer satisfaction:
A. is easy--just estimate the economic utility provided by all the marketing mixes.
B. is difficult because consumer satisfaction depends on the level of consumer aspiration.
C. must be done quantitatively.
D. uses MIS techniques.
E. None of the above is true.

22-33.
D
Comp.
Med.
p. 638-39

Consumer satisfaction:
A. is a highly reliable standard for evaluating macro-marketing effectiveness.
B. is easy to measure because it is a highly personal concept.
C. is the objective of all macro-marketing systems.
D. depends on consumers' level of expectation.
E. None of the above is true.

22-34.
A
Comp.
Med.
p. 639

When evaluating macro-marketing:
A. the evaluation is necessarily subjective.
B. the best approach is to consider the profit generated by individual firms within the overall system.
C. one must determine how efficiently the society's resources are used.
D. one must consider each individual firm's role in the marketing system.
E. All of the above are true.

22-35.
A
Comp.
Med.
p. 639

MACRO-marketing:
A. is probably best evaluated by how individual consumer-citizens vote.
B. can be evaluated with quantitative measures of consumer satisfaction.
C. is concerned with how efficiently individual companies use their resources.
D. is easier to evaluate than micro-marketing.
E. All of the above.

22-**36.**
C
Comp.
Easy
p. 639

MICRO-marketing effectiveness is _____ to measure than MACRO-marketing effectiveness.
A. harder
B. not any easier or harder
C. easier

22-**37.**
E
Comp.
Easy
p. 639

MICRO-marketing effectiveness can be measured by:
A. the profits of business firms.
B. the opinions of middlemen.
C. consumer complaints.
D. attitude research studies.
E. All of the above.

22-**38.**
A
Comp.
Med.
p. 639

Satisfaction with a firm's marketing efforts can be roughly measured by
A. its profit.
B. the firm's impact on the macro-marketing system.
C. the size of its target markets.
D. All of the above are true.
E. None of the above is true.

22-**39.**
C
Def.
Med.
p. 640

According to the text:
A. macro-marketing costs too much in the United States--given the current objective.
B. marketing never costs too much.
C. micro-marketing often does cost too much.
D. micro-marketing always costs too much.
E. all macro-marketing systems cost too much.

22-**40.**
D
Def.
Easy
p. 640

According to the text:
A. both micro-marketing and macro-marketing usually cost too much.
B. neither micro-marketing nor macro-marketing costs too much.
C. macro-marketing costs too much in the United States.
D. micro-marketing often costs too much.

22-**41.**
B
Comp.
Med.
p. 640

A study revealed that when consumers are dissatisfied with a product or an individual business
A. most of their complaints are fully resolved--if they are just reported.
B. a majority of their complaints are never reported.
C. a marketing manager should just ignore most complaints because they are the result of dealing with consumers.
D. All of the above are true.
E. None of the above is true.

22-42.
D
Comp.
Hard
p. 640

A marketing manager should
A. know that most consumer complaints do not require a response because the consumer's dissatisfaction is beyond the control of the firm.
B. recognize that many consumers who complain are trouble makers and that not much can or should be done about their complaints.
C. assume that most customers who are dissatisfied will complain, but that people who are satisfied will be silent.
D. be concerned that many of the complaints that are reported are never resolved.
E. recognize that a "complaint" box isn't needed if the firm is really market-oriented in the first place.

22-43.
D
App.
Med.
p. 640-41

Which of the following is NOT an explanation for why MICRO-marketing may cost too much in some firms?
A. Some managers feel that customers are eagerly awaiting any product they produce.
B. Production managers focus on designing products that are easy to make.
C. Financial managers reduce finished-product inventories and force "out of stock" situations.
D. Marketing managers do target marketing.
E. Some managers don't see a business as a "total system" focused on customers.

22-44.
E
Comp.
Easy
p. 640-41

MICRO-marketing may cost "too much" because of:
A. advertising that is not targeted.
B. inefficient distribution channels.
C. cost-plus pricing.
D. production-oriented product planning.
E. Any or all of the above.

22-45.
E
Comp.
Med.
p. 640

Which of the following is NOT likely to cause micro-marketing to cost "too much?"
A. A company with a poorly designed product relies on aggressive promotion to try to "get rid of the product."
B. Sales managers who stick with "old" channel relationships.
C. Ad campaigns selected for "creative" appeal, without support from marketing research.
D. Reliance on cost-plus pricing.
E. ALL of the above can cause micro-marketing to cost "too much."

22-46.
A
Comp.
Med.
p. 641-42

The reason that MICRO-marketing costs too much in many firms is that:
A. the marketing concept has not been accepted and implemented.
B. most new products are not necessary to meet competition.
C. marketing is not really needed.
D. advertising is usually ineffective.
E. None of the above--marketing never costs too much.

22-47.
E
App.
Easy
p. 641-42

MICRO-marketing will probably continue to cost too much as long as:
A. the marketing concept is not accepted.
B. traditional middlemen resist change.
C. firms do "mass marketing."
D. some managers believe that anyone can run a business successfully.
E. All of the above.

22-**48.**
C
Def.
Easy
p. 642

The text argues that MACRO-marketing in the United States:
A. costs too much because many consumers are dissatisfied.
B. is a growing concept.
C. does not cost too much.
D. tends to decrease consumer welfare.
E. costs too much because satisfying consumers costs too much.

22-**49.**
D
Comp.
Med.
p. 642-43

Most critics of marketing who argue that marketing managers help create monopoly or monopolistic competition feel this leads to:
A. restriction of output.
B. higher prices.
C. reduction in the national income.
D. All of the above
E. None of the above.

22-**50.**
A
Comp.
Hard
p. 643

When companies in a market-directed economy try to find "little monopolies" for themselves,
A. success is likely to attract more competitors--and squeezing of the innovators' profits.
B. they will fail.
C. this reduces innovation, new investment, and economic growth.
D. the allocation of resources will be the same as in a purely competitive economy.
E. this forces consumers to buy new--possibly more expensive--products that they do not want.

22-**51.**
B
Comp.
Med.
p. 642

Monopolistic competition--which is typical in our market-directed economy--is caused by:
A. manipulation of markets by business firms.
B. customer preferences.
C. consumers' unwillingness to pay for differentiated products.
D. All of the above.
E. None of the above.

22-**52.**
C
Comp.
Hard
p. 642

The monopolistic competition that is typical of the U.S. economy
A. always leads to higher prices, but it may not lead to higher consumer satisfaction.
B. is a problem because it does not result in products that reflect consumer's social values.
C. is the result of consumer preferences.
D. is the result of manipulation of markets by business firms.
E. All of the above are true.

22-**53.**
E
Comp.
Med.
p. 643

Advertising
A. always results in higher prices for products.
B. is a waste of resources.
C. costs so much that it reduces the chance to achieve economies of scale in production.
D. guarantees a product's success.
E. None of the above is true.

22-**54.**
C
Int.
Med.
p. 643

Regarding our MACRO-marketing system:
A. consumers would be better off if our macro-marketing system were in pure competition--rather than monopolistic competition.
B. marketing makes people buy things they don't need.
C. advertising can actually lower final consumer prices--if it helps achieve economies of scale.
D. monopolistic competition leads to higher prices, restriction of output, a waste of resources, and greater consumer dissatisfaction.
E. All of the above.

22-**55.**
E
Def.
Easy
p. 643

Regarding our MACRO-marketing system, advertising:
A. creates jobs and raises personal incomes.
B. may lower final consumer prices if it results in economies of scale.
C. encourages innovation.
D. stimulates investment and generates economic growth.
E. All of the above.

22-**56.**
D
Comp.
Med.
p. 643

According to your text, critics of advertising
A. argue that it lowers consumer prices--and thus results in "less than satisfactory" profits for firms.
B. often overrate the positive effect that monopolistic competition can have on the economy.
C. who think that a lot of advertising is annoying simply don't know what they're talking about.
D. claim that firms use clever ads to persuade consumers to buy whatever the firms want to sell.
E. base their evaluation on fears that advertising increases economies of scale.

22-**57.**
D
Int.
Med.
p. 643

Regarding our MACRO-marketing system:
A. marketing makes people materialistic by creating "false values."
B. advertising generally raises prices and wastes resources.
C. marketing tries to satisfy "unwanted demand" rather than "genuine wants."
D. satisfying consumer needs and wants is a dynamic, on-going process.
E. none of the above.

22-**58.**
D
Comp.
Easy
p. 644

Marketing:
A. creates materialistic values which did not exist before.
B. turns consumers into puppets.
C. seeks to create "unwanted demand" rather than satisfy "genuine needs."
D. reflects existing social values in the short run--while reinforcing these values in the long run.
E. All of the above.

22-**59.**
C
App.
Easy
p. 646

Which of the following is NOT a trend this is affecting marketing strategy planning?
A. growth of JIT and ECR.
B. struggles of post-communist economies.
C. less attention to distribution service.
D. more attention to quality.
E. faster new-product development.

22-**60.**
B
App.
Easy
p. 646

Which of the following is NOT a trend that is affecting marketing strategy planning?
A. more attention to targeted media.
B. focus on lower stockturns at higher margins.
C. slower real income growth in U.S.
D. growth of mass-merchandising.
E. growth of larger, more powerful retail chains.

22-**61.**
A
App.
Easy
p. 646

Which of the following is NOT a trend that is affecting marketing strategy planning?
A. fewer vertical marketing systems.
B. geographic shifts in population.
C. more attention to service technologies.
D. growing role of cross-channel logistics coordination.
E. greater use of database-directed promotion.

22-**62.**
D
App.
Easy
p. 646

Which of the following is NOT a current trend affecting marketing strategy planning?
A. growth of interactive agencies.
B. less regulation of business.
C. growth of intranet and DSS systems.
D. declining use of interactive bidding and proposal requests in organizational purchasing.
E. aging of the baby boomers.

22-**63.**
E
App.
Easy
p. 646

Which of the following is NOT a current trend affecting marketing strategy planning?
A. more attention to environmental issues.
B. growth of ethnic submarkets.
C. collapse of many dot-com startups.
D. growth of teen submarket.
E. shift from an emphasis on exporting of current products to diversification.

22-**64.**
A
App.
Easy
p. 646

Which of the following is NOT a current trend affecting marketing strategy planning?
A. slower new-product development.
B. growth of value pricing.
C. HTML e-mail and instant messaging.
D. more attention to profitability, not just sales.
E. international expansion by retailers.

22-**65.**
E
Int.
Easy
p. 647-51

Improving both micro-marketing and macro-marketing may require:
A. tougher enforcement of present laws.
B. better-informed and more socially responsible consumers.
C. more attention to consumer privacy.
D. more social responsibility by businesses.
E. All of the above.

22-**66.**
B
Int.
Med.
p. 650-51

Better performance of our market-directed MACRO-marketing system may require:
A. newer and tougher laws--because the present laws don't protect competitors enough.
B. more consumer responsibility.
C. less emphasis on consumer privacy.
D. None of the above.

22-**67.**
A
Comp.
Easy
p. 651

If we accept "consumer satisfaction" as the objective of our MACRO-marketing system, this means that:
    A. each consumer should decide how best to satisfy his or her own wants.
    B. government planners should choose the kinds of products to be produced.
    C. "home economists" will be the best judges of what should be produced.
    D. not every consumer should be allowed to decide his or her own wants.
    E. consumer educators should choose what products should be produced.

22-**68.**
B
Comp.
Med.
p. 651

Regarding our MACRO-marketing system, the text suggests that:
    A. consumers' freedom of choice should be reduced--for the good of society.
    B. some changes may be necessary--but consumer-citizens should vote on these changes.
    C. marketing managers should limit consumers' freedom of choice.
    D. marketing people may not be necessary in the future.
    E. All of the above.

22-**69.**
C
Int.
Hard
p. 651-52

The best way to improve the operation of our MACRO-marketing system--given the current objectives of our society--is:
    A. to encourage marketing managers to produce only what they feel is good for consumers.
    B. to eliminate the middlemen.
    C. to do better marketing strategy planning and implementation.
    D. to spend more on advertising.
    E. to move toward a centrally planned economy.

22-**70.**
E
App.
Easy
p. 651-52

Suppose you were able to start new cities on a planet in outer space. Suppose also that these cities will be self-supporting. Further, they will be democratic--with the objective of maximizing consumer welfare--measured by the level of consumer satisfaction. The economic decisions will be made through the "market mechanism." Which of the following statements might be made by some of the settlers?
    A. "The price of food is too high."
    B. "Middlemen should be eliminated."
    C. "Advertising expenditures are too high."
    D. "Marketing costs too much."
    E. All of the above are likely to be made.

22-**71.**
D
Comp.
Hard
p. 652

Regarding the future of marketing, the text suggests that:
    A. marketing managers should decide whether it is in consumers' best interests before their firms produce new products.
    B. continued growth of GNP is a MUST for our macro-marketing system.
    C. marketing will be regulated less in the future.
    D. marketing people may be even more necessary in the future--especially if consumers begin to value the "quality of life" more than material goods.
    E. All of the above are true.

22-**72.**
E
Comp.
Easy
p. 644-52

The future poses many challenges for marketing managers because:
    A. international competition makes it even harder to gain a competitive advantage.
    B. consumers' needs are becoming more subtle.
    C. the needs of the disadvantaged are not yet being met very successfully.
    D. environmental damage is no longer a hidden cost.
    E. all of the above.

NOTE TO INSTRUCTOR: The remaining questions in this chapter are all based on MARKETING CASE ANALYSIS. They require students to read and analyze short marketing cases--and then identify and apply concepts learned in previous chapters of the text. Because these are all application questions, we have not classified them according to level of difficulty. Most of the questions are "medium" in difficulty.

NOTE THAT THESE QUESTIONS DO NOT NECESSARILY COVER MATERIAL THAT WAS DISCUSSED IN CHAPTER 22. In general, these are integrating questions based on material discussed in previous chapters. Thus, these questions are well suited for use on a final examination.

Read the following case carefully before answering questions 22-73 through 22-81.

JEWEL CRAFT, INC.

Jewel Craft, Inc. is a leading producer in the United States women's costume jewelry and accessories market. Its brands are well known and are sold by department stores and better women's stores. Several stores in a city may carry Jewel Craft's brands because most of Jewel Craft's customers will not consider any other brand.

Jewel Craft's sales force calls on one wholesaler in each state. Gemco, Inc., of Boston, Massachusetts, is the Jewel Craft distributor in that state. Gemco stocks and sells women's accessories (noncompeting lines) for several manufacturers like Jewel Craft. Wholesalers are allowed a 20 percent markup by Jewel Craft--but pay the freight charges to their warehouses. Jewel Craft's policy of using one wholesaler per state comes from its desire to control its distribution. Jewel Craft uses national magazine advertising and also supports a cooperative ad program with retailers.

Jewel Craft's prices allow for a 40 percent retail markup--an attractive percent when one considers that Jewel Craft's products require little in-store selling because of their well-established reputation.

Recently, Jewel Craft was approached by a watch producer with the idea of expanding to watches under the Jewel Craft name. It was argued that although national watch sales have leveled off, Jewel Craft could enjoy growing sales for several years because of the fine reputation the company has achieved. If watches are added, Jewel Craft will use its present policies regarding distribution, pricing, and advertising. Further, it will offer the wholesalers and retailers an attractive "package" deal as an incentive to carry Jewel Craft watches. Middlemen will be required to carry the watches if they wish to handle the jewelry and accessories.

22-73.
E
App.
Med.

Jewel Craft jewelry and accessories would be in which product class--given the information in the case?
  A. Homogeneous shopping product
  B. Staple product
  C. Convenience product
  D. Impulse product
  E. Specialty product

22-**74.**
D
App.
Med.

Gemco, Inc. is a:
A. commission merchant.
B. selling agent.
C. manufacturers' agent.
D. merchant wholesaler.
E. manufacturer's sales branch.

22-**75.**
C
App.
Med.

Jewel Craft's distribution policy--at the wholesale level--is:
A. selective distribution.
B. direct distribution.
C. exclusive distribution.
D. intensive distribution.
E. for the wholesaler to be the channel captain.

22-**76.**
D
App.
Med.

Jewel Craft's distribution policy--at the retail level--seems to be:
A. direct distribution.
B. exclusive distribution.
C. intensive distribution.
D. selective distribution.

22-**77.**
C
App.
Med.

A sales invoice sent by Jewel Craft to Gemco is MOST LIKELY to include the following item:
A. F.O.B. buyer's warehouse.
B. F.O.B. seller's factory--freight prepaid.
C. F.O.B. seller's factory.
D. F.O.B. delivered.

22-**78.**
D
App.
Med.

When selling Jewel Craft's jewelry and accessories, a retail clerk's major role usually would be:
A. missionary selling.
B. supporting selling.
C. retailing.
D. order taking.
E. order getting.

22-**79.**
B
App.
Med.

The degree of brand familiarity for Jewel Craft products--among its present consumer buyers--is:
A. no brand recognition.
B. brand insistence.
C. brand preference.
D. brand rejection.
E. brand recognition.

22-**80.**
E
App.
Med.

Jewel Craft's selling price for an item which retails for $10 would be:
A. $5.20.
B. $7.00.
C. $8.00.
D. $6.00.
E. $4.80.

22-**81.**
B
App.
Med.

If Jewel Craft adds the watch line, which federal law might be most directly violated if it carries out its plan to require middlemen to handle BOTH the watches and the jewelry?

   A. Robinson-Patman Act
   B. Clayton Act
   C. Sherman Act
   D. Wheeler-Lea Amendment
   E. Magnuson-Moss Act

Read the following case and then answer questions 22-82 through 22-91.

CONSERVO PRODUCTS, INC. (CPI)

CPI, with annual sales of $200 million, is a well-known producer of a variety of paper products, almost all of which are made from recycled materials. Picnic plates account for about 70 percent of CPI's sales. The rest of the firm's sales comes from custom-designed materials--such as box liners and spacers, small boxes, and disposable products--like trays, towels and napkins.

CPI's picnic plates are sold through "sales reps" to grocery wholesalers and retail grocery chains. The sales reps are paid a 5 percent commission on all sales in their assigned territories. They usually handle related--but noncompeting--lines for several other manufacturers. Along with their selling duties, the sales reps help CPI with local advertising and sales promotion efforts.

Orders for the custom products are obtained by area managers who are paid a straight salary to call on business and institutional customers. The area managers are trained paper specialists and often help their customers design the products they order.

The picnic plates are priced to give CPI a 90 percent markup on the cost of producing the product--with the cost figured by taking the total factory cost for the previous year and dividing that total cost by the number of units produced and sold during that period. The firm's invoices read "F.O.B.--Delivered" and "1/10, net 30." Customers are allowed to deduct 3 percent from the face value of the invoice for buying plates in carload quantities, and another 2 percent for advertising them locally.

The custom products are sold "F.O.B. mill"--with CPI offering a price for each job. Competition is strong from many other manufacturers who are able to offer very similar products which meet the customers' specifications.

CPI forecasts that sales will increase to $250 million by 1999. However, much of this growth is tied to picnic plates--a market in which the firm has about a 7 percent market share and faces aggressive price competition from many smaller firms with greater brand familiarity. Further, CPI has been late with more than 50 percent of its plate orders due to scheduling conflicts with orders for custom products.

22-**82.**
E
App.
Med.

CPI's product line includes:
- A. only convenience products.
- B. impulse products and natural products.
- C. specialty products and supplies.
- D. shopping products and raw materials.
- E. staple products and component parts.

22-**83.**
A
App.
Med.

The picnic plates seem to be in the _____ stage of the product life cycle.
- A. market maturity
- B. market growth
- C. market introduction
- D. sales decline

22-**84.**
A
App.
Med.

For the picnic plates, CPI seems to be facing:
- A. monopolistic competition approaching pure competition.
- B. a pure monopoly situation.
- C. pure competition.
- D. monopolistic competition approaching pure monopoly.
- E. an oligopoly situation.

22-**85.**
E
App.
Med.

CPI uses:
- A. a direct-to-customer channel system for all its products.
- B. dual distribution.
- C. an indirect channel system for all its products.
- D. a direct-to-customer channel system for the plates and an indirect channel system for the custom products.
- E. an indirect channel system for the plates and a direct-to-customer channel system for the custom products.

22-**86.**
A
App.
Med.

The "sales reps" who sell CPI's plates are:
- A. manufacturers' agents.
- B. limited-function wholesalers.
- C. the firm's own order takers.
- D. selling agents.
- E. merchant wholesalers.

22-**87.**
D
App.
Med.

For its plates, CPI uses _____ pricing.
- A. flexible
- B. demand-oriented
- C. target return
- D. average-cost
- E. penetration

22-**88.**
E
App.
Med.

CPI offers the grocery wholesalers and retail chains:
- A. cumulative quantity discounts.
- B. All of the above.
- C. P.M.'s
- D. brokerage allowances.
- E. cash discounts for paying their bills quickly.

22-**89.**
A
App.
Med.

Regarding shipping costs:
A. CPI pays the shipping costs for the plates, while its customers pay the shipping costs for the custom products.
B. CPI uses freight-absorption pricing.
C. all of CPI's customers take title to the products at the point of loading and pay all shipping costs themselves.
D. CPI pays the shipping costs for all its customers--keeping title to the products until delivery.
E. CPI uses zone pricing.

22-**90.**
E
App.
Med.

For the custom products, CPI uses _____ pricing.
A. demand-backward
B. penetration
C. average-cost
D. target-return
E. bid

22-**91.**
D
App.
Med.

CPI's sales forecasts for picnic plates are not likely to be achieved unless the firm can improve its:
A. pioneering advertising.
B. paper coating machines.
C. below-average product quality.
D. customer service level.
E. above-the-market prices.

Read the following case and then answer questions 22-92 through 22-98.

SURE FOOT, LTD.

Sure Foot, Ltd. produces high-quality shoes and boots for serious hikers.

Sure Foot's shoes have suggested retail prices ranging from just under $40 to about $150. Usually, the retailer buys the shoes for about 50 percent less than the list price, and the retailer pays the freight charges from Sure Foot's plant in Maine. Sure Foot's credit terms are 2/10, net 30. Although Sure Foot's brand appears on every shoe--the firm does very little mass selling, except for a limited program of cooperative advertising and some sales promotion at walking events.

Sure Foot's shoes are carried by "better" sporting goods stores all across the nation--although usually in fairly small quantities. Its main showroom is in Boston, where two salaried salespeople handle most of the firm's large accounts. Sure Foot's products are also sold by seven independent "field reps" who are paid a 5 percent commission on all sales. Each of these field reps is responsible for a several state territory--emphasizing mostly the small stores in or near major cities. The field reps carry Sure Foot's products as a minor line--but none of their lines are competitive with each other.

The walking shoe market is supplied by 7 large firms and 50 or more smaller firms. While these firms are competitive, they do vary their materials, styles, prices, and promotion. The "high-quality" market is supplied by only 5 firms--Sure Foot being the largest. While these firms are also competitive, they generally offer a more limited assortment of materials, styles, and prices because the "high-quality" part of the market is not as large--and does not appear to be growing any more.

22-**92.**
C
App.
Med.

How are Sure Foot's shoes seen by most of its target market?
A. Impulse products
B. Staple products
C. Heterogeneous shopping products
D. Homogeneous shopping products
E. Specialty products

22-**93.**
A
App.
Med.

Assuming that Sure Foot wants to be in only the "better" stores--and mainly in large metropolitan areas--it seems to be seeking:
A. selective distribution.
B. exclusive distribution.
C. intensive distribution.

22-**94.**
D
App.
Med.

Sure Foot's "field reps" are:
A. selling agents.
B. missionary salespeople.
C. brokers.
D. manufacturers' agents.
E. merchant wholesalers.

22-**95.**
A
App.
Med.

The nature of competition in the hiking shoe market is:
A. monopolistic competition
B. monopoly
C. oligopoly
D. pure competition
E. Both A and B.

22-**96.**
C
App.
Med.

Sure Foot's geographic terms are probably:
A. F.O.B. freight allowed.
B. F.O.B. buyer's factory.
C. F.O.B. shipping point.
D. F.O.B. delivered.
E. None of the above--Sure Foot uses zone pricing.

22-**97.**
D
App.
Med.

"Credit terms" of 2/10, net 30 mean that Sure Foot is offering customers a:
A. functional discount.
B. quantity discount.
C. seasonal discount.
D. cash discount.
E. cooperative advertising allowance.

22-**98.**
A
App.
Med.

Sure Foot is probably in what stage of the product life cycle in the "high quality" market?
A. Market maturity
B. Market growth
C. Market introduction
D. Sales decline

Read the following case before answering questions 22-99 through 22-106.

ELECTECH, INC. (EI)

EI produces a line of semiconductors for electronics products manufacturers. These items range in price from $5-$100 and are used in products the buyer is producing. EI also designs and builds computer networking equipment. The prices of these items range form $5,000 to $100,000. These are used to control production equipment. Usually, they are custom-made to the specifications of the buyer--the firm which will use the product in its own production process.

EI sells nationally through independent sales reps--paid on commission--who work in the large industrial centers across the country. EI is more concerned with the quality of these reps than with the number of them. All of them also sell other lines. EI also uses five full-time salaried salespeople who work out of its corporate headquarters under a sales manager.

The home office salespeople are "technical specialists" who sell almost all the networking equipment, while the "reps" mostly sell the semiconductors. Sometimes, however, the reps will send in leads to customers who want networking equipment. EI also sells some of its semiconductors through a Los Angeles wholesaler who carries stock for West Coast customers.

There are many producers and importers of semiconductors in the U.S.--but several firms have captured large shares of the networking equipment market. EI has held its own, and in fact, over the past five years has increased its market share of these products to over 25 percent--because of its better technical designs.

Industry-wide prices of the more or less homogeneous semiconductors have been forced further and further down over the last seven years--as have industry profits. The price of networking equipment is set by adding a standard markup percent to the direct cost of the items--for overhead and for profit. Following industry practice, all prices are quoted at the seller's factory.

EI publishes a catalog which is revised periodically. And it exhibits in most equipment trade shows.

22-**99.**
C
App.
Med.

What kind of products are EI's semiconductors FOR MOST CUSTOMERS?
  A. Supplies
  B. Installations
  C. Component parts
  D. Accessory equipment
  E. Raw materials

22-**100.**
B
App.
Med.

What kind of products are EI's networking equipment?
  A. Component parts
  B. Accessory equipment
  C. Installations
  D. Raw materials
  E. Supplies

22-**101.**
D
App.
Med.

EI's independent sales reps are:
A. selling agents.
B. rack jobbers.
C. specialty wholesalers.
D. manufacturers' agents.
E. desk jobbers.

22-**102.**
A
App.
Med.

What kind of distribution is EI seeking for its networking equipment?
A. Direct distribution
B. Exclusive distribution
C. Selective distribution
D. Intensive distribution

22-**103.**
B
App.
Med.

What is the nature of competition for networking equipment?
A. Monopoly
B. Monopolistic competition
C. Pure competition
D. Oligopoly

22-**104.**
A
App.
Med.

What promotion method is EI using when it publishes catalogs, and exhibits in trade shows?
A. Sales promotion
B. Publicity
C. Advertising
D. Personal Selling

22-**105.**
D
App.
Med.

EI's geographic terms are probably:
A. F.O.B. delivered.
B. F.O.B. buyer's factory.
C. F.O.B. freight allowed.
D. F.O.B. mill.
E. F.O.B. basing point.

22-**106.**
A
App.
Med.

In which stage of the product life cycle do semiconductors appear to be?
A. Market maturity
B. Sales decline
C. Market introduction
D. Market growth

Read the following case carefully and answer questions 22-107 through 22-114.

PUMP SYSTEMS, INC. (PSI)

Pump Systems, Inc. (PSI) produces two major kinds of water pumps. The smaller pumps range in price from $5-$30, and are used in drinking fountains and soft-drink machines. Most of these pumps are bought by manufacturers of these machines and built into their product. PSI also builds larger pumps used in swimming pools and reservoirs. The prices of these items range from $250-$500. These are usually purchased by contractors who build the pools and reservoirs.

PSI sells nationally through sales reps located in the large industrial centers. These reps handle the selling function for PSI in their geographic areas and provide market information. They usually do the same thing for 10 to 20 similar manufacturers of noncompeting products--and are paid on a commission basis.

There are no other producers of the smaller pumps in the United States--because PSI has patent protection. As a result of this, management has decided to follow a policy of pricing high--to maximize profits--while the patent lasts.

Several competitors are in the market for the larger pumps. Industry prices and profits of these pumps have dropped in the past few years as a result of firms trying to increase their market shares. The product design has remained fairly stable over the last few years--and one firm dropped out as it saw that it would lose more money with its "me-too" product. Industry sales are increasing--but at a very slow rate. The price of these products is determined by adding a standard markup percentage to the variable cost of the items--to cover fixed costs and profit. For instance, pump Z has variable costs of $250 per unit, and a markup of 40 percent of this cost is added to the $250 to get its selling price. Management has estimated that fixed costs applicable to this product are $200,000 per year.

PSI publishes a product catalog which is revised annually. Also, it exhibits in most trade shows. PSI follows a policy of charging the same price to all customers--so all will have the same costs at their own plants. All purchases are shipped directly from PSI's factory to its customers--and title passes at PSI's factory.

22-**107.**
B
App.
Med.

What kind of products are PSI's small pumps to most customers?
A. Supplies
B. Component parts
C. Raw materials
D. Accessory equipment
E. Installations

22-**108.**
E
App.
Med.

What kind of products are the small pumps for customers who use them to replace worn pumps in their own machines?
A. Component parts
B. Raw materials
C. Accessory equipment
D. Installations
E. Supplies

22-**109.**
E
App.
Med.

PSI's sales reps are:
  A. selling agents.
  B. company salespeople.
  C. full-line merchant wholesalers.
  D. rack jobbers.
  E. manufacturers' agents.

22-**110.**
A
App.
Med.

What pricing policy does PSI use for its small pumps?
  A. Skimming pricing
  B. Price lining
  C. Target return pricing
  D. Prestige pricing
  E. Penetration pricing

22-**111.**
A
App.
Med.

What stage in the product life cycle do PSI's large pumps seem to be in?
  A. Market maturity
  B. Sales decline
  C. Market introduction
  D. Market growth

22-**112.**
A
App.
Med.

What is the contribution to fixed cost and profit of PSI's pump Z?
  A. $100 per unit
  B. $75 per unit
  C. $50 per unit
  D. $25,000
  E. Cannot be determined unless you know the sales volume.

22-**113.**
D
App.
Med.

What is the break-even point for pump Z IN DOLLARS?
  A. $200,000
  B. $100,000
  C. $2,000,000
  D. $700,000
  E. $500,000

22-**114.**
C
App.
Med.

What kind of promotion is PSI using when it publishes catalogs and exhibits in trade shows?
  A. Advertising
  B. Publicity
  C. Sales promotion
  D. Personal selling

Appendix A

Economics Fundamentals

True-False Questions:

A-1.
True
p. 656

Economists usually assume that customers have a fairly definite set of preferences.

A-2.
True
p. 656

Economics is called the dismal science because it says that most customers want more products than they can afford to buy.

A-3.
True
p. 656

The "law of diminishing demand" says that if a firm raised the price of its product, a smaller quantity would be demanded.

A-4.
False
p. 656

If a firm lowered the price of its product, the "law of diminishing demand" says that the quantity demanded would decrease.

A-5.
False
p. 656-57

A "demand schedule" for a television manufacturer would show how many new TVs are to be produced each month during the current production year.

A-6.
True
p. 656

A demand schedule shows the relationship between price and quantity demanded in a market.

A-7.
True
p. 657

A demand curve is a graph of the relationship between price and quantity in a market--assuming that all other things stay the same.

A-8.
False
p. 657

Most demand curves are upward-sloping--to the right.

A-9.
False
p. 659

If demand is elastic, then total revenue would decrease if price were lowered.

A-10.
True
p. 659

If demand is elastic, then total revenue would decrease if price were raised.

A-11.
False
p. 659

If demand is inelastic, then total revenue would increase if price were lowered.

A-12.
True
p. 659

If demand is inelastic, then total revenue would increase if price were raised.

A-13.
False
p. 659

Elasticity of demand is defined in terms of changes in total costs of production.

A-14.
True
p. 659

If total revenue remains the same when price is raised or lowered, then we have the special case of "unitary elasticity of demand."

A-15.
False
p. 660

A demand curve cannot be both elastic and inelastic.

A-16.
True
p. 660

A single demand curve can have both elastic and inelastic parts over different price ranges.

A-17.
True
p. 660

The availability of substitutes is one important factor affecting whether the demand for a product is elastic or inelastic.

A-18.
True
p. 660

When a large number of substitutes are available, demand will tend to be more elastic.

A-19.
False
p. 660

When few substitutes are available, demand will tend to be more elastic.

A-20.
True
p. 661

Most supply curves slope upward, indicating that suppliers will be willing to offer greater quantities at higher prices.

A-21.
False
p. 662

If supply is elastic, the supply curve will be nearly vertical.

A-22.
False
p. 663

The equilibrium point is where the quantity and price that sellers are willing to offer are greater than the quantity and price that buyers are willing to accept.

A-23.
False
p. 663

The equilibrium point is that point at which the quantity demanded would not change if price were either lowered or raised.

A-24.
True
p. 663

Some customers get a consumer surplus because they would be willing to pay more than the market price.

A-25.
True
p. 664

The elasticity of the firm's demand curve, the number and size of competitors, and the uniqueness of the firm's marketing mix all affect the nature of the competitive situation.

A-26.
True
p. 664

Pure competition exists when a market has homogeneous products, many buyers and sellers, and ease of entry for buyers and sellers.

A-27.
True
p. 664

In pure competition, individual producers have perfectly flat demand curves while the industry demand curve is down-sloping at the equilibrium price.

A-28.
False
p. 665

In pure competition situations, each seller usually has a lot of control over his price because of the lack of competitive substitutes.

A-29.
True
p. 665

Oligopoly conditions develop when a market has homogeneous products, a fairly inelastic industry demand curve, and relatively few sellers.

A-30.
True
p. 666

In an oligopoly situation, a "price war" will cause all sellers to lose sales revenue.

A-31.
False
p. 666

Monopolistic competition develops when a market is dominated by one large seller and a lot of small firms.

A-32.
True
p. 666

In monopolistic competition, sellers feel they have some competition in a market and consumers see competitive products as heterogeneous.

A-33.
False
p. 666

A firm in monopolistic competition faces no competition, so it can set its price at any level.

A-34.
True
p. 666-67

In monopolistic competition, individual firms have down-sloping demand curves.

Multiple Choice Questions

A-**35.**
B
Def.
Hard
p. 656

The "law of diminishing demand" says that:
  A. if the price of a product is lowered, usually the same quantity will be demanded.
  B. if the price of a product is raised, a smaller quantity will be demanded.
  C. the demand for any product will tend to decline over time.
  D. the more of a product a person buys, the less utility that particular product offers him.
  E. if the price of a product is lowered, a smaller quantity will be demanded.

A-**36.**
C
Def.
Easy
p. 656

A "demand schedule:"
  A. shows how much a firm is willing to sell at a particular price.
  B. is published regularly by the U.S. government and other governments.
  C. is a table which shows the relationship between price and quantity demanded in a market.
  D. is usually the same for all products.
  E. Both B and C are true.

A-**37.**
D
Def.
Med.
p. 657

A demand curve:
  A. shows what quantities would be supplied at various possible prices.
  B. shows how total revenue increases as prices decrease.
  C. is usually up-sloping from left to right.
  D. is formed by plotting the data from a demand schedule.
  E. All of the above are true.

A-**38.**
B
App.
Easy
p. 659

If a firm's total revenue DECREASES when the price of its product is reduced from $80 to $40, the demand for this product between these two prices is:
  A. unitary elastic.
  B. inelastic.
  C. elastic.
  D. Cannot tell from what is given.

A-**39.**
A
App.
Easy
p. 659

If a firm's total revenue DECREASES when the price of its product is raised from $50 to $55, the demand for this product between these two prices is:
  A. elastic.
  B. inelastic.
  C. unitary elastic.
  D. Cannot tell from what is given.

A-**40.**
C
App.
Easy
p. 659

If a firm's total revenue INCREASES when the price of its product is reduced from $90 to $50, the demand for this product between these two points is:
  A. inelastic.
  B. unitary elastic.
  C. elastic
  D. Cannot tell from what is given.

A-**41.**
C
Def.
Med.
p. 659

When a demand curve is INELASTIC:
A. if price goes down, then total revenue stays the same.
B. if price goes up, then total revenue stays the same.
C. if price goes down, then total revenue goes down.
D. if price goes up, then total revenue goes down.

A-**42.**
C
Math.
Hard
p. 659

In the following table, select the quantity interval in which demand is elastic.

PRICE	QUANTITY (UNITS)
$40	10
30	16
20	22
15	28
10	40
5	60

A. 28-40 units
B. 40-60 units
C. 10-16 units
D. 16-22 units
E. 22-28 units

A-**43.**
A
Comp.
Med.
p. 660

The elasticity of demand for a particular product depends upon:
A. the availability of substitutes.
B. the producer's costs.
C. the availability of raw materials.
D. the quantity the producer is willing to supply.
E. All of the above.

A-**44.**
D
Def.
Easy
p. 660

The elasticity of demand for a particular product depends upon:
A. the importance of the item in each customer's budget.
B. the urgency of the target customers' needs.
C. the availability of substitutes.
D. All of the above.
E. None of the above.

A-**45.**
B
Comp.
Med.
p. 660

Lack of good substitutes for a particular product affects its demand curve as follows:
A. Makes it more elastic
B. Makes it less elastic
C. Makes it unitary elastic
D. Doesn't affect it at all
E. Cannot be determined without knowing the supply curve

A-**46.**
E
App.
Med.
p. 660

Which of the following products would have the MOST ELASTIC demand?
A. Water supplied by a local utility company
B. A Minolta automatic camera
C. A new home which has not yet been built
D. Mercedes automobile
E. An individual farmer's wheat

A-**47**.
D
App.
Med.
p. 660

Which of the following products would have the MOST INELASTIC (or least elastic) INDUSTRY demand?
  A. Videotape recording system
  B. Microwave ovens
  C. Oranges
  D. Gas for heating homes
  E. Chicken

A-**48**.
B
Def.
Easy
p. 661

A supply curve:
  A. shows the quantity of products that would be demanded at various possible prices.
  B. is generally up-sloping from left to right.
  C. is not affected by suppliers' costs.
  D. generally slopes in the same direction as the demand curve.
  E. All of the above are true.

A-**49**.
D
Comp.
Hard
p. 662

Which of the following statements about elasticity of supply is TRUE?
  A. A product's elasticity of supply is calculated directly from its elasticity of demand.
  B. In the long run, the supply curve for most products is highly inelastic.
  C. If a product's demand curve is inelastic, then its supply curve also must be inelastic.
  D. In the very short run (after the growing season has begun), the supply curve for most agricultural products is highly inelastic.
  E. All of the above are true.

A-**50**.
D
App.
Hard
p. 662

Given generally elastic demand and supply curves for an industry, an INCREASE in supply will (all other things being equal):
  A. lower price but not change quantity demanded.
  B. increase price and increase quantity demanded.
  C. increase price and decrease quantity demanded.
  D. lower price and increase quantity demanded.
  E. not change anything else.

A-**51**.
B
App.
Med.
p. 662

The SHORT-RUN market adjustment for a homogeneous product, like wheat, following a decrease in demand would most likely be:
  A. an increase in production.
  B. a decrease in price.
  C. a decrease in production.
  D. a decrease in demand for available substitutes.
  E. an increase in price.

A-52.
C
Comp.
Med.
p. 663

Which of the following statements about demand and supply interaction is TRUE?

A. A market is said to be in equilibrium when the elasticity of demand equals the elasticity of supply.

B. For a market to be in equilibrium, the price and quantity that buyers are willing to accept must be greater than the price and quantity that suppliers are willing to offer.

C. The interaction of supply and demand determines the size of the market and the market price.

D. Demand determines price.

E. All of the above are true.

A-53.
A
Def.
Easy
p. 663

The "equilibrium point" is where:

A. the quantity and price sellers are willing to offer equal the quantity and price that buyers are willing to accept.

B. the quantity demanded equals its cost.

C. the market price is at its minimum.

D. the elasticity of demand equals the elasticity of supply.

E. the market price is at its maximum.

A-54.
D
Def.
Hard
p. 663

"Consumer surplus" means that:

A. consumers just get their money's worth in any transaction.

B. consumers don't consume all the products they buy.

C. the price consumers have to pay is more than the value to them.

D. some consumers get more than their money's worth because they would be willing to pay more than the equilibrium price if they had to.

E. there are more consumers than products to satisfy them.

A-55.
D
Def.
Easy
p. 664

A market situation with homogeneous products, many informed buyers and sellers, and ease of entry is a _____ market situation.

A. oligopoly

B. monopolistic competition

C. monopoly

D. pure competition

E. both B and C

A-56.
C
Def.
Med.
p. 664

Pure competition develops when a market has:

A. uninformed buyers and sellers.

B. heterogeneous products.

C. many buyers and sellers.

D. limited entry for buyers and sellers.

E. both C and D.

A-57.
E
Def.
Easy
p. 664

Pure competition occurs when a market has:

A. homogeneous (similar) products.

B. easy entry for new sellers.

C. many buyers and sellers.

D. informed buyers and sellers.

E. All of the above.

A-58.
C
Comp.
Med.
p. 664

A FIRM faces an almost perfectly flat or horizontal demand curve in a(an) _____ market situation.
   A. monopolistic competition
   B. monopoly
   C. pure competition
   D. oligopoly
   E. None of the above--demand curves are always down-sloping.

A-59.
C
Comp.
Med.
p. 665

A firm in pure competition will:
   A. advertise its product to tell potential customers about its unique product.
   B. be able to set its own price level.
   C. have to accept the going price.
   D. be able to increase its total revenue only by lowering its price.
   E. All of the above.

A-60.
A
App.
Med.
p. 665

Rico Hardware is an industrial supply firm that sells standard screws, bolts, and other small hardware items to construction companies. Rico competes with many similar firms nationwide and sells its merchandise at "the going rate." Rico seems to be operating in an environment that is close to:
   A. pure competition.
   B. monopoly.
   C. monopolistic competition.
   D. oligopoly.

A-61.
D
Def.
Easy
p. 665

Oligopoly situations develop when a market has:
   A. relatively few buyers.
   B. elastic industry demand.
   C. heterogeneous products.
   D. relatively few sellers.
   E. All of the above.

A-62.
D
Def.
Easy
p. 665

An oligopoly market situation has:
   A. relatively few sellers--or a few large firms and many smaller firms which follow the lead of the larger ones.
   B. essentially homogeneous products.
   C. fairly inelastic industry demand.
   D. All of the above.
   E. None of the above.

A-63.
C
Def.
Med.
p. 665

A market which has relatively few sellers, homogeneous products, and fairly inelastic industry demand is an example of a(an) _____ market situation.
   A. pure competition
   B. monopolistic competition
   C. oligopoly
   D. monopoly
   E. Any of the above.

A-**64.**
B
App.
Easy
p. 665

Which of the following would probably be an oligopoly in a U.S. market?
A. a gift shop at an art museum.
B. U.S. Steel (USX).
C. a "7 to 11" convenience food store.
D. a Ford car dealership in a small town.
E. all of the above.

A-**65.**
A
App.
Med.
p. 666

Renee Gray is responsible for price setting at her firm. The last time she raised her price, competitors left their prices at the lower level and she lost customers. Now she wants to increase her market share with a lower price, but she is concerned that her competitors will "follow" her to the lower price level. Gray is probably operating in an environment of:
A. oligopoly.
B. pure competition.
C. monopoly.
D. monopolistic competition.

A-**66.**
E
App.
Med.
p. 666

Which of the following is the best example of an oligopoly situation?
A. grocery retailers in Miami.
B. a community in the mountains with one electric power company.
C. a farmers' market with many farmers selling peaches.
D. a small airport with two airlines going to different destinations.
E. most of the aluminum in the U.S. is sold by three producers.

A-**67.**
B
App.
Med.
p. 666

In which of the following situations would the seller(s) be most likely to face a "kinked" demand curve?
A. a medium-sized airport with one gift shop.
B. a small town--some distance from any others--with three "off brand" gasoline stations at the major intersection.
C. men's clothing stores in downtown Las Vegas.
D. a small community with one electric power company.
E. a farmers' market with one farmer selling honey.

A-**68.**
B
Comp.
Hard
p. 666

In oligopoly situations:
A. prices tend to be rigid and similar--because of price-fixing agreements.
B. price wars may occur if a firm seeks to increase its market share by cutting price.
C. a firm faces an INELASTIC demand curve if it raises price.
D. the quantity offered changes a lot due to the lack of a fixed market price.
E. All of the above are true.

A-**69.**
D
Comp.
Hard
p. 666

"Kinked" demand curves:
A. are sometimes found in pure competition.
B. are inelastic above the "kink" and elastic below the "kink."
C. are typical of monopolistic competition.
D. tend to encourage a stable price in a product-market.
E. both C and D are true.

A-70.
B
Comp.
Med.
p. 666

Which of the following statements about oligopoly situations is TRUE?
  A. "Price cutters" face fairly elastic demand curves."
  B. Cutting prices can lead to everyone losing sales revenue.
  C. Many large sellers are competing with each other.
  D. Essentially heterogeneous products are offered by many competitors.
  E. None of the above is true.

A-71.
C
Int.
Hard
p. 666

Which of the following statements about the competitive environment is TRUE?
  A. In monopolistic competition a seller has a down-sloping demand curve due to the lack of any substitute products.
  B. In pure competition, an individual firm is usually faced with a very inelastic demand curve.
  C. Firms in oligopoly should avoid price cutting.
  D. The industry demand curve in oligopoly is usually horizontal.
  E. All of the above.

A-72.
B
Comp.
Med.
p. 666

Monopolistic competition occurs when an individual firm
  A. obtains complete control over prices--through collusion.
  B. differentiates its product from competitors--in the eyes of some customers.
  C. develops products which have no substitutes.
  D. obtains complete control of the supply of a product.
  E. All of the above.

A-73.
C
Def.
Easy
p. 666

A market with several firms competing, some promotion, and some differences among products is in a(an) _____ market situation.
  A. monopoly
  B. pure competition
  C. monopolistic competition
  D. oligopoly
  E. Any of the above.

A-74.
D
Def.
Easy
p. 666

Monopolistic competition exists when:
  A. each competitor has its own kinked demand curve.
  B. there is only one firm in the industry.
  C. no substitute products are available for consumers in this market.
  D. each firm in the market has differentiated its product from its competitors--in the eyes of some customers.
  E. both B and C.

A-75.
A
App.
Med.
p. 666

Which of the following is the best example of a monopoly situation?
  A. A movie theater with one snack bar for popcorn and soft drinks.
  B. Jewelry stores in Paris.
  C. A farmers' market with many farmers selling sweet corn.
  D. The only Domino's Pizza in a large university town.
  E. A small town--some distance from any others--with only three drugstores.

A-**76**.   Which of the following is MOST likely to be competing in monopolistic competition?

C   A.   a soybean farmer

App.   B.   a steel producer

Med.   C.   a restaurant

p. 666   D.   an oil producer

                E.   an electric utility company

Marketing Arithmetic

True-False Questions:

B-1.
False
p. 670

An operating statement is a simple summary of a company's assets, liabilities, and owners' equity at a particular time.

B-2.
True
p. 670

The main purpose of an operating statement is to determine a company's net profit over a specified period of time--and present data to support that figure.

B-3.
False
p. 671

The three main components of an operating statement are costs, assets, and profit.

B-4.
True
p. 671

The three main components of an operating statement are sales, costs, and profit or loss.

B-5.
True
p. 671

Monthly operating statements might be used to uncover unfavorable trends in sales, costs, and profit.

B-6.
False
p. 672

Returns or allowances are subtracted from net sales to find gross sales on an operating statement.

B-7.
False
p. 672

Net sales is the total value at cost of all the products sold during an operating period.

B-8.
True
p. 672

The total value AT COST of all the products sold during an operating period is the cost of sales.

B-9.
False
p. 672

"Cost of sales" equals the total value of all the products purchased during an operating period plus freight in.

B-10.
True
p. 672

Gross margin (or gross profit) is the amount left over after the cost of sales is subtracted from net sales.

B-11.
False
p. 672

Gross margin (or gross profit) is the amount left over after the cost of sales is subtracted from gross sales.

B-12.
False
p. 672

A company's gross margin must cover all the costs of making and selling the products, and hopefully leave a reasonable net profit.

B-13.
True
p. 672

The term "net profit" refers to the amount the company has earned from its operations during a particular period.

B-14.
False
p. 672

Net sales and net profit are the same thing.

B-15.
False
p. 673

The net cost of delivered purchases equals the original invoice cost of purchases plus purchase discounts minus freight charges.

B-16.
True
p. 673

Purchase discounts should be subtracted from the original invoice cost of purchases to get the net cost of purchases.

B-17.
False
p. 674

"Expenses" (on an operating statement) usually include the cost of sales--both purchased and produced.

B-18.
True
p. 675

A measure of the number of times the average inventory is sold during a year is stockturn rate.

B-19.
True
p. 675

The stockturn rate shows how rapidly a firm's inventory is moving.

B-20.
False
p. 675

It is impossible for a firm's stockturn rate to equal 1.0.

B-21.
False
p. 675-76

When calculating operating ratios from an operating statement, the denominator is usually net profit.

B-22.
True
p. 675-76

Operating ratios (calculated from an operating statement) show various items from the statement as a percentage of net sales.

B-23.
False
p. 677

Markups (expressed as a percentage of selling price) cannot be converted to markup percents expressed as a percentage of cost without knowing the actual selling price or the actual cost.

B-24.
True
p. 677

A 33 1/3 percent markup on selling price equals a 50 percent markup on cost.

B-25.
False
p. 678

A retailer's "markdown ratio" is calculated directly from its operating statement.

B-26.
True
p. 678

Markdowns are generally considered to be due to business errors, while returns result from customer errors.

B-27.
False
p. 678

Return on investment is a measure of the dollar resources the firm has invested in a project or business.

B-28.
True
p. 679

Return on investment and return on assets are both measures of how effectively a firm uses its resources.

B-29.
True
p. 679

The ROI ratio might be improved by earning at least the same net profit while reducing investment.

Multiple Choice Questions

B-30.
E
Def.
Easy
p. 670

The main purpose of the "operating statement" is to:
  A. show which products or customers are most profitable.
  B. show the sources of sales data.
  C. calculate the net profit for the company.
  D. present data to support the net profit figure.
  E. both C and D.

B-31.
C
Def.
Easy
p. 671

The basic components of an operating statement are:
  A. net sales, cost of sales, profit.
  B. gross sales, gross margin, expenses, net profit.
  C. sales, costs, and profit or loss.
  D. sales, costs, and expenses.
  E. gross sales, gross margin, net profit.

B-32.
D
Math.
Med.
p. 672

Ms. Treadway's athletic shoe store had gross sales of $62,500 in January. Compute her NET SALES for the month from the following data.

    Sales returns $2,500
    Purchases $5,000
    Markdowns $2,000
    Stockturn rate   3

A. $59,500
B. $5,500
C. $48,000
D. $60,000
E. $3,500

B-33.
B
Math.
Med.
p. 672

Given the following information, calculate the firm's NET PROFIT (or LOSS).

Returns and allowances	$ 60,000
Gross sales	$460,000
Cost of sales	$200,000
Expenses	$100,000
Gross margin	$200,000

A. $ 85,000
B. $100,000
C. $ 50,000
D. $160,000
E. a loss of $200,000

B-34.
C
Math.
Med.
p. 672

Given the following information, calculate the firm's COST OF SALES.

Beginning inventory	$ 50,000
Purchase discounts	$ 10,000
Ending inventory	$ 60,000
Purchases	$200,000
Freight-in	$ 10,000

A. $180,000
B. $285,000
C. $190,000
D. $120,000
E. Cannot be determined without knowing the firm's net sales.

B-35.
D
Int.
Med.
p. 672

Regarding operating statements:
A. gross sales are the actual sales dollars the company will receive.
B. net sales minus expenses equals the cost of sales.
C. "gross sales" minus expenses equals the cost of sales.
D. gross margin equals expenses plus net profit.
E. gross margin is the money left after all expenses are subtracted from net sales.

B-36.
A
Def.
Med.
p. 672

When a firm subtracts its cost of sales from its net sales, the amount left over is called:
  A. gross margin.
  B. return on assets.
  C. net profit.
  D. expenses.
  E. gross sales.

B-37.
E
Def.
Med.
p. 675

Stockturn rate equals:
  A. net sales minus gross margin divided by average inventory at retail.
  B. cost of sales divided by average inventory at cost.
  C. net sales divided by an average inventory at selling price.
  D. sales in units divided by average inventory in units.
  E. All of the above EXCEPT A.

B-38.
E
Math.
Easy
p. 675

The cost of sales for a company is $400,000 and its net sales are $800,000. What would its stockturn rate be if its average inventory at cost is $100,000?
  A. 3
  B. 2
  C. 1
  D. 8
  E. 4

B-39.
B
Math.
Med.
p. 675

A farm supply store starting with a $40,000 inventory at cost expects to sell $400,000 (cost of sales) of merchandise in the coming year. It plans to turn over its stock 10 times during the year. How much merchandise must the shop purchase during the year?
  A. $200,000
  B. $400,000
  C. $420,000
  D. $440,000
  E. None of the above.

B-40.
D
Math.
Hard
p. 675

What net sales are required to obtain a stockturn rate of 5--given an average inventory at cost of $100,000 and a gross margin of 50 percent?
  A. $100,000
  B. $1,500,000
  C. $600,000
  D. $1,000,000
  E. $400,000

B-41.
D
Math.
Med.
p. 675

Given the following information, calculate the firm's stockturn rate.
  Net sales $480,000
  Gross margin %   50%
  Average inventory at cost $ 40,000

  A. 7
  B. 10
  C. 3
  D. 6
  E. Cannot be determined from data given.

B-42.
E
Comp.
Easy
p. 676

Which of the following statements about operating ratios (which can be calculated from operating statements) is TRUE?
  A. By comparing operating ratios from one period to another, a firm can identify areas that may need special attention.
  B. These ratios are often used for control purposes.
  C. These ratios are calculated by dividing operating statement items by net sales.
  D. By comparing its operating ratios with competitors' ratios, a firm may be able to obtain a better idea of how it is doing.
  E. All of the above are true.

B-43.
C
Math.
Med.
p. 676

If net sales on the operating statement for Brandywine Company were $200,000--and gross sales were $240,000--what would the cost of sales be if the gross margin was 20 percent?
  A. $140,000
  B. $168,000
  C. $160,000
  D. $120,000
  E. Cannot be determined without knowing Brandywine's expenses and net profit.

B-44.
B
Math.
Easy
p. 676

True Blue, Inc.--which had a net profit of $200,000 last year--had a gross margin of 40 percent and expenses of 30 percent. What were its net sales in dollars?
  A. $700,000
  B. $2,000,000
  C. $1,000,000
  D. $800,000
  E. Cannot be determined with data given.

B-45.
B
Math.
Med.
p. 677

If a wholesaler takes a 33.3 percent markup on selling price, what is the approximate markup on cost?
  A. 80%
  B. 50%
  C. 20%
  D. 100%
  E. 33%

B-46.
D
Math.
Med.
p. 677

If a wholesaler's markup on selling price is 50 percent, what is the markup on cost?
  A. 33 1/3%
  B. 66 2/3%
  C. 50%
  D. 100%
  E. Cannot be determined without knowing the dollar amount of the markup.

B-47.
E
Math.
Med.
p. 677

In making a purchase from a wholesaler, a retailer is told that a certain item will earn a 100 percent markup on cost. What markup on selling price will this be?
  A. 75%
  B. 100%
  C. 66 2/3%
  D. 200%
  E. 50%

B-48.
A
Math.
Med.
p. 677

If a wholesaler takes a 50 percent markup on its cost, this is equal to a
_____ markup on selling price.
    A. 33 1/3%
    B. 200%
    C. 100%
    D. 20%
    E. 50%

B-49.
E
Math.
Hard
p. 677

Aiwa Industries sells directly to auto parts retailers and is trying to set a price on a
radar detector so that its retailers can sell it for $100. If the retailers need a 30 percent
markup--and Aiwa can produce the item for $35--what markup could Aiwa take for
itself?
    A. 35%
    B. 100%
    C. 30%
    D. 70%
    E. 50%

B-50.
E
Math.
Hard
p. 677

A hardware retailer who seeks a markup of 50 percent recently bought a new item for
$15.00. To determine its selling price, it should add _____ to this cost.
    A. $40.00
    B. $80.00
    C. $10.00
    D. $20.00
    E. $15.00

B-51.
C
Math.
Med.
p. 677

A drugstore buys toothpaste from its wholesaler for $30.00 a case. This retailer uses a
25 percent markup. The retail selling price for a case of the toothpaste will be:
    A. $37.50
    B. $120.00
    C. $40.00
    D. $22.50
    E. There is not enough information to tell.

B-52.
E
Comp.
Med.
p. 678

Regarding markdowns, which of the following statements is TRUE?
    A. The markdown ratio is calculated by dividing the sum of markdowns and
       allowances by net sales.
    B. Markdowns are required because customers' will not buy at the original
       marked-up price.
    C. Markdowns are generally considered to be due to "business errors."
    D. Gross margins are roughly equal to markdowns.
    E. All are true EXCEPT D.

B-53.
B
Comp.
Easy
p. 678

Markdowns:
    A. do not affect the profits of a business.
    B. are not shown on an operating statement.
    C. are similar to allowances--and are subtracted from gross sales on an operating
       statement.
    D. are generally caused by "consumer errors."
    E. All of the above.

B-54.
E
Int.
Hard
p. 678

Regarding "operating statements," which of the following statements is FALSE?
A. Stockturn rate can be calculated directly from a detailed operating statement.
B. Gross margin must be larger than expenses for a business to make a profit.
C. By comparing the results from one statement to another, management can see trends.
D. The markdown ratio cannot be calculated directly from a detailed operating statement.
E. The purpose of the operating statement is to determine the firm's ROI and ROA.

B-55.
D
Def.
Med.
p. 678

"Return on investment" means:
A. sales divided by investment.
B. investment divided by net sales.
C. net profit before taxes divided by the assets used to make the profit.
D. net profit after taxes divided by the investment used to make the profit.
E. None of the above.

B-56.
D
Def.
Easy
p. 678

Which of the following would NOT be shown on a firm's "balance sheet"?
A. Liabilities
B. Net worth
C. Assets
D. Net sales
E. All of the above would be on a firm's balance sheet.

B-57.
E
Math.
Med.
p. 679

Given the following information, calculate the firm's "return on investment" (ROI).

Net sales	$20,000,000
Net profit (after taxes)	$ 500,000
Investment	$10,000,000

A. 20%
B. 50%
C. 10%
D. 2.5%
E. 5%

B-58.
E
Comp.
Med.
p. 679

Other things equal, a firm can increase return on investment (ROI) by:
A. decreasing investment.
B. reducing expenses.
C. increasing profit margins.
D. increasing net sales.
E. Any of the above.

GIVEN THE FOLLOWING INFORMATION, ANSWER QUESTIONS B-59 THROUGH B-64.

Gross sales	$650,000
Returns	$40,000
Allowances	$10,000
Markdowns	$20,000
Beginning inventory	$50,000
Ending inventory	$30,000
Expenses	25%
Stockturn rate	10
Investment	$250,000

B-59.
E
Math.
Easy
p. 672

Net sales are:
   A. $560,000.
   B. $530,000.
   C. $650,000.
   D. $610,000.
   E. $600,000.

B-60.
A
Math.
Hard
p. 675

Given that the stockturn rate is 10, the cost of sales is:
   A. $400,000.
   B. $70,000.
   C. $60,000.
   D. $65,000.

B-61.
A
Math.
Hard
p. 672

The gross margin is:
   A. $200,000.
   B. $175,000.
   C. $250,000.
   D. $320,000.
   E. $130,000.

B-62.
A
Math.
Hard
p. 672

The net profit is:
   A. $50,000.
   B. $120,000.
   C. a loss of $75,000.
   D. $215,000.
   E. $85,000.

B-63.
D
Math.
Hard
p. 679

The return on investment is (assuming a 50 percent tax on net profit):
   A. 12.3%.
   B. 25.0%.
   C. 9.9%.
   D. 10.0%.
   E. The return is negative because the firm had a loss.

B-64.
D
Math.
Hard
p. 678

The markdown ratio is:
A. 20%.
B. 25%.
C. 15%.
D. 5%.
E. 10%.

GIVEN THE FOLLOWING INFORMATION, ANSWER QUESTIONS B-65 THROUGH B-70.

Gross sales	$240,000
Returns	$20,000
Allowances	$20,000
Gross Margin	25%
Markdowns	$30,000
Beginning inventory	$50,000
Ending inventory	$50,000
Expenses	$40,000
Investment	$50,000

B-65.
C
Math.
Easy
p. 672

Net sales are:
A. $140,000.
B. $155,000.
C. $200,000.
D. $180,000.
E. $220,000.

B-66.
B
Math.
Med.
p. 672

Given that the gross margin percent is 25%, what is the cost of sales?
A. $75,000.
B. $150,000.
C. $55,000.
D. $12,500.
E. $50,000.

B-67.
C
Math.
Med.
p. 675

The stockturn rate is:
A. 4.
B. 5.
C. 3.
D. 1.
E. 2.

B-68.
B
Math.
Hard
p. 672

The net profit is:
A. $15,500.
B. $10,000.
C. $65,000.
D. $23,000.
E. a loss of $90,000.

B-69.
E
Math.
Hard
p. 678

The markdown ratio is:
   A. 33.3%.
   B. 18.1%.
   C. 9.5%.
   D. 16.7%.
   E. 25.0%.

B-70.
A
Math.
Hard
p. 679

Assuming a 50 percent tax on net profit, the return on investment (ROI) is:
   A. 10%.
   B. 20%.
   C. 15%.
   D. 5%.
   E. the return is negative because the business lost money.